Acclaim for

One of the distinctive characteristics of the book that contributes to its readability is how, following the introduction of a theoretical concept, the authors provide numerous real-life examples and vignettes to bring the point alive.

This book addresses topics and themes that I believe would make sense to anyone who is interested in understanding and improving their relationships with other people in their lives.

The book is of course addressing topics and themes that will be very relevant to CPE students and practitioners of spiritual care practice, but also I think, to students and practitioners in any number of human science health professions, such as: art therapy, psychology, nursing, medicine, social work, and rehabilitation personnel, to name a few involved in counseling and helping people with 'existential issues'; any one whose work brings an investment in what the authors call "relational habitat maintenance". Also included here I think would be self-aware people in education and teaching, as well as in management and human resources in business.

Like any good piece of art, this book should be enjoyed again and again, because the reader will find new and different lessons each time, based on their own changing embodied experience and intentional reflection.

Leslie Gardner PhD. Associate Faculty, St. Stephen's College, Edmonton, AB and Professional Program Evaluator

✳ ✳ ✳ ✳ ✳

I would have loved to have this book during my CPE journey as all of the topics and themes are relevant and make sense for spiritual care practitioners and would have helped in providing a foundation or base from which to work. The book is full of helpful references for the various subjects discussed which I would have found invaluable, and will find invaluable going forward.

Kathy Brown MDiv. Spiritual Health Practitioner, Peter Lougheed Centre, Calgary, AB

✳ ✳ ✳ ✳ ✳

If each student within SPE/CPE were to read this book we would have reason to believe in a better understanding for not only the practitioners but for the profession on the whole. When people understand better what spiritual care can offer there is a much better opportunity to build a profession that is considered with a greater rigor.

I fantasize about the book being the main text in a course on spiritual care as well as being a reference book for students within CASC and other spiritual care associations in various parts of the world.

Jane Smith-EivemarkDMin. Registered Psychotherapist, Hamilton, ON, and CASC/ACSS Emeritus Certified Spiritual Care Practitioner and Supervisor-Educator

✳ ✳ ✳ ✳ ✳

The Authors

Joyce E. Bellous, PhD is a university professor, transformational educator, leader, consultant, mentor, social interaction theorist, and international speaker. She designs and offers a variety of personal assessments to develop team-building skills and is valued for helping people reflect on their experience so they can work effectively with others by enhancing their social and emotional intelligence. She has expertise in analyzing human systems and encouraging productive involvement in them. Her primary research interest is human spirituality. She has published several books on education, theological and collaborative reflection and social literacy. She developed the Spiritual Styles Assessment and is currently developing a literacy approach to lifelong learning based on the Styles in order to develop four reading strategies for creating learning environments that enhance social interaction and allow people to practice being different from one another, yet at the same time well-integrated with each other.

Margaret B. Clark, DMin is a Certified Spiritual Care Practitioner and Supervisor-Educator in Spiritual Care (CPE) within the Canadian Association for Spiritual Care/Association canadienne de soins spirituels (CASC/ACSS). Her lifetime CPE activities span parish, healthcare and academic settings in the United States and Canada. Over the course of five decades she has developed adult enrichment and outreach programs in rural faith communities, worked as a hospital chaplain and hospital-based Clinical Pastoral Education (CPE) supervisor, and taught graduate level courses in theological reflection and spiritual assessment. As part of redeveloping CPE in Alberta, Canada, she designed and co-facilitates a graduate course on the Sacred Art of Preceptorship, enabling CPE supervisors to locate educational seminars within theological colleges and place CPE students at multiple healthcare and community locations for apprenticeship with specially prepared spiritual care practitioners, working in collaboration with the supervisors. In recent years, she has enjoyed opportunities to serve others through CPE mentoring and spiritual direction.

THICK LISTENING AT THIN MOMENTS
THEORETICAL GROUNDWORK IN SPIRITUAL CARE PRACTICE

IV

THICK LISTENING AT THIN MOMENTS
THEORETICAL GROUNDWORK IN SPIRITUAL CARE PRACTICE

Joyce E. Bellous and Margaret B. Clark

TALL PINE PRESS
Edmonton, Alberta

Tall Pine Press
2655 Sir Arthur Currie Way, Edmonton, AB T5E 6S8, Canada
Web: www.tallpinepress.ca   E-mail: tallpinepress@gmail.com

Library and Archives Canada Cataloguing in Publication

Title: Thick listening at thin moments : theoretical groundwork in spiritual care practice / Joyce E. Bellous and Margaret B. Clark.
Names: Bellous, Joyce Edith, 1948- author. | Clark, Margaret B. (Margaret Beckwith), 1946- author.
Description: Includes bibliographical references and index.
Identifiers: Canadiana 20220243298 | ISBN 9781777666330 (softcover)
Subjects: LCSH: Spiritual care (Medical care)
Classification: LCC BL65.M4 B45 2022 | DDC 615.8/52—dc23

Contents

Acknowledgements

As the book comes to fruition, we express heartfelt thanks to those who accompanied us from its beginning to its completion. We begin by acknowledging Ken Bellous and Tall Pine Press. The support and encouragement received has contributed greatly to our perseverance in traveling through the various phases of publication. We also express gratitude to those who were there in the beginning when ideas for the book were still dim yet were nurtured through shared visioning, teaching and collaboration with Zoe Bernatsky, Elaine Nagy and Carol Potratz.

As ideas formed and chapters were written, we benefited from those who were willing to read our chapters and provide feedback to us. These people spanned various parts of Canada and the United States, they include Emily and Tom Baril, Leslie Gardner, Caryn Macdonald, Kathy Marshall-Spate, Joanne Olson, Zinia Pritchard, Craig Traynor, Jean Waters, Brent Watts and KC Young. Their contributions to our thinking and the rigor of our writing are deeply appreciated.

In Clark's experience, co-authoring an article in the *Journal of Pastoral Care and Counselling* (2020) with Darlene Pranke on the Alberta Consortium for Supervised Pastoral Education Program helped focus the changing landscape of Clinical Pastoral Education (CPE) not only in Alberta and Canada but also globally. Later, when developing clinical vignettes for Chapter 8, Clark gained a great deal of insight and awareness about viewing a shared passion for CPE Supervision through different cultural lenses during her conversations with Do Bong Kim, whom she met in Edmonton, Alberta. He is now a CPE Supervisor and consultant with the Holistic Healing Institute at G-Sam Hospital, Gunpo-si, Gyeonggi-do, South Korea. Clark is very grateful to Darlene Pranke and Do Bong Kim for their collegiality and collaboration.

As part of writing this book, Bellous published Spiritual Care as the Foundation for a Child's Religious Education in the journal *Religions*

(2021). She benefitted from interactions with colleagues who read the article. The topics of worldview formation and four types of literacy from that journal article have enriched multiple chapters in our book. Bellous brings scholarly integrity to her consultations, collaborations and ongoing theoretical pursuits.

Once the book was written, Bellous and Clark asked for feedback and critique on the book and it's with deep gratitude that we thank Kathy Brown, Leslie Gardner, Jane Smith-Eivemark and KC Young for reading our book in its entirety. Their comments, critique and commendations brought us to the finish line with a sense of gladness and heartfelt appreciation.

In addition to being co-authors, Bellous and Clark each have circles of people with whom they've shared the experience of writing this book. Margaret Clark expresses her gratitude to the following: Mary Clark, her beloved sister; KC Young, who faithfully sojourned these years of book-writing in all their twists and turns; her treasured "Sophia Sisters" (Lorraine Nicely, Yvette Plessis, Barbara Purin and Jean Waters) and "Pilgrim Companions" (Dolores Kueffler, Therese Mughannam-Walrath and KC Young). Lastly, Margaret thanks those friends and colleagues with whom she's talked about this endeavor and from whom she's experienced tremendous grace and goodness: Emily and Tom Baril, Pamela Brink, Christina Cathro, Bonnie Donohue, Sarah Donnelly, Veronica Dunne, Bonnie Herring-Cooper, Meg Jordan, Do Bong Kim, Evelyn Marcon, Joanne Olson, Nel Ouwens, Leon Remus, Ruth Stevenson and Lori Stewart. It's been a true blessing to sojourn with such wonderful company.

Joyce would like to thank Ken for his collaboration as husband and business partner for all the conversation that stands behind this book. Many conversations with family and friends have nurtured her thinking. She is indebted to Caryn Macdonald, a constant, collaborative thoughtful friend, who reflected with her on many aspects of the book. The work Bellous does as an organizational learning consultant enhanced her understanding of the complexity of theories presented in these pages. Over the years, many students and clients have made it possible for her to think more fully about the perspectives that shape the groundwork and architecture of the book. Every piece of writing is built upon collaboration that underlies its final presentation in the pages of a book. Bellous is continually grateful to family and friends who have improved her thinking through their interactions with her.

Lastly, as they reflect on the final product, Clark and Bellous are profoundly aware of how writing this book has changed them both. Their impact on each other, as they worked through the text, has shaped new approaches to their own practice of spiritual care. Bellous and Clark are spiritual care educators with very different backgrounds and life stories acquired across significantly different experiences. Through writing this book together, they gained something new from the experience, and are deeply grateful to each other. As its authors, they hope this book will provide the richness and rewards to its readers that it has given to them.

May 25, 2022

Introduction

Reading this book is not for the faint of heart. It's for people in the field of spiritual care who have passion, curiosity, imagination, and a hunger for complex, multidimensional learning. The field of spiritual care is broad. It includes coursework in seminaries, theological colleges and other educational institutions where academic theoretical groundwork advances spiritual care practice. It also includes those who participate in and supervise programs of Clinical Pastoral Education (CPE), together with professional associations that accredit those programs and certify spiritual care professionals. Most broadly, this book is for all who see spiritual care as an attitude toward the world and as a way of being in relationship with others that is rooted in our common humanity.

Creative Collaboration

Two spiritual care educators with very different backgrounds and life stories joined together to write this book. Dr. Joyce E. Bellous has over three decades of research into human spirituality in collaboration with an international cohort of Philosophers of Education and Religious Educators. She authored numerous articles and several books. For sixteen years, she led Ministry Reflection Seminars at McMaster Divinity College, Hamilton, Ontario. For five years, she was a full professor at Taylor Seminary in Edmonton, Alberta, where she continues to teach a graduate course, titled "Adult Learning in Spiritual Care Contexts", a course for those in western Canada seeking CPE supervisory certification.

Dr. Margaret B. Clark served in rural faith communities in Montana for twelve years. She was employed for twenty-two years at the University of Alberta Hospitals in Edmonton, Alberta, as a certified Spiritual

Care Practitioner and Supervisor-Educator in Clinical Pastoral Education (CPE). For seventeen years she taught graduate courses on "Theological Reflection in Professional Practice" as well as "Spiritual Assessment in the Promotion of Health" at St. Stephen's College, Edmonton. She co-authored a book with Dr. Joanne Olson, titled *Nursing Within a Faith Community: Promoting Health in Times of Transition*.[1]

Bellous and Clark first met in 1998 during the inception of structures that have since become the Canadian Association for Parish Nursing Ministry (CAPNM). They reconnected in 2015 when CPE in the province of Alberta underwent losses that required major changes. At that time, Bellous, Clark, Sr. Dr. Zoe Bernatsky and Rev. Elaine Nagy developed a course, titled "The Sacred Art of Preceptorship", which they taught at St. Stephen's College in order to establish a Spiritual Care Preceptor role within what was to become the Alberta Consortium for Supervised Pastoral Education (AC-SPE).[2] Concurrent with AC-SPE development, Clark, Bellous, Bernatsky and Dr. Carol Potratz collaborated on assessing the competencies found in Canadian seminary degree programs, in the Canadian Association for Spiritual Care/Association canadienne de soins spirituels (CASC/ACSS) and in a broader spectrum of spiritual care associations in North America. Their work, together with initiatives led by Dr. Jo-Ann Badley of Ambrose Seminary in Calgary, Alberta, contributed to the drafting of core competencies that have become part of a Collaborative Spiritual Care Program of Studies for spiritual care learners in Alberta and beyond. The success of these collaborations involved partnering with representatives from five graduate theological colleges in Alberta.

Theoretical Groundwork

Clark and Bellous strongly agree that theoretical groundwork is what fosters the development of competence in spiritual care professional practice. Theoretical groundwork also shapes spiritual care as it's carried forward by ordinary people around the globe who faithfully and conscientiously tend to needs of the human spirit. The word "theory" is ancient and meaningful, deriving from the Greek noun "theoria" (contemplation, speculation) and verb "theorein" (to consider, speculate, look at). From its inception the meaning of "theory" has been tied to action. Its earliest usage was associated with spectators in a theater who view a play and are part of the action. Spectators look at what's happening on stage, react emotionally to the story being portrayed and respond by heckling, silent awe, tears, laughter, and applause to show what they think and how they feel. Contemplating and speculating on human activities gives rise to making observations and reflecting on them as we formulate principles that motivate action. It's this further appreciation of theory, as a set of principles on which the practice of an activity is based, that has captured our imagination as authors.

The book's title, *Thick Listening at Thin Moments*, includes the subtitle "theoretical groundwork in spiritual care practice." The book is about theories that work in spiritual care. Why have we taken a theoretical approach? Let's consider two ideas about the word theory. First, based on what we've already shared, a good theory is built from a set of observations that eventually become principles we apply to good effect in specific situations. Second, a theory is a set of ideas that become principles we apply in practice because they've been abstracted from many situations over time. If we apply a theory and good outcomes result, we're confident that what we've abstracted (generalized) from experience is reliable and useful in future situations and, further, using the theory will likely bring about good outcomes. In good theater, the audience comes away with new theories about the human condition and about consequences of human action they may eventually apply in their own lives.

Suppose a young man named David holds the theory that 'it's best to be polite when meeting new people'. This has become his theory due to all the times that being polite resulted in friendliness with people he was meeting for the first time. Since he values friendliness, and friendliness makes him happy (which is a good outcome), being polite is a theory he applies whenever he meets someone new. Being polite when meeting new people provides David with benefits he values and wants to continue enjoying. But being polite doesn't guarantee his happiness—using a theory is not magic. Using a theory requires discernment and intentional reflection. Being polite is David's way of being open to the likelihood of happiness, but again, it's not a guarantee.

In general, we rely on a theory because we think there will be good outcomes from its use. But a theory may fail to provide good outcomes if it isn't based on sufficient experience. David needs to exercise good judgement as he applies his theory. If he's alone in a dark alley in a strange city, he must use judgement as he considers being polite as the best theory to use if a stranger were to approach him from behind wielding a knife. Up to now, David's theory has provided good outcomes, but this is because most of his life was spent in essentially friendly environments. When he's alone in a strange city, he needs to expand his theory about meeting new people.

If David wants to be a spiritual care practitioner, he'll do a lot of thinking about his approach to theory. Aspects of theory require practitioners to use good judgement as they apply theory to practice. Good judgement depends on the learning they experience as they move through academic and Clinical Pastoral Education (CPE) teaching/learning environments. As they become more experienced, practitioners can

- Become consciously aware of their theories
- Use good judgement when applying theories to specific situations
- Have a comprehensive understanding of a situation when applying a theory
- Develop a range of theories from which to choose
- Learn from a situation whether one theory or another is best to use
- Gain an understanding of the larger contexts within which a situation exists
- Realize a theory is no guarantee of good outcomes but is a reasonable approach to new and complex situations.

In summary, theories are tied to actions that occur as we live our lives. Principles for action are learned perceptually and conceptually. Contemplating and speculating on human experience goes hand in hand with recognizing best practices and carrying out these practices through what we're calling "thick listening at thin moments."

The Concepts of Thick Listening and Thin Moments

Spiritual care is a timeless practice. This book is about spiritual care that seeks to provide textured spiritual support for those going through times of change and transition. When people experience change and transition it's as if they're standing in a doorway between two worlds. It's our view that the ability to be fully present to other people as they go through threshold experiences is a unique skill set. We call this skill set *thick listening at thin moments.*

Thick listening is action. It's something we do. In the language of competency-based spiritual care practice, thick listening is a spiritual care practice. It's a quality of listening that is "thick", not only with attentiveness to the other, but concurrently with attentiveness to oneself. It's an ability to be fully oneself while being fully present to another. It's an ability to practice the safe and effective use of self in skilled, meaningful and relational ways. Thick listening grows and matures with experience.

A thin moment is something we notice in our own or in someone else's experience. In that noticing we pause to look at, contemplate and show reverence for the layered awareness of being in more than one place at a time that's characteristic of a thin moment. Thin moments have a liminal quality. They occur in spaces between worlds. They're moments of loss, trauma or exhilaration—to name some examples—that surprise us by happening *after* life-as-usual and *before* a new-normal sets back in. Thin moments are more than life-changing events. They're touchpoints that take a person to their very core. It's this quality of a thin moment that spiritual care practitioners learn to recognize. Like thick listening, the ability to discern thin moments is a spiritual care competency. The following examples have grounded Bellous and Clark in their appreciation of thin moments.

A thin moment for Bellous—As part of writing the book, we wondered what we might say about thin moment experiences from our own stories. Bellous recalls one such moment as she was walking with a friend along a trail in Edmonton she had travelled as a girl. The trail led over several train trestle bridges she and her girlfriend Connie used to ride their bikes along. In response to a question her friend asked about her mother, Bellous paused and laid her hand on the rail of the bridge. In that moment, it was as if years were swept away, and she was standing beside her mother's car the last time they stood together.

Bellous was living in Weyburn, Saskatchewan at the time. Her mom had driven all the way from Edmonton to see her in her new home. Her mom was renowned for getting lost and lived up to her reputation this time. It was dark by the time she drove up to the house. Bellous can still experience the feeling of running out to see her and standing in an embrace together on the street. She can still feel cool air on her skin and feel her mother's body holding her.

As she stood by the trestle railing, with one hand resting on it, she was back with her mother. It was November. Her mom died the following February, just three months later. That hug by the car was the last time she felt her mother's strong, upright body. The memory was triggered, felt, as distances between those worlds melted and became thin and transparent, as she stood still, on a train trestle bridge with a friend, Caryn, who knew how to wait with her.

A thin moment for Clark—Clark, too, recalls a time when she was in Desenzano, Italy, visiting locations that are historically associated with Saint Angela Merici, foundress of the Ursulines (a Roman Catholic religious community). In her early spiritual formation, it was Angela's charism that impacted Clark's life—and has continued to do so over many decades. Angela remains an influential force in Clark's spiritual care practice.

While sitting on a tiny bench in Desanzano, across the cobblestone street from where Angela is believed to have been born, Clark experienced Angela sitting right there beside her. In the silence between them there was a feeling of profound nearness, woman to woman, as graces originating in Angela's vision from the 16th century streamed through time and space. It was a thin moment of deep connection, in which Angela's words—written as counsel to leaders of her Company centuries earlier—sounded in Clark's ears. It was as if Angela spoke directly to her, saying "I am now more alive than when people saw me in person; and I see you, and I know you, and I am praying for you to never lose courage and hope."

Like Bellous and Clark, we all have thin moment experiences that have shaped and formed us. These thin moments, too, invite thick listening, contemplation and speculation. Our lives are interconnected. What we do and say influences others, just as what they do and say influences us. This is what it means to be human. When we pause to listen thickly to our own and others' thin moments, our lives come into focus in new ways. We're changed by social interactions that are embodied in spiritual care—whether this care is expressed through professional spiritual care practitioners, family members, neighbors, work colleagues, social acquaintances, or strangers.

Understanding Thick Listening at Thin Moments as a Complex Competency

While thick listening (as one competency) and the ability to recognize a thin moment (as another competency) can be observed and assessed separately, they're intended to be integrated as the cohesive, seamlessly exercised complex competency of *thick listening at thin moments*. When carried forward in combination by professional spiritual care practitioners, and also ordinary people who tend to the needs of the human spirit, this twofold competency comes alive in the here-and-now to foster right relationship, healing and wholeness.

We use the term *complex competency* to highlight the multifaceted nature of thick listening at thin moments. Complex competency is a term found in literature pertaining to learning foreign languages, introducing new competencies to existing competence, combining learning methodologies and finding common ground for interprofessional collaboration.[3] In this book, a *complex competency* is comprised of two or more distinct competencies that have been personally and professionally integrated and embodied as something new, a cohesive and seamlessly exercised complex set of spiritual care skills.

While theoretical groundwork relevant to the complex competency of thick listening at thin moments is the focus of this book, it's noteworthy that thick listening at thin moments is not found on any of the lists of competencies developed by spiritual care associations in North America. With respect, we leave the work of cultivating competency-based spiritual care education and evidence-based spiritual care practice pertinent to each association to the members of those associations who have expertise in formulating education, certification and professional practice standards.[4] For our purposes, we've chosen to use a competency—thick listening at thin moments—with which spiritual care professionals will be able to identify, while at the same time leaving to others the possibility of applying ideas from this book to their competency lists and standards.

Chapter Summaries

Spiritual care assumes that spirituality and healthy spiritual experiences are central to personal and social well being. Throughout this book, we use the words "personal" and "social" to convey how spirituality, spiritual experiences and spiritual care are integral to the ways people formulate meaning personally and, at the same time, become more aware of others through social interaction. No one is formed in isolation. One of the central messages we hope to convey throughout the book is the essential role that the humanity of the other, and of ourselves as practitioners, plays when we develop thick listening at thin moments. Reverence for the humanity of the other—for humanity in general—is at the core of engaging in thick listening and recognizing thin moments. The following chapters build on bringing theoretical insight to the task of learning thick listening at thin moments.

This book presents theories that apply to spiritual care practice. Following the central premise of Action Science, which is discussed throughout the book, we propose that *all action is theory driven,* as David's example demonstrates. However, the practical application of theory requires a set of skills and abilities that influence whether its application will result in good outcomes. Spiritual care practitioners want to enjoy good, evidence-based, outcomes with patients and clients. Good outcomes provide practitioners with the hope and energy that sustains them as they continue caring for people. In introducing and summarizing the content of the book, we provide an overview of theories presented in each chapter.

Chapter one presents three foundational perspectives on spiritual care practice. The first is a view of human spirituality, defined throughout the book as "a sense of felt connection," which is sometimes also expressed as "a felt sense of connection." The two expressions are interchangeable. The second foundational point of view comes from brain research and theoretical psychology. Since spiritual care practice aims to help people investigate and express their worldviews, it's essential for practitioners to understand how worldviews form in the first place. The third section of the chapter describes elements of Action Science, which is a process of reflecting on one's own thinking and acting that is at the heart of thick listening at thin moments.

Chapter two examines the idea and practice of faith, and connects faith with intentional reflection. In addition, chapter two outlines an understanding of contemplative mindfulness as a companion to intentional reflection, an understanding that broadens and deepens a spiritual care practitioner's comprehension of the ways faith impacts the faith stories they listen to when with clients and patients. This chapter also includes a distinction between spiritual and theological reflection and invites readers to let each type of thinking inform the other. As part of the relationship between theological and spiritual reflection, the chapter offers an approach that explores and reflects on inherited content in one's worldview that each of us has built up from birth onward, and that's firmly in place by early adolescence. The chapter concludes with a case study based on Rose, a woman who moves through Clinical Pastoral

Education (CPE) to become a well-educated spiritual care practitioner.

Chapter three provides an outline of human development based on the work of German-American psychologist Erik Erikson, who is widely referenced in spiritual care practice. Alongside his developmental approach, his eight ages of man [sic], the chapter includes four themes relevant to his work and to spiritual care practice. In addition, we describe each of his eight ages of human development and include issues, themes, and concentric circles of support that arise during each age, and that offer key questions that inform spiritual care practice.

Throughout the book, we urge readers to reflect on personal and social implications of care for the human spirit. Chapter four provides a framework that outlines a capacity every human being has for entering into and sustaining meaningful relationships, and that summarizes this human potential as the capacity of being *made for relationship*. The importance of embodied spirituality is discussed by unpacking the physical characteristics of the human body that enable one person to connect well with another, using insights from American psychologist Daniel Stern's concept of "a present moment" and also research on mirror neuron theory. Hospitality is also discussed as a human aptitude for connection as well as an attitude, standpoint and frame of mind that works toward helping rather than harming another. As mentioned, focus on the humanity of the other is paramount to learning the complex skill of thick listening at thin moments. The chapter points to the positive ways we're created for relationship, through the way our brains and bodies work so that we can persist with the aim of creating safety for one another.

Chapter five focuses on otherness, a subject that draws its understanding from many disciplines. A core aspect of spiritual care practice is the safe and effective use of self. This use of self must be informed by knowledge of self and other that allows a practitioner to hear and be heard by people who differ greatly. The chapter begins with exploring layers of self and other knowledge that need to be addressed if practitioners hope to engage others with respect and understanding. The chapter provides a framework for exploring difference by explaining three global patterns based on research into these patterns, with the aim of offering practitioners interpretative clues to help them negotiate the faith stories they listen to as they encounter people who live in unfamiliar contexts and tell very different stories about the meaning they attribute to life and experience.

Throughout the book, a central theme has to do with forming, informing, and transforming worldviews through intentional reflection and contemplative mindfulness. Chapter six explores the use of healthy reason as people reflect on their worldviews in the context of spiritual care experiences. The chapter outlines how reason impacted the previous century and notes two core ideas associated with reason and intuition. These two ideas (*dianoia* and *nous*) are foundational to understanding Action Science. The chapter includes practices for using reason based on Socratic conversation and Aristotelian deliberation.

Chapter seven provides an overview of competency-based learning and the steps to build mastery in the complex competency of thick listening at thin moments. The chapter explores a hermeneutical stance as it applies to spiritual care practice and addresses how change impacts what we come to know about ourselves and other people. The chapter goes on to present four reading strategies that facilitate appreciation of the "living human document", a phrase widely used in CPE to portray how practitioners provide spiritual care to clients and patients. The chapter concludes with a discussion of how a competency is constructed and how competence is developed in spiritual care practice.

Chapter eight picks up the theme of learning mastery in the complex competency of thick listening at thin moments by focusing on what competent spiritual care practice looks like clinically. The emphasis is on narrating lived experiences through vignettes and case studies. The chapter goes on to explore the work of American philosopher and educator Hubert Dreyfus, as viewed through a lens of spiritual care practice. His seven stages of skills acquisition are described, from novice to practical wisdom, and portrayed through clinical examples. Movement from stage to stage along the path of Dreyfus's progression offers spiritual care professional associations a theoretical framework by which to create rubrics and scales for assessing spiritual care practice.

Honoring a Time of Liminality

During the years 2019 to 2022, as we worked on the book, the whole globe trembled on an unknown threshold. As months passed, we witnessed waves and variants of the SARS-CoV-2 (COVID-19) virus, and observed myriad thin moment experiences that were both personal and social. We've seen global patterns come to life based on different approaches to public health initiatives, mandates and restrictions. We've observed people grappling with questions such as "In what can I put my faith? Who can I believe?"

In the midst of these questions we've lived in a period Charles Dickens captures by saying, "It was the best of times and the worst of times," in the opening line of his book, *A Tale of Two Cities*.[5] It's been a time of extremes—an age of wisdom and foolishness, an epoch of belief and incredulity, seasons of light and darkness, hope and despair. We've been faced by factions that hold astonishingly different interpretations of what's going on. During all these events, there's been a constancy of spiritual care lived out by professionals and ordinary people. This care was evident in our streets, homes, workplaces, and healthcare settings. Caring for the human spirit is essential during liminal times such as the one we're living through.

When we first envisioned collaborating on a manuscript dedicated to the topic of theoretical groundwork in spiritual care practice, we agreed it was a book that needed to be written. Back then, we didn't know exactly why. Now we understand. Care of the human spirit is essential during liminal times. So we offer our readers a co-authored book written during the turbulence of the second decade of the twenty-first century. We believe this book intimates a way forward for making human life better as we genuinely 'meet' each other's humanity. Our sense of the spiritual care that could make human life better is based on theoretical perspectives throughout the book that explore thick listening at thin moments. It's our hope you will come to share the confidence we feel in the significance of spiritual care as a way to improve the world we all share. Into your hands!

Chapter 1

Exploring the Territory

Introduction

This chapter examines three conceptual and theoretical foundations operative in spiritual care and its practice. First is the concept of spirituality. How is it described and defined in the literature? How do we understand and appreciate spiritual experiences in ourselves and others? What is spiritual care, and how does it attend to needs of the human spirit? What is the working definition for spirituality used in this book? Each of these questions will be considered in the early pages of the chapter.

A second conceptual and theoretical focus is how worldviews form from a perspective of psychology and brain research. Meaning produced through neural processes, as well as social and spiritual activities, results in a worldview we hold by the time we're 11 or 12 years of age. Worldviews develop through social interaction and inform us over a lifetime of human experience. One's worldview has the potential to mature through conscious reflection on experience, something facilitated in spiritual care encounters.

Lastly, the chapter looks at Action Science. This is a field of inquiry developed by Chris Argyris and Donald Schön[1] aimed at promoting reflection on and exploration of the reasoning and attitudes which underlie human action. It assumes that every action is theory driven, i.e. every action is rooted in the assumptions we hold and out of which we operate, with every theory-in-use fueled by a type of logic that happens inside one's mind. The purpose of Action Science is to help people unpack their thinking and feeling processes, and align what they do with what they say. This inner work is at the heart of spiritual care education, and equips practitioners to engage with others at reflective and explorative levels.

At the core of their professional functioning, spiritual care practitioners listen to people who are formulating meaning derived from lived experience. Having theoretical grounding that informs their listening is integral to optimal professional practice. Unpacking spirituality, worldviews formation and Action Science can serve as a foundation to what this book calls thick listening at thin moments, core concepts that will be developed in chapter two.

In its most general sense, spiritual care refers to caring for the human spirit and recognizing the human spirit as self-transcending. By self-transcending, we refer to a human capacity to get beyond ourselves, beyond our own limited physical self. As an example of this human capacity, we can fall in love with someone so that the other person becomes more important than we are to ourselves. While in love, we get beyond ourselves.

From another point of view, we've written this chapter at the outset of the Coronavirus pandemic of 2020. A term that cropped up, as people witnessed acts of kindness that appeared everywhere, was the term 'Caremongering'.[2] It's a concept that garnered global attention and led to the writing of several reports and research articles as well as the establishment of numerous FaceBook groups and postings.[3] It attests to the fact that human beings can choose to focus on caring for others, even strangers, in contrast to the scaremongering that could be just as rampant. Choosing to care rather than scare is indicative of the truth that people have a capacity to transcend their own interests, and consider and respond to the interests of others. This observable situation supports the view that a "person alone" is an ontological contradiction.[4]

What is the nature of that contradiction as we focus on spiritual care? Human beings are both material and spiritual entities. Our psychological, physical, emotional, relational, communal, racial, gendered, historical, social and anthropological dimensions exist within spiritual/material realities. Spiritual care assumes that spirituality and healthy spiritual experiences are central to personal and social well-being. If this generalization about the human condition is accurate, it's also true that people differ greatly, depending on the physical and social setting that someone occupies, and the place where someone grew up. Spiritual care relies on having a firm grip on understanding the patterns that form around our common humanity as well as the unique differences that characterize people. Spiritual care keeps open to these two dimensions of the human condition (common humanity and personal uniqueness) as practitioners listen to faith stories that people tell them.[5]

If we say that spirituality refers to a human capacity for recognizing self-transcendence, of our ability to get beyond ourselves, we may also be aware of conflicts and controversies that arose during the pandemic. As an example, the issue of wearing masks inside private and public places, where social distancing wasn't possible, was marked by public protests globally. There were people who adamantly refused to wear masks; for them, to be compelled to do so was an infringement of their rights. From another point of view, wearing a mask wasn't seen as protecting the one wearing it, rather it was a sign of the wearer's willingness not to pass on the virus. The controversy was heated. It impacted teachers as children re-entered school in September of 2020. There were some parents who protested mask wearing because they saw it as an infringement of their children's personal freedom, while other parents wanted their children to enter a setting where they were protected from a virus others might bring to school.

We raise the issue of mask wearing because it points out that, while we have the capacity to transcend our own interests, that capacity needs educating. In order to situate openness to, and understanding of, different ways of life at the centre of caring for others, we begin by exploring the territory spirituality inhabits. We also discuss religion and culture as ways to understand how to respond to spirituality's role in human experience. To begin, we investigate current ways that spirituality is described and defined. Following that analysis, we outline aspects of spiritual experiences that have been recorded and used to show that these experiences are common to humanity, and that the occurrence of recorded spiritual experiences is on the increase. In terms of our capacity for self-transcendence, and its need for education, the rest of the book explores the nature of spiritual care education.

In this chapter, we pose a challenge to healthcare definitions of spirituality by describing emotions that aren't typically included in the way the word is defined in that setting. In order to frame spiritual care in its essence, we unpack a practice called Action Science to establish the role that spiritual care has in helping people heal. Action Science proposes that every action is theory driven. Spiritual care practitioners help people examine the theories (assumptions) they're currently using to see if these are still the theories they want to continue relying upon.

At the core of their professional functioning, spiritual care practitioners keep in mind, as they listen, the two dimensions noted above (common humanity and personal uniqueness). As a result, in discussing Action Science, we provide a case study to offer an overview of the global human experience of poverty in a particular person. We also explore how worldviews form. In this chapter we provide a working definition for spirituality that's used throughout the book. Our purpose in this chapter is to liberate the word spirituality from some of its current contexts so the term is more useful in the public domain.

Situating Spirituality

As mentioned, the purpose of this chapter is to situate spirituality within its broadest scope conceptually so that spiritual care can be effective. Spirituality is often linked to religion and we want to probe that relationship. As we investigate the way the term spirituality is used currently in healthcare settings, which is one of the main contexts within which spiritual care practitioners are educated, there's a conceptual framework that helps sort through the data. In this framework, there are three possibilities underlying the discussion. The first possibility is to say that religion and spirituality are virtually the same and the two terms can be used interchangeably. Some definitions presented in Appendix 1 (e.g., Hodge et al., #6; Pesut, B., #8) make that claim.

A second possibility is to say that religion and spirituality are entirely different and have little or nothing to do with one another. There's at least one definition in Appendix 1 (e.g., Puchalski et al., #9) that describes spirituality without reference to religion. A third possibility is to say that spirituality and religion are related in such a way that spirituality applies to everyone and religion concerns some people. In definitions that coalesce under this third possibility, spirituality is often described with respect to world religions as well as to atheistic or agnostic points of view. The third option is the position we take in this book. The reason we rely on the third option is that it most closely conveys the view that every human being is spiritual.

We will unpack the claim that spirituality is more than religion, but at this point it's important to provide an analysis of definitions we've gathered to see how the healthcare field uses the term. One compelling observation to make about the definitions gathered to date (there's no claim we've been exhaustive in Appendix 1) is that spirituality is perceived as overwhelmingly positive. In every case, spirituality provides for meaning and purpose. This emphasis is understandable insofar as spirituality is an essential aspect of human nature. That said, an exclusively positive perspective on spirituality misses the full range of experiences that accumulate within the human spirit. We say more about the painful side of its impact later on.

Most (but not all) of the definitions gathered distinguish existential concerns from spiritual ones by introducing a transcendent aspect. That is, spirituality is different from ordinary problems of existence because it has to do with the supernatural, which some descriptions refer to as God, but, again, not all do. As mentioned, one of the definitions includes transcendent aspects of all world religions and refers to the idea of an ultimate purpose as the orienting aspect of the human/spiritual relation, which, as a result, takes spirituality outside of the domain of religion. (Reinert & Koenig, Appendix 1, #10)

If we drill down into these definitions of spirituality, sometimes they refer to action—spirituality is about recognizing and celebrating important values. In other descriptions, spirituality is a state of being, which typically offers people connection to self, others, nature and a transcendent Being or a life principle. As a state of being, spirituality is an ongoing experience that provides positive support to one's life through a feeling of *being with* others.

The idea of connection appears in almost all the definitions. Spirituality links people to others. Yet some definitions refer to 'individual' spirituality, which is interesting, if not misleading, since it's generally described as a state of *being with* others or an ability to connect with others. Individual implies separateness rather than connection; it suggests standing apart rather than *being with*. In this book, we prefer the term personal to individual. We prefer to emphasize that the personal is always formed in the company of others—the personal always has social influence. The human spirit gathers life experiences into a meaningful whole, which isn't to suggest the meaning we make from experience is without internal conflicts and contradictions.

For one thing, the personal meaning system that's produced through experience begins at birth, when we're helpless and need adults to act as meaning makers with us. It's often our helplessness, our dependence on others throughout life, and disappointments that can result from our need for others, which must be addressed through spiritual care.

This isn't to say that spiritual experiences themselves *always* involve other people. But rather, meaning produced through spirituality typically results in a worldview we hold by the time we're 11 or 12 years of age. Worldviews develop through social interaction and inform us over a lifetime of human experience/social interaction. One's worldview has the potential to mature through conscious reflection on experience. We explore the forming of a worldview more thoroughly later in this chapter.

Throughout this book, we use two terms, personal and social, instead of individual and collective or individual and communal/community. The work of being spiritual is best conveyed through ideas implied by these two terms. One aim of spiritual care is to help people have greater success in appropriating meaning personally, and at the same time, become more effective in social interaction. No one is formed in isolation. Working out an adult worldview that we intentionally choose to hold, by reflecting on the one we formed when we were young, is meaningful work that's supported through spirituality, spiritual experiences and spiritual care.

Spiritual Experiences

What is a spiritual experience? There seems to be ample evidence that these experiences inform ordinary human life. One starting point is found in the work of British zoologist Alister Hardy (b.1896). He entered Oxford in 1914 and read Zoology under his tutor, Julian Huxley, who was the grandson of T.H. Huxley—the man who was "known as Darwin's Bulldog for his fierce defence [sic] of the theory of Natural Selection."[6] Hardy studied under the strong influence of radical skepticism about religion and God's existence. That skeptical view was referred to as *mechanical materialism* and was the proposed certainty that the human body was essentially a machine without a soul.[7]

The reason Hardy's research matters to spiritual care practitioners is because of its roots in scientific investigations he initiated that have taken place for over 60 years. His research ignited interest in spirituality. After he retired as professor of Zoology at Oxford, Hardy gave all his energy to investigating what he called spiritual experiences. As a result, he was certain that all human beings (members of the species *Homo sapiens*) have the potential for spiritual awareness.[8] He further argued that spirituality has a biological basis: the way the human body is formed and the manner in which a person becomes a member of a social group allows people to experience what can't be seen, touched, tasted, heard or smelled, i.e., people are capable of having transcendent experiences that go beyond what's usually available to our five senses.

Hardy was unpersuaded by mechanical materialism. What he did subscribe to was a belief that "certain forerunners of *Homo sapiens* 'consciously chose' to attend to the spiritual dimension of their awareness," with the result that they received its benefits in terms of the "strength to cope with the dangers and difficulties of their physical and emotional environment."[9]

This positive view of spirituality's effects on people has continued to gain strength in the literature. As one example, American psychologist Lisa Miller made use of a 1997 study that was a landmark scientific article published in the *American Journal of Psychiatry*.[10] Its research provided evidence of beneficial dimensions of spirituality. Its conclusions were empirically derived. That study uncovered the significance of "a personal relationship with the transcendent" and argued that the relationship makes crucial and valuable contributions to "good health, mental well-being, fulfillment and success."[11]

A central aspect of Miller's view is that a relationship with the transcendent must be personal and personally sought, secured, and lived out in the daily exercise of one's values and behavior because that connection builds what she calls an inner spiritual compass. In her view, this compass is an innate, concrete faculty. Like emotional intelligence, it's part of our biological endowment. She asserts that it can be educated. We would add that, without civility, an intentional and respectful awareness of difference, this compass might be thrown off kilter if human differences are disdained within a social setting.

Miller notes that her evidence for an inner compass is "hard, indisputable, and rigorously scientific."[12] Is she making the case for religion? She cites a twins study carried out by Kenneth Kendler that asked about the relationship between spirituality and religion. He concluded that, in his research with nearly 2000 adult twins, "in people's lived experience, personal spirituality is a different concept from adherence to religion or choice of religious denomination."[13] Miller notes that, in Kendler's research, "spirituality did not meaningfully correlate with one specific religious [group because] there are highly spiritual people who [don't] adhere to any specific religious [group]."[14]

Miller provides a caveat when it comes to the relationship between spirituality and religion. She notes empirical research that methodologically identified what is *not* meant by personal spirituality. In her data, spirituality is unrelated statistically to strict adherence to a religion or a creed if there's no sense of personal choice or ownership. In other words, healthy spirituality involves personal choice and ownership. One of the functions of spiritual care is to listen for the ways personal choice and ownership are given voice.

In light of the definitions and discussion so far, when considering spiritual care, practitioners focus on common human aspects of spirituality as their starting point. But how does one recognize spiritual experiences, if religious language isn't used—or if a different language is used that's unfamiliar? In the chapter on Otherness, we look at ways to address difference. But first, we examine patterns that have been identified in spirituality research that indicate a relationship with the transcendent.

In 1969, Alister Hardy founded the *Religious Experience Research Unit* (RERU) at Oxford University in Britain with the "purpose of making a scientific study of the nature, function and frequency of reports on [what he called at the time] religious experience in the human species."[15] It's important to note that he didn't speculate on God or God's existence, but focused on human spirituality. British Zoologist David Hay continued Hardy's research and provided a summary of the data he gathered in 2000, which he compared with the data gathered in 1989.

The comparisons Hay drew indicated a significant upsurge in people's reports of spiritual experiences in Britain between 1987 and 2000. In addition, his Australian colleague David Tacey concurred with his findings by using data from his own country. It's noteworthy to add that, during this time period, while reports of spiritual experiences increased, church attendance declined. In his book, *Something There*, Hay notes that an increase in spiritual experiences and a decline in church attendance was evident across Western Europe.

Hay didn't speculate on that inverse relationship, but provided a useful description of spiritual experiences. Instances of spiritual experiences include the following qualities:

- A patterning of events that persuade people the events were meant to happen due to a transcendent providence
- Awareness of the presence of God
- Awareness of prayer being answered

- Awareness of a sacred presence in nature
- Awareness of the presence of the dead
- Awareness of an evil presence.[16]

Hay gives specific examples of these experiences as recounted by those who offered them to researchers at the *Religious Experience Research Unit*. In his summary, Hay provides spiritual care practitioners with vital and valuable approaches to understanding a client's experience, for at least two reasons: there's evidence that spiritual awareness is universal—everyone is spiritual—and spiritual awareness is expressed by qualities Hay identifies. Attentiveness to these patterns and qualities can prove foundational to effective listening, assessment and intervention in spiritual care.

It's important to pick up an aspect of Hay's research that differs sharply with definitions analyzed in the previous section. Hay notes two types of awareness in which people perceive the presence of the dead or of an evil presence. There's nothing in definitions or descriptions gathered from the healthcare field to compare with either of these two types of awareness. As mentioned, the way spirituality is conceived in healthcare at present is to see it as a positive, beneficial aspect of someone's life. We don't mean to diminish these positive benefits—but if spirituality were only positive, would anyone need spiritual care?

In addition, the positive attributes of spirituality need to be balanced by Miller's research. She makes it clear that spirituality doesn't provide positive benefits under the conditions she cites, e.g., if there's no sense of sacred relationship. Further, as authors, we both know people who grew up in religious environments in which, as children, they were drowning in guilt and fear. Unhealthy teaching and practice hurts people. Spiritual experiences can introduce people to confusing emotions, such as guilt, anger, shame and depression.

Spiritual Care and Difficult Emotions

In a significant book, *Shadows of the Heart*,[17] American developmental psychologist Evelyn Whitehead analyzes the underbelly of human spirituality by looking at what she refers to as negative emotions. She does so by identifying the upside of these emotions as she explores, what she calls, the good news about bad feelings. Whitehead points out that bad feelings may make us miserable, but they often come bearing gifts. She asserts, and supports the idea persuasively, that emotions are both personal and social. In particular, she points out that

> our feelings do not exist for us alone: emotions are social strategies directed toward our interaction with other people…emotions…are not just directives to ourselves, but directives from others to us, indicating that we have been seen; that we have been understood; that we have been appreciated; that we have made contact.[18]

The personal and social aspects of emotion are another layer of awareness that identifies *connection* as a central feature of spirituality. During spiritual care, practitioners pay full attention to the personal and social implications of a client's or a patient's situation, as a way to ensure that connection is established.

In short, emotions are an opportunity for connection because every emotion involves what Whitehead calls arousal, interpretation and movement.[19] She identifies an upside to distressing emotions and links each of four negative emotions to a benefit:

- Anger challenges us to right a wrong; calls us to decisive action to protect from harm something we judge to be of genuine value: *Anger* leads to action in pursuit of justice.
- Shame affirms the necessary boundaries that support our sense of self; warns of risks of premature exposure; protects the privacy that makes genuine intimacy possible: *Shame* is one of the roots of personal dignity.
- Guilt reminds us of the shape of our best self; alerts us to discrepancies between our ideals and our behavior; defends the commitments and value-choices we've made that give meaning to life: *Guilt* supports our sense of personal integrity.
- Depression alerts us that something has become intolerable; ordinary depression (not clinical) invites us to re-examine our lives; its misery motivates us to face challenges or the losses we have been avoiding: *Depression* can ready us for mature grieving and open up an opportunity for change.[20]

The positive aspects Whitehead links to negative emotions are surprising. Yet Whitehead isn't dismissing the power of negative emotions;

rather, she's calling us to channel that power towards a positive analysis of and healthy response to them. The task she sets out for people is made possible as we learn to reflect on meanings contained in the worldview that shapes our experience.

Meaning and Spiritual Needs

Up to now we've been saying that spirituality is universal. Why do we make that claim? From our point of view, based on an upsurge of scientific research about spirituality, the human spirit is an agent of and repository for accumulated meaning that's derived from exposure to experience. All human beings have a capacity for connection that allows them to develop a meaningful and positive way of being in the world. In the book, *The Spirit of the Child* (1998), Rebecca Nye describes the human capacity for connection as relational consciousness, which is grounded on human biology, but is a special kind of awareness that makes possible aesthetic, scientific and religious experience.[21]

In addition to its biological roots in Hardy's, Hay's and Nye's research, as a human capacity, in her book, *Educating Faith*, Bellous points out that spirituality builds meaning based on four additional existential processes, namely: sociological, neurological, cultural and psychological processes.[22] The psychological aspect of object relating unifies all five processes by organizing daily experience into a worldview.[23] Through all five processes, spirituality creates personal and social meaning out of daily life experience.

Through the spiritual work of relating to objects (e.g., people, events, places) from the time we're born and throughout life, the meaning we make from these encounters establishes and perpetuates assumptions, beliefs and values that form our worldview. That worldview shapes how people interpret what they can expect from life, from other people, nature, from the transcendent and of themselves. A formative worldview is at the heart of the way people live their lives.

Yet spirituality is an ambiguous term—it has more than one meaning. We've been speaking of it as a basic human capacity for connection. People also think of it as a way of life, e.g., a Muslim, Christian, Buddhist or an atheistic way of life. Some people incorporate both aspects into how they think about spirituality.[24] The two uses are important, but spirituality, whether a human capacity or way of life, is healthy only as long as essential spiritual needs are met in community (socially) and in someone's life (personally):

> Every human being has a spiritual need to celebrate, mark significant moments, bear witness to truths learned about life, play, tell their story, grieve, mourn, lament, connect with the past, pray, make significant journeys, express themselves symbolically, seek purpose and meaning, ask ultimate questions, have a satisfactory way to think and speak about the beginning and the end of life, survive, flourish, experience longing and enjoy its satisfaction, relax, cope with life circumstances, be seen, be heard, have a name that's remembered, be part of a larger community, organize experience meaningfully so as to make sense of it, maintain human dignity, see the future as hopeful, and experience transcendence.[25]

Meeting these spiritual needs is essential for healthful living. Personal meaning gathered into a worldview is intertwined with having our spiritual needs met socially or, sadly, of having them neglected by others and devalued by ourselves.

Spiritual care practitioners walk with people as they review the worldviews they've gathered. Worldviews may contain ideas, images and assumptions that no longer serve the purpose people want their lives to express. In addition, the meaning gathered may create harmful attitudes, practices and self-sabotaging strategies that, at some point in time, we may wish to reflect upon and even release ourselves from, so as to live in a different way. In order to reflect on our worldviews we need to understand how they came to be in the first place. Before we look at how worldviews form, we want to summarize how we're using the word spirituality.

Spirituality: A Working Definition

This book focuses on spirituality as a human capacity more than spirituality as a way of life. In 2006, Bellous published *Educating Faith* and offered a definition for spirituality as 'a sense of felt connection'. To come to this definition, she analyzed the human side of spirituality in the company of an international cohort of religious educators that included David Hay, Rebecca Nye[26] and David Tacey, mentioned earlier in this chapter.

Bellous' definition asserts that spirituality is more than religion and that everyone is spiritual, whether or not they're religious, a position Lisa Miller also takes, as discussed in the section on spiritual experiences. In this light, a focus of attention for spiritual care practitioners is to try to get behind what people present as their religious or non-religious beliefs and practices. As caregivers listen reflectively and aim to get a sense, not only of the person's belief statements, words or rituals, but also to hear the feelings or tone of the religious or non-religious experience that someone is trying to convey, they're involved in spirituality as a sense of felt connection.

When it comes to providing a working definition for spirituality, we note that the term is vague and ambiguous. It's ambiguous because it has more than one meaning: as a human capacity and as a way of life. It's also vague. Spirituality is used so widely that it seems to mean everything and nothing. Bellous had this point hit home when she attended a conference in the summer of 2019 at Laval University in Quebec where an international group of religious educators came together to discuss spirituality. The range of ways of conveying the term was astonishing! Its vagueness was strikingly evident. Why is this so?

We suggest it's the way with such words. They're hard to define. Spirituality doesn't lend itself to simple definitions, such as, 'a dog is an animal that barks' or 'a cat is an animal that meows'. In these definitions, there's a specific term (dog, cat), a category term (animal) and a descriptor term (barks, meows). The category is the same for dogs and cats but the descriptor term distinguishes one animal from the other. Using these definitions, we easily recognize dogs and cats we see on the street. It's not so simple with spirituality.

Another example might help. Let's take the two words baker and grocer. If we were to define baker we would start by saying that a baker bakes, and is someone who bakes bread, buns and other food items. When we define the word that way, we're pretty sure to recognize people who work in a bakery and distinguish those who are dressed in a certain way in the back by the ovens from those who provide service at the front counter. Of course, bakers could both bake and provide service, but we would be able to distinguish words for the tasks they carry out. We would say, Anne is a baker but sometimes she works in the front. For baker, the noun clearly conveys the verb: bakers bake.

But let's look at the word grocer. How do we define that term by saying what someone does? A grocer doesn't groce—there's no such word. In order to get a sense of what a grocer does, we have to pay attention to what they're doing. There's a range of possibilities—buying, selling, arranging, as some examples. If we use the word grocer, we need more information to recognize one when we see one in a grocery shop. The word spirituality is like the noun grocer and not like the noun baker.

Another way to define words like spirituality is to view them using the metaphor of a clothesline. There are appropriate words to hang on the spirituality clothesline. Other terms, by contrast, don't belong. For example, material aspects of life such as clothes, electronic purchases and food items don't belong on this clothesline. They're different and belong to other words. Material goods, by themselves, don't meet spiritual needs. Terms to hang on our spirituality clothesline might include the following:

> the personal; the social; a felt sense of connection; a human capacity; a way of life; engagement characteristic of really showing up; a developing worldview and one's reflection on it; thriving; purpose; meaning; core values, to name some words.

To carry the image further, and reinforce the research referred to earlier about how important it is to include a full range of experiences that accumulate within the human spirit when defining spirituality, the spirituality clothesline is like a neighbourhood in an old movie. It's not just pretty things that hang on the line. It includes not only fresh scented items but also some dirty laundry. The ugly hangs near the lovely. With a felt sense of connection there's opportunity for benevolence and malevolence, personally and socially. We can choose never to meet someone's gaze when they search for ours. We can ignore a loved one who's simply sharing our space. We can fail to show up, when it would cost us very little to do so. We can be desperately unkind. We can refuse to wear a mask during a pandemic because we're protective of our personal freedom, but also be, seemingly unaware of how important it is to hold a tension between personal freedom and the social good, as spelled out in a phrase often seen on notice boards: "my mask protects you and your mask protects me". There are endless ways one human being can hurt another, just as there are endless ways to offer meaningful, loving connection. While much of what we share about spirituality and spiritual care in the pages of this book highlights what's positive, we don't ignore the underbelly of human spirituality.

Forming a Worldview

Thus far we've discussed spirituality, spiritual experiences and spiritual needs. We've also made a number of references to the term 'worldview'. At this point, we want to explore how worldviews form from the perspective of theoretical psychology and brain research. Understanding how worldviews come into being will offer clues for thick listening, which is a concept central to spiritual care practice that will be discussed in the chapter on Faith. Our purpose is to unpack worldview formation to allow practitioners to hear as accurately as possible what people are conveying, and to discover deep-going opportunities that reach into and penetrate to the heart of the matter so that people can offer spiritual care.

Throughout the book, we define spirituality as "a felt sense of connection". That definition conveys how people make meaning from experience and form a worldview as part of their spiritual work. A felt sense is rooted in infancy.[27] At birth, an infant is a stream of sensations that eventually organizes into patterns that become concepts to use when thinking, feeling, investigating and deciding. These concepts show up in our faith stories. Sensory perceptions streaming into an infant brain (cortex) create cortical effects that gradually work into shapes and patterns: some of these effects form the concept 'me' and some form the concept 'not me.'[28]

British psychologist Josephine Klein[29] composed a picture to help us understand how we come to identify as ourselves. The way she explained it, identity slowly forms to include aspects that create the situation we find ourselves in as we interact with others. At the beginning, an infant fuses with its mother and doesn't distinguish itself from her. Over time, an infant emerges into a self. The term *emerge* refers to coming out of this merged connection between mother and baby. As Klein put it, "somehow the baby has to e-merge—come out of the merge. As babies e-merge, so do (m)others."[30] If all goes well, and we acknowledge this isn't always the case, a baby becomes aware of itself as distinct from its mother, which is a foundational experience for comprehending all other objects in the world, including other people.

At first, the child is a stream, or the stream is the child. The mother acts as skin might do, before the infant has developed what one might call its own skin—something to contain all its fluctuating sensations.[31] If all goes well, the mother acts as a container, a primary nurturing containment for the child's stream of sensations until the child becomes aware of its own skin. If she's able, the mother holds the child until the flow of input is steady for long enough to allow "pattern-making...pattern recognition, some organization and structuring, to take place."[32] The mother helps put things in perspective. If all is well, this process takes place between mother and child;[33] both mother and infant are active agents within and during it.[34]

The stream of sensations activates nerve cells. As a result, nerve cells or neurons converse with one another. They send electrical impulses to one another so that one nerve cell excites another.[35] These messages continue to move from neuron to neuron among networks of nerve cells[36] to form a communication system within the human body. As sensations enter the brain, they excite some nerve cells that are linked to the external world through a child's organs (e.g., eyes, ears) and to various parts within the body, for example, when bones or muscles change position.[37] This brain activity forms a child's perceptions of the world. Perception is a source of learning, establishes memories and constantly provides people with knowledge.[38]

A second set of nerve cells are linked to each other, not to the external world. It's this second set that are responsible for concept formation, e.g., mother, father, God,[39] sister, brother, women, men to name some that populate a worldview. In forming a worldview, concepts don't erase percepts. We have ongoing access to concepts and percepts. Percepts are sense based. Ongoing access to percepts and concepts is important in the process of learning. As we will discuss in the final section of this chapter, Action Science relies on our ability to perceive what we've missed in an environment and thereby allows us to rethink our concepts.

To Canadian psychologist Donald Hebb, it's the brain that thinks.[40] How does this work? The typical human being has the complexity of about one billion cell assemblies. This complexity is what makes the normal development of intelligence and human learning possible, including a capacity for abstraction and generalization (seeing patterns) that's fundamental to human thought.[41] A *percept* consists of cell assemblies excited by the senses; a *concept* forms by assemblies that are excited centrally in the brain by other assemblies—by their internal communicative interaction.[42] As far as adult thought is concerned, the development of new concepts is a process of modification and development of old ones.[43]

When we talk about formation of a worldview, we can ask about its content. Much of what's in a worldview is representational of the world it's inherited. That is, a worldview is based on a mental system, as Austrian-British economist F.A. Hayek pointed out in his research on theoretical psychology, that's "shaped by the conditions prevailing in the environment in which we live, and it represents a kind of generic re-production of the relations between the elements of this environment which we have experienced in the past; we interpret any new event in the environment in light of that experience."[44] It may be said that meaning making flows from interactions between these two sets of neurons—one externally linked and the other operating as an internal organization of meaning.

This second set of neurons forms concepts without relying on direct sensory input.[45] It's the communication among these neurons that makes conceptual learning possible. For example, let's consider what happens before a child comes up with the concept 'triangle'. As perceptions enter the cortex, the child sees an angle. The roundness and movement of the child's eye makes it possible to see other angles: a child looks at one angle of a triangle and then looks for others so that a triangle takes shape. As the process happens repeatedly, the child acquires the concept 'triangle', which is more than the sum of three angles—it's a new concept. Children can then recognize triangles, sometimes as soon as they see only one of the three angles.[46] These kinds of abstractions (a triangle) can't be per-ceived by the senses; they have to be conceived by central processes in the brain.[47]

Two essential aspects of learning are active in the brain: perceptual learning (sensations linked to the external world and the body) and con-

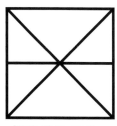

Figure 1 - Triangle perception

ceptual learning (stimuli that activate internally linked neurons that organize meaning). Con-ceptual learning works with perceptual learning—this point is at the heart of Action Science. In adult learning, new learning may be independent of direct sensory stimulation. Rather, it's expressive of the mental system to which Hayek referred: an association might have been set up by vision, and yet be manifest later by hearing a sound, or feeling a touch, for example, when we're triggered by a tone of voice or facial expression that we knew from the past.

By observing the process of acquiring data, (e.g., D.O.D. in the Ladder of Inference discussed later in the chapter), we catch a glimpse of conceptual learning; learning through the use of words and symbols. In a given situation, Action Science invites adults to look at and look for, more information than someone currently perceives so they can re-conceive the situation. Action Science serves as a learning process through which to re-engage and personalize one's inherited worldview. This classifying, conceptualizing process is the meaning-making labor everyone necessarily carries out; and as mentioned, creating meaning is a person's spiritual work. Psychologically, this can also be viewed as object relations work insofar as it's the unifying activity that produces meaning by considering the objects we encounter throughout life. Object relations theories explain our need for others, since they are "theories about our relations to the 'objects'—people and things—to which we are attached and which give meaning to our lives."[48]

Returning to Klein's picture, the process of thinking must be something like this: a sequence of events starts when central neural activity is a stimulus for communicating with other neurons, without needing the intervention of a sensory stimulus.[49] She notes that there's a difference "between fleeting and more enduring changes in the nervous system, making it possible for more central dominance to emerge.[50] To establish more central neural control is a victory of a person over an environment, enabling someone not only to adapt to the environment, but eventually to have agency within it. This is part of what happens as we e-merge, as mentioned earlier. As we're thinking, past memories can be drawn upon to evaluate current events, giving people the benefit of past experience before they need to take action. But again, we aren't always aware of all that it's possible to see. Look at the square diagram (see Figure 1). How many triangles do you see? Klein includes the diagram in her book and notes that she found fourteen triangles in this square.

The classifying process that shapes a worldview begins in infancy. The image of the homunculus[51] (see Figure 2), developed by Canadian neurosurgeon, Wilder Penfield, conveys where an infant's body initially records data; a baby begins to collect and organize perceptions that form their foundational picture of the world. We're all familiar with the way babies put everything in their mouths as they explore. The homunculus is a depiction of the sites where perceptions gather. In this way, a human being is a place where things happen, then becomes a self-recognizing object, and eventually, an agent of their own experience. It's both a perceptual and conceptual process. The network of these connections reproduces a multi-sensory, complete record of everything that's happened to a person. This memory bank is called an Engram; a storehouse of all that comprises a person's complex, multi-sensory memories.[52]

In order to situate the meaning-making work human beings do, and connect it with forming a worldview, let's go back to the idea of a felt sense. Klein's term, a felt self,[53] is the basis of self-consciousness that forms over time. Eugene Gendlin describes the innermost experience of a person that eventually develops the complexity of a felt sense, which is a stream of sensations (consciousness) organized into concepts and classified into patterns. Within a felt sense, one is aware of elements of this stream of consciousness in a studied, accessible and attentive manner.[54]

In terms of conceptual learning, there are two aspects of a worldview

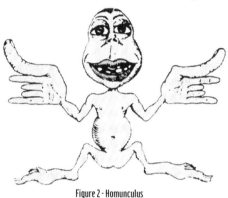

Figure 2 - Homunculus

called a map and a model.[55] Slowly a worldview map forms which consists of concepts and connections between these concepts, previously referred to as the Engram. The map isn't two-dimensional; it's multi-dimensional. It defines the relationship of everything to everything else. We can think of many maps within this map, just as we would think of a map of North America as composed of many smaller maps: Edmonton, Vancouver, New York, Chicago, small towns, villages, neighborhoods, someone's living room or someone's bedroom. The mental map has that sort of complexity and depth.

But at birth, there's no map—only the homunculus. Infants can't organize their picture of the world in an adult fashion because not enough has happened to get more than a blurry sense of what's going on.[56] As learning accumulates, based on inherited and personal experience, an internal meaning system will contain three elements: a sense of self, a sense of other people and things, and a sense of what goes on between these two.[57]

The second aspect of a worldview is the model, which is a representation of a given moment. The map and model each contain a self-concept. The model is experienced within a map; the map is its background.

A person adjusts to elements of a given moment that are active during social interaction, and the map has its full effect on how a given moment is read. Suppose something happens; an event occurs. To begin with, people test incoming experience against the map and their sense of whether the current instance is like or unlike the map. The map is the 'familiar' against which the model is scrutinized. Next, a person will judge whether an event resonates with how things should or should not be done. The map is the standard into which the model needs to fit.

If an event is congruous with (is like) the map then that's the end of it. If an event is unlike the map, people sense something should be done about the mismatch. A process of testing and finding congruity or incongruity is carried out until a given moment is like the map. Each worldview map is constructed from experiences that are unavailable to other people, even those who are close. As a consequence, as we encounter others, we have no sense of the whole map that stands behind a given moment *for them*. We gain no access to that map except by asking about aspects of it. If adults experience dissonance between map and model, they often react with what looks like defensiveness. It might not be defensiveness, however, but rather that a person is feeling an urge to correct the model so it can fit the map because, in the mismatch, they sense they've been misunderstood.

As experience accumulates, it's somewhat fluid; but over time the map reifies or solidifies. As it develops into a system of interlinking concepts, a new event is less likely to affect its overall organization. As mentioned previously, worldviews are established by early adolescence. The map is an internal organization based on past and semi-permanent connections composed of memories that create a personal meaning system that suggests what the future will hold. Any new event encounters a whole construction and can only modify behavior in light of the whole picture. The map is a relatively enduring structure that tells me who I am. At the same time, a given moment also says something about me. The map self and the model self interrelate during every social interaction. The map and model selves, under favorable conditions, are closely linked, giving a sense of continuity, identity, direction and value.[58]

The process of worldview formation results in embodied learning, as the examples of eye movement and the homunculus highlight.[59] Let's note that learning happens slowly and is ongoing. Its slowness is due to the complexity of which human thinking is capable.[60]

We've outlined differences between perceptual and conceptual learning. In addition, learning involves deciding. Human beings have a greater ability to steer behavior in a particular direction than other animals.[61] The ability to steer behavior depends on where we place our attention. As a worldview develops, neural structures come into being that involve an expectation of what will happen next and an impulse to do the next thing. One consequence of such structures is to make it possible for us to expect events to happen that haven't happened yet. These expectations give meaning to current events, so much so that an expectation can seem to be the same as the meaning.

All reflection is built on remaining awake to perceptions that influence our concepts. The classification of concepts occurs in the brain because the same entering event has the same effect whenever it occurs,[62] e.g., seeing the angle of a triangle. Concepts are the means for developing insight. But we're typically unaware of all that's available to be perceived in a given situation, as the square of triangles shows (see Figure 3). This is where Action Science can, once again, play an important role insofar as its methods require us to be intentional about approaching a situation in such a way that we notice what's actually there. As Action Science shows, there are directly observable data (D.O.D.) in most situations, and this data could make a difference to how we conceive what's happening. Data are there to be seen, but we don't necessarily see them, even though there's no repression of what's going on. Looking at Figure 3, what is the error in each of these triangles?

Figure 3· Directly observable data

We easily miss data that's present and is there to see, don't we?

Everything in our mental system is always there, but not readily available. We have a multi-sensory, complete record of everything that's ever happened to us. At the same time, we access the map in bits and pieces based on paying attention to a concrete moment of social interaction, especially if it's dissonant with the map. Conceptual learning involves intentional reflection on map and model.

A process of reading a situation introduces both planning and a feedback loop. Let's use the example of a spiritual care practitioner named John. He's hungry. He's also trying to finish drafting a verbatim for tomorrow's Clinical Pastoral Education (CPE) seminar.[63] He knows he can make a sandwich for supper and get back to work—but it would be the third lot of sandwiches he would eat that day. He's reading the situation, and his planning includes the following thought process:

> Hunger is satisfied by eating: I can eat sandwiches or think of all the other ways to satisfy hunger. I can buy sandwiches or consider all the other ways to get sandwiches. I can buy sandwiches at the corner store or consider all the other places to buy sandwiches.[64]

As John plans, a feedback loop emerges that tests his thinking. This demonstrates the fundamental building-block of the nervous system, i.e., its feedback loop. John forms a plan. A test is performed to determine whether the goal has been accomplished. Until the goal (hunger sated) is achieved, the feedback loop persists and repeats. John's hunger will be satisfied or his nervous system will continue triggering the feedback loop. According to authors Miller, Galanter and Pribram, taken together, planning and the feedback loop are referred to by the following acronym: TOTE (TEST, OPERATE, TEST, EXIT).[65]

During the process, there may be several turns in the feedback loop. Something is happening. TEST: John thinks, I'm hungry. OPERATE: action is taken; he checks the bread supply in the kitchen. There's no bread. He looks at the time. He starts walking to the corner store. TEST: he checks with the self-image on his map as he's walking. The idea of three meals of sandwiches in one day is incongruous with his self-image as a healthy eater and his goal to stay fit. ACT: at the store, he buys cheese and fresh fruit. TEST: he thinks that eating cheese and fresh fruit is congruous with his map's self-image as a health-conscious, fit man. He EXITS his plan, satisfies his hunger and gets back to work.[66]

While reflecting on the map and model together, John steers his behaviour in his intended direction.[67] The model is the active part on the map that accounts for where a person is in relation to the world as it's being experienced in a given moment (John feels hungry), in relation to the way he expects to be (a healthy eater), in relation to the good and bad places on his map (he wants to stay fit), as he lets feedback processes act gyroscopically. If our current sense of self is closely linked with the self on the map, we experience satisfaction (like John's buying cheese and fresh fruit, instead of more bread, at the grocery store) and this creates a feeling of congruence between 'who I am' and 'how I'm acting'.

Klein uses the metaphor of a gyroscope to describe human planning. A gyroscope is a spinning device used for measuring or maintaining orientation. There are objects used today that include gyroscopic elements, such as Apple IOS devices (iPhone, iPads) and compasses. Gyroscopic motion helps stabilize an object. On John's map there are good places (healthy eater, staying fit) and paths/orientations to those good places. There are also painful places on the map and paths toward more painful places. For example, in addition to feeling hunger, John might be thinking in a negative way:

> I'm alone tonight. Who cares if I eat sandwiches? My health can take a back seat. I'm going to finish this verbatim so I can make a good impression at tomorrow's CPE seminar. I must be seen as a skilled spiritual care student or I may not keep advancing toward professional certification. I always give in to bad eating habits.

Is it possible that some of John's paths are well worn? The feedback loop acts like a gyroscope to steer him toward one place rather than the other. A great deal depends on how he directs his attention to his map, model and his own thinking. This, in part, is what lies behind an emphasis on self-awareness in the formative work of CPE. Without self-knowledge, we can't truly know another as "other".

The image of a map is useful because it conveys the complexity of a worldview. It's important to recognize there are sub-systems going on within us at the same time. As we consider what to eat, we also want to finish our work. Thoughts about past behavior intrude. In every person's map, there are abstract partial selves, past dwellings, friendships, habits, school experiences and all that's ever happened from birth onwards. Depending on what John pays attention to, he may enter a thin moment experience, that we explore more fully in the chapter on Faith, something that's central to spiritual care practice. Thin moments unsettle the "familiar" of one's worldview map. John could feel at sea and sense he's being dashed against the rocks of his own unkind thoughts—his own unhealthy reasoning. Or worse, he may not even recognize he's being unkind to himself. He may believe it's the truth and there are no other options for his thinking. If he slows down his thinking and attends to what's moving and orienting him, he may gain perspective on the complexity occurring in this moment. This is where his CPE supervisor and peers can stand with him, as witnesses to his thinking, suggesting options that would be more central to the kind of person John wants to be. This is also where John, as a spiritual care practitioner, can stand with others as witness to their thinking and processing at critical junctures.

Such attention getting and giving is not an easy task. What's more, if John were continuously conscious of his entire map-based mental system of memories, he would be unable to get out of bed in the morning. That breadth of awareness is simply not possible for anyone. In the context of spiritual care, it's essential for a practitioner to realize that, while the map simile explains John's complexity, it's his sharing of his narrative that helps focus a CPE supervisor, CPE peer or spiritual care practitioner on seeing how a given model moment fits with his map.

John's personal narrative is a short form of what's in his memory bank. If he's a fully conscious person, he can give an account of himself. Klein refers to Hayek's description of conscious behavior in which people with a developed self-consciousness are able to give a summary of themselves, because they are able to

- Give an account of what they're doing or have been doing
- Take account of their actions and other simultaneous experiences of which they're also conscious
- Be guided to a large extent not only by their current perceptions but also by images that might be evoked by a given moment or model.[68]

In spiritual care, practitioners listen to faith stories and are aware of immense complexity within a person's narrative. The account is a partial representation of what's recorded in someone's mental system, which holds inherited as well as personal content.

Narratives give practitioners a way into a worldview. Ideally, being fully attended to by a caregiver allows people to hear themselves. Hearing oneself is essential to gaining a heightened sense of awareness of oneself. American literary critic Harold Bloom (1930-2019) taught Shakespeare for decades and summarized the bard's contribution to the development of personality:

> Literary character before Shakespeare is relatively unchanging. Women and men are represented as dying and aging, but not changing because their relationship to themselves has changed. Shakespeare's characters develop because they reconceive themselves...

which sometimes comes about because they overhear themselves talking, whether to themselves or to others.[69]

The content of our mental life is more than merely personal—we hear more than ourselves as we listen to what we're saying. As Klein put it, we don't begin life as individuals. We begin in relationship so that "relationships are at least as basic as individuals."[70] What is the relationship between inherited content and personal aspects of someone's worldview?

The idea of inherited content is supported by American sociologists Peter Berger's and Thomas Luckman's work on the social construction of reality.[71] It's confirmed by French sociologist Pierre Bourdieu's insight that every human body carries within a condensed map of the social body in which a person was reared—in a family, gender, race, economic bracket, community, city or village, country and in particular historical moments.[72]

As we mature, what are we to do with our inheritance? Over time, with more experience, maturing people may ask questions about their inherited content and the way they've been seeing themselves up to that point. When, as part of their spiritual care learning and certification processes, practitioners attend to their own thin moments and reflect on what's inherited, they may begin to question that content, as well as their concepts, in order to rethink how they want to live. This personal reflection can, in turn, sensitize professional practice in spiritual care so that they notice thin moments in clients and patients and reflect with them on what may be changing. Spiritual care is a relational resource within faith communities, healthcare facilities, social agencies and schools, as examples of places where practitioners come prepared to engage capacities of the human mind, to encourage people to be consciously aware of aspects of their worldviews and consider if ways they've been thinking and acting are the ways they want to continue to think and act.

Human beings have amazing capacities. We can steer behavior in a chosen direction. We also learn by looking around to take in data we either haven't noticed at all or haven't considered adequately. So the good news is, if worldview content doesn't go away, it can be reconceived. People have an ability to be mindful and learn from concepts they revise. Aspects of mindfulness, outlined elsewhere in this book, include insights that come from understanding the way worldviews form, as previously described above. Spiritual care practitioners accompany people as they 'look at and look for' data in a situation, as they bring their expectations to conscious awareness and brainstorm possible plans that might conform most happily with the kind of people clients and patients want to be.

If we consider the mind's complexity, we can incorporate insights from Harvard psychologist and educator Robert Kegan. In two books, he presents the view that human life in the twenty-first century is so complex, relationships are so complex, that we're *In Over our Heads*.[73] In order to live a satisfying life, the complexity we face requires us to learn new skills and sometimes to re-conceive ourselves in order to speak accurately from our own position, without forgetting our need for other people—that is, to maintain the social and the personal dimensions of our lives. Like learning, conceptually reframing our sense of self is a slow process.

While every human being has inherited content in their worldview and the memory system they form through experience, Kegan makes two important points that impact spiritual care practice:

- He invites us to consider "just how much can be understood about a person by understanding his or her memory system."[74]
- He assures his readers that the human "spirit is never at rest but always engaged in ever progressive motion, in giving itself new form."[75]

The changes we're capable of come through interactions with the environment (model moments) rather than through staying with internal processes (map) alone. Human beings organize; what we organize is meaning, as is evident from the way the brain works.

Part of those changes, re-conceiving a worldview, is based on being more aware of what's in our memory systems and accepting that our experience no longer fits with it,[76] or just as possibly, that it does fit but we want to be intentional about retaining it in our world view. When he aligns his developmental insights with faith and religion, Kegan points out that every one of us grows up with what he calls an orthodox faith— we grow up with it in our families of origin. What matters, in re-conceiving ourselves as we mature, is to realize that a family religion is not synonymous with a faith tradition. Rather, a family religion is one that operates powerfully and mysteriously in every family and is passed on to children by their simply being there. A family religion is nourished in private rituals and customs enacted in that dwelling. A family religion is the sum total of deep, idiosyncratic beliefs as to what life is really all about.[77]

In Kegan's view, we all have some kind of natural (family) religion. At the same time, we may all feel modernity's demand to reflect on our early experience. In the last century, Freud's best advice was to just walk away—erase those early concepts, even though his own object relations theory proposed that it's impossible to get rid of them.[78] Kegan's advice goes beyond Freud and suggests that, in order to become mature, we need to develop a new relationship with meaning we've made in the past. In this regard, we draw attention to Robert Kinast, who writes in the field of theological reflection, a topic we'll go into more fully in another chapter. In his gem of a book, *Making Faith Sense*,[79] he invites readers to explore the making of faith sense by means of personal, critical reflection on experience—as we might find in common sense, family sense, ethnic and cultural background sense, the world of work sense and a faith tradition's sense. In terms of personal reflection and consciousness development, Kegan and Kinast offer us a similar possibility for moving toward reconciling with the past.

Action Science Scenario

While most spiritual care practitioners may be unfamiliar with it, an effective method for reflecting on worldviews is captured in the practice of Action Science. The following scenario introduces Action Science as a strategy for personal reflection. In spiritual care, this strategy has potential to align with the core professional competency of spiritual assessment insofar as practitioners employ it as a way to help people sort through the meaning they've made from life experiences so they can ask themselves whether these are the ways they want to continue to think and to act.

Action Science in spiritual care helps people recognize assumptions that hold them back from having their deepest spiritual needs satisfied. Again, spiritual care thrives by helping people reflect on their existential experience. The scenario that follows involves a young woman who is neither neurotic nor psychotic, but her assumptions (theories) impact her parenting in ways that become obvious as she states them to another person.

Pre-Briefing

Consider a time when you were on an airplane, and someone was traveling with a baby. Or, by contrast, you may have traveled by air with an infant under a year's age. Ask yourself the following questions:

- What behaviors do you usually see when parents travel with infants on a plane?
- What do you think, feel and observe?
- What do you think parents are thinking/feeling while looking after a crying baby?
- How do you interpret the parent's assumptions and intentions?

What follows is a story about a baby and a mom on a plane. Please read it and make a few notes about your thoughts, feelings and observations as you read.

A Young Mom's Theory-in-Use

A friend of ours, a spirituality researcher, was on a plane from Vancouver to Toronto. Just before she got on the plane, she noticed a family that was travelling together, grandparents, siblings and their children. As she sat in her seat on the aisle, she saw one of the young women from that family seated in the aisle across from her, one row ahead of her to the right. As the flight began, she heard several babies crying. After an hour or so, only one baby was still crying. At about 90 minutes into the flight she looked around to see where this little one was sitting.

She was startled to realize that the infant was sitting in a car seat beside the young woman from the extended family she first noticed in the airport. As she continued to observe, she realized that, up to this point, she hadn't seen any behavior in the young woman to indicate there was a baby beside her. So our friend thought that a woman in the same row on the other side of the baby must be its mother.

She observed that young woman also. The woman on the other side of the car seat didn't touch or look at the baby but looked every so often at the young woman in the aisle seat. Our friend was confused. Then she noticed that the infant was reaching its hands up to the first young woman. The baby was looking at her and crying. From our friend's perspective, the baby seemed upset. She noticed that the young woman was looking at her phone most of the time and seldom looked at the infant. When she did look at the baby (about 10 months old) it was for very short times, with no eye contact. At that point, our friend leaned forward and asked the young woman if she might ask her a question. The young woman replied that yes, she could. Our friend asked, "Can you tell me what theory you're using as you sit with your baby?"

This bright, self-aware young woman was very clear about her theory. She replied that her theory was that the baby was most comfortable sitting in his car seat and that he soon would fall asleep. Our friend then said that she researched children's spirituality, and that, as she looked at the infant, she thought the baby was asking for her. The young mom looked at her baby. In a few minutes she undid the straps and picked up her child. She held the baby close. Our friend noticed that this mom appeared awkward at first but after 10 or 15 minutes, the baby settled down and fell asleep in his mother's arms. After a while, the mom put him back in his car seat where he slept for the rest of the flight.

Post-briefing

- Who are the players in this scenario?
- What was going on between the people on the plane?
- What were some of your observations? Did anything surprise you?
- What were some of your thoughts and feelings as you read the story?
- Did the story remind you of anything from your own experience?
- What did you observe about the young mom?
- What did you observe about our friend?
- Any further comments? Any insights? What might you have done in this scenario?
- Write down some of the theories that are at work in this scenario.

An Action Science Framework

The purpose of Action Science is to help people align what they do with what they say. As mentioned, the art of spiritual care involves practitioners in listening as someone walks through aspects of their worldview and begins to reflect on assumptions it contains. Action Science encourages people to state their assumptions and observe the data that's in front of them to see how and whether their assumptions match what they see, hear, smell, touch and taste.

There's a method to Action Science that draws out differences between what we say and what we do, based on our awareness of directly observable data (D.O.D.), so that we can ask ourselves about the fit between what we say and what we do. Sometimes, the absence of fit is referred to as hypocrisy (an amalgam in Greek, combining the prefix *hypo* meaning "under" and the verb *krinein* meaning "to sift or decide"). At times, everyone mismatches what they say and what they do; there are lots of reasons for the mismatch. Spiritual care is attentive to sifting out the congruence between words and deeds.

As we reflect on the airplane scenario, the young woman's theory matched her action but failed to take account of the directly observable data in front of her. Further, picking up the infant appeared to have the desired effect of putting the child to sleep. At this point, we want to put forward a perspective we use throughout the book: what we think shapes how we feel and directs how we act. Personal awareness involves more than thinking, feeling and acting. This complexity is conveyed through the Awareness Wheel Exercise in Appendix #2.

In spiritual care, practitioners who are aware of and practice Action Science can assist clients and patients in becoming aware of how they theorize. While this may sound dry and mechanical, it's quite the opposite. Self-consciousness includes content we're aware of and content we're unaware of. Sensory data, thoughts and feelings come together and contribute to the awakening of a person's capacity for reflection. This arousal is accomplished by helping people notice gaps between what they say they believe and what they actually do by going through what Action Science calls the Ladder of Inference. Here are some examples of Action Science and its potential for awakening consciousness.[80]

The Ladder of Inference:

- Directly Observable Data: (**D.O.D.**) What we see, hear, taste, touch, smell
- Inferred Meaning: (**I.M.**) Our personal interpretation of what's going on
- Behaviour: (**B**) What we do based on our interpretation of what's going on
- Reflective Questions: (**R.Q.**) Asking questions that challenge the status quo

- Actual Meaning: **(AM)** The other person's interpretation of what they meant
- Conflicted Values (result of a gap between what we say and what we do): **(C.V.)** Naming the values my behaviour violated

Example One:

D.O.D.: I've just presented my first verbatim to my Clinical Pastoral Education (CPE) group and someone asks me if I checked the client's name.

I.M.: He's trying to make me look bad, like I didn't do one of the first things expected when I enter a patient's room. He wants me to appear like an incompetent beginner.

B: I start to lie and say of course I checked the name (but can't remember if I actually did so).

R.Q.: What did he mean when he asked me that question? I ask him.

A.M.: He'd noticed that the patient's last name was the same as mine, and was humorously struck by this coincidence.

C.V.: I lied, but I place a high value on telling the truth. This is the gap.

Example Two:

D.O.D.: I'm a newly licensed pastor working in a downtown church. One afternoon the senior pastor enters the room where I'm meeting with the congregation's youth group and asks how I'm getting along. She points to one of the young people in the group and asks him to say something he likes about me.

I.M.: She thinks I'm not getting along with our congregation's youth and wants this young person to say something negative about me.

B: I roll my eyes, and try to be humorous by saying "Forgive me if I fold my arms".

R.Q.: After the group ended, I ask a pastoral team colleague if the senior pastor came into his room as well. The answer is yes.

A.M.: I realize the senior pastor was just doing her job and I don't know what she thinks of me.

C.V.: I was rude. I place a high value on being polite and respectful. This is the gap

Take some time to write out your thoughts about these two examples. As you continue reading the chapter, you may want to add to your notes.

Moving Deeper: Double Loop Learning and Fourth Order Thinking

Spiritual care aims at helping people reflect personally on the worldviews they hold. As people go through this Action Science exercise, their consciousness of what they think and feel may shift, as it did in the two examples above. Harvard psychologist and educator Robert Kegan analyzed this shift by describing double-loop learning and fourth order thinking. To support his view, he paid careful attention to Piaget's stages of development and noted something he thought was important. Instead of focusing on the stage achieved, he observed the movement that occurred as a person advanced from one stage to another. He asked questions about this movement—which he came to see as the movement of making meaning from everyday experience. From the perspective of spiritual formation, the human spirit is an agent of communication that accomplishes meaning making; human spirituality is the capacity to make meaning and reflect on the meaning made.

Drawing on object relations theorists such as Otto Kernberg and psychosocial theorists, especially Erik Erikson, Kegan concluded that the early dynamics of the formation of a self through meaning-making includes moving through two stages of consciousness to a third level of consciousness, at which point the self is organized as a system. We've adapted his overview to include the following movements:

First Level of consciousness:

- Sensori-motor: embedded in reflexes, then reflexes show up to the child as perceptions
- Mother shows up as separate, lose-able; infant expresses separation anxiety
- Pre-operational: embedded in perceptions, then perceptions show up as concrete experience
  1. Self emerges as an object

Second level of consciousness:

- Concrete-operational: embedded in the concrete, then concrete shows up as thought
  2. Self emerges as a role

Third level of consciousness:

- Formal-operational: embedded in thought, then thought shows up as organization
  3. Self emerges as a system, as a worldview

Fourth-order thinking:

- Using directly observable data to think about what we hold in our worldview by using double-loop learning.
  4. Self emerges as capable of reflection

The term double-loop learning refers to realizing what I'm thinking, feeling and doing as I consciously consider these thoughts, feelings and actions. In spiritual care education, this is the work of self-awareness and a maturing ability for the safe and effective use of self. On the Ladder of Inference, it's the place where we ask Reflective Questions (R.Q.). Double-loop learning moves the people in our two examples to realize that their actions violated important values they said they held. Double-loop learning involves comprehending "This is what I'm thinking" and then asking "Is this what I want to continue to think, feel and do?"

In Kegan's model of human development, he points to double-loop learning that moves people forward in their awareness of what's going on. In line with his thinking, directly observable data helps us think about what we hold in the worldviews we form from experience. If we are to address the complexities of modern life, the demands on twenty-first century adults require transformation that's every bit as fundamental as a child's need to leave behind magical thinking to acquire concrete thinking, and a school-aged child's need to transform concrete thinking into the abstract thinking that's required of adolescents.[81]

Action Science invites people to consider fourth order thinking as a level of consciousness, in which one's existing worldview becomes a new object for reflective consideration. To move to the fourth level, we stand back and inquire into the system we formed when we were younger. Action Science invites us to observe ourselves on a regular basis as we take action so that we can stand back and ask questions about what we're doing and what theories drive that action.[82] Using double-loop learning, we move to fourth-order thinking and stand back to observe Directly Observable Data (D.O.D., i.e., what's right in front of us) and ask what we want to do now. As we reflect on the question "is this what I want to continue to think, feel and do?", we may answer yes or no, or something quite different. The point is to ask the Reflective Questions (R.Q.).

During such inquiry, we carefully observe and ask whether the data we observe fits the worldview we're currently relying on. The Awareness Wheel Exercise, found in Appendix #2, provides a rich consideration of the cycle of self-awareness that includes sensing, thinking, feeling, wanting and doing as five dimensions of a reflective process that people learn to grasp as they become more aware of what's going on, both in themselves and in data that's operative in front of them. What would have happened if the young mom on the plane had gone through this process? Would she have looked at her baby, heard his crying, seen his arms reaching out in her direction, and picked him up earlier?

Action Science and Poverty: Personal and Social Implications for Action Science

At the beginning of the chapter we identified the importance of noticing both common humanity and personal uniqueness in the faith stories people tell. The following case introduces a global pattern (poverty) that impacts what people think is possible and that embeds itself in the worldviews they live by. It's our belief that many middle-class people (including a number in the field of spiritual care) don't understand the systemic nature of poverty sufficiently to adequately hear the faith story of someone who's telling us about their lived experience of poverty.

Pre-briefing
- Can you think of a time when your financial resources were very limited and you worried about whether there would be food on the table for your family?
- Have you been in the grocery store standing behind someone who didn't have enough money to pay for the groceries they'd chosen?
  ◊ Review what you experienced, felt, thought or observed in either circumstance?

◊ What do you think people are thinking/feeling when money is short?

◊ How do you interpret their assumptions and intentions?

Mary's Story

Mary is an Indigenous woman who was removed from her family and placed in the child welfare system as part of the "Sixties Scoop" in Canada.[83] She went to a Christian camp as a child and accepted the Christian faith in that context. She lost track of her family when she was very young, and lived with a white family who took her in. She stayed mostly in her bedroom, if she wasn't in school. Occasionally, the family would go out to dinner and leave her at home, locked in her room.

In her fifties, she was living in the spare bedroom in her daughter's rented house. She worked part time at a nearby Dollar Store. One Sunday, she attended a downtown church and met Sally, who taught at a local Seminary. As they got to know each other, Sally introduced her to other people at church and, as their friendship grew, the two women went for coffee together once a week.

One Sunday in church, Sally introduced Mary to Jane, who happened to be walking by as Mary and Sally talked about Mary's part time job situation. Jane listened to their conversation for a while and at one point said to Mary, "Why don't you just get another job?" Sally observed Mary's body language, as the air seemed to slowly seep out of her. They stood for a few minutes without talking. Then Jane said she had to get home to put on the family's dinner and left the conversation.

"How are you, Mary?" Sally asked, after Jane moved down the hall to get her coat. Mary looked at Sally and said quietly, "I feel like a gerbil in a cage that's trapped on its exercise wheel and can't get off."

Post-briefing

• Who are the players in this scenario?

• What was going on between and among Mary, her foster family, Sally, and Jane?

• What were some of your observations?

• Did anything surprise you?

• What were some of your thoughts and feelings as you read the story?

- Did the story remind you of anything from your own experience?
- What did you observe about Mary, Sally, and Jane?
- Any further comments? Any insights?
- What might you have done in this scenario?
- Write down some of the theories that are at work in this scenario.

If we consider the perspective of Action Science, there are many assumptions at work in this scenario, but we can also step back to take a wider view of what's going on.

In particular, taking into account the pattern of poverty for the working poor like Mary, certain elements of her situation emerge. In the exceptional book, *Nickle and Dimed*, American essay writer Barbara Ehrenreich[84] went undercover as a low-wage worker in three U.S. states to find out if non-skilled workers could make ends meet. She found a low paying job and lodgings in each of five pre-selected locations and concluded that it isn't possible to provide for oneself, let alone children, under the conditions of work that attend these jobs. For many people, earning enough to provide a roof over their heads isn't possible. Thus, some of the people she met lived in their cars.

If we take a few of her first-hand observations, and apply these insights to Mary, key issues come out. When people are working in a low paying store like Mary worked in, they are often part-time and without benefits. Additionally, they're on a list of part-time employees that has more people on it than the number of people who actually get work. They're frequently told that other people would be very happy to have their job, with the implication that they'd better be happy with it, or else. The impact this has on workers is unhealthy on many fronts. It leaves the impression that lots of people could do their job, so they're not personally valued or appreciated. They have no job security.

Likewise, Mary learns to be on guard and chronically vigilant, and therefore in a chronically stressed situation. At any time, she could have her purse searched for drugs or for theft or be tested for drugs, so she's always on alert for trouble at work. On occasion, no time is allotted for a coffee break, to go to the washroom or have her lunch. She can be told at the last minute she's not needed for the shift that she thought she had. Also, work shifts are not put up for her to see until a few days before the next work period begins, so she's never sure if she'll be working in a given two-week period. Given the systemic uncertainty of this environment, she believes it's not safe to ask for time off to see a doctor or dentist, regardless of how she's feeling.

There's no consideration given to Mary with regard to what she does while at work. She's asked to stock shelves or do cash, regardless of comments she's made about her health (e.g., she has a back problem that makes stocking shelves very painful), or about her preferences (i.e., what she believes she's actually good at doing). She can be asked to lock up at any time, which means staying late and walking home in the dark. This opportunity is presented as a compliment.

These aspects of Mary's work situation create a setting in which "just getting another job" seems impossible, not simply because she can't count on when she'll be called into work or when her shift might be cancelled, but because she's caught in the cage she described in the scenario. She's entangled by an emotional milieu that conveys she's easily replaceable and of little worth. In her experiences, Ehrenreich saw and felt the debilitating impact of these work environments, even though she's middle-class, well educated and successful personally.

While Ehrenreich's research was carried out in the United States, the pattern of poverty for the working poor is a global reality. In order to hear assumptions, images and generalizations Mary makes about her life, we must understand what poverty has done to her. That includes her emotional, social and relational poverty as well as the financial distress and uncertainty that dogs at her heels. As their friendship continued to develop, Sally came to realize that Mary would never have a roof over her head that she could count on. The idea of a secure retirement was something Mary wouldn't even imagine for herself.

A pattern of poverty is a system that shapes multiple aspects of low-wage workers' lives through its relentless and pervasive power structure. Understanding poverty and other common human patterns is at the heart of spiritual care. In the case of poverty as a global pattern, material needs are not inferior to spiritual needs. Karl Marx was correct to point out that without material resources, it isn't possible for people to live a fully human life.[85] Material and spiritual resources are equally important to human flourishing. Spiritual poverty and material poverty are equally dehumanizing. Mary's expectations for her life were formed during the relational and economic poverty of her early years.

Conclusion

We live in a secular age. But secularism isn't the same as it was in the last century. What's unique about secularism now is that spirituality is a well-researched, widely experienced aspect of the human condition. If we think of secularism as anti-religious, that's no longer accurate. Twenty-first century cultures insist that we become culturally aware and respectful of people who speak, relate, dress, and worship differently than we do. Those who choose not to worship God, or something like God, are equally deserving of respect and engagement.

When weighing terms used in the chapter, we explore how spiritual experience, spiritual needs, spirituality and spiritual care support a person who wants to reconsider their worldview by understanding how the brain works in human learning. The human spirit has the capacity to create and sustain healthy felt connection with the self, others, nature and the transcendent. As we interact with other people, and their way of being in the world is taken into account and respected, the capacity to make and sustain a healthy sense of felt connection can flourish. A human capacity for felt connection is also at the heart of spiritual care.

In summary, as authors, we believe that those who engage in spiritual care create and sustain a healthy sense of felt connection with clients and patients. In chapters that follow, we look directly into what spiritual care includes. Suffice it to say, it goes well beyond looking after the physical needs of a human body, but doesn't discount the value of the body or underestimate how material and relational aspects of human interaction, for both good and ill—as in the case of poverty—can heal or harm the human spirit. Spiritual care reaches into the inmost being of people in a way that's not intrusive but that establishes a felt connection with them.

Take Away Questions for Reflection

- How does thinking about spirituality as a "felt sense of connection" fit with your current understanding of spirituality? Are there other important ideas you would add?

- How would you trace the major landscapes of your worldview map? What were some of the significant model moments that formed you?

- What differences do you notice between perceptual and conceptual learning, in yourself or in someone else?

- When you consider the gifts that negative emotions offer us (E. Whitehead), can you think of any examples from your own life?

- When you read "every action is theory driven", what meaning does this phrase have for you?

- What was your reaction to the question asked of the young mom on the airplane?

- What Ladder of Inference scenario would you like to create?

- What was new learning for you in reading this chapter?

Chapter 2

Faith, Thick Listening, and Intentional Reflection

Introduction

Every human being has faith in something or someone. We couldn't be mentally healthy unless that was true. We generally think of faith as positive and strengthening, as we pointed out in the previous chapter. It's also true, however, that people may put their faith in someone or something that can have negative effects on them. For example, people may put faith in their own unimportance. They may put faith in someone who's lying to them or stealing from them. To understand how faith works, we have to take a broad view of it.

In this chapter we hope to shed light on faith as "being in relationship with" others – whether persons, places, things, or with that which transcends the limits of tangible knowing.[1] Rather than quoting one or several of the many definitions of faith found in various fields of study, where each definition makes an assumption of relationship, we choose to write about the relational core at the heart of human nature. That is to say, to be human is to be incomplete and in process; to know only in part. It's also true that a "person alone" is an ontological contradiction.[2] Relationship is the universal baseline common to all expressions of self-transcendence and the orientation toward wholeness. Being in relationship is integral to every concrete experience of having faith in something or someone.

While faith is about relationship, we first want to look at the concept itself. There are three moving parts to faith. There's an agent of faith—the person that exercises faith. There's an object of faith—the something or someone that an agent puts faith in. And there's the relationship between

41

the agent and the object that may be healthy or harmful. The relationship between agent and object influences how a person sees the world, feels about their experience and shapes how they take action. When it comes to spiritual care, it's essential to learn about the relational core and three moving parts of faith insofar as spiritual care practitioners are positioned to help people unpack the ways they think about and use faith in their lives.

Faith is universal. It's viewed as a constitutive human dimension,[3] a necessary element of everyone's life. What we put faith in matters a great deal. In fact, human beings are compelled to put their faith in someone or something as they grow up and mature in the world that surrounds them. This is due to the conceptual connection between trust and faith, which we'll look at more fully later in this chapter. Faith is also something we need to think about intentionally. Some questions to reflect on personally and socially include the following:

> Who or what am I in relationship with? Where do I tend to invest my faith? Why do I do so? What's happening to my faith as I invest it? What's happening to family, friends, acquaintances, as well as to me as I continue to invest faith in the things, people, ideas and places that I do? Is my faith growing with my life experience and gaining interest, or is it buried so deep in me that I can't access it? What's faith like? What's it like to be in relationship with others—both tangible and intangible others? How do I exercise faith? What would it be like not to have faith? Is that even possible? What would happen to me if I more intentionally exercised faith?

In this chapter, our purpose is to position faith at the very center of spiritual care. Faith is the primary outcome of the spiritual work of connecting with other people, the world, nature, the transcendent, and with ourselves. We grow and mature in our faith as we engage with the spiritual issues in our lives, and learn how to be in relationship with self and others. This chapter explores the nature of faith, and situates it in its broadest human context. We want to be clear that faith in God, or a Transcendent Other is only one aspect of faith's exercise. Exercising faith is an existential necessity. In order to describe faith in its broadest sense and in its relational core, we begin the chapter by examining the three moving parts of faith and reflect on those dynamics.

Later in the chapter we'll look at how concrete experiences of exercising one's faith can be purposefully reflected upon. Toward this end, we'll introduce and differentiate two concepts—spiritual reflection and theological reflection—and focus on intentional reflection as a framework within which to expand our understanding and appreciation of worldviews, analogies for faith, the ways of story, and the art of seeing with eyes of faith. Each of these approaches to the exercise of faith and to spiritual/theological reflection is viewed through a lens of "thick listening at thin moments".[4] This phrase emerged while Clark was developing a course on theological reflection at St. Stephen's College in Edmonton Alberta, Canada. She brought together insights from two authors, Walter Brueggemann and Thomas Groome.

Brueggemann was asked to write a Forward for a book by Maria Harris, titled *Proclaim Jubilee! A Spirituality for the Twenty-first Century*.[5] The basis for the year of *jubilee* is found in the Hebrew Scriptures. Harris offers a compelling argument that a living jubilee is a comprehensive spirituality that would have a positive political, economic and moral impact on individuals, families, faith communities, organizations and nations. Her book considers the consequences of living out the implications of jubilee for today, and for the twenty-first century.

> In Brueggemann's Forward to her book he says: Harris' explication of the themes invites us, along with her, to 'thick listening', which is one of her ways of speaking about prayer. This book is all about thick listening that understands and relishes the deep touch points that take place between suffering and imagination, touch points that can produce energy for the 'healing of the world' that is now our urgent human vocation.[6]

Groome, promoting his book *Sharing Faith*,[7] used the word *disciple* to speak about a form of apprenticeship in which a person holistically engages everyday life experiences by concentrating on interior movements that flow from life, to faith, and back into life. He went on to speak about a belief within Celtic spirituality which perceives certain times and places, encounters and events, as thin moments occurring when and where the separation between worlds is thin.

When the two phrases are brought together, the interpretive lens and spiritual care practice we develop in this book comes into focus: *thick listening at thin moments*. The essence of this lens can best be appreciated by means of the question: Can you imagine *thick listening* as a quality of multidimensional, contemplative mindfulness that understands and appreciates the deep interfacing between everyday life experiences and *thin moments,* where separation brought about through differing world-views, paradigms and filters becomes increasingly thin and transparent? These three concepts—multidimensional listening, contemplative mindfulness and the deep interfacing of everyday life with breakthrough experiences—are threaded through the chapters of this book, and will be addressed more fully in later chapters. This is the imagining, especially as it's subsumed into spiritual care practice that, as Brueggemann put it, can produce energy for the healing of the world that is now our urgent human vocation.

Thick listening at thin moments is an approach that involves a spiritual care practitioner in the following: being in an ongoing relationship with self and others, having concrete experiences within that relationship, reflecting on those experiences, and embodying this reflection through meaningful action. It's steeped in spiritual and theological reflective practices, and optimally occurs when one person walks with another through the meaning-making process that comes to form a life. Thin moments (e.g., falling in love, happiness, grief, trauma, amazement, disbelief, as some examples) arise in the midst of everyday living but are not restricted to chronological time. Rather, such moments can exist as enduring markers to which a person returns whenever circumstances associated with the event are reawakened. A person who has experienced the trauma of sexual abuse, for example, has the original thin moment experience but can also be vulnerable to memories of that original experience in further sexual involvements. In their origins and continuing impact, thin moments emerge.

Making Sense of the Three Moving Parts of Faith

If we think linguistically about the word faith, and its exercise, there are two aspects: the noun *faith* and the verb *to believe*. The noun and its adjective are conveyed in the following sentences:

- Noun: The faith of his parents is Christianity.
- Adjective: She is a faithful friend.

The second aspect of faith, the verb to believe, is conveyed in the following sentences:
- She believes in a Divine Presence.
- As an economist, he believes in The Market.

We can also write the fourth sentence differently, to express faith's exercise (action):

- He puts his faith in The Market.
- He exercises faith in The Market.

Faith is a noun, an adjective, and is connected to the verb believing. In a later chapter, we look into belief, disbelief and unbelief. The seeds of those thoughts are found here, in an understanding of faith. Always relational, faith, belief, disbelief and unbelief involve an agent of faith in relationship with an object of faith. The quality of that relationship is typically spoken about as confidence, trust, reliance or conviction but in disbelief or unbelief, the relationship can be spoken about in terms of suspicion, lack of confidence, and skepticism. In its core, faith is exercised by placing trust in someone or something. As people exercise faith, their practice becomes an attitude of the heart, i.e., a disposition or aspect of their character. When people exercise faith, there's an observable element, i.e., they can be counted on to act in certain ways. Placing confidence in a person or thing alters thought and action with respect to that person or thing. Exercising faith (believing) changes a person just as much as exercising one's muscles changes the shape of one's body. For example, we can hear a young woman say she's putting more and more faith in her ability to swim and we can observe her demonstrating more and more confidence while she's in the water. She's increasing her faith in the idea that the water will hold her up so she doesn't have to fight it as she improves the way she swims. Interestingly the word confidence derives from the Latin word for faith, which is *fides*.

Faith refers to content (what we believe in, e.g., that water in a swimming pool will hold us up). When content is tested through practice or exercise (the swimmer swimming in the pool), it builds an attitude that becomes a disposition and also a way of life. In this sense, the exercise of faith implies movement; it's not static, but rather is a relational investment. Further to this, the word disposition indicates what we can expect from something. For example, water is disposed to be liquid at room temperature, solid at freezing temperatures and gaseous at high temperatures. In the same way, if faith is exercised consistently, we can count on a person to act in certain ways. We can count on our swimmer to swim confidently. Swimming with confidence is part of her way of life. We wouldn't expect to see her be so frightened that she refused to jump into the pool and swim, unless there was a serious event that had shattered her confidence in believing that water will hold her up.

So, to summarize, let's return to our original description of the three moving parts of faith. In the example of our swimmer, the swimmer is the agent of faith. The belief that water will hold her up is the object of faith. Swimming with confidence is the relationship between the agent and the object of faith.

Reflecting on Dynamics of Faith

Faith is complex. To begin with, people give intellectual assent to the objects of their faith. An object may be a perceived threat (I believe I'm not safe with that person) or a general theory about the world (I believe people of a certain type are not safe to be with). Or, from another perspective, some people believe they should "Look out for themselves! No one else will do it for them." In general, those who give intellectual assent to an idea feel bound to act according to implications of the statements they prize. That said, it's also true that a dynamic of faith is captured in the relationship between what people say they trust and what they actually rely on in daily life. Intellectual assent implies there's congruence between a belief and the action flowing out of it. There may, however, be incongruence between beliefs and actions. As an example, those who believe in only looking out for themselves may in some circumstances ask for help and expect to receive it. In this case, we must look at a broader context in order to understand why someone suddenly asks for help when their stated belief is to be self-sufficient.

Part of understanding faith and how it operates involves reflecting, or looking back on the congruence between what we say and what we do. In this regard, it's not enough to look, believe and act; it's also necessary to 'look again'. This is the activity of *respect* (from the Latin, re = back + specere = look at). It's fair to say that respect is a pre-condition for reflection and reflection is integral to exercising faith. When we ask what faith is, we also pose a question about human experience. While faith is essential to being human, and everyone exercises faith, establishing consistency between what we say and actually do is not so easy. If our swimmer stopped swimming one day and refused to enter the water, but still wanted to say she believes the water will hold her up, we would need to know a great deal more about her story. We would need to look again. At first glance, her behavior fails to support the content of her belief. The relationship between agent and object of faith has shifted from confident swimming to something that's incongruent, i.e., refusing to enter the water. If a spiritual care provider were to sit down on the edge of the pool with this woman, and recognize her incongruence as a thin moment experience, a natural starting point for conversation would be to engage the woman in reflecting on what has shifted. What event shattered the swimmer's confidence? Respect, in this scenario, is an expression of thick listening, and shared reflection with the swimmer would be a pathway to meaningfully explore the thin moment at play in the swimmer's incongruent behavior.

As mentioned, faith is both content and practice. Practice may be expressed as loyalty to a tradition that's consciously chosen as a way of life. In this sense, our thoughts and overall disposition may be oriented to living with fidelity, holding fast to our integrity and keeping our word. It's belief put to use. Faith's exercise implies a kind of contemplative mindfulness that informs what we do: we observe ourselves acting congruently with what we claim to believe. The attitudes we rely on undergird our faith practices. For example, in situations where we come to a crossroads, our disposition of faith may be what leads us to prefer a way of loving the world, of acting hopefully about the future rather than being fearful, skeptical or unbelieving, even if skepticism was something we learned from our family tradition when we were young.

Maturing faith holds an attitude about the world that may also be informed by a consciously chosen tradition that guides our way of life. This use of the word 'tradition' (from the Latin, trans = across + dare = give) refers to giving over or handing down a way of life from one generation to another. One's tradition can be derived from common sense, family sense, ethnic and cultural sense, the world of work sense, and a faith tradition's sense.[8] As we mature, contemplative mindfulness helps us make faith sense of the narratives we've learned to live by and those we consciously choose.

When a way of life is organized around formal religion, faith may include coming to grips with God or the transcendent. Faith holds sure in the object of its trust. If a person believes in a loving God, faith may be experienced as a heightened sense of awareness of God, a confident reliance on God's attributes. As such, it's a way of perceiving the world, self and others through the lens of those attributes.

The image of God we hold is integral to the faith we practice. Historically, images of God have been eco-centric, anthropocentric and theo-centric. God images have also been personal and social. There are faith traditions with one God, many gods, and no god. There is also literature on God representations, concepts and images that are based on personal experience and psychologically formed during childhood that may be experientially modified throughout one's life.[9] However understood, faith and belief develop over a lifespan through complex interactions with nature, self, others and an Other.

Perceiving and conceptualizing are at the core of these complex interactions. People observe what's familiar to them, but do so through filters of attachment, aloofness, curiosity, repulsion, anguish, optimism, as some examples of human experience. We said earlier that faith is the primary outcome of the spiritual work of connecting with other people, the world, nature, the transcendent and with ourselves. Further to this, believing is an outcome of faith: it's the action, energy and accrued lived experience of faith continually influencing daily life. An essential human task is to learn to use faith in a healthy and meaningful way, whether or not people place faith in God. Once again, the potential for faith to produce positive effects in people depends on the relationship between the agent and the object of faith's interest.

Suppose a little girl exercises faith in her mother. As they go for a walk, they come to a playground. The child says she wants to play on the slide. She climbs up the steps. As she sits at the top, her mother stands at the bottom of the slide. The mother looks steadily at her daughter and says she'll catch her little girl. The child fixes her gaze on her mother's face. She glances down the slide and is afraid but looks back to a familiar face that hasn't turned away. The child pushes off from her safe resting spot, keeping her eyes on her mother. Her mother catches her. The relationship between mother and child is carried through their mutual gaze and expressed in their shared success.

In this scenario, the little girl is the agent of faith. Belief that her mother will catch her at the bottom of the slide is the object of faith. Successfully sliding and being caught is the relationship between agent and object. Of note in this situation is the gaze shared between daughter and mother. Sometimes referred to as a transitional object of faith, the physical focus on which the little girl rests her faith is the mother's face and gaze, not the slide. As yet, she is still afraid of the slide. Under favorable conditions, faith addresses fear. It's the opposite of giving in to fear.

Faith tries things out and, failing or succeeding, goes on trying. While it may be possible to avoid slides in a playground, every human being must exercise faith. We may put faith in trustworthy and untrustworthy people. Based on her trust in her mother's gaze and the experience of being caught, this little girl is likely to put faith in trusting other people, and perhaps the world in general.

We learn about faith as infants. Consider an infant who plays a game of peek-a-boo with his father. The father, the game and the baby constitute an activity in which the infant is learning through a relationship with his father to trust that his dad exists even though the baby can't see him. As they play the game, the baby learns to have faith in things unseen. Faith is active when we can't make use of our five senses. Faith is the consequence of experimenting with trust. We put faith in something or someone with the result that we acquire certain beliefs about the world.

If conditions are *favorable*, the beliefs we form about the world encourage us to exercise trust in other people and in things around us rather than succumbing to fear and refusing to trust what we can't see, smell, hear, taste or touch. If conditions are *unfavorable*, we may learn to mistrust others who prove to be untrustworthy. If faith is placed repeatedly in something or someone that's untrustworthy, mental health may be at risk.

Suppose a young boy is standing on a staircase at the entrance of his home. He's on the fifth step from the bottom when his dad enters the house and tells the little boy to jump into his arms and he will catch him. The boy hesitates. One of his feet remains on the stair and the other slides a little way closer to its edge. He looks at his father. The boy waits. Again, the father tells him to jump. The boy looks uncertain. The father raises his voice and orders him to jump. The boy jumps as the father turns away and steps aside. The boy crashes to the floor. While the boy is lying on the floor crying, the father stands over him saying he has told him time and time again not to trust anyone. Cultivated mistrust, manifest in the young boy's distress and hesitation, can produce misgivings, suspicion, doubt, skepticism and contempt. This little boy may grow up to exercise the strong belief that he can't trust other people.

Analogies for Faith

In addition to faith's three moving parts, faith (being in relationship with self, others, and Other) is also the underlying structure of human existence. Faith cuts across secular and religious lines. It's an attitude that integrates the experience of a whole person—an entire self. In its integrative role, faith influences action as it organizes our perceptions of life so we can make sense of what's happening and act in such a way that we seek what's best for others and ourselves, both personally and socially. The important work of making faith sense by unpacking the influences of faith's three moving parts is where spiritual care practitioners can accompany others with thick listening and an ability to cultivate spiritual and theological reflection. If human beings want to be well, they're compelled to make sense of life. Thick listening relies on analogies that depict faith experiences. People who find themselves at thin moments frequently use the language of analogy as a way of explaining what they're going through. Images from nature and everyday life are drawn upon to convey the angst or exhilaration being experienced: "I'm hanging in there, like last year's leaf in this year's wind", or "I can hardly contain myself; it's like breaking out of a shell that's confined me for years!" These images invite respect and reflection.

We use analogies because faith fills in gaps in our experience between what we're able to touch, taste, see, hear or smell and realities we can't perceive or test empirically. Faith attends to depths that can't be plumbed with a measuring stick. Faith organizes connections between what can be and can't be experienced directly. This feature of faith is as true for scientists who study the atom as it is for those who trust an invisible God.

Faith focuses on realities beyond mere seeing. For twentieth century science, reality is only what is measurable—a view now challenged by scientists themselves. For example, John Polkinghorne is an English theoretical physicist, theologian and Anglican priest. He asserts that faith operates in theology and science in the unique ways that each discourse explains the world. He argues that science and theology have to express their belief in the existence of unseen realities, whether it's about quarks forever hidden within nuclear matter or the invisible reality of a divine presence.[10] The justification for confidence in things unseen is the same in each case.

In Polkinghorne's words, for science and theology, "the appeal to what isn't directly perceptible makes sense of a great deal of experience that is more accessible to the senses,"[11] which illustrates the way an infant has confidence his father exists while playing peek-a-boo by covering his eyes and then experiencing his dad's absence. Playing peek-a-boo prepares a child for elements of a faith story that include understanding that something we can't perceive with our five senses still exists. Similarly, this function of faith operates for the little girl who feels confident that her mother will catch her when she gets to the bottom of the slide. With more and more experiences that are favorable, confidence increases. These two children practice faith; this practice integrates their experience and is expressed by the worldview they're forming.

Practicing faith is an attitude of the heart, a disposition or aspect of character in the agent of faith. We can also say that faith (being in relationship) is an attitude that integrates the experience of a whole person. According to American philosopher James Pratt, to say faith is an attitude is to say that it's the responsive side of human consciousness. In his view, faith acts consciously as it responds to what is beyond sense experience (beyond what we see, hear, taste, touch, smell). Faith as an attitude is found in mental states such as attention, curiosity, expectancy, feeling, imagination and reaction.[12] And faith is more than a mental state insofar as it's expressed in action. That said, as an attitude, it's "a subjective response to the power or powers that people conceive as having ultimate control over their interests and destinies; [it's an] attitude of a self toward an object in which the self genuinely believes."[13] It's the attitude of an agent toward an object of faith, whether it's a thought, image or idea, as it is in some faith traditions.

Insofar as human beings are compelled to make sense of life, we do this by narrating the meaning that surrounds and undergirds what we experience. This often includes using figures of speech. For example, the geological image of an archipelago acts as a simile to reveal how faith integrates experience[14] through imagination. Human experience is like an archipelago—a landform in which islands are surrounded by an expanse of water so that their surfaces can be seen and explored but their roots and interconnections under the water can't be seen. These connections must be imagined, but it's reasonable to believe they exist.

Developing this analogy further, science focuses on landforms; faith focuses on what lies between. Landforms can be charted and their materials tested. Faith connections can't be verified through measurement. Rather, they are believed. Studies of landforms will be repeated and variances assessed. In contrast, studies of faith connections will be described, story upon story, in believable patterns of lived experience.

Human beings can't look at islands without making assumptions about the deep-water connections among them. Even casual observers sense there's something there. People make sense of life by including the islands and the deep water—science and faith. Faith's role is to help make sense of the geography of human experience and to orient thinking about life as a whole.[15]

The Art of Seeing with Eyes of Faith

Seeing by faith is an aesthetic skill that compares with the moment an artist sees the picture she will paint before she actualizes her vision in the final product. Faith sees like an architect in a moment of designing a brick and mortar building with paper and pencil. Faith sees like a gardener who observes her garden each year and is confident that next year this or that plant will be even more beautiful. Faith sees like an interior designer who knows what a room will look like before he's done, while rough materials still clutter the floor. Imaginative engagement with personal and social experience builds bridges between what's familiar and what's extraordinary and makes faith sense of it all.

Each of the 'faith sees like' scenarios named above is nonverbal, includes contemplative mindfulness, and can be perceived through a lens of thick listening at a thin moment. Spiritual care practitioners can witness a nonverbal pause prior to action as people approach experiences of trauma, loss or distress. For example, rather than using words, a mother's focus may be on offering comfort even in the midst of feeling helpless—as she reaches her hands through the open holes of an incubator bassinette to touch the tiny body of her seriously ill newborn baby. Each thin moment invites thick listening. By being in relationship at such critical life junctures, a felt sense of connection is formed between practitioner and client. This sacred space allows a client to pull back layers of meaning, fill in silhouettes with substance and story to find words to bring the scenario to life. Thick listening allows someone to see more deeply and meaningfully into their experience.

Faith sees with the eyes of the heart, as captured in the words of Saint-Exupery's *The Little Prince*, "it is only with the heart that one can see rightly; what is essential is invisible to the eye."[16] Faith is a capacity to see what's not yet visible and work for its realization with sustained and sustaining passion. Like a dress designer who takes shapeless material and sees how to sew it into garments that fit the body and soul of a woman, faith allows the materials at hand, and people close by, to be part of the fabric of the final product. Faithful seeing is the heart's intellectual work within the domain of the dwelling mind.[17] Faithful seeing brings the intellect to bear on the problems of life. Seeing by faith relies on a sense of felt connection between artist and work, or a mother and her hospitalized infant.

Lastly, faith—as an attitude toward life, others and oneself—is "the intuition to hope [which] is a significant and essential aspect of what it is to be human."[18] Hope grounds faith, and faith gives assurance to what is hoped for.[19] Regardless of different traditions, faith and hope complement one another in the human enterprise. The experience of our little girl who was caught by her mother at the bottom of the slide will integrate life in particular ways that others will be able to observe. She will be hopeful about the trustworthiness of others, as she imagines she will be caught again. Likewise, the experience of our little boy who tried to jump into his father's arms, only to crash to the floor, will integrate life in particular ways that others can observe. He may not be hopeful enough about the trustworthiness of others to try again—with his father or anyone else.

Thus faith is related to hope. Recall that at the beginning of the chapter, we said that people generally think of faith as positive, as strengthening. But we acknowledge that people may trust someone or something that harms them. At this point, and for purposes of this chapter, we suggest hope anchors a person's orientation to believing in the trustworthiness of others, like the gaze between our little girl and her mother. Confident faith is strengthened by hope. Hope is rooted in our awareness of our incompleteness (our knowing only in part). Hope invites us to risk being in relationship with others. In contrast, hopelessness is a sorrowful form of silence; it's an absence of confidence. It's a sense of the non-existence of safe, trustworthy arms catching our little boy at the bottom of the stairs. Hope moves us beyond our settled opinions to search for what's trustworthy. Hope amounts to expecting something good to come from our efforts. It's anchored in the present but can see beyond existing constraints. Hope delivers us from the tyranny of the present and from feeling we must grab as much as we can before all opportunity passes away forever. With hope, we're able to live in the light of eternity rather than being driven by madly relentless urges to seize the day.[20]

The Centrality of Contemplative Mindfulness

Throughout this chapter we've made use of the term *contemplative mindfulness* to describe a standpoint that understands and appreciates deep interfaces between everyday living and experiences that take the familiar and tear it asunder, what we referred to as thin moments. Contemplative mindfulness is a quality of thick listening that can turn inward as self-observation and outward as perceptive accompaniment of others. It can inform what we do. It can also help us pause before doing anything at all, and especially something of significance. Contemplative mindfulness is integral to making faith sense of the worldviews, paradigms and filters we've learned from our family traditions as well as those we've consciously chosen in the process of maturing.

In professional spiritual care practice, to be mindful is to be watchful, aware, attentive, and thoughtful. To be contemplative (from the Latin, con = with + templum = consecrated space) is to position oneself within the sacredness of *this particular* moment-in-time, and *this precise* situation or circumstance. It's to be "in the temple with" another or others. Every human encounter holds the potential of playing itself out on holy ground and existing within a habitat of what Austrian Jewish and Israeli philosopher Martin Buber calls 'meeting'. Contemplative mindfulness is a type of sustained attention that's directed inward to self, and outward toward others or the Other. It's the intentional, thoughtful beholding of something or someone.

While it's not the language used in Clinical Pastoral Education (CPE) programs, we believe spiritual care practitioners learn about contemplative mindfulness during supervised small group seminars by means of standard tools for in-depth reflection. From one's first CPE course, through to completion of professional certification as a Spiritual Care Practitioner or Board Certified Chaplain, engaging verbatim, critical incident, and case study frameworks is grist for the mill in learning and practicing spiritual care in such a way that thick listening can ripen through contemplative mindfulness.

There are three main reflection tools that are part of CPE learning. The verbatim tool studies a single conversation by capturing initial impressions about the context, person or people involved, and the reason for choosing that particular experience. Development of the verbatim includes examining the conversation from theological, psychological, and sociological points of view, and then reflecting on one's spiritual care functioning through self-critique and learning aptitudes. A critical incident is an experience of significance to the report writer—something that's had an impact or raises questions—perhaps questions about the spiritual care practitioner's beliefs, values, attitudes and behaviors. Here again, resources from theology and the behavioral sciences are drawn upon in carrying forward the reflection.

Lastly, case studies are used to view more long-term, multidimensional and nuanced spiritual care experiences. Anton Boisen, one of the founders of CPE, favored case studies and they have more recently been featured in the work of George Fitchett as a preliminary way to approach spiritual care research.[21] In the Canadian Association for Spiritual Care/ Association canadienne de soins spirituels (CASC/ACSS), a thoroughly documented case study is one of the professional papers required for certification. Details spelled out in the Standards include that the case study describe the spiritual and religious care of an individual or group, and will include the following elements:

- A description of the context in which the care is provided,
- Background information about the patient/family/group,
- A spiritual assessment,
- Spiritual care strategies and interventions,
- An analysis of the patient/family/group dynamics that includes awareness of and sensitivity to diversity,
- Verbatim sections and/or descriptive vignettes that indicate the nature of the interaction,
- A summary of the certification candidate's closure/referral/continuing involvement with the patient/family/group, and
- A reflective assessment of the candidate's strengths/limits and learning areas within this spiritual and religious care relationship.[22]

What each of these tools requires of fledgling as well as experienced spiritual care practitioners is an ability to engage in thick listening, acquire contemplative mindfulness, and know how to step forward relationally in the face of another person's thin moment experience.

The education is broader than a single conversation, critical incident, or case study. Contemplative mindfulness requires practitioners to direct their attention to experiences that involve witnessing a client's storyline, something that may lie beneath what's immediately presented. It includes hearing narratives, noting significant happenings, identifying key players and layered interactions, and being aware of systems involved in the storyline. Contemplative mindfulness is at the heart of reflecting spiritually and theologically from within one's own or another person's exercise of faith. Contemplative mindfulness is about grappling with the wit and wisdom of saying "don't just *do* something *be* there!" It transcends reflective practice[23] and participates in contemplative practice.

What does this mean? According to Drake & Miller,[24] the contemplative practitioner's distinctiveness rests on *being*, and *being* is experienced as unmediated awareness characterized by openness, a sense of relatedness, and by awe and wonder. Drake and Miller see this as a sense of relatedness that goes beyond Buber's I-Thou,[25] insofar as it goes beyond all shades of duality to a place of communion with the other as other. Such experiences, while grounded in the skills and competencies of reflective practice, transcend deliberative and reflective knowing with "careful attention and quiet wonder."[26] Contemplative mindfulness in the face of lived experiences in spiritual care opens the practitioner to a multitude of dynamic points of entry into what's going on: it liaises the ways of story (sacred habitats where clients can pull back layers of meaning and surrender vagueness to clarity), and it allows a practitioner to find words to bring significant scenarios to life. When contemplative mindfulness engages one's own or another's faith story, the outcome is "new truth and meaning for living."[27]

The Ways of Story

The faith stories we tell orient the way we think about the world and convey how we link events meaningfully. Our stories are comprised of many thin moments that invite explanations of what holds life together, even as these explanations may shift and change over time. In spiritual care education, practitioners understand the importance of narrative insofar as the storying of events helps people make faith sense. As previously described, spiritual care scenarios are carefully and systematically reflected on in CPE programs so they can be better understood. The goal for spiritual care practitioners is to exercise thick listening at the client's thin moments by appreciating the ways of story, helping in the unpacking of meaning, and assisting in spiritual/theological reflection on life patterns. With careful attention and quiet wonder, a spiritual care practitioner can perceive a client's lifetime faith story as it emerges in the contours of an immediately experienced spiritual care event.

Let's draw on an analogy to tease out some of the nuances of this sort of thick listening. A client's thin moment may involve the loss of a loved one. This loss can be viewed as a fragment of a deeper story of loss that shapes this person's worldview. While the current loss can feel unique and overwhelming, it remains a fragment that's connected to all of the other fragments in the person's loss narrative. As such, it's tied to the person's beliefs and assumptions about loss. In this light, theoretically considered, a spiritual care practitioner might imagine a riverbed[28] as an analogy for someone's faith story. Just like in a river, some of the person's inherited knowledge about loss forms its bedrock and is solid and firm, virtually unchanging. Thus, in the experience of thick listening, a spiritual care professional might notice the person saying "God never gives you more than you can deal with." The person's belief statement can be viewed as a faith resource. Yet, the bedrock leaves channels so that other beliefs and assumptions held by the person are organized in observable patterns. These may be sensed as the person expresses thoughts and feelings within the current experience of loss, e.g. "I didn't have time to say goodbye." Some of their ideas may be like the shifting sand that moves sluggishly along the hard rock in response to the water's currents, sounding like "Oh, if only I had arrived sooner...run that red light...had exact change for parking...." Lastly, some beliefs and assumptions may be fluid, like the water that flows freely and changes with circumstances, expressed by saying, "I'm devastated!...I can't believe he's gone!...Why is this happening to me?"

As an agent of thick listening, the spiritual care practitioner stays present to all the person's words and deeds, noticing what's bedrock, what's a tributary, and what's shifting or free flowing. Without judgment, the spiritual care professional tunes into subtle healing movements while accompanying the person, discerns meaning-making perceptions as these come into focus, and mirrors the person's beliefs and assumptions about loss in such a way that, hopefully, this new loss story will become a healing fragment as it finds its place in the whole of the person's life.

As we consider a worldview by using the analogy of a riverbed, it's important to notice that we don't get a worldview by satisfying ourselves that it's correct. Nor do we keep our worldview because we're satisfied we're correct. As discussed previously, our worldview derives from lived experience, as perceived through human consciousness and freedom. It acts to filter what we see, hear and understand. As we first begin to believe anything, what we believe isn't a single idea; it's a whole system of ideas;[29] it's an impression of something foundational and beyond our individuality. The deepest layers of a worldview are the inherited background, the bedrock, that we get early in life and against which we distinguish what's true from what's false.[30] A worldview emerges from foundational experiences that are informed by other people's filtering mechanisms that sift through flowing waters and shifting sands. As a consequence, we use our filters to decide whether our beliefs and assumptions ring true or false,[31] as we assess whether someone is trustworthy or untrustworthy, and can be counted on as a faith object.

So we might say that all thinking is grounded on believing, i.e., on holding inherited knowledge that we consider to be reliable, with some assumptions we seldom doubt. Even for the most broadminded person, some ideas are steady and reliable like the rock floor at the bottom of a river, or to use another analogy, like the hinges on a door that allow the door to open. In both analogies, faith is an axis for expressing comfortable certainty. It exists at a point where we're no longer struggling[32] to differentiate what's true from what's false. Yet if we reflect intentionally, we aren't hasty or superficial. Rather, we've created a way of life.[33] Faith must find its resting place within a way of life and in a faith story that makes sense so that, in living our lives, we make sense to other people.

This understanding of faith is similar to a Hebrew perspective. The precise meaning of faith to the ancient Hebrews was "hold God."[34] What was this faithful grip on God like? It was a faith that instinctively trusted the self-revealing divine presence that accompanied Hebrew people through their thin moments of struggle and discovery. To hold God was to have a comfortable grip on God; it was to believe in God's trustworthiness. For the Greeks, Philo in particular, faith was a kind of certainty.[35] What sort of certainty was it? It was faith that had stopped struggling and was at ease in the spaciousness of a dwelling mind. This attentive mind, relying as it does on thick listening, doesn't rush to action but allows itself the space to reflect, feel and consider what's going on without anxiety. These ancient understandings shed light on faith and faith stories as trusted forms of life, worldviews, reconfigured over time through personal and social experience, yet held securely.

From another perspective, faith develops through hearing and seeing, that is, by way of sense experience. This hearing and seeing, however, accrues in a particular way in the light of faith. Through hearing, faith forms the layers of assumptions from infancy onward that German philosopher Ludwig Wittgenstein described using the analogies of the bedrock and the hinges on the door. This hearing happens communally, so that personal identity forms in association with a group. Our social identification is accomplished through verbalized, embodied interactions. What we hear, we hear together. Yet hearing is also personal: we hear what we're able to hear at any given moment.

Hearing, both with others and alone, accumulates meaning within a worldview, and couples with seeing in a specific way. Returning to the geological image of an archipelago, faith integrates experience through the spiritual skill of imagining. In Christian spirituality, St. Ignatius of Loyola constructed exercises for faith's way of seeing that are similar to the archipelago analogy. He grounded these exercises in biblical scenarios, on which he invited people to reflect.[36] His invitation included a technique often referred to as the "application of senses." A person following this approach can read and also imagine the scenario and then apply the five senses of seeing, hearing, touching, tasting and smelling to it. As a result of this sensual immersion, the person becomes imaginatively involved in the biblical scenario and, from within this experience, previously unseen connections are perceived. This way of seeing deepens meaning. The spiritual exercises of Ignatius provide an opportunity to bridge biblical narratives and personal narratives. In this way, through seeing by faith, a person builds on the bedrock of their worldview and faith tradition and learns to navigate the flowing waters and shifting sands of their personal faith story.

Differentiating Spiritual and Theological Reflection

As mentioned, life experience is organized into a worldview by the time we're 11 or 12 years old. Worldviews filter what we see, hear and understand. They express our fundamental relationship with all that surrounds us. We trust this picture of the world and put faith in it. Worldviews inform the exercise of faith and the exercise of faith continues to shape our worldview. Both processes are intimately connected. They play out in the day-to-day events of our lives and contribute to the ongoing construction of our faith stories. Later chapters discuss the role of worldview and human development, how we relate with others and also how we reason based on these worldviews. The current task is to consider how we intentionally reflect on experiences that shape our worldview and break into our awareness as thin moments, inviting us into the work of spiritual and theological reflection.

This work involves a fourfold trajectory: being in relationship (something integral to having faith in something or someone), having concrete experiences of being in relationship, reflecting on these experiences, and embodying reflection through meaningful action. In this sense, the exercise of faith isn't static; rather, it involves a deep longing to understand what's happening, to seek right relationship, and to willingly pursue sources of wisdom for the living of one's life.

While there's a reflective quality innate in all human living, it's often not until we reach adulthood that we begin to intentionally look again (respect) and look back (reflect) on experience to gain greater comprehension of what's going on in a particular situation, and ask ourselves whether we want to take an active role in reshaping our worldview. In order to organize reality meaningfully, and reflect on it intentionally, we need a narrative to give shape to our worldview. This narrative expresses part of the mental mapping that occurs during worldview development, where concepts and connections between these concepts gradually take shape on the landscape of lived experience that defines the relationship of everything to everything else.[37] We need stories, analogies and signal events that enable us to self-reflect and make faith sense in our everyday lives. These stories depict the three moving parts of faith in concrete ways; they portray the dynamics of congruence and incongruence, and reveal our encounters with trustworthy as well as untrustworthy people and things. One's faith story emerges at the intersections of personal narrative, social connection, experience with tradition and cultural analysis, as well as intentional spiritual and theological reflection.

Let's focus on this last point of intersection. What is intentional spiritual reflection, and intentional theological reflection? Are they the same or different? We propose that differentiating between the two types of reflection is important in being able to use both in professional spiritual care practice. In a book by O'Connor and Meakes titled *Spiritual and Theological Reflection: A Canadian Qualitative Study on Spiritual Care and Psychotherapy*, the terms *spiritual reflection* and *theological reflection* are identified neither as synonyms nor as antonyms. Rather, they "embrace many similarities and differences."[38] A key variable in the practice of these types of reflection is educational background. For O'Connor and Meakes, spiritual reflection is carried out by professionals whose formal education is in a discipline other than theology, for example, by a nurse, occupational or physical therapist, social worker, psychologist or physician. Practitioners in all these occupations see spiritual care as belonging to their scope of practice.

Sources of knowledge pertinent to spiritual reflection are found in an abundance of literature that addresses concepts such as spirituality, spiritual health, spiritual suffering and spiritual distress (diagnostic terms listed by the North American Nursing Diagnosis Association/NANDA), religious or spiritual problems (a diagnostic criteria found in the fifth edition of the Diagnostic and Statistical Manual of Mental Disorders/ DSM-V of the American Psychiatric Association), spiritual beliefs and values, spiritual resources, spiritual assessment and spiritual history taking. From this broad array of topics, some authors and professional groups are developing inroads for a needed depth of field in the study of spiritual reflection. Authors described by O'Connor and Meakes include Paul Pruyser (clinical psychologist), Harold Koenig (physician, psychiatrist, epidemiologist), Froma Walsh (social worker), Ken Pargament (clinical psychologist, researcher), Lorraine Wright (nurse), Beverley Clarke (physiotherapist), and Sue Baptiste (occupational therapist). Given the widespread popularity of a term like spiritual reflection (especially when contrasted with the less popular, religiously identified term theological reflection), it's important for practitioners, researchers, theorists and educators in professions that see spiritual care as integral to their practice to pursue in-depth development, analyses and discussion of methods and models for spiritual reflection.

Theological reflection is exercised by those with formal studies in theology as a body of knowledge, including world religions and diverse faith traditions. Spiritual care professionals, faith group leaders, psycho-spiritual therapists and people who are affiliated with a chosen faith community typically exercise theological reflection. The distinction between spiritual reflection and theological reflection is important to spiritual care practitioners who are educated in both theology and the behavioral sciences and whose professional practice includes spiritual as well as theological reflection.[39] It's imperative that spiritual care professionals access, study and learn from resources such as O'Connor's and Meakes' book insofar as it offers a structure to help navigate theological reflection. Navigable structures are integral to the development of spiritual and theological insight, with their implications for competent spiritual care practice.

Something inferred but not explicitly stated by O'Connor and Meakes is a suggestion that principles used to understand theological reflection can serve to inform theoretical approaches to spiritual reflection. This is thought-provoking and significant in its implications for spiritual care. It's also a hopeful possibility. If the key difference between practicing spiritual vis-à-vis theological reflection is the study of theology as a body of knowledge, and if theoretical work originating in the area of theological reflection can be relevant to constructing a depth of field in spiritual reflection, there may be hope that all allied professions who see spiritual care within their scope of practice might come together in valuing and exploring both approaches to intentional reflection. We proceed in the light of this hope, using language that's ambiguous (has more than one meaning and is therefore applicable to spiritual and theological reflection) but also explicit enough to be practical and usable.

Constructing Intentional Reflection on Lived Experience

There are several foundational concepts to consider in the construction of theological and spiritual reflection as forms of intentional reflection. First, we look at the concept of model. It's typically understood, based on approaches to theological reflection cited in previous as well as following paragraphs, that a model is a framework for reflection. Further, many theological reflection models found in the literature have methods by which the model can be applied.

For purposes of our chapter, we prefer to shift away from this understanding of model by drawing attention once again to the work of F.A. Hayek. He highlights two aspects of worldview formation—a map and a model, and states that a model is "a representation of a given moment".[40] A model is experienced within a worldview map; the map is its background. We access the map in bits and pieces by paying attention to given model moments of social interaction, especially those that are discordant with our map. In this sense, both map and model can be viewed as sources for the kind of intentional reflection that will have an impact on one's conceptual learning and the reconceiving of one's worldview.

According to Hayek, *map* is the big picture of accumulated experience that's multi-dimensional and multi-layered, and defines the relationship of everything to everything else in a worldview. A *model* is a moment of social interaction, experienced within a map, which serves as its background. The map is the 'familiar' against which the model is scrutinized; it's the standard into which a model is supposed to fit in order to give continuity, identity, direction and value to one's worldview.[41] When the fit is there, we seldom scrutinize what has occurred. Sometimes, however, there's a lack of fit between *map* and *model*. This may create dissonance, and the tension that gives rise to a "thin moment" in which the safeguards of one's familiar are shaken up. This *model* moment of social interaction can be a *source* for intentional reflection. In spiritual care, thick listening that occurs at a client's thin moment may involve noticing an embodied reaction or uncensored utterance as the indicator of dissonance or tension. Caring and respectful engagement with the client—in this thin model moment—may be what opens relational space for the person to risk talking about what's unfamiliar and unsettled, a space that will potentially expand their awareness and broaden their worldview.

This understanding of *model* as a moment-in-time of lived experience, set against the backdrop of one's broader life narrative and faith story, finds affinity with conceiving of *model* as a source for intentional reflection. It's an understanding that situates *model* with *map* rather than with *method*. This isn't to deny or dismiss the value of methods in carrying forward spiritual reflection or theological reflection. It cautions, however, against using method as a technique, application or routine that may miss the thin moment in a client's actual experience. If *model* is a source for reflection, *method* must be activity that flows out of engagement with the *source* (especially dissonant thin moments). Rather than being about models as frameworks to which methods are applied, our thinking proposes that the *method* is thick listening. Thick listening is the method for hearing what's happening in a thin moment. Thick listening at thin moments, as *method*, is the heart of spiritual reflection and theological reflection. These ideas about *map, model, source*, and *method* are different from but not incompatible with existing literature.

According to O'Connor and Meakes, frequently referenced approaches to theological reflection found in the literature include those developed by James and Evelyn Whitehead, Patricia O'Connell Killen and John deBeer, Robert Kinast and Howard Stone and James Duke.[42] All these authors point to lived experience as the integral source for doing intentional reflection. Insofar as lived experience is both personal and social, it engages and is engaged by further sources for reflection. The Whiteheads refer to three-sources (sacred tradition, contemporary culture and personal experience). Killen and deBeer have two sources (experience and tradition). Kinast's focus is on the primacy of experience (with theology at the service of experience). Lastly, Stone and Duke emphasize thinking as having sources in both embedded theology (values, beliefs, practices, and attitudes that shape a person's life) and deliberative theology (articulated beliefs and lived values).

Note that Stone and Duke's embedded theology is similar to what we've been calling the inherited content in one's worldview. Translating embedded thinking into deliberative thinking is something undertaken in spiritual care education as well, especially in CPE. Having occasions to say what one believes and disbelieves, and also to grapple with meaning that's related to bedrock beliefs or disbeliefs, is inherent in the reflective emphasis of all CPE learning. In an educational climate that constantly asks about beliefs, values, assumptions, social location and the safe and effective use of self in professional practice, CPE students struggle with the ways their inherited content can appear like channels in the river's bedrock. Interacting with peers, supervisors and clients who come from other storylines can be unsettling, and cause shifting sands and fluidity of interactions to muddy the waters. It's hard work. Learning at a level of intense and intentional reflection is full of effort. But, if CPE students persevere, they may discover their capacity for contemplative mindfulness, competency in thick listening at thin moments, and arrive—as spiritual care professionals—at sacred points of intersection with others where they have the privilege of being witnesses to clients as they give voice to their deliberative thinking.

A final consideration about intentional reflection on lived experience has to do with looking at *social interactions*. We wrote earlier that a *model* represents a moment of social interaction that either fits or doesn't fit with the contours of one's worldview map. A person navigates these social interactions relationally, informed by perceptual and conceptual learning. While most social interactions give continuity, identity, and direction to our life story, there are those characterized by incongruence and dissonance that we've identified as "thin moments"—points of interaction with someone or some thing that invite us to pause and enter more deeply into the landscape. As we reach adulthood, and consider whether or not we want to take an active role in reshaping our world-view, it's these thin moments, points of entry into our map, that invite us to purposefully look again and look back at our storyline with a view to greater comprehension of what's gone on, or is going on.

Whether we're doing spiritual reflection or theological reflection, points of entry give rise to questions; these questions can serve as navigational tools in exploring one's worldview and faith story. Some typical questions include: Who are the people involved? What are the signal events? When have these events occurred—developmentally, historically and culturally? Where have they occurred—socially, geographically? And why does something stand out as a thin moment? Points of entry into the landscape that surrounds a thin moment need to be approached with curiosity, careful attention and quiet wonder. They are always relational, and necessitate thick listening.[43] The landscape entered into is multi-dimensional and multi-layered, and contributes to defining the relationship of everything to everything else.

Navigating Intentional Reflection

Thus far we've said that the *map* is about worldview, the *model* is a moment of social interaction against the backdrop of the map, and *thin moments* are model experiences that evoke dissonance or lack of fit with one's worldview so that they invite intentional reflection. As such, thin moments are the main source for spiritual and theological reflection. Thin moments serve as points of entry to the map's landscape. These points of entry serve as navigational pathways into a thin moment source

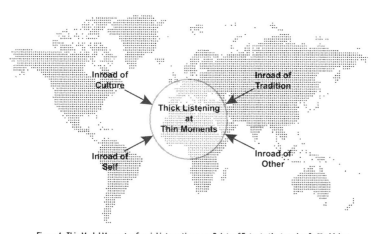

Figure 4 - Thin Model Moments of social interaction open Points of Entry to the terrain of a Worldview

for reflection. Lastly, we've proposed that the *method* for intentional spiritual and theological reflection is thick listening at thin moments.

For purposes of our book, there are four key and interconnected points of entry to one's worldview map: self, other, tradition[44], and culture.[45] These entry points find resonance with what previously referenced authors identify as sources. Each point of entry serves as a way into the broader terrain being explored. Further, as intentional reflection is pursued, each way-in connects with what we've been discussing as the three moving parts of faith. To stand on the landscape of one's worldview is an act of faith. A person or group carrying forward intentional reflection is the agent of faith, the source being engaged is the object of faith, and the relationship between agent and object is what one intentionally reflects upon. Navigating thin moments through in-depth attention to self, others, tradition and culture is integral to considering whether or not to take an active role in reshaping one's worldview.

There are two further points to be made. First, as discussed elsewhere, the relationship between agent(s) and objects of faith may be healthy, unhealthy, or even harmful—influencing how the person or group sees the world, feels about the experience and takes action. Thus, for example, if a person's faith story includes coercion "in God's name," clergy abuse, or ethical impasse based on church teachings, it may be nearly impossible for that person to engage tradition—especially the institutional aspect of faith tradition—as an object of faith and as a source of information, insight and wisdom.

Second, whatever the initial touchpoint of connection (self, other, tradition, culture), all four pathways to information and insight will be impacted by reflection. Thus, for example, focusing on the source (thin moment social interaction) will implicate reflection on tradition, culture and self; focusing on culture will implicate a person's views about others, self and tradition. Like touching a square of gelatin dessert, no matter the point of contact, the whole square jiggles. So too with spiritual and theological reflection. All four points of entry to the map intersect and are interconnected. Again, the trajectory of intentional reflection is that of being in relationship, having concrete experiences of being in relationship, reflecting on these experiences, and embodying this reflection through meaningful action. Reflection follows experience and requires a pause prior to action. We're identifying the pause as reflecting on the source (thin moment) and intentionally engaging spiritual and theological reflection. Now, let's see how this theoretical groundwork plays out in the story of Rose.

Rose's Intentional Reflection in Clinical Pastoral Education (CPE)

While many references to thick listening at thin moments used in this book are described as if a person were in a clinical experience with a client, there's also need for describing the thick listening at thin moments that can occur within the matrix of experiences comprising Clinical Pastoral Education (CPE) itself. Since not everyone who practices spiritual care enters into this kind of learning environment, there may be resonance with other types of coursework, internships, or professional assessments. What follows is intentional reflection on Rose's CPE narrative as she navigates various points of entry into the map of her worldview through thin moments in her spiritual care education.

> This is the story of Rose, a fifty-two year old woman exploring professional spiritual care. Rose is married, has three young-adult children, and worked as a high school teacher for ten years. When the family moved from a small town in one of the rural provinces of Canada to the province's capital city, Rose found herself reflecting on what she might do next. She could return to teaching, or she might explore a sense of calling she'd felt for a long time to serve in ministry. While she wasn't interested in ordained ministry, a series of events transpired that lead Rose to wonder if she was being called to work in the field of spiritual care or chaplaincy. In order to explore this possibility, she applied to take a program of CPE in tandem with several courses at a nearby theological college.
>
> After being accepted to the CPE program, and placed at an acute care hospital for her clinical hours, Rose turned her attention to her peer group and supervisor, engaged in the reflective seminars that comprise essential aspects of the program, and worked on the written assignments that invited her to reflect on all aspects of her learning. Rose's first on-call experience threw her off balance. She wasn't sure how to put it into words. After much consternation and doubt, she decided to bring this on-call event to the CPE inter-personal relationships (IPR) seminar for discussion and feedback. Subsequent to that seminar Rose decided to do some intentional reflection. This became an ongoing practice in her CPE process, which spanned several years and involved

completion of a Master's degree in theological studies. What follows is a summary of instances when Rose chose to engage the four points of entry to her faith story through inroads of self, other, tradition and culture. Each "turning to" is narrated in the present tense, includes Rose's experience of thin moments, and is coupled with conceptual elements currently under consideration as she is 'navigating intentional reflection'.

Turning to the inroad of 'self'—In bringing her first on-call experience to IPR, Rose is both the agent and object of faith. In particular, Rose wants to reflect on trigger moments (in which there was dissonance between her map and model) that occurred as she was called to five patient care scenarios over the 24-hours[46] she carried the on-call pager. These five calls included three patient deaths. As Rose prepares to bring her experience to the group, she takes stock of her emotions and body sensations. Her heart is pounding, hands are sweaty, and she feels cold in her bodily core. She's restless and a bit jittery, waiting for an opening in the group's process. When she starts to talk, she's aware of her mind going blank intermittently, her voice wavering near tears, and her thoughts seeming to come out in short, scattered phrases rather than coherent sentences. She talks about the pager going off five times, twice during the late night and early morning hours. While each call was unique and meaningful in her encounters with the people involved, she says she felt triggered and was overwhelmed by the sheer number of calls. She questions her competence and fit for this kind of work.

After Rose shares these aspects of her experience, there's a deafening silence in the group. This serves to intensify her anxiety, and uncertainty. It's at this point in time that Rose starts to pray and, thankfully, feels God with her. This felt sense of God's presence calms her mind and emotions. She waits in the silence until one of her more experienced CPE peers speaks. He says, "Rose, I'm deeply moved by your experience and want to support you in any way I'm able. How are you doing now, with us, after sharing this overwhelming experience?" With these words, Rose feels the door for deeper sharing opening, and she walks through.

She talks about one call to a medical unit where, after walking into the patient's room, she was immediately aware of being the only white person there. The patient died as she stood at the foot of the bed with the patient's husband and children standing on either side, holding their wife and mother's hands. When she asked about praying together, she was soon aware of being a Christian who was with a Somalian Muslim family. She asked if they had a customary prayer they wanted to say, and they immediately began praying in their mother tongue of Somali. Rose said she felt useless, like an outsider. She wanted to leave but stayed in the room. When the family finished praying, they thanked Rose profusely saying, "Thank you for praying with us at this sorrowful time." Rose says she left the room confused and bewildered.

Before waiting to hear feedback from her peers and supervisor, she goes on to tell about another call during which she was asked to talk with an elderly man, near death with lung cancer. The man asked to see a chaplain. He had some things he wanted to get off his chest. After their initial introduction, the man started to talk about 'sins of his past'. These included being abusive to his wife and three children—hitting them, expecting them to do whatever he asked, even acting sexually toward his two daughters. He wanted Rose to forgive him "in God's name." He didn't want to die with the guilt and remorse he felt. Rose asked a few questions about when he last saw his family. He shared his wife had died, and his children had been geographically distant for decades. They didn't want anything to do with him. He knew death was near. So he turned again to Rose to ensure God's forgiveness. Rose was struggling. All of a sudden images of her uncle Toby started popping into her mind. She didn't know why they were there. She tried to focus on the patient, and managed to get through a prayer for forgiveness. As she prayed, "in your name we pray, Amen", the patient's eyes closed in death. Again, Rose says, she left the room confused and bewildered.

Now Rose pauses. She's emotionally spent. She feels vulnerable and uncertain. These *others* who have listened to her story, her peers and supervisor, hold a great deal of power. There's a *culture* of CPE, of which Rose is aware, where group interactions may be respectful, healthy and supportive—or they can be invasive, analytical and potentially abusive.[47] She's heard stories of both, and is still too new to CPE to entirely trust what might happen to her. Thankfully, her supervisor and peers engage Rose with support, compassion, and encouragement. She receives feedback about the differing *racial and faith traditions* she encountered when she was with the Somalian family. She becomes aware of how racially protected her life has been, growing up in the *culture* of a small, rural town where all the people were white. She also receives feedback about the flashes of her uncle Toby invading that moment with the dying elderly man who had just confessed his physical and sexual abuse. Her supervisor wondered if Rose had ever explored therapy in order to learn more about her unremembered childhood experiences with this uncle. She said she hadn't but this might be an important thing to do.

After her IPR experience, Rose thought about how spiritual and theological reflection on her first on-call had been a way to learn about herself. Using the image introduced earlier, she could see that the corner of gelatin dessert touched was a *self* source that reverberated with learning about *others* (the Somalian family, elderly man, and her CPE supervisor and peers), her *faith tradition* of being Christian while praying with Muslims and sensing God's presence when she was anxious in IPR. She also learned about several *cultural* nuances that were as yet barely coherent to her, i.e. how racism and sexism existed on the margins of her life, and how stories about CPE group interactions were a real issue as she felt her vulnerability and the power differential among her supervisor and peers following her open, intimate sharing.

Turning to the inroad of 'other'—Having encountered life-changing experiences in the course of her first CPE program, Rose continues with CPE learning. On another occasion she brings a verbatim to a clinical seminar for review by her peers. This seminar focuses on a client, methodically described by Rose, as the object of faith; while she and her peers are the agents of faith. The seminar commences with an unscripted role play in which Rose is the client, a man we'll call Bob, who is 50 years old, a husband, father and successful criminal attorney and who has just received a terminal cancer diagnosis. One of her peers is the spiritual care practitioner, and others in her group play the parts of a nurse and the patient's wife. In this context, Rose gains intimate appreciation for the patient's thin moment experience as she steps into his feelings of shock and emotional confusion; it's as though the wind has been knocked out of him. As Bob, Rose experiences what it's like to have a peer respond to her spiritual needs. Following the role-play, and its debriefing, Rose circulates copies of her verbatim report. She relates preliminary information about Bob and goes on to read her spiritual assessment, theological reflection, psychological and sociological concerns, self-critique and her lessons learned.

The corner of gelatin dessert touched in this clinical seminar is that of *other* as a source of insight and wisdom. It's an instance in which there's the *other* of Bob as patient, and the *others* of Rose's supervisor and peers. Both are points of connection for her insofar as she learns, through contemplative mindfulness, how to listen to Bob's multi-layered grief and loss in light of his terminal diagnosis. She uses a spiritual history tool developed by Christina Puchalski and her colleagues[48] to carefully assess to what extent Bob considers himself spiritual or religious, how important his faith *tradition* is to him, what he considers his faith or religious community to be, as well as what role he'd like his faith to play going forward. In addition to learning about Bob, Rose learns more about the *culture* of healthcare and inter-professional collaboration. She realizes spiritual care can be practiced differently by a variety of health care professionals. She appreciates her profession's uniqueness in its depth approach to the field of spiritual care, including the integration of theological and religious content when doing assessments and interventions. Slowly but surely, in relationship with her CPE peers and supervisors, Rose is gaining confidence in her *self* and in her competence as a spiritual care practitioner.

By now, Rose is aware that palliative care is the sub-specialization of spiritual care to which she feels most drawn. This requires her to read topics such as hospice and palliative care, total pain and its management, and death and dying. Literature in this field is abundant and empowers Rose to bring greater depth of knowledge to her thick listening at palliative patients' thin moments. In continuing to learn about inter-professional collaboration, she benefits in a particular way from a study out of the University of Ottawa, that features inter-professional education in palliative care using popular literature.[49] As well, in the course of her research, she comes across a doctoral dissertation in which palliative care and St. John of the Cross's description of the dark night of the soul are co-related and considered in great depth.[50] She's amazed with this discovery insofar as it brings her to understand how an aspect of her Christian *faith tradition* can be integrated with her growing interest and competency in palliative care. As her spiritual care practitioner identity develops, she has a greater sense of how to demonstrate the safe and effective use of *self* when relating with clients and colleagues. She's done significant therapeutic work, and now knows herself in ways she could never have imagined prior to CPE. This has benefitted not only her professional functioning but also her marriage and family life. She appreciates from experience what she's heard many times, that unlike other professions where stethoscopes, high-tech machines or sophisticated monitoring systems serve as tools of practice, she *herself* is the tool of her profession. It's who she is, personally and professionally, that she brings with her to every spiritual care moment of meeting, contemplative mindfulness and thick listening event.

Turning to the inroad of 'tradition'—Eighteen months after Rose commenced her first CPE program, she finds herself mid-way to completion of her academic degree and in her fourth CPE course. Recently, she took part in a sweat lodge ceremony conducted by the woman Indigenous Elder who's part of the health care team. Sitting in profound darkness, heat, and the sacred smells of the smudge circulating through the lodge, Rose remembers a number of interfaith experiences she's had with Hindu, Islamic, Buddhist, Jewish, Sikh, and Indigenous families while carrying out her spiritual care practice in acute and long-term healthcare facilities. In her pondering, she realizes that the object of her faith in this moment is tradition, especially faith tradition—something that's been a significant part of her overall learning. She's cherished her in-depth studies of the sacred texts and history of her Christian faith. She's integrated theological reflection into clinical reports (verbatim, critical incident, case study), including a focus on foundational spiritual attributes[51] as well as standpoints (certitude, self-assurance, exploration) and some theological themes.[52] These resources regularly inform her spiritual practices and professional relationships. From having gone deeply into her own faith tradition, Rose can more clearly appreciate parallels and dissimilarities with other faith traditions. With the benefit of learning from theology and the behavioral sciences, Rose comprehends the core meaning of tradition as something multi-faceted, involving the handing down of beliefs, ceremonies, texts, symbols, stories, teachings, practices, rituals and music from generation to generation. She recalls viewing the movie, *Fiddler on the Roof*,[53] with its lively rendering of the song "Tradition", in which Tevye reflects on the contrasting societies within his small town of Anatevka. In that song, tradition isn't only about religious faith, it's also about gender role assignments, military occupation, and the coexistence of a number of diverse cultures.

The corner of gelatin dessert touched in her pensiveness is that of *tradition* as a source of insight and wisdom. Following her sweat lodge experience, Rose spends time learning about interfaces of faith and culture, revisiting the concepts of spiritual/religious/cultural traditions and social location,[54] human rights, cultural competence/humility/ safety found in the Canadian Association for Spiritual Care/Association canadienne de soins spiritual (CASC/ACSS) document on *Competencies of CASC/ACSS Certified Professionals*.[55] She remembers the many times she's heard people say, upon learning she was a spiritual care practitioner and part of a health care team, that they were spiritual but not religious. She grapples with the dissonance experienced by so many people regarding faith, spirituality, theology and religion.

She's aware her own faith tradition has been instrumental to her sense of *self*, calling and vocational fulfillment, but also acknowledges that other people's experiences may be more conflicted due to dogmatic and hierarchical coercion. Rose comes to understand that tradition and culture, in their differing ways, have impacted her professional identity, her theoretical knowledge as a spiritual care practitioner, her professional ethical conduct, and how she assesses and uses intervention skills. While she's aware her learning in this area will be lifelong, she decides that—since her cognizance was sparked by participating in the sweat lodge experience—she'll read the *Final Report of the Truth and Reconciliation Commission of Canada*,[56] giving special attention to its ninety-four Calls to Action, and she'll consider ways she can incorporate greater consciousness of *tradition* in her spiritual care practice.

Turning to the inroad of 'culture'—Four years into her parallel studies of a Master of Theological Studies degree and CPE learning, Rose considers her endgame. She's nearing completion of her thesis at the college, and is eyeing professional Standards for becoming a Certified Spiritual Care Practitioner—referred to as a Board Certified Chaplain in a number of North American spiritual care associations. While on a week-long holiday in the mountains with her husband, Joe, Rose finds herself thinking back on all the events that have brought her to where she is now. She and Joe, her most intimate *other*, spend hours talking together as they walk the beautiful mountain, meadow and marshland trails. Rose remembers when she first awakened to the possibility her uncle Toby had sexually molested her. She expresses heartfelt gratitude to Joe for accompanying her to several therapy sessions dealing with sexuality in their marriage. Rose's therapeutic work has had a profound impact on her sense of *self*. She and Joe talk about how shocked they were to realize they are implicated in *cultures* of racism and sexism, even though the small town in which they grew up, married, and raised children was exclusively white. Several years ago they spent time reading aloud to one another, the book *White Fragility* by Robin DiAngelo.[57] They also read critiques of this book by people of color. They grappled with ubiquitous race and gender-based social constructs. They watched a number of movies and YouTube films related to the cultural variables of politics, economics, health, education, language, law, ethnicity, immigration, family systems, the environment and religion. Rose and Joe discuss the shifts in social discourse that have occurred over the past several decades—how polarized family and neighborhood gatherings have become, and how a new language expresses the binary thinking, false equivalencies, and social impasses currently at play. As their holiday time wanes, Rose makes it a point to share how important her *faith tradition* has been in her CPE and spiritual care experiences. How much she's known her need for God. And also how much her mind and heart have opened to faith traditions beyond her own. In this regard, Rose talks about how spiritual reflection has helped her grasp underlying concepts related to spirituality, spiritual assessment, spiritual problems and spiritual care, and how theological reflection has enabled her to wrestle with her image of God and rework her worldview to include authentic respect for others' beliefs and practices. It's amazing for Rose and Joe to hike, canoe, eat out, take drives and think back—doing this as a couple. On the last day of their very unusual, deeply enriching holiday, Rose and Joe gather leaves, twigs and pebbles. They build a huge campfire, roast marshmallows, and drop a leaf or twig or pebble into the fire to signify losses, discoveries, struggles and growth experiences. It's the perfect ending.

The corner of gelatin dessert touched by Rose's and Joe's holiday is that of *culture* as an object of faith and an inroad to insight and wisdom. For Rose, cultural learning isn't abstract. She continually meets people in her spiritual care experiences that are dealing with one or other of the cultural variables discussed with Joe. She has also come to understand systems thinking,[58] and can see its functioning in myriad ways. Lastly, insofar as her CPE occurred in healthcare settings and some of it happened during the COVID-19 pandemic, Rose found it fascinating to read *The Great Influenza: The Story of the Deadliest Pandemic in History*, by John Barry while being steeped in her existing pandemic experiences.[59] As she read his book, there were so many comparisons to be made. There's so much to discover about how the medical profession as a whole, and public health in particular was sorely tested by the 1918 pandemic and is being tested again in the 2020s. Given the cultural interconnections of global travel, cross-species viral spread, and the economic, gender and racial complexities related to societies that are impacted by a global health crisis, Rose believes it's likely additional pandemics are yet to come.

Readiness for professional certification—Throughout her CPE experience, Rose has used intentional spiritual and theological reflection to navigate the four points of entry as inroads to self, other, tradition and culture. She found that, by attending to thin moments at each point of entry, as she observed the objects of faith she put her trust in, she was able to learn a great deal about professional spiritual care in a multi-dimensional and multi-layered way. This involved her plunging deeply into several psychological theories, Erik Erikson's stages of psychosocial development, and specific therapeutic modalities for spiritual care practice. She worked with theological, spiritual and religious understandings in ways that integrated what she knew conceptually with how she relates to others so that she could incarnate her beliefs and values relationally. From within the rigor of CPE, Rose grew to better appreciate the map of her life narrative and faith story as she reflected on it deeply and in the company of supervisors, peers and her husband. In this work, Rose recognized thin moments in her own experience of the shifting sands and fluidity in the riverbed of her worldview. She grappled perceptually and conceptually, but has come to a sense of self that's tested, trusted and open to further growth. Later in the year, after completing her degree, Rose plans to begin the process of seeking professional certification as a Spiritual Care Practitioner.

Conclusion

In summary, faith is essentially human. It's rooted in the relational core at the heart of human nature. It comprises three moving parts: an agent, an object and the relationship between them. Faith is both content and practice. It's built up through multi-sensory experience from the time we're born. Faith produces a worldview, life narratives and habits of the heart that come together as ways of seeing and ways of being in the world. Faith is anchored in the hope that people can be counted on to act in certain ways.

For spiritual care professionals, being in relationship with patients, long term care residents, inmates, deployed soldiers, congregational members and other clients involves learning the strategies of *thick listening at thin moments, contemplative mindfulness* and *spiritual/theological reflection* with people who are in the human enterprise of making faith sense. The story of Rose is an example of how a practice of intentional spiritual and theological reflection can accompany learners through CPE experiences, so they grow into competent Spiritual Care Practitioners. More will be said about a number of these topics in other parts of our book. For the present, we reiterate that every human being has faith in something or someone, and central to the spiritual care practitioners' role is a commitment to walk another through the meaning-making process that comes to form a life. This involves being present in order to help people unpack faith dynamics, worldviews, joys and sorrows, stories and discoveries of faith in action.

Take Away Questions for Reflection

- When you think about the three moving parts of faith (agent, object, and the relationship between them), how would you describe these terms using a spiritual care experience?
- What analogy would you choose for depicting the term "faith story"?
- Have you ever experienced thick listening? How would you describe that experience?
- Can you think of a thin moment experience in your life? If you were to re-visit this thin moment as a source for spiritual and/or theological reflection, which inroad (self, other, tradition, culture) would you start with?
- What meaning does the term "contemplative mindfulness" have for you after reading this chapter?

Chapter 3

Spiritual Care and Human Development

Introduction

Spiritual Care professionals complete their education within academic and clinical settings, drawing on knowledge from both theology and the behavioral sciences. While it's not our intention to delve into the history of almost a century of growth and change in the field of modern pastoral and spiritual care education, we want to raise and respond to the question of why we select Erik Erikson's psychosocial theory as the focus of this chapter on human development. It's notable that, with the emergence of Clinical Pastoral Education (CPE) in the mid-1920s, pastoral and spiritual care studies focused significant attention on understanding the psychological make up of human persons.

Since its beginning, theorists, schools, traditions, and specializations in psychology and human development intersected with theological/spiritual/religious studies to become an integral part of CPE learning over the decades of the twentieth century.[1] Likewise, current reflections on the development of chaplaincy and spiritual care education propose learning models that are complex and multi-dimensional.[2] This is a field that deserves its own in-depth description, investigation and analysis.

For the purposes of this book, with its emphasis on personal and social aspects of human spirituality in fostering personal and social well-being, Erikson's psychosocial theory provides a broad framework through which to view development across the lifespan. It features and values the social nature of human beings and the important influence that social relationships have on development. Further, it acknowledges the importance of holding competing ideas of ethnic, religious, national and cultural identity in a kind of tension of differentiation, something that's relevant to a fuller understanding of human growth and worldview formation. Finally, it's a theory that supports links between ego strength and the gaining of practical skills and competencies—including the spiritual care competency of thick listening at thin moments. Along with its merits, we acknowledge that Erikson's theory has its limitations, and will try to point these out as we delve more fully into its key elements.

Overall in this chapter, it's our purpose to outline Erikson's work and ask if spiritual care practitioners need to consider what he does and doesn't offer as they help people sort through the combination of factors that exist at intersections of spiritual health and social location, i.e., gender, race, social class, age, ability, religion, sexual orientation and geographical setting. People in society don't think alike or experience reality in the same way. Acknowledging multiple worldviews and psychosocial realities is at the heart of spiritual assessment and intervention.

Introducing Erikson

Erik Erikson (1902-1994) was a leading German-American figure in the fields of psychoanalysis and human development. His essay "The Eight Ages of Man" is found in an important book on child development, *Childhood and Society*, which was first published in 1950.[3] Erikson focused attention on how people develop, or fail to develop, aptitudes and attitudes about themselves and others that allow them to become productive, satisfied, adult members of society.

Insofar as Erikson's theoretical insights are frequently taught in spiritual care settings, both academic and clinical, it's important to understand his historical context and worldview. Born in Frankfurt, Germany, of mixed Jewish and Danish heritage, not knowing the name of his biological father, Erikson struggled with issues of identity. In the early 1930s, after he and his wife emigrated from Germany to the United States, Erikson worked as a child psychoanalyst in Massachusetts, Connecticut, South Dakota, and California. In those settings, he reflected on the phenomena of identity struggle and identity growth. This reflection contributed to his groundbreaking approach to developmental theory. He learned to hold competing ideas of ethnic, religious, national, and cultural identity in a kind of tension of differentiation that he saw emerging at each significant growth age. He came to understand that the healthy holding of this tension supports a maturing person through turbulent times of working out personal relationships to self and others. He identified unhealthy ruptures in the developmental process that may interfere with reaching maturity and that show up in a person's inability to relate fully and freely to self and others.

A helpful image in conceptualizing human development is that of the rings in a tree's growth. Each year development occurs but some years are marked by disease, drought, fire or other injuries. Rings continue to form, but those produced during a harmful event retain the damage. So it is with humans. Growth occurs throughout one's life, some wholesome and some scarred. Early life events impact later ages of development as a person traverses new tensions of differentiation.

Persevering through difficulties, and learning from challenges, marks the life of most people. These are the people whom spiritual care professionals encounter in hospitals, faith communities and public agencies. The traces of struggle are present and become growth opportunities through which to renegotiate and heal old wounds. Spiritual care is that care which recognizes and responds to the needs of the human spirit when faced with trauma, ill health or sadness. Spiritual care addresses the need for meaning, self worth, self-expression, faith support, and perhaps, for rites, prayer, ordinance, sacrament, or simply for a sensitive listener.[4] As we outline Erikson's developmental theory, we identify issues, themes, supportive contexts and key questions that inform spiritual care practice. The elements that we pick out of Erikson's perspective on human growth fit well into spiritual care education as well as with professional practice.

Languaging, Historical Context and Worldview

Although we claim there's a good fit between spiritual care and Erikson's model, there remains a concern we want to point out at the beginning of the chapter. Our concern has to do with the language he uses to describe humanity. Spiritual care involves listening to someone put a faith story into words. According to Hadrian Lankiewicz,[5] the word 'languaging', originally coined by Merrill Swain in 2006, has become a popular term and applies to many disciplines from philosophy to psychotherapy, linguistics and education. Undergirding the idea of 'languaging' is a belief that language conveys meaning and enables people not only to become conscious of themselves within their social location, but also allows them to make sense of the world around them.

Languages people use give voice to a historical context and a world-view they hold. But whose language do we use when describing human-ity as a whole? What about cross-generational, intercultural and broadly diversified languaging? How do we make sense of enduring insights, such as those offered by Erikson, when they're delivered in a language that no longer fits a practitioner's current historical context or worldview?

As authors, this is a concern we faced when writing about Erik-son's developmental theory. To be true to his language is to use words that emanate from a worldview solidly situated in Caucasian, Western, Neo-Freudian, male-oriented, mid-twentieth century North America. In today's world, racial and gender exclusive language is offensive and ques-tionable. Thus, to use Erikson's original words is to risk offense. At the same time, to modernize his language might dilute his enduring insights and theoretical contributions and also fail to acknowledge the exclusive-ness of the situation in which he was writing.

We wanted to broach this dilemma directly. Writing and working in the 1950s, and until the end of the twentieth century, Erikson was fo-cused on a particular perspective. He's very clear that, to him, favorable conditions for a child are found within a home in which adults create and sustain monogamous, heterosexual, childbearing and committed households. The parameters are very different in the twenty-first cen-tury. Conditions for a child's life are found within environments created by diverse relational configurations. That said, Erikson's thorough and insightful work is at the heart of what many understand to be descriptive of human psychosocial development.

Another question his work raises is whether he accurately describes female experience in his overview of human development. Again, he's writing in the 1950s when it's common to use male pronouns to con-vey the entire scope of human experience. So how are we to read his references to boys, men and male pronouns?[6] On one hand, it would be wrong to assume he's only talking about male experience in his eight ages theory. This is for two reasons: firstly, he studied cultures other than Cau-casian Western ones and brought sensitivity and insight to his task. He's deeply critical of racism, which he thinks of as an expression of radical immaturity.[7] If he's strongly critical of racism in American cultures of the 1950s, is it reasonable to think he's unaware of and insensitive to gender issues? We don't know. That conversation isn't included in what he says about human development.

Secondly, asking the question about gender differences is an important way to read his work as a theory for human development. If we take his eight ages theory seriously, will we be able to see what went wrong for women who grew up in Caucasian Western cultures during the mid-twentieth century? Will we be able to distinguish some of the patterns that disadvantaged women, and may still hinder their freedom to achieve an authentic self and social expression, as we compare Erikson with the typical experiences of girls and women? This second point is a deep and ongoing problem. In order to work with the second reason for allowing the eight ages framework to act as the measure for human development as a whole, we're assuming Erikson provided the right standard for taking its measure. So, we don't have a simple problem if we raise the gender issue. We have a complex problem, one worthy of more in depth reflection. Therefore, we treat the gender issue in its own chapter.

Four Existential Themes and Eight Developmental Ages

So what role does Erikson's theory play in the work of cultivating authentic, therapeutic, spiritual care relationships? We suggest that the ages Erikson outlines form a backdrop to themes, issues and key questions that emerge during spiritual care engagement. If we consider that the nature of healthy human development was his primary focus, an additional interest of ours is to ask about narratives that don't necessarily conform to his framework. It's important to us that the richness of otherness is seen, heard, appreciated and meaningfully respected.

Further, while his eight ages life cycle descriptors are often the primary focus of his work, some of the themes that emerge in his essay remain important throughout a person's lifespan. Spiritual care practitioners work with his eight ages theory and his themes as they accompany people who want to reflect on the faith story that gives shape to their lives at important junctures. In this chapter, we outline the eight ages framework in the following paragraphs. But first we list and comment on themes in Erikson that include the following:

Erikson's Four Existential Themes:
- Mutual regulation—Erikson described the emotional reciprocity between parent and child as *mutual regulation*. He believed that

mutual regulation is essential for healthy personality development. Parents who achieve mutual regulation with their infant foster a *sense of trust* in the child and a generalized belief that the world is a safe place. Where mutual regulation fails, infants learn *mistrust.*

- Holding on and letting go—In the second age, called autonomy vs. shame and doubt, Erikson viewed muscular maturation as the foundation for experimentation with two sets of social modalities: holding on and letting go. It's at this age that a child begins to explore and move away from the trusting environment of parents. To hold a child too close at this time can become restrictive or restraining; to let go too soon can be destructive in the sense of conveying neglect or boundary ambiguity.[8]

- Congruence—This is the idea that what's inside a person will match favorably with what that person expresses outwardly; e.g., initially, an inner state of feeling loved is congruent with a loving parental reality, or an inner state of anxiety is congruent with an anxious parental reality. Over time, being congruent is a personal issue.

- Dissonance—The tension of differentiation, traversed throughout one's lifespan, can give rise to discordant thoughts, feelings and actions. Contradictory beliefs, ideas or values expose dissimilarities between what's inside a person and what's expressed outwardly. Dissonance can give rise to feeling like an impostor, well captured in the words, "If you really knew me, you wouldn't like me," which suggests evidence of a sense of internal division and abandonment, sometimes expressing a sense of loss and division that begins at birth.

Mutual regulation, holding on and letting go, congruence and dissonance may show up in someone's faith story as practitioners listen to questions about life experience that reflect a person's difficulty or confusion with some of the dimensions of these themes.

Differentiating A Situation and A Sense Of

Before we lay out Erikson's eight ages framework, two theoretical perspectives he relied on help spiritual care practitioners understand another person. The first is what he calls *a situation*; the second is his description of *a sense of* something.

For Erikson, there are three processes that converge in *a situation* that's under analysis. These include the somatic process (the person as an organism), the ego process (the person as a self) and the societal process (the person as a member of society). Each process can be distinguished for the purpose of inquiring into someone's self-presentation and also to enhance self-awareness. Erikson consolidates these three parts into a whole when he writes, "we find that the three processes…are three aspects of one process—i.e., human life."[9] He notes that the words 'human' and 'life' have equal weight for understanding the embodied story that a person conveys about his or her lived experience.

To explain *a situation*, he tells of a little boy whose grandmother died. The boy went on to experience epileptic-like symptoms. Erikson treated him, and through observation, he asserted that this little boy experienced the following as part of his *situation*:

- Somatic tension: brain lesions in the boy's brain and the resultant violent acts
- Individual anxiety: the boy's fear that his mom might die
- Societal triggering: stress due to being a Jewish boy in a Gentile neighborhood who was connected to intergenerational trauma after WWII and Jewish concentration camp experiences of his extended family members.

The boy's situation produced internal and external (embodied) signs that Erikson could read as he attended to him carefully.

The other expression Erikson developed is the phrase 'a sense of' to convey that—to continue with his example—this boy expressed the three aspects of his *situation* internally and externally. Erikson proposes that detecting *a sense of* something happens through testing and analysis. To him, an experience of *a sense of* something comprises three dimensions:

- Experiencing that's accessible to introspection (through personal awareness)
- Behaving that's observable to others (through social awareness)
- Emerging inner states that are determinable through testing and analysis.

Given his theoretical perspective, we can draw on Erikson's understandings to explore, for example, the definition of human spirituality as "a sense of felt connection" that was presented as a working definition for spirituality in chapter one. In addition, interpreting *a sense of* can include perceiving someone's well being, illness or apprehension by relying on these three dimensions that are available to investigation and reflection.

For spiritual care practitioners, there may arise *a sense of* what a client or patient is going through in their *situation*. For instance, a practitioner may experience an inner state of empathy, trepidation or concern when first encountering the other. The meeting of two people allows their inner states to comingle through inroads of engagement, inquiry and listening. For example, both people may experience introspective wondering about whether or not the other can be trusted. Outer behavior may or may not immediately communicate trustworthiness. Practitioners may notice that clients aren't looking them 'in the eye', as we say in western cultures. In contrast, there may be *a sense of* the other as someone who can be trusted.

As implied earlier, spiritual care practitioners engage with, observe and assess people as they accompany them by drawing on Erikson's insights into their *situation* and the *sense of* what they're experiencing while they remain in that situation. From the perspective of spiritual care, three parts of *a situation* are framed using some different language that includes the following:

- There's a somatic element related to the embodied person (e.g., in illness or as a search for health and wellness)
- There's an introspective element related to the immediate context (e.g., uncertainty/anxiety about the condition of health) and an ego context (loneliness, isolation, longing, companionship and intimacy)
- There's a bridging opportunity through communication that takes account of the broader psychosocial context (e.g., living during the COVID-19 pandemic)

In spiritual care, the initial engagement with a patient or client often includes a felt sense for the spiritual care practitioner. This *sense of* may be empathy or concern but it's an initial aspect that draws the practitioner toward a more in-depth assessment process.

Along with a felt sense, the practitioner observes and is curious so that following the other person's embodied narrative motivates the inquiry. If we think of the little boy mentioned earlier, a spiritual care practitioner would be attuned to issues of grief that might be impacting his anxious ways of acting. Learning about his Jewish heritage would provide access to the deeper layers of the boy's hyper-vigilance, loss and trauma.

The spiritual care practitioner's three dimensions of a situation are similar to the way Erikson proposes that we understand a given *situation*. Paying attention to Erikson and spiritual care ways of describing a situation is extremely useful to spiritual care practitioners as they witness as well as listen to the embodied faith story that someone is telling them.

The Eight Developmental Ages

In this section, we identify elements of Erikson's eight ages that pertain directly to spiritual care practice. For each age, there's an initial summary of core concepts and their meanings. Then, from within these summaries, we identify spiritual care implications, issues Erikson raises, themes he names and the institutions he picks out as essential support for that age of human development. Issues, themes, institutions and key questions are highlighted in specific paragraphs. Again, it's beneficial to turn to the image of a tree's growth rings in light of this notion of concentric circles—whatever impacts a young tree or person (scars, disruptions) will be evident in the older tree or person as he or she perseveres through difficulties and moves toward maturity.

One caveat: due to Erikson's exclusive references to male pronouns, we'll use male pronouns to outline his eight ages framework for human development. Not to do so is to fall into the trap of false gender neutrality that does nothing to clarify the role that being female plays in the formation of a human being. If we use gender inclusive language in these next sections of the chapter, we beg the question that we want to explore by simply assuming that Erikson has accurately and adequately described female experience. This move is related to the ongoing, complex problem of the gender issue referred to earlier.

1. Basic Trust versus Basic Mistrust *[Infancy]*

Erikson establishes the foundation for someone's whole life by showing how initial experiences for an infant build toward one of two possibilities: basic trust or basic mistrust. In his research, he observed that the first indications of basic trust are seen in an infant's ease of feeding, depth of sleep and relaxation of bowels. For him, a positive parent/infant relationship is characterized by mutual regulation and an infant's first social achievement is letting mother go out of sight without undue anxiety or rage.

During the early years, an important sense of one's embodied, inner/outer subjectivity emerges that can be described as "an inner population of remembered and anticipated sensations and images of familiar and predictable things and people."[10] Erikson's point is also picked up in the section on how worldviews form in chapter one. He chose to use the word trust to describe the foundational response to the world that infants may make. To him, trust consists of naïveté and mutuality: as he noted, one can trust others if they provide consistent and dependable experiences for us.[11]

In spiritual care, establishing initial rapport with a patient, long term care resident, congregant or client is foundational to meaningful communication, assessment and intervention. If the person carries wounds inflicted by mistrust or by trusting too much and experiencing radical disappointment, there may be suspicion or aloofness expressed during the initial encounter. Accepting and accommodating mistrust as an aspect of the attempt to initiate spiritual care conversations can open space for inquiry and allow a natural testing for safety. Often another person's caution isn't a personal assessment of the spiritual care practitioner, but rather, may be due to the discomfort felt about the institutional religion with which the spiritual care practitioner is identified.

Issues: (These may arise and recur throughout one's lifespan)

- Somatic trust: Do I trust my own body? Relational trust: Do I trust other people? Do I trust myself with other people? Do I experience mutual regulation? Have I experienced over-regulation by others? Do I over-regulate myself? Have I experienced neglect? Can I self-regulate? What's the relationship for me between fear and anger? What's my sense of the inner and outer parts of me? Is there congruence between the inner life and its outward expression? Do I feel integration between my inner and my outer life? Trust about the future: Does life feel predictable or unpredictable? How do I experience my own memories?

  ◊ Of note is that, even under favorable conditions, there remains a sense of inner division and universal nostalgia for a paradise lost, which may include a sense of having been deprived and/ or abandoned. Characteristic of these early years, there develops what Erikson calls Projection and Introjection. He considered these two contrasting responses to be sources of deep and dangerous defense mechanisms. In his view, with Introjection, we feel and act as if an outer goodness has become an inner certainty. In Projection, we experience an inner harm as an outer one: we attribute to others a malevolence that actually is in us.[12] In spiritual care practice, we no longer use Erikson's definitions of these two terms as he defined them. Currently, the term Projection evokes the depiction of a projection machine that sends images onto a movie screen. The screen in this case is another person. The images we project may be negative or positive, rendering the other person as safe or unsafe, trustworthy or untrustworthy. Introjection is less often referenced in spiritual care literature, but it's observable as reverse projection, i.e., viewing the projection machine of another person sending images onto the screen of oneself. Messages of respect/disrespect, affirmation/criticism, and the like, are taken into the self and incorporated as part of one's sense of worth—or its lack.

◊ Further, throughout life, there will be crises of love, trust, faith in or animosity toward one's adversaries. A person may acquire a sense that "I'm alright, I'm being myself or becoming what others trust that I will become." This personal sense of integration needs support from a meaningful wider sense of belonging. In general, the emergence of meaning is a sustaining, embodied confidence. To Erickson, the essential role for institutional religion is to support this personal sense that "I'm alright." To him, the role of religion is to provide *Care*. In Erikson's explicit assertion that religion's primary role is to care for people, there's an implicit criticism of religious contexts that fail to do so, or in some cases, actually produce harm.

Themes:

- Mutual regulation that builds toward self-regulation. Finding integration between inner and outer life. Answering positively the questions: Can I trust myself? Can I trust others? Can I trust the future? And becoming aware of and content with the meaning one is making about life.

Concentric Circles of support:

- Self; others, organized support through the family and institutional support through organized belief systems or religion.

Key Question:[13]

- Is my world safe?

2. Autonomy versus Shame and Doubt *[Early childhood]*

Erikson's second age undergirds human experience over a lifespan by his description of the foundational, embodied feelings of shame and doubt, insofar as these are contrasted with independence and self-care. For Erikson, shame is based on a sense of being completely exposed, bared, unprotected, of being 'looked at', as if one is an object, and therefore one feels self-conscious. As self-conscious, a person feels visible while not being ready to be seen—often expressed as an impulse to bury one's face in one's hands or sink into the ground.

In hospital settings, it's not uncommon for patients to have a physician and accompanying residents come into the room, especially prior to surgery. Many times, there's little rapport building going on while, at the same time, a patient is questioned about very personal matters. The quandary for the patient is one of conceding trust to the doctor as a health authority who's needed in this time of physical vulnerability, but also a feeling of exposure and objectification. It's a moment where shame and doubt can take hold, lessening one's sense of autonomy during an already difficult moment.

To Erikson, when people feel shame, they may want to force the world not to look at them and not notice their exposure. They may want to destroy the eyes of the world.[14] With shame, someone may wish for invisibility and turn rage against himself. With shame, there's an increasing sense of being unimportant and small by comparison to others, which is linked to a child's ability/inability to stand up for himself, be independent and different in size or importance when compared to the adults or other children around him.

In Erikson's model, visual shame (a feeling of being seen when one doesn't want to be seen) precedes auditory humiliation, which is a sense of personal unworthiness or disgrace. In the experience of auditory shame, the phenomenon of 'voice' becomes an active dynamic. Voice is not only external (e.g., "Shame on you") but internal—speaking when people are all by themselves, when no one is watching and when everything is quiet, *except* for the inner, influencing sounds of (e.g., "Shame on me") in which a person is coming to grips with self-sufficiency versus ignominy. For Erikson, too much shaming can lead to a secret determination either to not exist altogether or to get away with things through hiding and secrecy. He notes that there's a limit to any person's ability to see himself as reprehensible and malevolent, and to believe in the infallibility of those who judge him.[15]

To Erikson, doubt is the brother of shame and is conveyed by a sense of having a 'front and a back', and of things happening behind one's back. The behind of our bodies can't be easily viewed by a person, and is susceptible to be invaded by or dominated by others. To 'have another's back' is to support another's independence when he's being vulnerable to attack. To 'have backbone' is to be self-supporting, autonomous. To Erikson, these attacks may come in the form of criticism, of too much control, or as over-protection.

In the face of these messages, a person may experience doubt, inadequacy and low self-esteem. There's also a sense of doubt that connects with what one's own body produces, e.g., by the bowels. This is the age of toilet training. On the positive side, learning to control bodily functions leads to a feeling of independence. Erikson viewed muscular maturation as the foundation for experimentation with two sets of social modalities: holding on and letting go. That is, what one has clung to or left behind can form a substratum for later and more verbal forms of tension between autonomy versus doubt.

All of these feelings are included in the bedrock of a worldview. As such, a person may encounter situations wherein they're able to resolve humiliation through self-acceptance and acknowledgement of limitations. Or, they may be stuck in doubt, inadequacy, tentativeness, suspicion, intense fear, low self-esteem and an over-dependence on external authorities. The tensions children face at this age continue to impact people over a lifetime and include one's sense of and willingness to engage with:

- Love versus hate
- Co-operation versus willfulness

- Freedom of self-expression versus the suppression of self-expression

Positive development at this stage comprises the movement from a sense of self-control without loss of self-esteem to a sense of lasting goodwill and pride; this is in contrast to the possibility that a sense of loss of self-control and an experience of foreign over-control may move a person toward a lasting propensity for doubt and shame.[16] Doubt can be expressed as a loss of face and the fear of being attacked from behind.

In terms of shame and doubt, institutional needs are addressed by the principle of law and order, which apportions limitations, establishes appropriate privileges and affirms human rights and obligations. To Erikson, autonomy won't lead to doubt and shame if people enjoy rightful dignity, lawful independence and a sense of justice within political and economic spheres.

As we consider some of the contexts for spiritual care in light of Erikson's model, when people are in hospital, they feel vulnerable and depersonalized, e.g., they all wear the same posterior exposing gowns. They need to know someone has their back and will advocate in the event of distressing actions on the part of health care staff or even their own loved ones. It's not uncommon for mixed agendas to emerge at a time of health crisis. Many involved in caring for a patient or client have their own needs as well; if these needs take over, the needs of the patient may get lost.

A setting in which patient needs got overlooked was part of a dilemma health care professionals faced during the COVID-19 pandemic in retirement homes for the elderly. During the first wave of the pandemic there were places where spiritual care professionals were invaluable within the health care team. Their role as patient advocates took many forms, including facilitation of information, provision of a caring presence and mediation of ethical questions or concerns. The sensitivity and awareness spiritual care practitioners brought to these settings, allowed them to recognize themes associated with doubt and shame that continue to impact the elderly based on the emergence of these themes when they were young. This knowledge enabled spiritual care practitioners to notice and respond to underlying distresses that increased for the elderly during a time of new and unique vulnerability in those healthcare settings.

Issues: (These may arise and recur throughout one's lifespan)

- Am I able to hold on and let go in a balanced, healthy way? Does my holding on have destructive aspects in the form of cruelty, or is it expressed positively in the ways I care for others? Does my letting go involve a letting loose of destructive forces or can it be expressed by a relaxed 'let it pass' or 'let it be' approach? In another vein, am I able to experience a sense of self-control without loss of self-esteem? Do I experience lasting goodwill and a sense of personal pride? Or, am I stuck with a sense of loss of self-control and of foreign over-control? What are my experiences with doubt and shame? Lastly, can I establish appropriate limits and freedoms within a given lifespan? This is an issue that's best served by healthy experiences with mutual regulation.

Themes:

- Shame, doubt, self-worth, visibility/invisibility, voice (inner/outer), holding on and letting go.

Concentric Circles of support:

- Self, family, larger social world, institutional support from organized and predictable law and order.

Key Question:

- Can I do things by myself or do I always have to rely on others?

3. Initiative versus Guilt *[Pre-school]*

At this point, there's a new and vigorous unfolding of hope and responsibility to indicate the age of initiative versus guilt. For Erikson, initiative is observable in experiences of crises that are characterized by fumbling and fear but that are resolved so that a child suddenly seems to 'grow together', is more activated, more activating, more loving and more relaxed, brighter in judgment and appears to be 'more himself'. In addition, there's access to surplus energy that permits the child to forget failures quickly and approach what seem to be opportunities that are desirable, yet uncertain and potentially dangerous.

Initiative adds to autonomy an undiminished and a more focused sense of direction, characterized by a quality of enterprise, planning and confronting of a task for the sake of being active and on the move, instead of expressing defiance or protested independence. During this age, a child is 'on the make,' so to speak, asserting control and power over the environment. Of note, it's at this point (only) that Erikson specifically mentions girls and distinguishes their approach to this age from boys: boys are on the make, according to him, and take pleasure in attack and conquest through intrusive actions.

To Erikson, girls focus on making themselves attractive and endearing; indirectly snatching and catching rather than intruding or invading. As female authors, we're not sure how to respond to Erikson's assertion about the development of girls and women insofar as this is the only age in which Erikson refers to females. That said, it's fair to observe that, if Erikson is accurate, a girl's initiative at this age would involve her in becoming as skillful as possible in understanding and responding to other people—her achievements would be primarily adaptive and relational.

The logical and psychological danger during this age is a sense of guilt over the goals one contemplates and the acts one initiates in an exuberant enjoyment of new physical skill and increased mental power. Tensions during this age include the following three splits that may signal one is stuck and persistently divided within oneself:

- Potential human glory versus potential total destruction
- Over manipulating the self versus exercising moral responsibility
- Paralysis, inhibition, impotence versus exhibition or over-advertising the self.

Parental roles that employ mutual regulation are significant as they balance a child's exuberant growth potential and initiative. Parental guidance can support and increase self-observation, self-guidance and appropriate self-chastisement during this age.[17]

At this point, a child can gain insight into the institutions, functions, and roles that permit responsible participation. Children find pleasurable accomplishment in wielding tools and weapons, in manipulating meaningful toys and in caring for younger children. Of note regarding this age, Erikson laments a tendency for the human conscience to remain partially infantile throughout life, which is, to him, the core of all human tragedy. Under this unfortunate condition, people do to others what they wouldn't want others to do to them.[18]

But the child is also eager to learn, share obligation and responsibility and work on projects cooperatively. Children enjoy combining with others to construct and plan and are willing to profit from teachers and to emulate ideal prototypes. Under favorable conditions, work provides a sense of identity without infantile conflict. A realistic identity as a responsible worker is possible. By doing things together children have the opportunity to practice equality. The institutional support for this age is found in the health of one's economic ethos and in the presence of positive and supportive heroes.

When the dynamics of initiative versus guilt arise in spiritual care settings, they're often lived within adult bodies. Issues of manipulation can easily arise if one feels helpless and powerless. Grabbing attention, seeking special treatment from staff, and/or becoming critical of discrepancies between institutional versus homemade food may be ways to self-soothe in the face of feeling overwhelmed in a healthcare setting.

In congregational, community or agency settings, a person may dramatize their failures in order to draw attention to a deep need to be seen in the conundrum they're trying to manage. Spiritual care practitioners can willingly and wisely help to hold the relational tension that can erupt as people try to work together, by offering their skilled listening and responses that can open space for deeper reflection and self-sharing. In general, when people struggle with the relational implications of the skills they need to acquire at this age, behind coping behaviors may lay the niggling feelings of guilt and the fear of failure. Whenever these feelings emerge during someone's life, being present to the struggle is central to meaningful spiritual care practice.

Issues: (These may arise and recur throughout one's lifespan)

- Can I take initiative? Do I recover, find resolution if I fail? Can I move on? Do I have the willingness to undertake, plan and attack a challenge to achieve its resolution? Can I focus on making, constructing and producing things? Do I manage a sense of guilt if I feel my initiative meets with disapproval or criticism, or if others view me as overbearing? Do I have a sense of responsibility for my successes and failures? Do I experience sufficient, healthy, mutual regulation that helps me explore and find my purpose and place in the world?

Themes:
- Tensions cover the following extremes: Paralysis, inhibition and impotence versus showing off or over-advertising the self.

Concentric Circles of support:
- *Self*, family, communal world, institutional support from a healthy economic ethos, also the presence of positive versus negative heroes.

Key Questions:
- Am I good or bad? Do I start projects? Am I skillful? Do I work well with others?

4. Industry vs. Inferiority *[School age]*

At this point, schooling in some form begins for children. They're thrust into a public and impersonal world and all their efforts are channeled into that landscape—for better or for worse. Schooling includes systematic instruction. Erikson refers to Sigmund Freud and his view that this age is a latency period—a time of reduced sexuality Freud believed occurred between approximately ages seven and adolescence. He saw it as a hiatus in sexual development. Erikson points out that other interests become important. It's as if a child forgets or sublimates a predisposition from the previous age to attack, attract, snatch and intrude, and settles into the task of learning to win recognition by producing things, either through play or from active productivity.

This age requires steady attention and persevering diligence. *It is a socially decisive age.* Children acquire the fundamentals of technology characteristic of their era and develop abilities through the use of tools and utensils. School seems to be a culture all by itself, with its own goals, limits, achievements and disappointments. Success and inclusion at school is powerful for a child's sense of industry or for a child's sense of inferiority.

In the COVID-19 pandemic, tensions of industry and inferiority were very much alive as great emphasis was placed on the role of health care professionals as heroes and heroines who stayed with patients through thick and thin. Among these professionals were spiritual health practitioners, clothed with personal protection equipment, who mediated communication between patients and their loved ones. Their interventions were often focused on fundamentals of technology characteristic of the present era rather than an earlier age. Phones, FaceTime, WhatsApp and others such platforms for Android and IOS devices were invaluable in bringing the faces of loved ones back and forth between locations outside the health facility and locations in the Intensive Care Unit. Having an arms length from the immediate demands of physical care, being trained in the essentials of infection control, and being viewed as part of the health care team, spiritual care professionals were available to attend the spiritual and emotional distress felt by both patient and loved ones in the face of traumatic fear, radical separation, and the need for felt connection. Building on their developmental industry and applying this to the industry of smart phones and tablet devices to bridge direct contact was integral to whole person health at a time of dire need.

To Erikson, this age brings about the following issues, themes, circles of support and key questions that stay with people over the course of their lives.

Issues: (These may arise and recur throughout one's lifespan)

- Can I create and make things? Do I receive positive recognition for my ability to be productive? Am I viewed as competent in comparison to others, or am I seen as inferior? Am I rewarded for my achievements, or compared negatively to others' achievements? Can I be diligent, steady and patient with acts of creation? Can I find and pursue genuine interests, and practice the skills required? Am I able to learn from others, establish a rudimentary grasp of the technology that's situated within my cultural setting, and show up positively in my educational setting?

Themes:

- Achievement, recognition, school success. But if children accept work as their only obligation, and "what works" as the only criterion of being a worthy person, they may become conformists and thoughtless slaves of technology and also of those who are in a position to exploit them. The danger to children at this stage is a sense of inadequacy and inferiority that prevents them from becoming agents of their own experience.

Concentric Circles of Support
- Self, family, schooling, other organized settings children involve themselves in, e.g., service clubs/sports, religious institutions and the social world in general.

Key Questions:
- What am I good at? What do I like doing? What am I not good at?

5. Identity vs. Role Confusion *[Puberty and Adolescence]*

Adolescent growth, physically, sexually and relationally, is prominent during this age. That growth includes, and in some ways focuses on, genital maturity. A young person's emerging identity finds its strength in the support offered by the social world. A person at this age is trying to manage personal, work-related and socially related skill development that will eventually lie at the heart of an ongoing sense of identity. As a consequence, in general, adolescents return to some issues they experienced in their early years.

The adolescent task is to integrate ego abilities, different aspects of one's identity, the vicissitudes of the libido, aptitudes with which one is naturally endowed and opportunities derived from social roles. Ego identity is the accrued confidence that the inner sameness and continuity cultivated in the past is matched by the sameness and continuity of one's meaning for others, which is often established by finding a career, meaningful work and loving commitment.

The danger of this age is role confusion—which is an ordinary, existential experience and not to be thought of as unusual. Yet if a person is not comfortable in being himself, he may relive old tensions of trust/mistrust, autonomy/shame and doubt, and/or initiative/guilt at this age. The adolescent body, as young people experiment with behaviors and mannerisms they see in heroes, peers and love interests, may introduce confusion. They may test things out, as well as experiment with risk-taking behaviors. Adolescence is rife with cliques, stereotyping, inclusion/exclusion maneuvering and ideological thinking.

In general it's not uncommon for spiritual care professionals to encounter issues related to identity and role confusion when serving people in faith communities, public agencies and health institutions. What is it that brings a person to a pastor, chaplain or spiritual health practitioner? The move is often related to asking core questions, such as: Who am I (now, and in these circumstances)? How are others seeing me at this time? A concern for new personal understanding may show up in a circumstance of relational transition when a person shifts from being husband to father, or to being an "ex", or becoming a widower. It may be when one first becomes a mother and experiences the unique bonding of having a child placed in her arms—a bonding that's felt at the core of her being—that fathers also experience. It may arise when one confesses to wrongdoing, e.g., embezzlement, vilification, or perhaps gross dishonesty. The need for connecting with a spiritual care provider may arise when someone seeks counsel about getting a girlfriend pregnant, or 'coming out' to one's parents, or struggling with self-pleasuring behaviors.

Each concern is unique in its complexity and identity versus role confusion implications. To be met non-judgmentally, with compassion, at such times of inner distress and struggle can be life saving, literally. This is a time for spiritual care practice to convey empathy and respectful curiosity. It's a time for meeting the other as 'other' in the sacred space of a caring and confidential relationship, in which one who's coming for help is given voice. The care provider holds the tension of another person's pain. This holding requires inner discipline and single-hearted focus. The task is to be present rather than spending effort trying to do something for the other person. Out of the posture of presence, the other may find inner resources to move forward in trust, autonomy, initiative and industry.

As part of the listening presence of a caregiver, there may arise issues, themes and key questions Erikson identified that emerge during this age of identity and role confusion.

Issues: (These may arise and recur throughout one's lifespan)

- How do I appear in the eyes of others as compared with what I feel I am? How do I connect roles and skills cultivated earlier with work and life identities that need to be chosen? Who are my allies? Who are my adversaries? Do I tend to look to idols and ideals as guardians of my destiny? What qualities do I admire in myself and other people?

Themes:

- The dangers of role confusion regarding sexuality and work identity. Youth may express an over-identification with heroes, cliques or crowds. Falling in love is a central aspect of adolescence along with the failure and disappointment that attends it. Adolescents may be clannish and cruel in response to another young person's identity confusion.

Concentric Circles of Support:
- Self, family, schooling, organized institutions, e.g., service clubs/sports, religious institutions and the social world in general; ideologies, nationalisms and the economic ethos of the times.

Key Questions:
- Who am I? Where am I going?

6. Intimacy vs. Isolation *[Young adulthood]*

Erikson points out that the strength acquired at any new age is tested by taking chances with what was most vulnerably precious in the previous one. In this case, the young adult has worked to establish a sense of personal identity and now becomes willing to fuse that identity with another and/or others. This is the realm of intimacy.

Intimacy refers to a capacity to commit to concrete affiliations and partnerships and to develop the ethical strength to abide by such commitments, even though they may call for significant sacrifices and compromises. Intimacy includes qualities of care, tenderness, affection and closeness. It also includes a capacity to appreciate and understand someone as other than oneself and to value people with whom cooperation, conciliation and compromise can be shared.

The danger at this age is that intimate, competitive and combative relations are all experienced with and against the selfsame people, e.g., one's parents and close friends. Positively, if people can work out the challenges of intimacy, they can develop an adult ethical sense.[19] This involves both vulnerability to what is attractive about another and an ability to step back and ask meaningful questions about oneself in relation to the other. The act of stepping back may be at the service of intimacy, or it may be a kind of detachment and standoffishness that refuses to commit to concrete affiliations and partnerships. A posture of aloofness and indifference can grow into what Erikson calls isolation, i.e., a condition of being inaccessible and distant from the closeness that characterizes intimacy. In isolation there may often be overwhelming loneliness.

A focus in Erikson's writing about this age is sex. Up to now, according to Erikson, sex is mostly of an identity searching kind or a genital combative kind. In addition, sex can be mistakenly viewed as a permanent state of reciprocal sexual bliss. With sex, in order to work through tensions of intimacy and isolation, the goal of mutual regulation is central.[20] Mutual regulation is based on Erikson's perspective mentioned earlier in the chapter that focused on monogamous, heterosexual households, in which he situated what he refers to as a "utopia of genitality," or what could be called sexual intimacy, which he describes in the following way:

- Mutuality of orgasm
- With a loved partner
- Of the other sex
- With whom one is able and willing to regulate the cycles of mutual trust, work, procreation and recreation, so as to secure to offspring, too, all the stages of a satisfactory development.

The world Erikson describes, as mentioned, doesn't necessarily capture the world that patients and clients who come for spiritual care will experience or value today.

When Erikson speaks about the overall, guiding activities of a healthy, mature human life, he refers to Freud, who was once asked what a normal person should be able to do well. Erikson draws attention to Freud's formulaic response: "to love and to work." For Freud, "love" meant both *genital* love and genital *love*; "work" meant a general productiveness that wouldn't pre-occupy the individual to the extent of losing the right and capacity to be a genital and loving human being. In today's world, there are different work/love anxieties. The balance implied in Erikson and Freud about becoming a loving human being, may encounter different demands. Still, the tension of productivity and genital love continues to be an issue and is expressed differently in the diverse cultures, races, religions, gender identities and ideologies that characterize modern multi-cultural societies. In Erikson's framework, during this age, intimacy develops along with mutual regulation as adults work out what it means to be workers, lovers, friends, colleagues, parents and citizens.

Intimacy is multi-dimensional as a human capacity: it's the willingness and ability to commit to concrete affiliations and partnerships. Descriptors of intimacy are numerous: closeness, tenderness, companionship, affection, confidence, understanding, familiarity, compassion and caring, to name some examples. In most faith traditions, intimacy is at the heart of spiritual practices and the sense of felt connection. One of the sacred privileges of being a spiritual care professional is witnessing intimacy during the rituals acted out by members of a particular tradition. For example, in a privileged moment of family inclusion, a spiritual care practitioner may be witness to the intimate love communicated in a gaze between the parents of a fasting Muslim family at the moment the fast is broken by a single sip of water.

For those who work in hospitals, practitioners may be invited to hear words spoken by a neonatal ICU physician who realizes that a newborn baby won't live for more than a few minutes or hours. Clark was involved in a situation like this one. As the baby's parents realized their only child's life wouldn't last, they asked for someone to baptize their little on. Clark was on-call. The ICU physician conveyed the parents' wishes to her. As she thought about how to carry out the sacred ritual with this infant, she knew the ceremony always involved speaking the child's name. Just before the baptism began, she heard the physician say, "Her name is Hope. Her parents have decided to call her Hope." The rich intimacy of this moment remains with Clark as she recounts the privilege it was to participate in Hope's baptism.

In another scenario, sacred and intimate moments may arise as a despairing person, sitting on the precipice of a tall building, reaches for the hand of his pastor who's there with emergency personnel. Practitioners might be invited to remain quietly with a Buddhist monk who sits wordlessly for hours, in the presence of a deceased believer, and in this way, gives honor to the time of a soul's rebirthing. Intimacy is experienced in times of aloneness, loneliness and solitude, and as one example, as a spiritual care provider is waiting with an old married couple, lifelong friends, as they realize death is coming to one of them. This intimacy is felt when long-time caregivers grieve the loss of a patient to dementia or death. Intimacy has many names and many faces. Spiritual care is rich with them.

Issues: (These may arise earlier and recur throughout one's lifespan)

- Am I able to allow my hard-won sense of identity to fuse with another and/or others in order to experience intimacy? Am I able to commit to concrete affiliations and partnerships, or do I isolate myself from such commitments for fear of ego loss or due to the complexities that deep closeness would cause for me? Am I able to find a work/love balance that's meaningful and supports my sense of being a loving human being? Am I also comfortable with being on my own? Do I like myself?

Themes:
- Loss and recovery; holding on and letting go; life satisfaction; congruence; dissonance; meaningful work; authentic self-love in tandem with satisfying intimacy and commitment to those who are close, and a general responsiveness to a wider social world.

Concentric Circles of Support:
- Self, family, friends, organized institutions, e.g., community, social, political, economic and religious, as well as the social world in general.

Key Question:
- Am I loved and wanted?

7. Generativity vs. Stagnation *[Middle adulthood]*

This age draws attention to maturing human beings and their potential roles as teachers, learners and people who create institutions for the well being of society as a whole. For Erikson, generativity is the concern to establish and guide the next generation and has to do with productivity and creativity. Without the impetus of generativity, of caring for others however that's expressed, concern only for oneself can creep into a person's life and move that person toward self-indulgence, self-preoccupation and what Erikson refers to as stagnation. Such a person is stuck so that inner lethargy and personal impoverishment give rise to pampering oneself as someone might pamper a child—to the exclusion of showing any concern for other people.

As people move into their middle years, questions of achievement and/or inadequacy can rise to the fore. It's not uncommon for spiritual health practitioners to hear the lament of someone who feels their incompleteness, restlessness and self-dissatisfaction. These feelings may be especially acute at a time of illness. Oddly, these years often see illnesses related to the endocrine system, surfacing as hormone imbalance, and resulting in hysterectomies and prostate surgeries. The physical focus of generativity may be lost, leaving a person to ponder what there is to show for the fruitfulness in their life.

Generativity can manifest in many ways. Some of the work of spiritual care has to do with teasing out a sense of life's abundance—whether that abundance is conveyed through progeny, a body of work, or some other outcome that expresses the generous way one has lived in relationship to self and others. It's also true that during the middle years people may throw off their commitments and reconstruct their values. This attempt to do things differently may result in marital infidelity, job abandonment or taking financial gambles. Accompanying individuals, families and communities through times of upheaval and disruption is a significant role for people who offer spiritual care.

In Erikson's view, this age expresses itself in the following issues, themes and key questions, that provide a framework for care givers as they consider how to walk beside people who are going through this phase of development.

Issues: (These may be insistent and require resolution)

- Can I care for myself, for my family (however defined or understood – e.g. those served in work or community contexts) and others in the world? Am I attuned to my important role in teaching, learning from and nurturing the emerging generation?

Themes:

- Loss and recovery; creativity and productivity; holding on and letting go; congruence; dissonance; nurturing and supporting a younger generation.

Concentric Circles of Support:

- Self, family, friends, organized institutions, e.g., community, social, political, economic and religious, as well as the social world globally.

Key Question:

- Will I provide something of real and lasting value to the world?

8. Ego Integrity vs. Despair *[Maturity]*

Erikson's eighth age points to an intergenerational confluence wherein the dependence of children on adults interfaces with the dependence of adults on their children or the younger generation. Maturity is characterized by constancy and meaning and by what Erikson called a "post-narcissistic love of the human ego."[21] This points to the human capacity to transcend self-interest and express a spiritual sense that's grounded in life's fullness, however perceived. Ego integrity appreciates not only the dignity and solidarity that originated in a person's past experiences and different pursuits, but also the accidental coincidence of one's unique historical moment. A primary issue during this age is the acceptance of one's 'one and only life cycle' as something that had to be and that, by necessity, permitted no substitutions. The final lines of Mary Oliver's poem "A Summer Day" precisely capture this essence when she writes: "Doesn't everything die too soon? Tell me, what is it you plan to do with your one wild and precious life?"[22]

In the age of ego integrity, one knows that death is certain and will eventually come, but people don't fear it in advance. In addition, ego integrity implies that people have the emotional integration to participate as either a follower or a leader and realize that both types of responsibility are needed. With ego integrity, a person is confident that maturity accepts either role, as the need arises. Erikson summarizes the impact of this stage of life by saying that healthy children won't fear life if their elders have integrity enough to not fear death.

But if people are unable to embrace this final life tension with contentment, despair may be an outcome. According to Erikson, despair expresses a feeling that time is running out and there's deep existential anguish as time passes too fast. He notes that despair may be covered over with the expression of disgust, antagonism, and regret.

Spiritual care in this age is rife with anamnesis, a focus on reminiscence. With the guidance of spiritual care, remembering may take the form of life review therapy, writing a memoire, investing time and energy in making a quilt or other creative craft that depicts the recollections that are personally meaningful. The unique role of spiritual care practitioners accompanying those in this time of their lives is to help them reflect on the cumulative threads from each of their developmental ages that are woven into their faith stories. These threads express a life narrative. In the act of weaving them together, people consider the question of how the threads give shape and meaning to what they have become.

Spiritual care practitioners offer to help people sort through the evidence of Erikson's global themes of mutual regulation, holding on and letting go, congruence, and dissonance. They help people ask themselves how these themes are manifest in their lives and how they create the chapters of a faith narrative. Spiritual care accompaniment is often characterized by episodic encounters as people reflect on some aspects of the issues, themes and key questions that typify human development. In addition, a practitioner may have opportunities to hear about the circles of support that gave shape to the life someone lived. Sometimes reminiscences are of short duration and are characterized by a degree of incoherence. The point of accompanying someone isn't so much to reach conclusions or summarize everything, it's about listening to issues and experiences as they are shared, and having the willingness and ability to sojourn with someone until life ends.

Erikson's development approach identifies the following issues, themes and key questions that form a foundation for the spiritual care work that practitioners focus on as they accompany people through to the end of life.

Issues: (These may be insistent and require resolution and release)

- What is my sense of readiness for physical decline, loss of friends and family, diminishment in my health? How do I experience the advancement of death? Do I see it as a fullness of life and greet it without fear, or do I feel time is running out and experience deep anguish or disgust? Do I feel that I'm facing this age of my life with contentment and gratitude, or do I struggle with regret?

Themes:

- Integrity, contentment, the discernment to hold on and to let go, living a meaningful, congruent and satisfying way of life that doesn't disdain other ways; integration; willing participation in following and/or leading as situations arise and abilities permit; and acceptance of death.

Concentric Circles of Support:

- Self, family, friends, organized institutions: local community, social/national obligations, political, economic and religious commitments, as well as the social world globally.

Key Question:

- Have I lived a full life?

Conclusion

In this chapter our purpose was to outline Erikson's work and convey how spiritual care practice benefits from considering what he does and doesn't offer as providers meet, engage, assess, and accompany people within healthcare contexts, faith communities and public agency settings. Erikson focused attention on how human beings develop, or fail to develop, aptitudes and attitudes that allow them to be productive, satisfied members of society. He described psychosocial ages of development and pointed to the tensions that characterize each one of the eight ages. At the beginning of the chapter, we offered an image of tree rings that form each year as a tree grows and pointed to each year's effects insofar as they reflect concentric circles of impact of early development on later vitality. Erikson's ages, like the tree rings, create and contain the experiences that shape each life. During spiritual care, specific issues, or the cumulative effects of life experience, are allowed a voice.

While Erikson's work begins by describing childhood, spiritual care professionals, more often than not, meet people in adult bodies. Even for pediatric chaplains and those responsible for children's activities in faith communities or communal agencies, the focus of attention is on a family unit rather than solely on the child. Growth, both healthy and scarred, is happening or has already happened by the time spiritual care interventions occur. What makes "that care which recognizes and responds to the needs of the human spirit"[23] significant and therapeutic is its recognition that persevering through difficulties, learning from challenges, and finding peace in being oneself is a sacred activity. Spiritual care is about "meeting", in the sense of Buber's "all real living is meeting."[24] The "I" of the practitioner meets the "Thou" of the one served in a holy "Between" where skilled and sensitive listening fosters reciprocal, empowering and healing dialogue.

In each age, Erikson identifies life long themes that help spiritual care practitioners situate a patient's or a client's faith story within a broader context. These themes include the following:

- Holding on and letting go
- Congruence between one's inner world and what's demonstrated outwardly
- Positive experience with mutual regulation
- Success at self-regulation
- Productivity and progress
- Working on healing and wholeness by seeing problems as emerging from one's past
- Loss and recovery

Spiritual care practitioners find themselves facing these themes as they journey alongside people who tell them the faith stories that are currently shaping and directing their lives. Erikson is an extremely rich source of insight into someone's story. Our intention for this chapter is to provide spiritual care practitioners with insight, perspective and hope, even though leaving some aspects of Erikson's theory of human development in question.

As Erikson concluded his essay on the eight ages, he mused about completing his task in a circular fashion. He observed that the Webster's dictionary definition of trust (Erikson's first ego value) was "the assured reliance on another's integrity" (Erikson's last ego value). What one arrives at in the end derives from the beginning; the beginning is the end, to paraphrase the American poet T. S. Eliot.[25] This is the great mystery that opens up to the activities of a spiritual care professional. No matter the point of entry to another's faith journey, the whole is present in the part. Meeting and accompanying another, whether for brief or lengthy periods of time, is a theoretically informed, skilled and sacred service.

Take Away Questions for Reflection

- When you read about Erik Erikson's four existential themes, what spiritual care stories come to mind? How do they put flesh on the bones of Erikson's theoretical ideas?

- Is there one of Erikson's eight developmental ages that especially speaks to you? If so, which one? What meaning does it have for you? How have you experienced this age in your personal life? Where have you seen it clinically in your spiritual care?

- How might the key questions at the end of each developmental age assist you in an initial spiritual assessment? How might these questions help you listen thickly to someone's faith story?

- What is the value of having a developmental theory as part of one's approach to spiritual care practice?

Chapter 4

Made for Relationship

Introduction

Up to now, we've focused on spiritual care as a professional practice that takes place in hospitals, long term care facilities, the military, businesses, prisons, not-for-profit organizations, churches, counseling centers and schools. These places include a focus on caring spiritually for patients, residents, armed forces personnel, staff, prisoners, clients and students in each location. In this chapter, we propose that spiritual care can't be confined to these settings or to the provenance of professionals. Spiritual care is a profession, but it's more universal than that—it's an attitude toward the world. It's also an attitude that belongs in happy homes and healthy cities.

In this chapter, we draw attention to the value of spiritual care as something from which all can benefit, whether receiving it from or offering it to someone else. As human beings, we're made for relationship. We're interconnected, and bound to one another through "a sense of felt connection". How might our ideas about spiritual care change, or do they change, if we think of it in the broadest possible terms? In her book, *Learning Social Literacy*, Bellous introduces an ecological metaphor that she calls relational habitat maintenance.[1] If we step back to widen our horizon, what would it look like if we attended to the spiritual needs of others the way some people love and garden the earth? What if we saw our personal and social worlds as relational habitats calling for the seeding, cultivating and nurturing of spiritual care as care for the human spirit?

Our purpose in this chapter is to advance theoretical groundwork supporting the possibility that spiritual care can be extended to everyone we meet, whether it's through a simple greeting with strangers on the street to whom we give full attention, even for a few seconds, or to husbands, wives, parents, children, partners, friends, a work cohort, bosses and neighbors in our communities and cities, and also people around the world who are strangers to us. We propose that hospitality in spiritual care be viewed as an attitude, standpoint and frame of mind; a human capacity embodied within and oriented toward all peoples of the world as we meet them. As a broad-based, inclusive attitude that conveys equity and respects diversity, spiritual care is compellingly attractive. We invite readers into this perspective based on real and ordinary aspects of what human beings are capable of doing and being.

An attitude of spiritual care begins with the realization of our common humanity. In this chapter, we look first at research that began during Charles Darwin's time, when many theorists were enchanted with the idea of how human and animal domains are linked by their emotional expression. Following that section, we look at the why of spiritual care, and then move through a number of human potentialities that are available to those who want to develop the ability and willingness to care spiritually for others. The human body is a storehouse of experiences, beginning with birth, whose contents are sorted throughout life into the worldview each one of us lives by. Human beings have the ability to pay attention to the stories emanating from that worldview—referred to throughout this book as faith stories—which are conveyed bodily. They also have the know-how to help other people sort through what they're thinking, feeling and doing in order to be healthy and whole, in order to live a fully human life.

Our purpose in this chapter is to challenge all of us to be attentive, attuned and available to others, and to ourselves, as a way to achieve widespread spiritual health. In the sections that follow, we describe ordinary human capabilities to show that people are made for relationship, and also to say that people need to give and receive spiritual care in order to realize the full potential of what it means to be human.

Embodied Spirituality

Toward the end of his intellectual career, Charles Darwin (1809-1882) wrote a book titled, *The Expression of the Emotions in Man and Animals*.[2] A 200th anniversary edition celebrating his birth has an introduction and commentary by American psychologist Paul Ekman who drew attention to the fact that Darwin, along with others of his day, wanted to establish continuity among species in order to show how human and animal domains share certain aspects of being.

Darwin's evolutionary view was in stark contrast to notions of creation circulating widely at the time. But, if we stop and think about it, it was perfectly reasonable for people to believe that every organism on earth was created independently.[3] Look at a mouse, then look at an elephant. Based on their outward differences, why would anyone think these two beasts share some of the DNA that's responsible for continuity between them?[4] Yet today, it may be a small group of people who doubt that DNA is a largely shared heritage that signifies connections among all living, breathing creatures. Most of us have appropriated aspects of Darwin's point of view.[5]

His work on the continuity between emotional expression among animals and humans was picked up and popularized by Paul Ekman, notably in the television series, *Lie To Me,* but also through his website, which helps people improve their emotional awareness of other people by detecting clues found in facial expressions.[6] Such clues parallel insights discussed in the chapter on Otherness, where we quote Mary Douglas's view that there are patterned ways people express themselves that can be read in the human body—something every person has. Spirituality, far from being perceived as abstract and immaterial, needs to be viewed as embodied self-expression, that's grounded on the human capacity for experiencing a sense of felt connection.

As with the chapter on Otherness, patterns we examine in this chapter offer interpretive clues in the practice of spiritual care. The clues we suggest allow spiritually sensitive people to notice threads and themes in a person's narrative. That said, we caution that a person's story is always more than what can be observed or embodied at a given moment. A faith story can't be *reduced* to the patterned ways people express emotions, as one example. Indeed, the television series based on Ekman's analysis of facial expressions that convey the Facial Action Coding System (FACS) impresses its audience with a consistent realization—being able to read a facial expression doesn't mean observers know what's going on in someone else's mind or heart. As a consequence, while someone might detect worry, fear or contempt on another person's face, because those emotions are conveyed through patterned muscle arrangements that are fairly consistent across animal and human domains, the actual meaning behind the emotions is more complex.

The practice of thick listening at thin moments recognizes that faith stories are based on personal and social realities. Assessing an embodied behavioral pattern and remaining open to someone's uniqueness are not mutually exclusive aspirations. Rather, they are two aims that can be simultaneously exercised in what we call I-Thou relating, here and elsewhere in the book. In this deep awareness of another person, there is always a respected *other*, a Thou, in Buber's terms. Spiritual care practitioners are neither distant nor detached. It is, for example, with interest and engagement that a practitioner reads a facial indicator of anger that's combined with the verbal clue "Why is this happening to me?" This combination of facial and verbal clues isn't an invitation for spiritual care practitioners to provide explanations or elucidations. Rather, it's a thin moment, a sacred space within which to receive and support the other's emotion as he or she struggles with the meaning behind the 'why' of what's happening. The combination of bodily and verbal clues is like a conduit through which personal and social realities of one's faith story can be expressed.

Once again, spiritual care requires us to keep in mind common human patterns at the same time that we pay full attention to the personal uniqueness that's embedded in someone's faith story. That is, empathy is in play. I must keep in mind that I can't read someone's mind just because I accurately decode a facial configuration that conveys, for example, anger. We have to hear the story behind an arrangement of particular facial muscles that convey specific emotions.

Conveying the "Why" of Spiritual Care for Everyone

In the chapter on Exploring the Territory, we say that everyone is spiritual, whether or not they're religious. There's good scientific evidence to support that claim. The research is growing. In addition, everyone has spiritual needs that, when satisfactorily met, create a healthier world than if spiritual needs are unmet. Further, spiritual care addresses human need as its most fundamental task. As a result of meeting spiritual needs, a sense of felt connection can be established between caregivers and patients or clients, or family and friends, so that physical and mental conditions that bring someone into care can be softened and made more bearable. In this chapter, we suggest that a felt sense of connection can be experienced within all the worlds we inhabit.

In this regard, we return to the phrase *relational habitat maintenance* used earlier. A relational habitat is a place in which one is embedded and invested.[7] The prime location for relational habitat maintenance is wherever one calls home, among people one calls family, friend, colleague or associates. These habitats are characterized by involvement and concern for others, as well as concern for ourselves, especially given the personal and social resources that our investment requires and that it provides.

This chapter implies a role for including spiritual care in all relational habitats and social environments. It can be offered to all who need it and that means everyone. But why does it matter that we offer spiritual care to others, in whatever situation we're in—whether professional or personal? A short answer is found in the nature of spirituality itself. We have a capacity for felt connection and a human need for it. We need to feel connected to others, nature, the transcendent and ourselves in order to live a truly human life. Positive, health-giving meaning has power to support us in everyday events, and sustain us in unexpected, unwelcome crises that come our way and that leave us to suffer loss. Health-giving meaning transports us beyond ordinary, limited human existence. Health-giving meaning is built through a sense of felt connection, i.e., through spirituality.

The essential work of spiritual care relies on spirituality as a human capacity that develops and grows through relationship. A strong theme in this book is that healthy spirituality is formative of someone's full capability for being personal and social—of being authentic in the fullest sense, and at the same time, being well integrated with others.

Relational Complexities and Present Moments

Let's clarify the field of spiritual care a bit more fully by applying a framework identified by Sigmund Freud. Because he focused on illness, he described two aspects of mental illness that he worked with—neurotic and psychotic problems. In terms of spiritual care, we add a third category captured by ordinary experience, that of existential problems. An existential problem deals with ordinary aspects of everyone's everyday life. It refers to problems most of us expect to experience. If people describe an event, such as the death of a loved one, they typically count on others to understand, to some extent, what they're thinking, feeling and going through. This notion of the human capacity to share experience is also informed by the common expressions of emotion that Darwin and Ekman explored.

Freud observed that people with a neurosis have gone some distance away from how others tend to experience life, due to unresolved or catastrophic existential problems. A neurotic person has shifted from inter-subjective reality (shared by others) and has lost some contact with how others interpret what's going on. As a consequence, when a neurotic person describes his or her situation, other people don't or can't see it the same way, or they may suggest alternatives that tend to explain away (discount) the situation that someone with a neurosis is describing. As a consequence, the risk for I-It relating rather than I-Thou is high. The need for empathetic awareness in the face of what is foreign is very great.

With psychosis, the break with other people is complete. A person with a psychosis has little or no connection to inter-subjectivity. Freud noted that psychoanalysis (his talking cure) tends to work only with someone who has access to the interpretations of a therapist. He acknowledged the difficulty of working through his talking cure with people who have a psychosis. In his view, by using a method that relies on being able to sense a felt connection between patient and therapist (although he didn't use that expression) the patient must have some access to how other people see things—they at least have to believe that the therapist who listens to them is credible.

This is why Freud saw a therapist as a substitute for an absent father or a cruel mother, as two examples.[8] People with a neurosis or psychosis, like every other human, can benefit from spiritual care. While not therapists in the sense used by Freud, spiritual care professionals can contribute to a healthy relational habitat by avoiding subject-to-object (I-It) thinking and, while being cognizant of the limits of reciprocal engagement with people who aren't able to fully relate inter-subjectively, they can support a sense of felt connection with the other as *other* (I-Thou). Appropriate training, skills and competencies are called for in such situations.

Once again, as a human capacity, we rely on the human spirit to establish and secure a felt sense of connection with others, for example, by engaging in the particular kind of encounter that American psychologist Daniel Stern describes as 'a present moment'. In the last century, Stern was involved in research with mothers and infants to help understand the human experience of attachment and affect attunement. He wrote about that research in *The Interpersonal World of the Infant.*[9] But after observing deep connections between moms and babies for so long, Stern analyzed an interaction he thought all adults capable of as well. He called this deep engagement 'a present moment'.

In his elegantly written book, *The Present Moment in Psychotherapy and Everyday Life*, Stern provides a framework for thinking about the potential for human connection by describing a type of social interaction that's full of presence and participation. This is how he wrote about *a present moment,* which, to him

> is a special kind of mental contact—namely, an inter-subjective contact....[that involves] the mutual interpenetration of minds that permits us to say, 'I know that you know what I know' or 'I feel that you feel what I feel'. [During one of these moments, there's] a reading of the contents of the other's mind....[People] are capable of 'reading' other people's intentions and [of feeling within their own bodies what another is feeling]. Not in any mystical way, but from watching their face, body movements, and posture, hearing the tone of voice, and noticing the immediate context for their behavior, even though [these] intuitions need verifying and fine-tuning.[10]

Capacity for the relational connection that Stern describes finds it parallels in Buber's "meeting" and in Clark's "thick listening at thin moments." The embodiment of our human ability to care and the willingness to meet someone is at the heart of spirituality as a felt sense of connection. In addition, being in this kind of connected moment with another person, whether family, friend or client, is fulfilling at the deepest level. It's the essence of listening well and being present.

In summary, human beings have potential to help one another meet human and spiritual needs. We share a body, we convey emotions in patterned and predictable ways, we're capable of empathy and of realizing the need to listen because what's happening to someone else requires us to notice its foreignness; and finally, we have the capacity for connection that's captured in Stern's present moment. For all these reasons, it's crucial to know that human beings are made for relationship and to see that every relationship has the need for spiritual care—whether the relationship is personal, private or professional.

Neural Pathways and Hospitality in Spiritual Care

It's compelling to consider how research into human spirituality has advanced scientifically in the last 60 years. The discovery of mirror neurons in the early 1990s, quite by accident, by Giacomo Rizzolatti and his associate Italian scientists, provides a basis for our capacity to connect with others. A mirror neuron is a neuron that fires when an animal or human acts and when an animal or human observes the same action performed by another. Thus, the neuron "mirrors" the behavior of the other, as though the observer is also acting. Mirror neurons, along with the human tendency to express emotions facially and bodily, enable human beings to pick up another person's movements, their emotional state and their intentions, at least sufficiently enough to attend to that person and wait to hear what's going on.

In addition to mirror neurons, human beings have a many-branched Vagus (from the Latin "wandering") nerve that could be called the body's social-engagement system. When the "ventral vagus complex" runs the show, we smile when someone smiles at us and nod our heads when we agree with someone. We also frown when friends tell us of their misfortune.[11]

The Vagus Nerve Complex (VNC) is one of 12 cranial nerves and is the longest one. It extends from the brainstem to the abdomen by way of multiple organs including the heart, esophagus and lungs. This nerve complex is constantly sending updated sensory information about the state of the body's organs 'upstream' to the brain via afferent nerves— nerves that bring information toward the brain. As well, this system of nerves is efferent (referring to movement away from the brain), so that messages from the brain inform the rest of the body. Just as neurons in the brain form a communication system, as described in chapter one, the VNC promotes communication between brain and body.

From the perspective of Vagus nerve functioning, for our physiology to calm down, heal and grow we need a visceral feeling of safety.[12] When we're safe, the VNC is engaged and sends signals down to the heart and lungs, slowing our heart rate and increasing the depth of our breathing. As a result, we feel calm and relaxed, centered or pleasurably aroused. The Vagus nerve also registers heartbreak and gut-wrenching sensations, such as a dry throat, tense voice, racing heart and respiration that becomes shallow and rapid.[13] As mentioned, the science that studies the human body is advancing at a breathtaking pace. As an example, readers can easily find information online on psychological practices based on our increasing understanding of the role that the VNC plays in social interaction.[14] It may be instructive for spiritual care workers, concerned with personal and social implications of one person's affect on another, to gain the useful insights available in these psychological practices. An excellent resource, in this regard, that focuses connections between trauma and embodiment is *My Grandmother's Hands: Racialized Trauma and the Pathway to Mending Our Hearts and Bodies*, by Resmaa Menakem (2017).[15]

In the research on mirror neurons and the Vagus nerve complex, we can see how spiritual needs are unmet if people aren't seen, heard, accepted and believed, or if they hold a view of the future that's hopeless, to name a few unmet spiritual needs. What human spirituality makes possible is a felt sense of connection that's personal and social and that meets our deepest needs. The human spirit longs to be included personally in a network that matters, and in which people matter to each other so they feel woven into the social fabric of their small, particular part of the world.

Cultivating relational habitats where equity, diversity and inclusion thrive is fast becoming a critical necessity in the twenty-first century. If we're to survive and flourish as a civilization, we need to come together in support of healthy families, communities, social aggregates and the earth's environment. Once again, we've identified a topic that far exceeds the parameters of this book. That said, it's worthwhile to ask the question: What do inclusion and exclusion look like? In his inclusionary-status continuum, American psychologist Mark Leary identified a range of inclusion and exclusion behaviors. His summary identifies the following along the continuum he outlines:

- Maximal inclusion: others make an effort to seek out an individual
- Active inclusion: others welcome the individual but don't seek out him or her
- Passive inclusion: others allow an individual to be included
- Ambivalence: others don't care whether an individual is included or excluded
- Passive exclusion: others ignore an individual
- Active exclusion: others avoid an individual

- Maximal exclusion: others physically reject, ostracize, abandon, or banish an individual.[16]

While there's much that can be said about the word inclusion, for our purposes we draw attention to the two definitions of the term typically found in dictionaries. Using the online Google English dictionary provided by Oxford Languages, as one example, inclusion is: (1) the action or state of including or of being included within a group or structure, and, (2) the practice or policy of providing equal access to opportunities and resources for people who might otherwise be excluded or marginalized. The definitions turn our attention to systems thinking[17] and in particular the language of closed versus open systems. Indeed, inclusion begins with opening to something *other*. Also implied in the definitions of inclusion is a sense of duality, division and possibly opposition insofar as there can be haves versus have-nots within a particular setting. Those who have power advantaged positions and resources may include or exclude the have-nots, as depicted in Mark Leary's continuum.

Into this conceptualization, where tensions of I-It vis-à-vis I-Thou relating can emerge, we want to focus in on the value of hospitality. Hospitality implies a relationship between a guest and a host, wherein the host receives the guest with goodwill. Hospitality may involve more than including guests and visitors; it may welcome strangers. Interestingly, the word host in German is *Gastgeber*, meaning "guest-giver, the one who gives to guests;"[18] with hospitality, the relational outcome of guest-giving, is called *Gastfreundschaft* or guest-friendship.[19] Hospitality is an open system in which the space between host and guest quite naturally relies on and cultivates the gaze behavior of mirroring and engagement of VNC activity. Hospitality transcends mere inclusion. By fostering mutuality, equity and diversity, the practice of hospitality underscores a quality of human relating that's attested to in the sacred texts and teachings of many faith traditions.

As authors, we point out that hospitality happens in an interpersonal space that's invested with the work of relational habitat maintenance. In his book *Reaching Out,* Henri Nouwen explains that reaching out to other people requires the spiritual discipline of moving from hostility to hospitality. He writes

> In our world full of strangers, estranged from their own past, culture and country, from their neighbors, friends and family, from their

deepest self and their God, we witness a painful search for a hospitable place where life can be lived without fear and where community can be found...The movement from hostility to hospitality is hard and full of difficulties...But still—that is our vocation: to convert the *hostis* into a *hospes*, the enemy into a guest and to create the free and fearless space where brotherhood and sisterhood can be formed and fully experienced.[20]

As we grow in self-awareness, we realize we're capable of hostility as well as hospitality. We're capable of both I-It and I-Thou relating. If we want to cultivate an attitude of offering people spiritual care, Nouwen's insights into hospitality can help us examine how we're thinking about others, especially those we view with hostility, as enemies, foreigners and strangers, many of whom may be in our immediate circles of relationship as family, neighbors or co-workers. We all have lists of those we consider less deserving of attention, of relational investment, or that we may think deserve to be outside the boundaries of our positive regard. Until we admit our tendency towards hostility, we can't freely embody hospitality.

To Nouwen, in order to open up so that hostility becomes hospitality—creating spaces that are safe, welcoming and full of attentiveness—we need to first ask these questions:

What is currently occupying, or preoccupying the space? What keeps it from being open? What current and tangible relationships in our lives are marked as those who are in and those who are out?

In asking these questions, Nouwen highlights three relational dyads parent/child, teacher/student and professional/client as near-at-hand work sites for reflectively navigating the path from hostility to hospitality. If we don't invest in relational habitat maintenance with those close to us, we won't be able to authentically reach out more broadly to people in other cultures, faiths, languages and diverse orientations. Lastly, in what ways do we receive the other as *other* while also being true to ourselves?

As he reflects on hospitality, Nouwen draws attention to the dialectic of receptivity and confrontation. He says "[really honest receptivity means inviting the stranger into our world on his or her terms, not on ours."[21] At the same time, receptivity invites confrontation by facing another with one's authenticity, from the Latin (*con* - "with" + *frons, front*-"face"), because the open space being traversed "can only be a welcoming space when there are clear boundaries." It is an important dialectic of receptivity and confrontation that Nouwen introduces here. As we encounter genuine differences, we come face to face with conflict and potentially, with losses, e.g., of the certainty and ease that typified our lives before the encounter. As Nouwen says, how do we receive the other while also being true to ourselves?

How are receptivity and confrontation to be lived out together? Returning to Stern's insight about relational complexities and the present moment, we propose that the space between host and guest is punctuated by a series of present moment encounters during which the self and the other differentiate in healthy ways. This won't happen without an immersion into something philosopher and contemplative Edith Stein discusses as a phenomenology of sensual and emotional empathy.[22] She insisted on the primary realization that the object of our contemplation is foreign to us. But we want to be clear; an event in question may be foreign, but the person before us is *not* strange; he or she is also human and respected as such. We're made for relationship. We have compelling and essential aspects of humanity that link us to one another. Yet if we are to value our differences and preserve our authenticity, in sacred hospitality, we're compelled to ask questions Nouwen poses, so that embodied hospitality and empathy are interdependent during present moments that characterize relational habitat maintenance.

Attentiveness and Spiritual Care

What every human spirit requires is attention from others, attentiveness from those who matter to us and even from strangers. Greeting people on the street matters to spiritual care. Attending to others refers to the just distribution of attention, which is an embodied presentation of the self that includes pausing, regulating our gaze behavior and modifying our body's expression to attune to another person and fully take that person into account. Several sections of this chapter address the topic of spiritual care and inclusion. If we take Leary's point about inclusion and exclusion, we see that inclusion is built on a willingness and ability to offer another person our full attention.

In his book, *The Pursuit of Attention*,[23] Charles Derber analyzed the concept of attention to make the point that attention is a commodity; it's like money. Giving attention to someone signals the social value they hold for us. Derber believes attention is more important than wealth as a sign of personal and social worth. People who easily get attention are seen as valuable, as movie stars and athletes can attest. In this respect, we're suggesting an affinity between the concepts of inclusion, attention and social value.

Messages that convey our lack of worth are learned from experience. The attention that creates and sustains a personal sense of having value is focused on someone's whole being, rather than on a particular feature of his or her life. Likewise, a sense of having value can be traumatized; ramifications of such wounding may be carried viscerally for years.

Two stories capture this mind/soul/body connection. One woman told us, as a teenager living in Eastern Canada, that a group of her classmates took her into the woods and tied her to a tree. They left her there all night. No one came to her rescue. Her parents had no idea she was in trouble. After a few hours, she gave up crying for help. Since that time, her sense of self-worth has been encumbered by a belief that people won't remember her name, even though she has a successful career and is highly esteemed for her expertise. Remnants of her traumatic abandonment are embedded in her nervous system, and sustain an enduring sense of loss. Another woman tells the following story:

> She recalls being in a campground as a tiny child, about three years old. It had a beach with access through the woods. One afternoon she and her two older brothers went to the beach, following their father. Close to the woods her father started to run. She tried to keep up in her little flip flop sandals. Somehow her brothers managed. Her father led them through a patch of mud just before entering the woods. Her brothers negotiated it and kept running. As she ran into it she got stuck, sinking ankle-deep in mud sucking at her feet. She screamed for help. No one came.

> Close by, a family spotted her terror. She remembers the boy's name, Billy. He attended her brother's karate class. His mother pulled her out of the mud. She remembers a large fluffy towel the woman wrapped her in before she washed her feet with warm water. She can't say how long it was before her family realized she was missing. It had to be a long time. Billy's mom got water hot in a campground, brought a towel, and washed mud off her little feet. She knew Billy's mom was kind but no one is mother or father at three years old except one's own parents. They didn't come. Billy's mother took her back to her family's camping spot.[24]

This woman told her story like any survivor. From her facial expression, it was clear she was back in the camp, stuck in mud. This is one of many stories she can tell about her childhood.

Children feel in their bodies the loss of being seen. If adults forsake them, the loss creates unresolved tension—pressure that troubles all their relationships, until they experience healing. Neither of these women is neurotic or psychotic. Their traumas occurred within ordinary households. Their inability to gain attention when they were desperate resulted in a lost sense of personal value. An outcome of this loss is that these women don't easily show up within a relational habitat.

Recognition allows a person to show up to other people. As an example, even as limits are set on children, if they feel recognized and have a sense that adults understand how they interpret their experience (whether or not adults interpret behavior in the same way the child does), the young can find limit setting tolerable and may even feel relieved at being 'caught', since it's a way of showing up to others. If children don't feel recognized, they may resent limit setting as a violation of identity, which is what it is.[25]

Even among adolescents and adults, being held responsible for our actions is another way to receive attention. While it may be uncomfortable, if other people hold us accountable, we come to see they care about us: they care about how we act and about the impact we're having on them; they care about the impact we'll have on other people, and therefore, ultimately the impact our behavior will have on us. What matters, as conflict is addressed through caring, is that empathy, respect and present moment encounters come to underlie the healing and restoring of relationships, even if we're caught doing what's harmful and unpleasant to other people.

In addition to recognizing people by focusing on their behavior, parents, teachers and spiritual care practitioners need to go a step further. They must be drawn toward and stay with a person consciously and intentionally if their attention to that person is to have its full effect in paying out value. As those who reflectively offer spiritual care know, it's easy to attend to people who have developed the requisite skills to draw our attention to them. These people receive attention easily, seemingly without effort, so we never see them as attention seeking. By contrast, people like the two women whose stories we just shared may have to work hard to get attention. They might be labeled as attention-seekers and perceived negatively. In offering spiritual care, the invitation is to attend as willingly to the awkward person as to those who acquire attention with ease. To this end, spiritual care practitioners discipline their thinking and notice judgments as they arise and refuse to see some people as deserving attention and others as undeserving. Skilled spiritual care practitioners are even-handed when it comes to paying attention to others. They seek to relate in an I-Thou manner, valuing each *other* they meet with equanimity. This balanced approach, something all people benefit from, is an aspect of thick listening at thin moments.

If attention giving is an aspect of the attitude of spiritual care, Derber notes a modern problem many people have. While attention-getting attracts recognition, attention keeping conveys that someone's value is secure and permanent. In his analysis of attention getting, keeping and giving, Derber asserts that Western culture is addicted to attention getting. He believes we're so driven to seek attention for ourselves that no one is left to give it. He points to a modern self that carries a unique distress: "Each person…has received the burdensome gift of an overgrown self. We enjoy the positive, attractive features of this self-orientation, but…fail to appreciate how much it costs us as well."[26]

The choice to pay full attention to one's children, spouse, co-workers, friends, neighbors, or clients in spiritual care is a contribution we make to sustaining a relationally satisfying home and social environment. It's at the core of relational habitat maintenance. Yet, can we tell if we're exempt from an insatiable desire for attention getting ourselves? Can we perceive whether we give others attention generously on the strength of our commitment to meet spiritual needs? Do we withhold attention as a means of exercising power over someone else? As in the case of unmasking hostility in order to move toward hospitality, unmasking one's desire for attention encourages people to not only seek and secure it, but also to give attention generously.

Giving attention is significant in terms of human survival and meaning making. Like all other human beings, spiritual care practitioners have these needs as well. If attention is a currency, and attention getting establishes personal worth, it also supports what Harvard psychologist and educator Robert Kegan points out, which is that "survival and development depend on our capacity to recruit the invested attention of others to us."[27] Apart from the innate human bonding associated with parenting, in order for us to survive, people have to be recruited to draw close and stay near. Parents, teachers, pastors and spiritual care providers may need help to cultivate the capacity for attachment (attention keeping) and attunement (attention giving) that's specific to a particular person's way of attention seeking.

Again, the need for attention begins in infancy. Infants learn to grasp physical objects and human objects in order to achieve their survival and maintenance—to remain alive in the world. An infant's capacity "to hold the mother with a recognizing eye is as fundamental to...development as is the prehensile capacity to hold a physical object."[28] The need to hold the attention of others follows us throughout our lives. As adults, our sense of self-valuation can rise or fall on the strength of attention we secure from those who are important to us—even from strangers. Engaging in concrete experiences that rely on gaze behavior and give attention effectively are the means for preparing the ground for thick listening at thin moments.

While we don't think of people as objects, we use the phrase "object of our contemplation" in several chapters of this book. Contemplation is the action of looking thoughtfully at something for a long time. It's an act of considering something with our full attention. While contemplation has been relegated to the domain of spiritual and religious practices, it has a broader value. The capacity to get and keep attention is an exercise in which people are trying to recognize and be recognized. Whether the object grasped is a thing or a person, infants, as an example, aim to accomplish a similar end: to make meaning with these objects, which are transitional objects of ordinary life. The term 'object' implies motion insofar as it's understood to be a material thing that can be seen and touched; it's a person or thing toward which specific action or feeling is directed. We saw this in an earlier chapter with the little girl who focused attention on her mother as she readied to go down a playground slide. Over time, the meaning we create by interacting with objects that move through our experience creates a sense of self that develops through experiencing them, which then is folded into the worldview we create. The meaning that contemplated objects in our lives hold for us is wrapped up into the worldview that shapes our faith story.[29]

Once again, the greatest inequality in any situation isn't based on money; it's due to an unequal distribution of attention. On a personal level, from infancy, our need for others is central to the development of mature humanity. Every human being needs to be seen, heard, recognized, believed.[30] On a systems level, professions such as spiritual care need to be incorporated into organizational charts and budget lines. Too often they're left out of an institution's considerations. Inequities in the distribution of attention are an understudied research area and beyond the scope of this book. That said, in this chapter, while we often start with the personal, ties between people and social systems are also important to highlight.

In the scenario that follows, personal and social aspects are evident in what Lisa Miller calls a shared spiritual connection between an older woman and young girl. The intergenerational transmission of spiritual sensibility is integral to a just distribution of attention. In order to establish what she means by shared spiritual connection, Lisa Miller described 'the nod' in her book *The Spiritual Child.*[31]

> She tells the story of seeing an older woman who may have been dressed up for a Sunday church service, with white gloves, no less. She entered a subway with a young girl walking beside her. Down at one end of the subway car a man who was very drunk was yelling out an invitation for someone to come and eat with him because, on the seat beside him, he had a large box of Kentucky Fried Chicken.
>
> As the woman and girl entered, they noticed that other passengers had moved as far away as possible from the drunken man and were trying to ignore him by looking down at their magazines or at their cell phones. The woman and girl paused, and the older woman nodded to the girl. Both of them turned toward the drunken man and sat down across from him. After a moment, he raised his voice and offered them some chicken. Again there was a nod. The older woman thanked him politely and said they'd just finished their lunch. In the next several moments, after several more offerings of chicken, the drunken man settled down quietly and continued to eat.[32]

In her analysis of the scenario, Miller says that the older woman, perhaps a grandmother, had a spiritual relationship with the girl that allowed them immediately to recognize what to do and how to act. Miller saw the nod between them as a signal that the relationship was securely established over a long period of time. She observes that the nod was spirituality shared between child and beloved elder: spiritual direction and values were conveyed and received through a loving relationship.[33] They understood one another. They were able to share their secure relationship with a man—a stranger—who needed it. Their generosity allowed him to regain some dignity.

This intergenerational action is an example of relational habitat maintenance. There are many people deeply invested in the ecological maintenance of the earth, an investment that's good for all of us. However, if we consider the spiritual need to connect meaningfully with other people, we would do well to put effort into maintaining relational habitats with equal attentiveness, even in public spaces. One of the most important lessons of COVID-19 is that it revealed deep social and personal needs for dignity to be upheld on behalf of every human being.

Creating Safety

When human spirituality is based on a felt sense of connection, it creates a feeling of safety. To American psychologist Bessel van der Kolk, "being able to feel safe with other people is probably the single most important aspect of mental health."[34] Even for a man who's drunk on a subway, "safe connections are fundamental to having a meaningful and satisfying life."[35]

In his important book, *The Body Keeps the Score*, van der Kolk, a medical doctor, describes the effects we can have on each other based on what we've been describing as the presence or absence of a sense of felt connection (although he doesn't use that specific term). He's clear that our effects on each other can go in two directions. From decades of experience with trauma patients, he observes that:

- Our capacity to destroy one another is matched by our capacity to heal one another.
- Language gives us the power to change ourselves and others by communicating our experiences, helping us to define what we know, and find a common sense meaning about what's going on—or what's gone on in the past.
- We have the ability to regulate our own physiology, including some of the so-called involuntary functions of the body and brain, through such basic activities as breathing, moving, and touching.
- We can change social conditions to create environments in which other people can feel safe and where they can thrive.[36]

van der Kolk points out that a human response to the effects other people have on us follows a certain pattern. Whenever we feel threatened,

- We initially turn to others; we call out for help, support and comfort.
- If no one comes, we resort to survival in fight or flight.
- If help still doesn't come, we revert to preservation by shutting down and we move into a state of freeze or collapse.[37]

Whether ordinary or traumatic, these human reactions to other people's impacts on us are tied to physiological, psychological and spiritual health. When we learn to pay attention to ourselves in a balanced and compassionate manner, we grow our capacity to reach beyond ourselves not only to get and keep attention, but also to give it to others. In the broad sense addressed in this chapter, we willingly offer spiritual care to others that allows them a deep and secure sense of safety and we become part of interpersonal and intergenerational encounters that nurture our relational habitats.

In the daily life of ordinary people, healing and wholeness are created out of some of the most accessible experiences. Let's look at van der Kolk's threefold pattern more carefully. Efforts to be relationally healthy start with an ability to seek out social contact if we feel threatened, to reach out when we're afraid and call for help if something is wrong. While positive acknowledgement of a first level call for help is common for many people, in some families, people learn it's not safe to call out for help. There are marriages in which spouses pay a high price for asking for help. In school classrooms, young people learn that teachers and other students might humiliate them if they signal a need for help. In the workplace, many people quickly learn that asking for help isn't smart; needing support can be dangerous. In highly individualistic North American cultures, where singularity is prized above all else, asking for help may be interpreted as weakness. If we need help, we must be lacking or incompetent. As a result, many people come to feel that reaching out isn't possible or safe—and that it certainly isn't wise.

What happens if people learn, as did the woman left overnight in the woods, that when they ask for help no one will provide it? If no one shows up to help, a second level response is to resort to survival in fight or flight reactions. Clenching one's fist in the face of a threat, or fleeing one's abusive home, are examples of fight and flight. If our second level response fails to keep us safe, we revert to third level self-preservation by shutting down and becoming paralyzed—we freeze: a body may go limp, someone may look 'spaced out', dissociated or in a state of collapse.[38] Under unfavorable conditions, a first response to reach out for help may be replaced by fight, flight or freeze reactions.

In contrast to healthy interaction, trauma almost invariably involves not being seen, not being mirrored, and not being taken into account during social interactions in families, schools, workplaces, religious settings, neighborhoods, on the street, or in socio/political or community organizations.[39] Yet, we can experience repair if someone turns to us, rather than turning away, or when someone's eyes light up as we enter the room.[40] The human body we all share is designed to help us seek healing and wholeness.

Why are we, as authors, giving so much weight to trauma, the absence of safety and the scarcity of attention? It's because these experiences are existential problems of our age. It's rare to live a lifetime without some exposure to personal and social wounding. As we said at the outset of this chapter, we want to open ordinary humanity to the attentiveness of spiritual care. Spiritual care is integral to the just distribution of attention. It engages the angst of trauma, loss, grief and recovery to which van der Kolk refers as he delves into losses people experience if they feel disconnected to themselves and others due to unmanageable, traumatic events they can't escape. van der Kolk's focus is on healing. His book is full of hope. He begins to unpack the problem of trauma by looking at human interaction, with all its scope and frailty. In his research, he sees human interaction as both curse and blessing with respect to spiritual and mental health.

As a therapist, van der Kolk sees his work helping people to 'acknowledge, experience, and bear' the reality of life—with all its pleasures and heartbreak—and identifies the greatest sources of suffering in the lies we tell ourselves (e.g., I'm invisible. I don't matter.)[41] When losses overwhelm us, reaching out, telling the truth by expressing our beliefs and letting someone pay attention to them with us, is the heart of becoming healthy. What does it take for someone to tell the truth? At its base, the freedom to tell the truth depends on feeling safe, even though telling the truth opens up the possibility that we'll be rejected or judged, and so we feel very deeply the potential for being harmed by self-revelation. Interestingly, a Hebrew word for truth—"*emeth*"—gathers around itself a number of terms such as faithfulness, reliability, stability and trustworthiness. These concepts depict a relational environment in which an *I* engages a *Thou,* thick listening pays attention at thin moments, mirror neurons and Vagus nerve interactions find resonance with others as *other.*

The social support that characterizes spiritual care isn't the same as simply being in the same room with other people. van der Kolk points out that many traumatized people feel out of sync with the people around them. The critical issue for him is reciprocity, which he defines as being truly heard and seen by other people and by feeling that we're held in someone else's heart and mind.[42] In this way, he links together Stein's embodied empathy, Stern's present moment, Buber's I-Thou relating and Nouwen's hospitality. Spiritual care thrives during encounters created by two or more people who share a deep sense of felt connection. If we recall the list of spiritual needs, the link to van der Kolk's assertion about safety is obvious: spiritual care meets people's spiritual needs for a felt sense of safety.

In order to feel safe enough to face what's going on, we need to be with people who are kind. Kindness matters in every context we're in—whether family, school, workplace or neighborhood. It's a core relational value among indigenous peoples around the world, within many faith communities and in literature related to professional pedagogy and ethics.[43] In a manner similar to the word *truth*, kindness (in Hebrew "chesed") gathers to itself a number of terms, such as goodness, respect, courtesy, beauty, mercy and steadfast love. van der Kolk quotes Jerome Kagan,[44] a distinguished Harvard professor, who said that "being benevolent rather than malevolent" in response to someone else is "probably a true feature of our species."[45] In van der Kolk's response to trauma, where he accentuates the need for a visceral feeling of safety going hand in hand with bodily calm and serenity, we find an inspiring invitation to all people who envision spiritual care as an attitude toward the world; an attitude that belongs in happy homes and healthy cities.

For van der Kolk, the foundation for healing is rooted in regulating our physiology, including some of the so-called involuntary functions of the body and brain through such basic activities as breathing, moving, and touching. For him, healing is based on an ordinary human capacity to keep breathing. This healing capability is something Dr. Joseph Edwards and Dr. Lynne Zettl have translated into a therapeutic modality called Self Regulation Therapy (SRT). Their mission is to heal the world one nervous system at a time and they have dedicated themselves to this mission by establishing the Canadian Foundation for Trauma Research and Education (CFTRE).[46] Their therapeutic approach enables practitioners, including spiritual care practitioners, to accompany people in balancing their nervous systems by diminishing excess activation and cultivating new, healthy neural pathways for flexibility in managing daily challenges and stressors.

So let's keep breathing. As authors, we've said that people are made for relationship. The essential work of spiritual care relies on human spirituality as a capacity that people can develop and grow into through relationship. van der Kolk and the CFTRE also promote a parallel assertion that our wounded selves are made for healing and health. The body's capacity for healing is expressed through research findings on mirror neurons, the Vagus nerve complex, attention getting/keeping/giving, relational safety and fight/flight/freeze coping abilities. Those who engage in spiritual care, whether professionally or in the broader sense developed in this chapter, can rely on such research as they foster the insight that, through offering and participating in ordinary processes such as breathing, gaze behavior, and acknowledging others as we encounter them, we can change social conditions to create environments in which people feel safe and can thrive, so that we steer our behaviour in a chosen direction.[47]

Mindfulness and Spiritual Care

If spiritual care rests on the attentiveness and safety we offer others, it's also grounded on an ordinary human ability and willingness to be mindful. In his book, *The Mystery of the Mind*, Canadian neurosurgeon and medical doctor Wilder Penfield described a mind's capacity for self-reflection and attentiveness. He was a colleague of Donald O. Hebb who developed the neurological research outlined in chapter one on the formation of worldviews, as both men worked at McGill University. Penfield developed a notion of mindfulness through scientific investigation of the brain. He examined active brains and came to see, to his surprise, that the mind is capable of what he called mindfulness.

Penfield's sister had epilepsy. In the 1970s, there was little help for her. In his medical practice he focused on performing brain surgeries that allowed him to work on people who were conscious as he probed different parts of the brain. As a result of his efforts, he helped his sister, but also opened up awareness to how brains function. His view on mindfulness isn't based on a religious perspective; it's based on scientific investigations of the brain and outcomes of his research. As we consider his view on mindfulness, once again we observe that the human body has inbuilt capacities that are activated by and supported through spiritual care, i.e., we're made for relationship, healing and health.

To Penfield, mindfulness is mental awareness that has specific attributes. In the bulleted summary that follows, we include Penfield's, van der Kolk's and our own analysis of what the mind can do. Mindfulness allows us to

- Focus attention so that learning occurs.
- Expend energy to pay attention.
- See what's going on: understand, reason, make decisions and put them into play.
- Make new decisions by distinguishing options and assessing good/ better preferences.
- Be conscious of the past and the present, and experience both at the same time.
- Access the meaning system we've been forming since we were young, based on personal experience.
- Decide whether the ways we've made meaning in the past continue to be useful to us and whether they're still the way we want to see the world and be involved in it.
- Hover calmly and objectively over thoughts, feelings and emotions and then take time to respond.
- Self-regulate: Inhibit, organize and moderate the emotional brain's typical reactions.

Penfield, in particular, summarized his research by saying that the ability of the brain for mindfulness is crucial for preserving our relationships with other human beings. That is, mindfulness is an ally to I-Thou relating, thick listening at thin moments, and embodied empathy. It's a human capacity that can couple not only the concept of contemplative mindfulness developed in the chapter on faith, but also spiritual practices and theological reflection in the many activities of broad-based spiritual care.

Gaze and Embrace

Throughout this chapter we have been drawing attention to a number of human potentialities that are available to those who want to develop the ability and willingness to care spiritually for others. This final section is on the significance of two kinds of human engagement: gaze and embrace. Spiritual care involves a foundational move toward rather than away from others. It's an initial and initiating move to connect and be hospitable during social interaction. As we include people, and offer them the hospitality of a present moment, we relieve their stress so they feel neither strange nor alone.

We all have the spiritual need to be seen and heard. We begin learning to be human by receiving our social value from others. This chapter has highlighted the importance of attention getting in a number of ways. Building on our social value, we learn to value ourselves. If our personal value harmonizes with our social value, we enjoy self-esteem. If our sense of our own value is out of sync with the social world, we may experience low self-esteem.

Like any other form of currency, social value is won, lost, invested, traded and squandered in games of attention getting, keeping and giving that establish individual success and social worth. But self-esteem is not an outcome of self-evaluation only. It's a function of attention we receive from others; and since all cultures make it possible for people to get it, attention that provides esteem is a distinct social phenomenon that can be analyzed to ascertain the value of a person's life.[48] In attempting to offer spiritual care, when we're with people who appear to attach too little or too much value to themselves, we're well advised to wonder how this condition came to be.

Appropriate esteem provides us with a satisfying feeling of well-being that gives us energy to go on trying to accomplish what we set out to do. People need appropriate recognition in order to feel well about themselves. If society is civil, the need for sufficient attention is tempered by compassion and understanding. As a consequence, people aren't driven to get recognition, they aren't addicted to getting it, nor do they suffer from isolation and aloneness. Claiming esteem as our due doesn't automatically deny the same to others. With appropriate self-regard, we learn to see others as sources of care and support from whom we may receive recognition and to whom we readily grant it.[49]

Looking at this through another lens, part of the human endeavor is knowing how to pay attention to our inmost being—that flow of awareness that plays a basic role in our behavior and is informed by a worldview that waters root and branch of our inner experience. Felt experiencing of what is within us is deeper and broader than can easily be put into words. Yet, infants are capable of it. In an infant, that awareness grounds their capacity to initiate, sustain, or end inter-personal experiences with others long before they can talk.[50] As ordinary human beings, we can pay attention to our inmost self. As we attend to ourselves, we also learn to offer ourselves the spiritual care we hope to give others. The two aspects of care go together—self-care and care of others. One without the other is a distortion. This is why there is so much emphasis given to self-awareness in spiritual care education. We can't engage others relationally if we don't engage ourselves reflectively.

Really hearing the meaning-making effort of another person, helping them feel safe and finding relief through an experience of being fully seen and heard is at the heart of spiritual care. But as spiritual care practitioners, and certainly as ordinary people, how do we manage our capacity to sustain authentic care? Isn't there a risk of drowning in concern for those who happen to be in our care (at home or in hospital beds)? And what if we get it wrong? What happens if we say the wrong thing? How do we know how much care is needed? These are essential questions to ask. An adequate response depends on how we view others and their capacity to heal.

When it comes to offering and participating in attention giving and getting, it's important to distinguish professional spiritual care relationships from a broader sense of spiritual care as an attitude toward the world. In professional relationships, the person offering spiritual care is the one who attends to spiritual needs of the other. If mutuality is the starting point of a relationship either person can give attention to the other. Attending is a response to two human longings: a yearning for inclusion and a yearning for distinctness.[51] Usually one's first experience of attending occurs in a humanizing gaze between parent and child. Previous sections of the chapter referred to this primary human phenomenon. Eye to eye gaze behaviour exists in adult relating also. In many cultures, it communicates inclusion and hospitality. It's important to be aware, however, that looking directly at another person can be perceived as aggressive and disrespectful in other cultures. Here it is best to divert one's gaze while speaking or listening in order to communicate attentiveness and respect. We use the phrases *contemplative mindfulness* and the *object of our contemplation* to convey its aspects. Spiritual care exchanges of mirroring and gaze behavior are situated in present moments through embodied empathy and conveyed during Clark's thick listening.

A second experience in caring for others involves what we might call an embrace. Just as gaze behavior marks inclusion, this type of engagement responds to a yearning for distinctness. "I" meets "Thou" in a holding environment that is characterized by greeting and hospitality. An embrace can be physical, social, and/or spiritual. The focus of attention is to welcome the other as other; to envision the relationship as being boundaried, encircled, enclosed, safe. As mentioned, we have the ability to regulate our own physiology through such basic activities as breathing, moving, and touching. By embrace we refer to the healthy holding of another person, until the time is right to release them.

In embracing,[52] one person with permission of another, unanxiously holds that other often anxious person. It's not simply the physical gesture of holding, which also characterizes attending based on the gaze behavior supported by embodied empathy during thick listening. It's holding that contributes to the self-regulating capacity of the one being held. Embracing is the ability and willingness to hold in the right way, at the right time, for the right length of time and for the right reasons. Its appropriateness lays the groundwork for healthy separation[53] since holding on "without constraining (the other person or oneself) may be the first requirement of care."[54]

Embracing is a way of being present to another so the attention we pay *is to them*, not to the problem. In spiritual care we respond to a person not a problem. If we react to a person by trying to mitigate a problem, we convey a lack of trust. Each person must address his or her own situation authentically for healing and distinctiveness to take place. Yet, an ability to be present to others when they're anxious, to acknowledge anxiety without becoming anxious oneself or immediately trying to relieve the distress is a feature of competent, usually professional, psychological help,[55] as well as of healthy emotional support through spiritual care. Embracing is an act of presence and hospitality that's needed if we hope to help the other eventually not to need us in the same way. Embracing can be conveyed without touch, as unconditional positive regard and authentic acceptance, achieved through appropriate, respectful gaze behavior.

To embrace others is to pay attention to the person behind a problem so that people can relax into the truth and kindness (*emeth* and *chesed*) and become able to trust and respect themselves. If we refuse to embrace, healing is at risk; if we refuse to let go, we no longer merely hold someone—we hold that person back.

Consider the following example of embracing as a model of the complexity implied in what we've been discussing. A young mother goes for coffee at a neighbor's house. They each have a child roughly the same age. We observe the interaction between one mother and her child. The child sits on her mother's lap while the two women converse. Then, the child looks at the other child playing. She gets down with a hand on her mother's lap and leans toward an enticing game. She watches the play and moves closer to toys and a partner her size. Then she climbs back on the lap. Her mother welcomes her but now the child sits on her perch and her whole attention is on the game played by the other child. Eventually, she gets down and joins the play.

The initial embodiment of safety on the mother's lap transfers over: the child leaves her hand on her mother's lap and leans further into the play. She may then return to the lap until a sense of safety and curiosity moves her again into the play. A sense of safety continues to show up during play with the other child and by establishing some distance from her mother. Being near and moving away is a game the young learn, under favorable conditions, as they begin to discover independence. In romantic love, the pattern repeats itself: nearness, distance, nearness again. Spiritual care is built through allowing the other to move toward and away from one's physical or emotional caring presence as new places of safety are secured.

Peeling off yet another layer of reflection, we note that the mother in this example is doing many things at once: conversing, drinking coffee, watching a clock and donating her lap to her child. The activity of embracing is built on self-donation—a mother's lap and a child's need for it. A mother gives herself to a child's need yet has time for friendship. Mother and child relax in their availability to each other. Availability is another example of social currency. Like attention giving and social valuing, availability is a human resource that may be abundant or scarce. If a mother is socially, emotionally or financially deprived she may be unavailable; if preoccupied, anxious or otherwise engrossed, she may not be present to her child. In the economy of human relationships, a person can seldom give to others what they have never received themselves, until they experience it personally. A mother who's capable of self-donation has experienced receiving attention, experienced attunement, and availability from others in order to turn around and bequeath it to her child. (While what we're saying is generally the case, it's sometimes astonishing what a human being can give to others despite the relational, financial and emotional poverty of their upbringing; rare perhaps, but also very real.)

In a healthy exchange, in which a mother gives and receives relational currency, a quality of mutuality is evident. Mother and child are equally valuable. Her availability is an offering to a child, expressive of her value to the child. In this sense, embracing is a form of self-donation in which both parties enjoy value, although needs differ. The mother holds the child, initially and after the child's first explorative ventures; she receives a child's need for her; a need that she values. Feeling her child's hand on her lap is assurance of the child's well being. It's a touch that is a gift. Self-donation involves giving, losing, valuing and regaining the self that offers support. It builds on attentiveness, attunement and availability and improves the health of one's relational habitat.

Tensions in self-donation arise, for not only mothers and their children but also for spiritual care practitioners and their recipients if one gives oneself while also losing oneself. Where there are urgent, foundational needs, one can get lost in responding to the other. If a mother appears to get lost for a time, due to a child's needs, self-donation requires her to regain herself. If a spiritual care practitioner appears to get lost for a time, due to another's needs, self-donation requires him or her to regain a sense of separate selfhood. We can't donate what we've lost. Regaining oneself implies not getting permanently lost, but temporarily and willingly giving priority to another's need. Regaining oneself is the appropriate reaction to giving oneself wholeheartedly for a time.

Self-donation is conscious, intelligent action, not addiction. If a compulsion to give is fueling spiritual care activities, this drive needs to be addressed by becoming aware of what's going on within oneself by contemplating one's own being. Each spiritual care professional needs to be able to carry out a full range of self-donation components: giving, losing, valuing, and regaining self. If there's no self at the foundation of an act of self-donation—a self that's capable of self-differentiation—there can be a risk of giving oneself away to another's need, even temporarily, that devolves into expensive periods of exhaustion, oppression or self-pre-occupation. If the young mother in our story is to care for her child, it's imperative that she be industriously self-preserving in doing so. Risks in this example are sometimes extreme if there's a lack of social value attributed to mothers or spiritual care practitioners.

Finally, in considering gaze behavior and embrace, it's noteworthy that in healthy spiritual care practice, we learn how to create an economy of attention, attunement and availability that allows us to be effective in caring and at the same time self-preserving. If we use the currency metaphor referred to earlier, getting and keeping secure attention is like having sufficient currency for self-donation. The amount of funds available, however, often depends on past and present experiences of being cared for by others. Again, we can't give to others what we've never received ourselves; we can't donate what we've lost, without engaging with new learning that's available if someone offers us spiritual care. With the benefits of therapeutic work and regular spiritual practices, we can all tell whether we have adequate funds to go on living and to go on caring.

Conclusion

In this chapter, we've focused on ordinary human capabilities that provide a foundation for offering not only professional but also broad-based spiritual care to other people, while also caring spiritually for ourselves. Emotionally and bodily, we have what it takes to offer our full attention to other people without losing ourselves in the process. In addition, so much of the potential for spiritual care depends on how we think and feel about ourselves and think and feel about other people. We've looked into some of the research about a number of concepts, including relational habitat maintenance, existential problems, facial action coding, mirror neurons, the Vagus Nerve Complex, exclusion, inclusion, hospitality, attentiveness, spiritual connection, relational safety, mindfulness, gaze behavior and embracing. All of these human capacities can be employed to make the world a better place because human beings are made for relationship. We can rely on that reality to increase the trust we exercise as we care for others, receive their caring, and acknowledge that all people are capable of growth and healing.

Trusting others depends on what we understand about the human condition. Spiritual care practitioners ask themselves what they might expect not only from other people but also for and from themselves.

What is reasonable to expect from others as we try to achieve mutual regard? These questions pick up on a theme that runs throughout this book, having to do with being available to others while also remaining grounded in attentiveness to ourselves. What does this imply? As we've mentioned, the twentieth century solution for so many people was to walk away and stay away from difficult relationships because we were losing ourselves in those relationships. In this chapter, we're saying that human beings are made for relationship. Can we imagine what a difference it can make to our relationships if we focus on meeting each other's spiritual needs and take on an attitude of spiritual care to life in general? How will we find ourselves in our relationships if we envision them as having more to offer than to frustrate our attempts to be authentically ourselves?

In the book, *In Over Our Heads*, largely through paying attention to feminist critique of the first book he wrote, Robert Kegan addresses the possibility of staying committed to our relationships while remaining authentically ourselves in them. He points out that

> There is no necessary *identity* between taking command of ourselves and taking leave of our connections. Increasing differentiation can be a story of staying connected in a new way, of continuing to hold on to precious connections and loyalties while refashioning one's relationship to them so that one *makes them up* rather than *gets made up* by them. Increasing autonomy doesn't have to be a story of increasing aloneness. Deciding for myself doesn't have to be deciding by myself. Autonomy is self-regulating but regulation might well be on behalf of preserving and protecting one's connections according to an internal compass or system, since abiding and journeying are contexts for transformational development. The capacity to take a more differentiated position in the context of our relationships can permit us to move closer to another person.[56]

In this chapter, we hope we've been persuasive that we're created for relationship. People don't do well if they're not seen for the very unique person that each of us is. But we need each other and we need to learn how to remain with the people that matter to us, without getting lost. In professional spiritual care, practitioners learn how to be themselves in a role that requires them to donate themselves to other people. Offering relational hospitality and embodied empathy are foundational to meaningful spiritual care giving, both professionally and in the broader attitude we've spelled out in this chapter.

We can attend to the people we live with everyday as well as strangers we meet on the street as people who comprise our spiritual care relational circles and who form part of our relational habitats. All of us are called to spiritual care as an attitude toward the world. If people don't get what they need spiritually, all of us are impoverished in the deepest possible way.

Take Away Questions for Reflection

- How does understanding spiritual care as "an attitude toward the world" fit with your current approach to spiritual care?

- When you read the phrase "relational habitat maintenance" what comes to your mind? Are there specific relationships you think about? How do you maintain healthy relational habitats? What does that maintenance look like in practical terms?

- How might Paul Eckman's approach to facial expressions influence your spiritual assessment? Have you visited his website (https://www.paulekman.com)? If so, what have you discovered there?

- What do you make of Daniel Stern's description of "a present moment"? Have you ever experienced such a moment? If you have, describe it in writing or share it with someone else.

- What did you make of mirror neurons and the Vagus Nerve Complex (VNC)? In what ways do these deep body connections affect your approach to spiritual care practice?

- What role can hospitality play when considering equity, diversity and inclusion in spiritual care practice? What do you make of Henri Nouwen's coupling of hostility and hospitality, and how might this duality have an impact of your spiritual care practice?

- Have you ever had an encounter with the kind of person described by Lisa Miller in her book The Spiritual Child? What are your thoughts and feelings as you think of how the older woman and child related to one another and to the man on the subway car?

Chapter 5

Meeting Another as "Other"

Introduction

In spiritual care education, practitioners draw on several fields of learning. These include philosophy, theology, psychology, sociology and anthropology. In this chapter, we focus on *otherness* as an essential aspect of spiritual care. The topic of *otherness* draws on all the above-named fields of study, but given that a chapter is limited in length, we focus on sociological and anthropological insights. That said, readers might note our reliance on the other fields as well. Our purpose is to underscore the importance of attending to difference and noticing how someone's faith story conveys ideas, images and assumptions that are *dissimilar* to our own. In spiritual care, these differences are respected, engaged, and *met* in Martin Buber's sense that "all real living is meeting".[1] This chapter considers tools, a framework, and three global patterns that contain useful insights as we listen to others.

As authors born in the twentieth century and living into the twenty-first, we're aware that *otherness* deserves careful attention. How difference is conceptualized, spoken about, systematized and dealt with in everyday social interactions and spiritual care interventions needs to be a focus of conscious awareness. Issues around otherness include polarization, stereotyping, segregation and prejudice but also respect, compassion, civility, and solidarity—all of which need to be in dialogue with each other.

A phrase carried forward in spiritual care circles from early in the twentieth century is "living human document."[2] This expression positions all human persons as sacred texts to be contemplated as revelatory of spiritual wisdom. When meeting another as 'other', it's a valuable practice for spiritual care professionals to notice questions that spontaneously arise in their hearts and minds. These questions undergird practitioners' thick listening insofar as they engage thin moment experiences of those being served in hospitals, congregations, prisons, social agencies as well as in many other places. In thick listening, a practitioner may wonder: (a) How is *otherness* present as I engage this client's lived experience and faith story? (b) What are the social and cultural variables being communicated? (c) How self-aware am I when it comes to interpreting cultural differences? (d) How skilled am I in meeting the other as other-than-my-self?

These questions of self-awareness and *meeting* resonate with Buber's philosophical assertions pertaining to I-Thou relating. Buber's major theme is that human existence is defined by the way we engage in dialogue with each other, the world and that which transcends the world, (e.g., God, Divine, Spiritual Essence). According to Buber, human beings may adopt two attitudes toward the world: I-Thou and I-It. In I-Thou relating, there's inter-subjectivity and recognition of the unity of being that exists between self and other. Differences may be in evidence but they're viewed within a framework of human-to-human communication; attention is focused on the wholeness of self, other and the relationship between them.

By contrast, I-It relating is based on subject-to-object thinking. Differences are observed and analyzed from a distant, detached stance. When two people meet in a spiritual care context, experiences that originated in different parts of the world or within different cultural, gendered, racial or economic spheres, to name some significant factors, come to life relationally and influence the quality of rapport that occurs.

Thick listening across differences requires consciousness of the I-Thou as well as I-It dynamics that may be at play when two people from dissimilar backgrounds meet. Each person in an encounter brings along a worldview, paradigms and filters through which their communication occurs. In thin moment experiences, where stress levels can be high for all involved, beliefs, values and assumptions may operate below the surface. This can result in I-It exchanges. Viewing someone as "Thou" requires spiritual care practitioners to pause, to be in the moment and become grounded in respectful awareness. Such here and now consciousness is rooted in spiritual care competency development.

Integral to professional education and certification, spiritual care practitioners seek proficiency in the safe and effective use of self.[3] The "I" in I-Thou relating must be authentic and attentive to dynamics that comprise one's unique social location,[4] beliefs, power, vulnerability and boundaries as these personal aspects impact relationships with individuals and groups. Those who meet others at thin moments must be knowledgeable about the circumstances in which their own life experience, subjectivity, values and biases enhance or compromise one's effectiveness. In a given moment, helpful questions include:

> Who is this other? Are there faith, culture, gender, race or other differences of which I need to be aware? Do I feel capable of engaging this person across the variances I'm noticing? To whom or where can I turn if I need assistance in providing optimal care?

Asking these questions can help practitioners carry forward spiritual assessments, provide intervention and offer follow-up.

In this chapter we cover topics that deepen an understanding of how to meet another as 'other'. These topics include interpathy, dialogue, I-Thou relating and embodied empathy. We also look at the big picture of 'otherness' by delving into three global patterns that shape human identities and worldviews. The global patterns chosen for this chapter are individualism, strong group dyadic membership and a location that's caught between these two patterns. The *caught betweenness* we describe is captured in the example of twentieth century white western female experience. We acknowledge that many groups experience this *caught betweenness* as a fundamental condition of their existence. However, as white western women ourselves, we focus on an experience with which we can fully identify. In this identification we hope to highlight patterns that other *caught between* groups can test as to the validity for them.

Interpathy, Dialogue and I-Thou Relating

If we recognize the 'I', we can move to consider the 'Thou' in I-Thou relating. We can also focus on the relation between I and Thou insofar as it's characterized by inter-subjectivity and human-to-human communication. This section introduces two concepts, interpathy and dialogue, that deepen our understanding of the quality of I-Thou relating. The terms are primarily taken from literature in pastoral counseling and cross-cultural studies.

David Augsburger coined the word *interpathy* in 1986.[5] It's meaning is linked with two other terms, sympathy and empathy. According to American theologian Roslyn Karaban,[6] sympathy is the spontaneous sharing and understanding of another's feelings based on one's own experience of something similar. As an example, if you're experiencing loss and grief, and I've also experienced loss and grief, I can feel with you in your loss and grief. Empathy goes beyond self and looks at unfamiliar situations from another's perspective. Suppose you're telling me about what it feels like to be a mother, but I've never been a mother. With compassionate imagination, I can feel with you as you talk about being a mother. We're different, but I can connect with you meaningfully and caringly. Of note here, is that the bridging of such a difference may still rest upon similarities in our worldviews, paradigms and filters. My empathetic response to you may even involve me in thoughts or perceptions that lie just below the surface of my awareness, which are based on similarities in our gender, culture, race or faith tradition.

Interpathy moves a person beyond what's familiar into what's unfamiliar. Interpathy requires felt connection and intentional cognitive envisioning of the other as 'other'. I must bracket my spontaneous assumptions and beliefs about you in order to appreciate you. I must recognize and respect that your thoughts might originate from another way of knowing than mine do; your values may grow from another frame of moral reasoning and your feelings may come from another set of assumptions. We may have nothing in common but our basic humanity. For me to relate with you meaningfully as a spiritual care practitioner, I practice a quality of self-emptying (referred to as *self-donation* in the chapter on Made for Relationship) that's grounded in respect, humility and unknowing. It's by way of this unknowing that I can learn from you across our differences. Who are you? What do you want me to know about you? What are you trying to say to me? What are you hearing me say to you? What's allowed, or not allowed, in terms of spiritual care relating? How do you want me to accompany you in this thin moment experience?

As mentioned earlier, in order to fully engage another as "Thou," we need a framework of human-to-human communication that gives attention to the wholeness of self, other and the relationship between them. This is where *dialogue* comes into focus as the conduit in Buber's practice of meeting, through which meaning making can flow both interpersonally and inter-culturally. In the following paragraphs we consider the term *dialogue* by drawing on insights of William Isaacs, Pope Paul VI, Nelle Morton and Paulo Freire.

To begin with, *dialogue* comes from two Greek words, "dia" (through) and "logos" (word, or meaning). For human beings, meaning tends to flow through words. It can also flow through nonverbal expressions. In dialogue, there's potential for people to converse in such a way they suspend opinions and, according to William Isaacs, think together in relationship.[7] In dialogue, people think from a center rather than their own positions and allow shared meaning to emerge and flow freely back and forth. This kind of conversing (verbal and nonverbal) is at the heart of thick listening. For the spiritual care practitioner, words spoken by a client imply underlying feelings, values, concerns and a storyline of meaning derived from prior lived experience. Discovering the wholeness of the other requires that we loosen our grip on certainty and personal insight, yet remain attentive to our own inner movements and subtle perceptions.

In this regard, drawing on insights from Pope Paul VI, in his words, dialogue is an attitude and a method.[8] As an attitude, dialogue discloses rootedness and openness. Another word for rootedness is worldview. It's the "I" we bring to each spiritual care encounter. Our openness allows us to see people on their own terms rather than through our lenses only. As a method, dialogue is a form of spiritual communication characterized by four qualities: clarity, meekness, trust and prudence. Each of these qualities contributes to the shared language, respect, generosity of interpretation, reciprocity and mutuality of the conversation. The spiritual care professional seeks to learn *about* the other by learning *from* the other. The client's voice may be thin, weak or silent due to trauma, grief or preoccupation with immediate concerns, but the voice is there to be discerned and heard.

In 1986, American theologian, feminist activist and civil rights leader Nelle Morton, in reflecting on this kind of listening, coined the phrase "hearing each other to speech".[9] She argued that the process of finding one's voice is integral to having agency for oneself. Dialogue is a place for discerning the voice of the other with whom one is engaged. This discernment is empowering for both parties insofar as it evokes empathy and solidarity.

South American social activist and educator Paulo Freire, author of *Pedagogy of the Oppressed,*[10] contributes to the idea of dialogue and spiritual care. His approach to a dialogical relationship highlights five ideas he believed are important for dialogue to occur. First, dialogue can't exist without humility. This notion parallels the idea of meekness in Paul VI's approach. Both terms are intrinsic to the charity of dialogue and the truths it explains. Second, dialogue requires hope. It can't be carried out in a climate of hopelessness. Third, faith in people is an *a priori* requirement for dialogue. The dialogical person believes in other people even before meeting them face-to-face. Fourth, dialogue is founded on love. If I don't love the world, life and other people, I can't enter into dialogue. Lastly, dialogue can lead to reflective thinking and transformative action. To Freire, human existence is nourished by the truth with which men and women name the world, and by speaking truth aloud they transform the world. Interpathy and dialogue are essential tools for spiritual care practitioners as they seek I-Thou relating.

Empathy as a Bridge between Self and Other

In the previous section, empathy was discussed as a quality of response that goes beyond sympathy and, with the help of compassionate imagination, looks at an unfamiliar situation from another's perspective. In this section we explore definitions and theories about empathy insofar as they hold potential to broaden and expand a spiritual care practitioner's capacity for empathetic listening. Definitions of empathy fall into two main groups. Some focus on putting ourselves into someone else's shoes. Along this vein, the Oxford English Dictionary defines empathy as the ability to imagine and understand the thoughts, perspective and emotions of another person.

A second group rejects the notion of projecting and focuses on walking alongside and receiving another. Brené Brown captures this second category when she says empathy is "simply listening, holding space, withholding judgment, emotionally connecting, and communicating that incredibly healing message of 'You're not alone.'"[11] While the second group of definitions offers an alternative to the idea that one person can fully comprehend another, the first group of definitions tend to be most commonly used. Yet both categories invite further reflection for spiritual care practitioners as they aim at I-Thou relating.

This is because empathy is not without problems of excess. If I consider empathy to be about projecting myself into someone else's experience, I must notice when empathy becomes invasive. I mustn't march into another person's space or story. When empathetic caregivers transgress those boundaries, they may hear another say something like: "that's not quite it; not exactly; you're not getting it; you don't understand what I'm going through!" This reaction may signal that empathy has become intrusive and fails to comprehend the other in a way that that person accepts and finds credible. On the positive side, a projecting view of empathy is built on believing in the value of the other; it's an act of valuing the other and of trying to enter lovingly into that person's experience because of the significance attributed to them. To be genuine, empathy that projects conveys the sense that the one empathizing clearly values the other. But empathy must stop short of an incursion into another person's story and must leave that person's story intact.

The second group of definitions has a different set of problems that can be just as troubling. As mentioned, synonyms for empathy in this second group imply coming alongside rather than entering someone's story. This way of practicing empathy emphasizes *getting with* rather than *getting in* the story. From this perspective, empathy is meant to convey that the other person is credible and significant. Those who empathize using this second approach convey their valuing of the other through unlimited, undivided attention, with a focus on approachability and receptiveness. But this approach to empathy may tend to trap the other in the snare of attentiveness.

As an example, Bellous was describing empathy to a group of people. Suddenly, a woman in the group said "I get it!" She went on to tell her story to the group. Her adult daughter had been diagnosed with cancer. This mom was desperate to know how her girl was doing and phoned her every day to ask. Her daughter finally told her not to call. The mom was devastated and still carried a sense of rejection. But as she listened to excesses of empathy, she realized she'd gone to an extreme of attentiveness—one that gave her daughter no breathing room and had become a burden.

Receiving someone empathetically must stop short of entrapment due to excessive attention, which can become an aggressive holding on to those who want to be released from this overly attentive gaze. People need to be able to escape our attention when they need their own space to work things out personally. Excess isn't always easy to figure out. As we express empathy to someone, we may get hurt in return, unless we understand how our approach is shaped by our own stories. The mom in our example believed she needed to show her daughter she was constantly on her mind. Her daughter didn't need that degree of attention.

German philosopher Edith Stein offers a third perspective on empathy[12] that she analyzed during her struggle as a prisoner of the Nazis. As a student of German philosopher Edmund Husserl (founder of phenomenology) she focused on thought as embodied experience. Her view of empathy provides boundaries to keep empathy from over-stepping in entrapment or invasion. The primary notion she insists upon is a realization that the object of our contemplation is foreign to us. The term "foreign" is integral to understanding Stein's phenomenology of sensual and emotional empathy. For her, in every instance, empathy refers to acts in which we grasp foreign experience. As someone is empathetic, they aim to sense not only what's presented by another person, but also what's *behind* that self-presentation, i.e., a personal narrative that brought someone to this point by way of experiences about which the one empathizing doesn't know.

By foreign, we refer to experience that isn't ours because it's not happening directly to us. Something like it may have happened to us in the past, but this particular object of attention isn't happening to us in the same way it's happening to another person: e.g., at this time, in this way or at this point in their personal history. If we convey a sense that we believe what's presented to us—although it isn't our experience and we don't presume to understand it completely—we make an enormous contribution to the practice of empathy by our act of thick listening.

As a consequence of Stein's insight, empathy isn't just about a helping person's capacity for projecting into or coming alongside the other. It takes two people (at least) for empathetic engagement to occur. Both parties remain involved authentically if empathy is to be successful. A working definition for empathy that seems useful at this point is the following:

> A fully participatory empathetic act conveys that we're deeply understood and understand, that we feel safe with another, even though we've been exposed; that our experience makes sense to at least one other person; and hopefully, finally, makes sense to us as well, which lets us know that we're neither crazy nor alone.[13]

Empathy is a bridge that reaches from self to other and from other to self. It creates a sense of felt connection and underscores the spiritual nature of this engagement. Along with sympathy and interpathy, empathy furthers the important work of thick listening at thin moments.

Leaving the Familiar: Foundational Considerations

In this section, we establish *otherness* as an ordinary existential experience, which is its purview in spiritual care. Everyone is born a human being but we become human in the company of particular people who demonstrate what it's like to be human. All early learning is situated in particularity. This is the only way we learn how to be human; it's true for every one of us—we're born incomplete and dependent on others for survival. As a result, during the early years, we're enculturated. We equate being human with being like a particular group of people. Our aim is to fit into that social milieu. If we remain with those people over a life span (which is the case in traditional societies) we may not notice our humanity as an object for reflection; it's simply the air we breathe. This continuity shaped human history for a long time, but is no longer the case. Modern nations comprise diversity. Experiencing *otherness* is inevitable and, for many, is an attractive feature of life.

It's when people differ from us that we bring to consciousness our own mode of experiencing the world.[14] That is, *otherness* poses a challenge to the way we think things are or should be. As such, *otherness* opens a pathway to self-reflection by compelling us to consider how we think, feel and act in concrete situations where differences exist. While not universally true, it can be said that a person's initial experience of *otherness* occurs with leaving home, with leaving one's familiar setting. It may be an experience of staying over at a friend's house, going to summer camp, travelling to a foreign country, emigrating from one's homeland, serving a prison sentence, joining the military or entering a religious community. Let's take an example of going off to college and living in a dormitory.

When you arrive you realize you have a roommate who comes from a very different home setting. She doesn't do things the way you do. As you were growing up, your family valued carefully squeezing the toothpaste tube so that not a single bit of toothpaste was left when the tube was finished. Your father puts an elastic band around the bottom of the tube as he uses it up. Your mother has a pretty ceramic holder that winds the tube gradually. She never wastes any paste. You have your own ceramic toothpaste holder that you brought to college with you.

On the first morning, you see your roommate grab her toothpaste tube unceremoniously in the middle and squeeze it without any regard for conservation. You're appalled. Based on first impressions, you begin to see your roommate as sloppy. Your opinion of her falls daily. As you experience the first weeks in residence, you find her less and less attractive. You begin to disrespect her. You're not sure you can stay in the same room with her. If, at this point, you pause and notice your thinking, you could begin to sense the extent to which your images, assumptions and ideas about what it means to be a good person have been brought into play. For you, the use of toothpaste tubes has been a differentiating criterion about whether or not people are acceptable as human beings. But you had no idea you held that assumption while you were still at home.

What's going on? An image for worldviews is that of a web of meaning.[15] Worldviews are made up of threads, like a spider's web. To pull one thread is to put stress on others—or sometimes, on all of them. If you remain committed to your own view of the right way to use toothpaste tubes, and feel superior to your roommate, it's unlikely you'll be able to maintain this living arrangement peacefully.

While you remain her roommate, you have some options. One option is to approach your roommate from an I-It perspective. Perhaps you decide to gossip about her with other students. You mention her behavior to your parents. They join you in disdaining her. You actively avoid her outside your room and make a show of sitting far away from her in classes you take together. This scrutinizing, distancing and detached stance undermines human-to-human dialogue and may develop into abuse under the following conditions: e.g., if you don't engage in self-examination, if you remain certain that your way is the only right way, if you want to please your parents, or if you enjoy a following of people who think just like you do.

To the extent that you're unaware of what's driving your behavior toward your roommate, and fail to critically reflect on your thinking, your action may escalate until she finds it impossible to be comfortable around you. It's possible she could leave university, or worse, we know young people who commit suicide because of personal and social isolation characterized and instigated by behavior such as yours. And, when you analyze it, this is bullying. First, you're significant to your roommate because she has to spend time with you. Second, because of your proximity to her, you are able to keep her under surveillance, noticing everything she does. Finally, she may internalize your treatment as self-disdain or even self-hatred. She may engage in self-harm and self-sabotage.[16]

On the other hand, you could approach your roommate from an I-Thou stance. You could recognize the unity of being that exists between the two of you. Differences may exist but, when viewed within a framework of human-to-human communication, giving attention to the wholeness of self and other, you could begin to see your roommate as interesting, joyful and spontaneous. This option requires you to reflect on your way of doing things. You might ask yourself: Where did I learn to roll up my toothpaste tube so as not to waste any toothpaste? Is mine the only right way to handle a tube of toothpaste? How did I arrive at the theory that the way one uses a tube of toothpaste is tied to being good, tidy and careful? If I reflect fully on the situation, might I even come to explore Colgate's research on recyclable toothpaste tubes and replace my toothpaste with a tooth tablet?[17]

If you choose the option of I-Thou relating, your grip on toothpaste tubes comes into question, together with your ideas about being a good, tidy, careful person. To welcome your roommate, you must to some extent look at your grip on your own perspective. That's the challenge *otherness* presents—it can be uncomfortable. When familiar actions of one person meet unfamiliar actions of another, there's a jolt to our awareness, a triggering of feelings, possibly including anger or fear, and we can feel destabilized. There's also a sense of loss. How intentionally we stay with these feelings, and what we choose to do with our discomfort, has implications for spiritual care.

Human maturity requires us not only to challenge the familiar but also to reflect on the way we think, feel and act. It's in this sense we suggest that encountering *otherness* is an opportunity for self-reflection and may include loss. We may be unable to remain absolutely certain about our point of view at the end of meeting *another*. Of course, we can gain insight and take pleasure in the compassion we convey to someone else. It's not all loss. Thoughtfully reflecting on the discomfort diversity poses is part of listening to someone as they convey what is foreign to us and that we initially find strange.

A Framework for Exploring Differences

In responding to the topic of the differences we experience when we meet another, this chapter explores several large-scale patterns that contain insights to use as we listen to someone else. In a previous chapter, we looked at poverty as a global pattern among the working poor and provided research-based insights to assist in listening to faith stories of people who work in low-paying jobs. Those insights serve as interpretive clues to help a spiritual care professional recognize beliefs and assumptions in the other person's faith story, especially if the other person's story differs from the worldview of the practitioner.

The process of identifying global patterns, providing research-based insights, and drawing on these insights as interpretive clues will serve as our framework for exploring differences. Spiritual care education gives serious attention to reflective practice.[18] Reflective practice finds affinity with the research-based insights of Action Science, Double-Loop Learning, and Fourth Order Thinking, as described in chapter one. In particular, for our university student, mapping theories-in-use provided interpretive clues and allowed her to reflect on her way of handling toothpaste tubes. As spiritual care practitioners relate with others, mapping theories-in-use can bring to light the assumptions embedded in their contemplation of another who is viewed as a living human document.

As authors, when we use the phrase reflective practice, we also refer to the multidimensional contemplative mindfulness that undergirds our framework. When reflective practice encounters a *thin moment*, it recognizes a separation from what's ordinary or familiar. In chapter two we distinguish reflective from contemplative practice. At this point we want to fold them together and remind the reader that contemplative mindfulness transcends deliberative and reflective knowing by incorporating careful attention and quiet wondering. In a *thin moment*, the terrain of another person's worldview is collapsing and they are encountering distance from the familiar. There's an opening between worlds that's increasingly thin and transparent. It's like standing on the threshold between two worlds and perceiving them both, but they disrupt each other. Reflective spiritual care practice thrives on thick listening at thin moments. But in order to thrive, it's essential that thick listening be theoretically informed and consciously accessible.

Self-reflection is crucial to knowing the other. Thus, knowing one's theories-in-use is integral to optimal spiritual care. The College student's theories-in-use had to do with the connections between using toothpaste tubes and being a good, tidy person. Again, Action Science proposes that every action is theory driven. Just as the mother of a crying baby on the airplane from an earlier chapter could be asked the question "Can you tell me what theory you're using as you sit with your baby?" spiritual care practitioners may ask themselves questions such as "Can I say what theory I'm using as I sit with Mr. Jones (a resident living with dementia in long term care)?" Questions about theories-in-use spur CPE small group seminar discussions to help foster the safe and effective use of self in spiritual care professionals.

The framework we propose for cultivating multidimensional contemplative mindfulness, as a quality of thick listening in spiritual care practice, includes: (1) global patterns, (2) research-based insights, and (3) interpretive clues. First, there are global patterns, or large-scale recurrences of concepts, thoughts and actions that can be distinguished from other large-scale human patterns. Returning to the example of poverty among the working poor, we learned from Ehrenreich[19] that low paying work cultures affect people of all ethnicities in much the same way, and can be distinguished from middle class work environments. When a middle-class church member met Mary, the woman in a low paying job, and said "Why don't you just get another job?" she spoke out of ignorance about poverty. Her theory about jobs was informed by middle class experience. The impact of her ignorance was hurtful. Even though they were both churchgoers, differences in their work cultures clashed because the middle class woman didn't have access to either lived experience or research-based insights about what it's like to be part of the working poor.

Research-based theories shed light on experiential clash points that occur when people with dissimilar backgrounds meet, and provide those who are committed to thick listening a means for better appreciating the impact of global patterns on spiritual care practice. Cultivating curiosity when meeting differences can lead to identifying, understanding, appreciating and incorporating global patterns into one's spiritual assessment practices. This can lead to interventions that engage the *other* with sympathy, empathy and interpathy.

Research-based insights can be gained from what is immediately available, such as the directly observable data (DOD) discussed previously in the Ladder of Inference exercise (see Appendix #2). From these initial insights, knowledge of the other accrues through asking questions that are explored through scholarly inquiry derived from a variety of fields of study. This body of thought is a foundation for knowledge that informs spiritual care practice. It can build over a lifetime, and add depth to a practitioner's over all competence.

There are also interpretive clues derived from global patterns and research-based insights that play a role in fostering thick listening at thin moments and I-Thou relating. The term *clue* comes from a Middle English word, *clew*, meaning a ball of thread or yarn. In a classic Greek myth, a young Athenian hero named Theseus entered his Cretan enemy's Labyrinth, which was known to be inescapable. His purpose was to kill the Minotaur, a monster responsible for the death of many young Athenian boys. Before he entered, he received a ball of yarn from Ariadne (daughter of the king of Crete). Using the yarn, he tied one end of it to the Labyrinth's entrance, made his way to its center, slayed the Minotaur and retraced his steps to find the way out. We can think of following a global pattern in the same way that Theseus used his ball of yarn. Directly observable data can anchor us as we explore unfamiliar, and sometimes frightening, passageways into and out of a global pattern.

The word clue also suggests bits of evidence, like the breadcrumbs Hansel and Gretel threw down in the Grimm's fairy tale to help them get out of the dark forest where their parents abandoned them during a famine. In spiritual care, interpretive clues occur during relational engagement, at intersections of thought, as flashes of insight or points of understanding, so that practitioners ask themselves, should I go this way or that way, as I follow a faith story.

Conceptual knowledge interfaces with integrated personal, professional competence to build caring relationships. As they look for clues, spiritual care practitioners benefit from the study of hermeneutics, i.e., the theory and practice of interpretation, which is used to highlight principles for interpreting sacred texts. When it comes to interpreting a living human document as sacred text, there's both wit and wisdom to aligning the phrase 'a hermeneutics of' with words such as suspicion, generosity, agitation, disappointment, respect and curiosity, as a way to situate a patient or client within perspectives that are identified by using these expressions.[20] Drawing on the work of German philosopher Hans-Georg Gadamer, more will be said about hermeneutics in the chapter on Competencies.

Returning to the global pattern of poverty, one can imagine that every spiritual care practitioner has a theory about poverty arising from their lived experience. Examples of theories might be: poor people need my help; unemployed people are on welfare because they're just not trying; being poor is a simple life—I wish I had a simple life; poor people are strong and resourceful. It's also noteworthy that a theory, whether obvious or concealed, can express itself in everyday settings as well as during times of stress. Once again turning to the two churchgoers, when the middle-class woman asked Mary, "Why don't you just get another job?" it was a response that revealed her theory about poverty . Telling someone to get another job fails to notice the hermeneutic of disappointment within which Mary is living, and is blind to the systemic disappointments that attend someone who's caught in low-wage work cultures.

When spiritual care professionals link their learning about the global pattern of poverty, research-based insights about the working poor, including complexities related to earning a living wage, perpetual job insecurity, and health implications of particular types of work, they're equipped with a ball of yarn needed for I-Thou relating. For example, suppose they meet Mary on a hospital Orthopedics ward at a time when a disk in her back has ruptured. Benefits of research-based interpretive clues and spiritual care assessment processes come together in a comprehensive way. A practitioner can offer interventions to promote Mary's health that take full account of her situation. As a living human document, she's mindfully attended to and appreciated for her unique goodness within the context of a particular thin moment event.

Selecting Global Patterns to Connect the Twentieth and Twenty-First Centuries

Thus far, in approaching the topic of differences, we've described attitudes and tools to aid self as well as other awareness, such as I-Thou relating, thick listening at thin moments, interpathy, dialogue, and embodied empathy. Multidimensional contemplative mindfulness makes good use of these relational attitudes and tools. In addition, comprehending otherness is based on our tripartite framework that includes global patterns, research-based insights and interpretive clues. Our purpose now is to select three global patterns that contain insights to use as we listen to someone else in their *otherness*. Each pattern was identified through research and picks out interpretive clues. This approach seeks to equip spiritual care professionals with questions rather than answers. It's the questions that arise during spiritual care that guide meaningful relating and offer a sense of felt connection. In this regard, the words of Rainer Maria Rilke are poignant.

> Be patient toward all that is unsolved in your heart and try to love the questions themselves, like locked rooms and like books that are now written in a very foreign tongue. Do not now seek the answers, which cannot be given you because you would not be able to live them. And the point is, to live everything. Live the questions now. Perhaps you will then gradually, without noticing it, live along some distant day into the answer.[21]

Like the pattern of poverty among the working poor, global patterns are large-scale and worldwide. Each pattern carries tensions within it. For example, if we consider the COVID-19 pandemic as a global occurrence, and look at different responses to it around the world, we observe a pattern in China we might compare to a pattern observed in the United States. While there's a great deal of diversity in each of these countries, in China, collective responsibility is paramount. In the United States, individual rights and personal freedoms are central. The history of each country contributes to the contrast in their approaches to the virus. In part, historical realities create a web of meaning in which global patterns find their expression and make their social and political impacts.

Since there's no way to analyze the abundance of large-scale patterns available for shared reflection, the chapter focuses on three deep and ongoing differences: western individualism, western mid-twentieth century white female experience and strong group patterns. As authors, we selected global patterns with which we're familiar. In addition, as women born in the twentieth century and living in the twenty-first, we're aware that writing authentically calls us to talk about what we know from experience so we can identify pertinent research-based insights and interpretive clues within these patterns.

We acknowledge and accept who we are as an aspect of exploring otherness. We invite our readers to do the same. It's only by authentically being who we are—in age, gender, ability, race, faith tradition, culture, and so much more—that we can truly "meet" in I-Thou relating. Our purpose is to note differences within the selected global patterns from our vantage point. From that place, the patterns offer and amplify a number of themes developed in the book, such as an overview of human development, the role of worldview in critical self-reflection and the centrality of relationships. All of these topics are intimately connected to spiritual care practice.

The Big Picture

Below, in Table 1, readers find an overview of the three global patterns we discuss in the rest of the chapter. Along with each pattern, there are references to a primary body of knowledge drawn upon for research-based insights (endnotes include a wider range of sources). Lastly, there are interpretive clues that show up in each pattern, as threads of evidence to follow during the practice of spiritual care. While it's natural to treat each pattern sequentially, in a linear manner, we invite a different approach. Imagine if you will, a three-stranded braid interlacing the global patterns, insights and clues. All three patterns are interconnected, as will become clearer in the pages that follow.

Table 1—Global Pattens, Insights and Clues

Global Pattern	Research-based Insights	Interpretive Clues
Western Individualism	E. Erikson (1950/1963)	Congruence: inner life and outward expression; singularity; self-made man;
Mid-twentieth century white western women in their caught betweenness as a locus of tension due to inaccessible individualism and unavailable dyadic membership	C. Gilligan (1982)	Voice; embodied knowing;[22] public/domestic dissonance; ambivalence;[23] identity tension;
Strong group dyadic membership	M. Douglas (1970)	'You are because we are' (ubuntu); family-based identity; communal/public identity

American psychologist Erik Erikson, American ethicist and psychologist Carol Gilligan, and American anthropologist Mary Douglas,[24] provide primary data for these three global patterns, all of which point to different ways of thinking about what it means to be human. While there are differences among them, we offer ways of explaining them that pick out their interfaces as well. Our aim is to explain *otherness* (social uniqueness) while prizing our common humanity.

Let's look first at the humanity that unites the human tribe. Douglas begins her search into patterned ways people express themselves by positing that most "symbolic behavior must work through the human body" and that, since every human being has one, we can compare the symbolic use of the body to help identify patterned behavior that resides in different cultural settings. If this point weren't true, we would never be able to make sense of one another when we travel. As outlined in the chapter, Made for Relationship, there are numerous linkages among human beings. In terms of the differences and comparisons that show up between these global patterns, we give an initial overview:

- Erikson provides a classic individualistic pattern in which what matters is demonstrating congruence between one's inner life and its outward expression, and an inner driven initiative that consistently demonstrates personal autonomy.
- Feminist perspectives are less individualistic and more ambivalent than Erikson's model implies and autonomy is constructed on a different body experience.
- Strong group members differ to a great degree from the inner/outer congruence anticipated in the mature development Erikson outlines. Individualism isn't seen as a human good; living congruently between a singular inner world and its outward expression doesn't capture core values of the strong group global pattern; private, personal autonomy isn't seen as a cultural value.

To offer interpretive clues for understanding these global patterns, we use some of Erikson's theories as a place to start. Our aim is to orient thinking about cultural, social, racial and gendered differences that show up as we interact with others. We build implications of individualism on his theoretical framework. His underlying assumption is that what we experience in our early years and adolescence informs the rest of our lives, as the rings of a tree metaphor conveys. His ages, themes and key questions are excellent starting points for allowing people to identify existential and spiritual issues at the heart of spiritual care practice, from the perspective of individualism.[25]

As one example, in the chapter on Human Development, we note Erikson's statement that girls and boys differ when it comes to how they initiate action and practice autonomy—one moves toward conquest, the other aims to attract. At that point, we said that, if his assertions were right, girls will focus on relationships. But we first have to ask whether Erikson's statement is descriptive (he simply records his observations) or prescriptive (he asserts what should happen). Generally, as authors, we think he's descriptive but we're well aware of people (including some women) who read descriptions such as his as prescriptions for how 'good' women should act.

Feminism grew in the mid-twentieth century to counter prescriptions about what women's lives should be like.[26] Through her research, Gilligan (b. 1936) identified gaps in how we typically understand girls and women. She offered a different perspective for female moral development in her best-known work, *In a Different Voice*. In that book, she asserts that girls focus on community and ethical relationships and attend to certain subject-object problems in ethics in a manner that differs from some implications of male development. While her book is about the ways women differ from men, it's important to observe that her research supports Erikson's observation about girls. If Erikson is right, girls focus on relationships; Gilligan's research shows that girls focus on relationships.

However, we must be clear that Erikson and Gilligan work from different points of view as they make their assessments. While both are psychologists, Gilligan is concerned with moral formation and framing a female outlook on it. In this chapter, moral refers to thinking, feeling and acting that surrounds the question of how one person should treat another and how people ought to treat themselves.

Erikson maps out personal, social and institutional influences that children face, and gain support from (or not), as they grow up. Gilligan asks what girls and women care about as they attend to others and themselves. Her research builds on, and contrasts with, the dominant moral framework of her time—Lawrence Kohlberg's moral development model.[27] Kohlberg built his model on research he carried out with 84 boys over a 20-year period.[28] Gilligan studied girls. In comparing the three global patterns, perhaps it's fair to say that Erikson describes what we go through and Gilligan/Kohlberg address how we respond to what's happening, as we make decisions about how to think, feel and act toward others and ourselves. It's important to note that these models have individualistic assumptions at the core. Erikson and Kohlberg support individualism and in Gilligan's case individualism shows up as a problem.

As we reflect on Erikson's approach, spiritual care practitioners can gain insight into what clients and patients may think, feel and do about the freedom and constraint they believe should characterize their lives. Understanding someone's sense of personal freedom to do or not do whatever one wants and needs is foundational to assessment in spiritual care. Gilligan began her book by outlining three core assumptions:

- The way people talk about their lives is significant.
- The language they use matters.
- The connections they make reveal the world as they see it and describe their impressions of the setting in which they're choosing to act.[29]

These core assumptions are similar to those spiritual care practitioners rely on as they listen thickly to those they meet. Gilligan compared her research to Kohlberg's, which he built on what he called an ethic of rights, in which individualism is primary, as is separating oneself from others as a way to maintain congruence between one's inner life and its outward expression. Gilligan's research constructed what she called an ethic of care based on a sense of responsibility within relationships, which also has making and keeping human connections as its goal.

These are significant differences, which isn't to say male and female ethics have nothing to say to each other. Yet, it's true that, in terms of them, justice implies that people are impartial benevolent observers and care implies that people are relational benevolent participants. For justice, a sense of harm is present when there's objective unfairness; for care, a sense of harm is present when there's subjective hurt. Listening to some of these assumptions in a client's faith story will offer insight into the choices people have made in the past and the moral values they believe are the principles that should guide their action.

Tensions Among Identities

The next sections pick out the three global patterns we choose to describe and the inherent tensions among races, cultures and genders. In this book, we focus on connecting the personal and the social to name how human beings try to be true to themselves and also well integrated with others. At this point, we look at otherness by focusing on the social aspect of difference. Our university students' example occurred between two white, Canadian women who achieved university entrance status. They had a lot in common. They both fit into a university setting. It was the difference between personal and family cultures that caused their difficulty. Based on our big picture chart, we explore patterns of individualism, white western female experience and strong group dyadic membership, but the main comparison is between the first and third patterns. We chose the middle pattern to point to the ambivalence conveyed in the expression *caught betweenness*—typified in bodies that don't fit the social image of a given culture, e.g., female bodies in a male dominated world, or those who are black skinned when white skin is the privileged social physicality.

In the first chapter of the book, there's a section on forming a worldview. In that section, we describe the inherited and personal content that shapes each person's picture of the world. We referred to French sociologist, philosopher, anthropologist and public intellectual Pierre Bourdieu (1930-2002). He observed that each person carries within a condensed map of the social body as well as content arising from personal experience.[30] Inherited content echoes dominant social preferences. Bourdieu expands his observation to relate what happens if people don't fit the dominant image. He grew up in a working class French environment. When he won a place in an elite French university, he saw in himself significant embodied differences that could have prevented him from being successful. Teachers and students read his otherness as a deficit. Based on his experience, he framed a theory about mismatches between the social body and the personal body. He summarized by saying that, if people's bodies (including values that attach to them) fail to resemble the privileged social body (and its preferences), they find it hard to succeed.

He gives an example of embodied mismatches. As a working class man, he spoke with what's called a big mouth—his mouth was very active as he spoke. Men in the elite university followed an aristocratic pattern of speaking with a small mouth—they pronounced words with very little mouth movement. Bourdieu realized that, if he wanted to succeed, he had to speak with a small mouth in order to convey his competence. In that setting, he learned to do just that. However, this was a double loss for him because, in his working class culture, it was women who spoke with a small mouth. In order to fit in, he compromised his working class maleness. However, he was at least able to make the shift. He was able to steer his behaviour in the direction of conformity. During his life, he became the most widely read public intellectual in France. His academic books were so popular they were sold in supermarkets.[31] Unlike Bourdieu's accommodation to privileged French culture, in Minneapolis, George Floyd was unable to change the colour of his skin to save himself from being killed by police. His murder fuelled the Black Lives Matter movement that erupted all over the globe in 2020. Our freedom to fit in and be recognized by the powers that be is limited by conditions, such as skin colour and gender, that for most of us, we simply can't change.

We chose western twentieth century white female experience as a third pattern—a place of caught betweenness with which we can identify—because women often exist in individualistic contexts where they find it hard or impossible to gain equal recognition for the values they hold. As a consequence, it can be difficult to flourish unless they deny or reject aspects of themselves. This sense of not being recognized as having equal value to the dominant culture is not exclusive to western white females.

We have another reason for including the third pattern. White western women are caught between an embodied way of being and the global pattern of radical individualism. Consequently, Bourdieu's option to accommodate isn't open to them. He adapted his way of speaking, but his body conformed to the elite culture. Women don't have that option. Like black skin in a white culture, most women inevitably show up as female and are linked through their labour.[32] Globally, most women still share responsibility for unpaid domestic labour and the birthing and care of small children. In the context of western individualism this difference can dis-privilege them.

Difference matters to spiritual care. Practitioners who listen to the clues inherent in these global patterns can more accurately perceive and understand the meaning people make of their obligations and responsibility to others and to themselves. Within the different patterns, and their embodied experiences, a person's reasons for doing one thing rather than another gains contextual meaning and relative importance or unimportance. However, neither individualism nor caught betweenness can explain the pattern of strong group dyadic membership. That being said, as we point out later, may be a bridge between individualism and strong group cultures.

Individualism

With this global pattern, the unit of social analysis is a singular individual. The emphasis is on living from the inside and living autonomously. Autonomy is the freedom and right to choose the rules one intends to live by, from within an environment of rules that are conveyed by family and culture as a person grows up (inherited worldview content). In this pattern, experience is defined in terms of self-conscious experience, i.e., I sense myself and I sense myself as an object of other people's perceptions of me. In being self-consciously aware, an individual is thought of as being in control of self-perceptions, so that individuals believe: I am what I think I am; this awareness implies the existence of an inner and outer self.

In this global pattern, an individual is thought of as capable of independent thinking and action, self-awareness, self-control, personal responsibility and self-directedness. If anything goes wrong with an individual life, the problem is found in one's personal history. Ultimately, individuals must go back and fix what's wrong if they want to be well. In addition, individualism insists that, because of the way people are constituted as unique and separate beings, individuals are held responsible for what they do, an assumption that the Western justice system relies on for meting out penalties and punishment for wrongdoing.

From the perspective of individualism, the world is made up of other people who are like me, who are potentially like me, who are not yet like me, or who are less than me. Ideally though, all other people are just like me in that they have the ability to accomplish whatever they set their minds to do. The belief in equality rests on the idea that individuals are equally able to pursue personal interests, but only if they're ambitious enough. Individuals are the determiners of their own destiny. If people fail, it's because they didn't try. People control their own aspirations. Individual interests are conceived as material necessities plus the various goods each person feels worth having in life. In general, individual interests are essentially material, but other values may be taken into account—still, they're personal, private and individually chosen. Since material interests may be scarce, in getting what an individual wants and needs, each one is in competition with all other individuals who also intend to get what they want and need.

Individuals are essentially discrete, complete, separate units who pursue self-fulfilment in an unfriendly, competitive social environment. The metaphor of economic exchange often typifies an individualistic approach to relationships. Each person's identity is located in an internal, private space bounded by a psychophysical entity—a mind/body. In that internal space, I experience only my own mind/memories, aspirations, desires, hopes and body. I only implies 'I'. I'm my own witness and the sole judge of my behaviour. The identity question here is *who am I*. An extreme form of relational isolation made possible by individualism is captured in the attitude that 'what's going on in you has nothing to do with me'.

Figure 5 - Male inner and outer Me

A typical white western perspective, with its male and female counterparts, lies at the heart of individualism's psychological/moral/ethical ways of thinking and acting. If we recall Erikson's framework, and lay Kohlberg's ethic of justice over those bones (Kohlberg's exclusively male research invites

Figure 5 - Male inner and outer life

the use of male pronouns here), at the center of western ways of being, there's a solitary individual who lives congruently between his inner life and its outward expression. He's able to walk away from commitments that no longer support his autonomy. He tries to be courageous and unencumbered by the demands and expectations of others—he does his own thing and can sing the song "I Did it My Way".

Being alone at the top of an organization is often an image that encapsulates the goal of individualism, and which expresses itself as achieving singularity. We realize that the solitary male may not be integral to Erikson, but support for this global pattern is evident in his description of human development, in which he asserts that maturity is about being true to oneself.

The literary form of the novel is important in understanding this individualistic interior living space. From one view, individualism emerged between about 1050 and 1200 in response to a sense of injustice inherent in harsh treatment that students experienced at the hands of their teachers in religious communities.[33] After that period, the notion of the individual tended to slip back into mainstream family systems in the Middle Ages. It re-emerged in Shakespeare's writing[34] in the 1600s, and again in Jean-Jacques Rousseau's 1700s novels, *Emile* and *Sophie*, and in his other political writing, e.g., *The Social Contract.*

In the mid-1900s, individualism typified youthful student protests in the U. S. and elsewhere in Europe and Canada. Perhaps it's already clear to readers that extreme individualism only works well for very few—those who are wealthy, unencumbered by commitments to other people and the planet, and who hold an elite status in which they can buy or coerce others to serve their interests on the strength of their wealth and power. For the rest of us, individualism is a seductive, elusive, treacherous myth. It's one that the Coronavirus in the 2020s exposed for its ideological failure to create a broad social consensus that was capable of balancing the personal and the social.

Strong Group Dyadic Members

Let's look at an example of strong group dyadic membership. Tony is a young man whose connection to family is fundamental to his reason for living and his sense of identity. At sixteen, he was devastated when a young cousin died in an automobile accident in the car he was driving. It threw his life into chaos. In strong group cultures, belonging to extended family is a person's most important identity marker. Tony's identity is rooted in whatever his extended family says it is. As a result of being shunned by the larger family, support and loyalty from his nuclear family couldn't fully compensate for his loss. Even though his parents and siblings stood by him, the loss of connection to uncles, aunts, grandparents and cousins brought his well being to a halt after the accident. For Tony, life is family. His loss of extended family support would have impacted his nuclear family negatively as well. Tony isn't an individual in the sense described in previous paragraphs. Something else is going on. He exemplifies strong group dyadic membership and his identity suffers when extended family connections seem irreparably ruptured.

Given the dynamics of individualism that lives at the heart of western psychological practices that show up in Erikson, Kohlberg and are questioned in Gilligan, there's at least a thread of continuity among these three theorists as they discuss human development, moral/ethical formation and empathy. By contrast, in this section, we explore a narrative about what it means to be human that characterizes what are called strong group cultures, which may comprise 70% to 80% of the world's populations.

Strong group cultures organize around complex social values, including what's called honor-shame. But shame functions differently in strong group narratives than it does in Erikson's *second age*, which he calls autonomy versus shame and doubt. One way to understand cultural tensions is to unpack honor-shame systems that typify strong group membership. This global pattern forms around a cultural/religious ethos that puts family at the core of social life. From its centrality, family shapes social interactions by relying on concepts such as filial piety and intergenerational veneration, and assumes that family solidarity is a person's most vital link to what it means to be human.

In strong group cultures, the basic unit of social analysis is the dyad, which implies that to be human is always to be joined to others. The term dyadic describes a person who's linked with at least one other social unit, in particular, an extended family. Each person is part of an undifferentiated family ego mass. During the dismantling of apartheid in South Africa in the early 1990s, the word "ubuntu" was frequently used to communicate a collective sense of South African identity. It's a concept that means a person is a person through other members; I am because you are; you are because we are. Without one's group, one ceases to be. Dyadic members need others to confirm and affirm who they are. Personal identity is shaped by internalizing social identity, an undertaking they hold to be necessary to someone's well being. The focus of moral activity is directed towards living up to demands and expectations of others who have power to bestow or withhold social honour. Coherence is an issue for strong group members, but that coherence isn't between one's inner and outer self; it's between the actions of each member and the public or social identity of the group.

In this global pattern, conscience literally refers to people's sensitive attention to the public group image, an identity that's also strongly gendered. Exercising conscience means aligning personal behaviour and self-assessment with the public image. Conscience is the internalization of what others say about, do to and think about us, since other members play the role of witness and judge as they evaluate every member's behaviour. For a strong group member, there's nothing on the inside that doesn't register on the outside. Emotional language is expressed in surface terms; e.g., anger is a gesture.[35] For dyadic members, the world is whole—

material and spiritual are unified—these dimensions freely communicate with and influence each other.[36]

In dyadic membership the identity question is *who do you say that I am*. Everyone is personal, but no one is individual: personal-ness is expressed by one's bodily presence, each one is unique, but *I* always implies *We*.[37] Even though people experience themselves as whole in relation to others, the personal emphatically depends on group embeddedness. For example, in the book, *I Rigoberta Menchu*, an Indigenous Guatemalan feminist and social activist wrote about her experience in terms of the strong group membership pattern that we're describing. In this light, all her people are family.[38] If a young Guatemalan man dies at the hands of the injustice she fought against, it's her brother who's died. Her connection to all Guatemalans is a social reality.

If individuals are constituted psychologically, strong group members are constituted sociologically. While an individual lives from the inside, the living space for strong group members is located between the surface of their outward psychophysical being and the bonds of attachment that connect each member to all others. With individualism, identity is private; with dyadic membership, identity is public. As a consequence, members don't go through the same stages of ego formation that are typical of Western individuals. Carol Gilligan, as one example, observed that women don't appear to go through these stages of development either. Her work resembles some of the distinctions made between individualism on one hand and dyadic membership on the other. We explore this point in the following section.

For the present, it's important to observe that extreme forms of strong group membership may have debilitating outcomes at the level of the personal.[39] News reports coming out of Wuhan, China early in the COVID-19 pandemic, showed families boarded into their apartments because they contracted the virus. Likewise, extreme forms of individualism have disastrous outcomes at the level of the social. Again referring to COVID-19, a belief in personal freedom and individual rights as rationale for refusing to wear masks and maintain physical distance had significant impacts on viral transmission rates and overall case numbers in the United States. In many ways, COVID-19 stands as a compelling example of the contrast between individualism and strong group membership as we've seen extreme expressions of the personal on the one hand and the social on the other. Extreme forms of the two global patterns sever the bond between the personal and the social. Our intention throughout this book is to identify ways of integrating the personal and the social in each human being.

Whether one is an individual or strong group member, it's possible to feel that one fits in if, in the one instance one conforms to the group, and in the other, one emphasizes self-sufficiency and has personal success due to having the requisite social value. But what if these two identities compete with one another for a particular person? If identities compete (e.g., someone is strong group in an individualistic culture) people experience themselves as a minority, which seldom refers as much to numbers as to differences between the ways of being in these two patterns. As mentioned, individualism works for a small number of people but its ideological global impact is immense, and both patterns can shift into extremes.

In the context of spiritual care, the touchpoints *otherness* creates may be conveyed through the faith story someone tells that communicates they have little or no social value due to these competing identities. For example, an Indigenous woman injured in a motor vehicle accident while passing through a large city on her way home after gathering medicine herbs at a sacred location miles away, speaks of feeling cut off from her community; isolated among caring strangers. The sense of isolation adds a feeling of nonexistent to the woman's health crisis. Her knowledge keeping and healing role in her Indigenous community is not recognized or valued in the urban hospital setting where she is receiving treatment. If identities compete, they may eventually cancel each other out. Both identities must enjoy social value if people are to flourish. If, during her hospital stay, the Indigenous woman doesn't enjoy social value for being Indigenous or for being a respected knowledge keeper, she is neither a self-sufficient individual nor a member of a valued community. She can seldom hide her socially unwelcome identities—as Bourdieu was able to do. It's not unusual for spiritual care practitioners to listen to faith stories of those trapped between two global patterns such that personal identity amounts to zero, and a wound of non-existence is embedded within a thin moment experience—a uniquely real form of spiritual distress.

The Indigenous woman's distress is captured by the term *Intersectionality*, a word coined in 1989 by Kimberlé Crenshaw.[40] She's a civil rights advocate and professor at UCLA School of Law and Columbia Law School. Crenshaw examined the story of a black woman who sought justice when she was denied a promotion at her workplace. The woman was a single parent and wanted to improve her family's life circumstances. She didn't get the promotion. She claimed the decision was discriminatory. She took her complaint to court, but it was thrown out.

As Crenshaw examined her case, she noted that the complainant was both black and female. In the company where she worked, all women employees were white and all black employees were men. The judge decided that, since she had two competing identities—i.e., she was a woman, like the advantaged white employees, and black, like the advantaged men employees—he would be granting her a double advantage if she got the promotion, so he dismissed her case. As Crenshaw notes, her two competing identities gave her no advantage at all; at their point of intersection, they cancelled each other out. Another author who examined minority experience, Geoffrey Dench[41] also described this identity problem. In his analysis, most frequently, when minority people have two identities, a subtraction takes place; if they cancel each other out, a person is left with nothing. This black woman was caught between two identities and was unable to achieve her personal and family goals.

Insofar as personal-professional identity is an intentionally studied topic in the education of spiritual care professionals, it's important for practitioners to be aware of a broad range of complexities related to identity. Knowing about the theories that inform the global patterns of individualism and strong group dyadic membership is vital, as is understanding the intricacies of competing identities, the discriminatory subtleties of intersectionality, and the ways in which social valuations affect health and human flourishing.

Caught Between and Standing on a Threshold

Early in this chapter, we describe how people learn to be human in the company of particular people who demonstrate what it's like to be human. This slow process of primary socialization is a universal phenomenon. During our early years we equate being human with being like a particular group of people. One's family of origin is the primary unit of belonging. However, as a consequence of the ubiquity of individualism, many people from strong group cultures exist in individualistic settings, and experience their social status as *caught betweenness*. They may be drawn toward an inaccessible individualism and at the same time lose the social value of their dyadic membership. If people are drawn forcibly by two competing identities that don't blend, they may come to feel as if they live nowhere as a whole self.[42] It's to these people we turn as we explore the third global pattern, mid-twentieth century white western women who experience an ambivalence that they share with other cultural groups.

Caught betweenness is felt socially. As Black activist Franz Fanon put it, a young black boy is at home inside his house but the moment he steps outside of it, he's a misfit.[43] Dissonance is the result of misalignment between primary and secondary socialization. The ambivalence created by dual identities operating in this way may leave people with a deep, inescapable sense that they belong nowhere. In general, we try to fit in with what's seen as important in cultural or sub-cultural settings. But environments aren't always friendly. For example, one seminary student reflects on her environment:

> As a woman and a Christian, there have been times in my life when I have felt disempowered on account of the gap between [the personal and social realities I face]. I sometimes experience the socio-cultural world of my church as androcentric and do not always feel like I 'fit' as a result. For example, it seems to me that the popular interpretation of sin as pride, wanting to be like God, self-righteousness, doesn't apply equally to women as to men. I experience myself differently. My failure and separation from God come about in the form of self-denial (food, sleep), lack of self-confidence, insufficient self-esteem, etc. I experience sin as an undervaluing of myself more than as an attempt to be like God. An androcentric definition of sin can disempower women by contributing to their failure or inability to identify and combat sin in their own lives.[44]

This woman finds it difficult to fit into Christian community due to a tendency to harm herself by thinking she has little value.

While we aren't saying only men succumb to spiritual pride and only women suffer low self-esteem, it's important to see that gender affects people's well being when it comes to feeling a sense of fit in social settings. But the issue of spiritual well-being isn't simply based on a feeling of fit, although it's essential. It entails an ability to find life meaningful and live it fully—once again, a goal Erikson proposed—so that aging is a time to see one's life as the only life that one could have lived, and to enjoy a sense of life satisfaction.

In this book, we operate on Freud's assertion that a fully human life encompasses love and work. At this point, for many people, western expectations have elaborated the notion of a fully human life to say that such a life enjoys meaningful work and relationally satisfying love. As American educator and psychologist Robert Kegan observed, these expectations get us in over our heads.[45] The social and emotional skills needed to manage work and love in the twenty-first century take us to a new level of consciousness that requires us to engage in mindful, contemplative reflection on our lives and on our impact on others.[46] We have to think about what we're thinking about. We need to ask ourselves whether the ways we act continue to be the ways we will choose to act in the future, as we consider our influence on other people and on ourselves. In spiritual care professional practice, this work of thinking about what we're thinking about is integral to one's effectiveness and overall competence. The invitation, and challenge, is to know ourselves well enough to accompany others as 'other'. To live our deepest joys, we must be willing to live the tensions of I-Thou relational learning.

In the third global pattern, focusing on twentieth century western white women coping within an individualistic milieu, the ambivalence inherent in their lives led to a level of domestic dissatisfaction that created the largest degree of change in family life the West has experienced in the last several hundred years. How did this change come about?

During the 1800s and 1900s, with consideration given to racial and ethnic variance, white western women lived in households where only men could work in public spaces. The rural and urban economies of pre-industrial communities relied on gender-based divisions of labor in which women provided unpaid domestic labor. The household contribution of wives and daughters to the production of goods and services was vital. It was meaningful work. With the Industrial Revolution, significant aspects of domestic productivity gradually left the home. Factories took over processes that women had carried out for centuries. We aren't saying this was a bad shift, but it left open the question of how women would find meaningful labor as they also tried to preserve their domestic roles and relationships. Further, two World Wars recruited women from the home to work for the war effort. In those public spaces, women experienced how good they were at what they did. It can be said that many women have never returned exclusively to domestic work since that time.

While it's a far more complex and nuanced topic than the limits of this chapter allow, overall, women's lives transformed dramatically in the last century. Subsequently, feminist consciousness has produced a wealth of literature, fueled significant political movements, and given rise to multiple racial and ethnic distinctions within women's narratives. Examples of women caught between individualism and strong group cultures can be found in the writing of female[47] and male[48] authors. In visual media, one has only to watch the popular historical television drama *Downton Abbey*, or see the movie *Hidden Figures*, to get a sense of the scope and complexity of these changes.[49]

Figure 6 - Female inner and outer life

Returning to Gilligan's work and reflecting on Erikson's assertion about girls, white western female perspectives include an image of women who care for others, and are therefore unable to walk away from their commitments, as long as their relationships are central to them. In this sense, they don't experience autonomy the same way as an unencumbered individual would. If we affirm Freud's assertion that a fully human life includes love and work, we see that, in the same way that individualism may spur people to pursue their own work at the expense of relationships, women may let caring for others take over all their interest and effort and not pursue work for its own sake. Women may make relationships their work, in the excessive way the mother did by calling her daughter every day to check with her because of the young woman's cancer diagnosis.

Further, whether or not a woman actually bears children, she has that capacity, which may seem inevitable during primary socialization. As a result, if we apply western individualism to women in order to depict their moral responsibility and maturity, it simply doesn't work. Every woman houses within herself not only an inner individual female self that's supposed to be congruent with its outward expression, but also a life-giving capability that binds her to the labor and life experience of all women. These two identities compete for attention. She's caught between them. She finds living as an unencumbered individual to be impossible but she doesn't benefit from solidarity shared with other white western females. So what can be learned from this third global pattern? What are its implications for spiritual care as I-Thou relating and thick listening at thin moments?

What if we look at *caught betweenness* with fresh eyes? What if we choose to think of western individualism and strong group membership dialectically? We wrote earlier that in neither world do people with competing identities find a complete, whole sense of self—unless both of their identities enjoy social value. If the social world bestows value on both identities (in this case white western women, but it could also be another caught between social entity), they might amount to one whole and satisfying life as a third option. Reflecting on both identities, and encouraging them to interact with one another, has the potential to transform *caught betweenness* into a type of liminality, i.e., a position that values both/and rather than either/or—as occurs when a person stands on a threshold between two large rooms and regards each as welcoming and valid. In this regard, we draw on the work of Brian P. Hall, who, in his book *The Genesis Effect: Personal and Organizational Transformations* writes

> Dialectical simply means two entities talking to each other. I may give a point of view on what I feel family means. My wife may have another view, and together we may come up with a third and different understanding that satisfies both of us. This is the basis of dialectical discussion or reasoning. It seems that values do the same thing. Two values interact to form a third.[50]

If we simply stay on opposing sides, there's polarization (dichotomous dualism). But it's possible to establish liminal contexts, which encourage dialectical communication inclusive of more than either identity. The dialectical works at points of liminality. It invites a conversation among the global patterns discussed in this chapter. Using a dialectical approach is a personal and social accomplishment; it's also a necessity in the twenty-first century.

What we choose to do in liminal spaces is important to the future. Human beings are capable of intentionally steering their behavior in a specific direction. Earlier we referred to the work of William Isaacs, who sees dialogue as thinking together in relationship, i.e., from a center rather than opposite sides so that shared meaning may emerge. Those who experience identity tension can meet at intersections of society where the terrain is uncharted, where social valuations are dynamic and not rigid. While there are people who cancel out the identities of the other, as did the judge in the black woman's case, there are those who are openly dialectical. Tensions can create fertile places for meaning making.

Spiritual care practitioners regularly enter liminal spaces as they meet people who are experiencing thin moments of loss, trauma, upheaval, and disorientation. The phrase *thin moment* suggests liminality. As worlds come together at a threshold, there's a lot that's happening at the same time. Identity boundaries may collapse. Someone may cross from wife to widow, active soldier to amputee, son or daughter to orphan. If tensions are fertile places, they're also places for thick listening at thin moments and I-Thou relating. This is essential work for spiritual care.

To summarize, the ideal of a solitary individual is hard to apply to women—which isn't to say women can't choose a singular life, if that's what they find meaningful and important. But pursuing this life is a different quest for them. Women experience ambivalence. Erikson's and Gilligan's research identifies a female tendency to maintain relationships at the expense of other considerations and this tendency may apply to women generally, not simply to mothers. Most western white women are pulled in two competing, powerful directions: toward themselves and meaningful work, and toward others and responsibility to care for them. This inner competition is difficult to avoid[51] and hard to resolve.

From a different point of view, these women may epitomize an opportunity to prize the personal as well as the social, but they must come to terms with this inherent tension in order to do so. This is a threshold women stand on in the twenty-first century, a model of liminality that upholds diversity not only of gender but also faith or race. What we choose to do in this liminal space depends on our willingness and ability to rethink our conceptions, to engage in conceptual learning and to practice living a renewed sense of what life requires. Social value and dialectical reason are keys to a successful resolution of competing identities. Returning to the work of Brian Hall, he says

> The value, whether in the written language or spoken word, is the tip of an iceberg... behind the dialectic there is an inner imaging and re-imaging process that is actually re-organizing the person's world view [sic] and all his or her consequent behavior. [One's] values are simply external indicators of this process.[52]

We can make friends with the inherited content in our worldview; we can come to terms with our dual identities, but we need social recognition and social value in order to do so.[53]

Valuing the broad spectrum of the third global pattern we've been discussing is integral to healthy spiritual care. Consider for a moment how far a solitary individual has to move into liminality in order to recognize the reality of ambivalence experienced by those who live in caught between places. A solitary, unencumbered individual finds it difficult to understand the limits of freedom implicit in living relationally with others, let alone dyadic membership. As spiritual care practitioners listen to faith stories, and unpack images, assumptions and values born of cultural, social, gendered and racial differences, they have opportunities to apply research-based clues about the three global patterns to these stories. Likewise, with social value and dialectical reasoning, they can offer healing to broken hopes and ameliorate confusion, anger and hopelessness that might accompany someone's inability to fit into the complex milieu of twenty-first century society.

Competition or Cosmopolitanism

Is it possible to approach *otherness* by embracing our own worldviews while remaining open to the worldviews of others? Consider our College student. Must she throw away her toothpaste tube to make the other student more comfortable? Does one student need to change completely, whichever one it is? What needs to change? What doesn't need to change? How do people who are trapped in competitive ambivalence treat their own way of being in the context of individualism and its infusion into so many of the ways we think, act, plan and practice life?

Moral theorist Kwame Anthony Appiah offers an antidote to competitive tendencies within *otherness* in his concept of Cosmopolitanism. His approach is woven together using two threads of thought. One thought is that we have obligations to others that stretch beyond kith and kin, and anchors citizenship. We share a common humanity that can't be set aside to secure private interests. The second thought is that this obligation isn't meant to neutralize important particular values, beliefs and ways of life.[54] As he uses the term, cosmopolitanism is a response to a need to live together in local and global realities and offers support to an attempt to be in relationship with other people who differ from us.

To Appiah, communal obligation derives from the thread of common humanity that unites the human tribe. Respect for difference arises from commitments, values, practices and concerns that people take on and that shape their personal worldviews. Cosmopolitan people are world citizens and citizens of their own hometowns, and are committed to those particular people who taught them to be human in the first place.

The approach Appiah promotes is more of an attitude than a solution. Cosmopolitan people belong both to their own city and to the universe; they are part of humanity as a whole and joined with a particular community. As he put it,

> Each person you know about and can affect is someone to whom you have responsibilities: to say this is just to affirm the very idea of morality. The challenge, then, is to take minds and hearts formed over long millennia of living in local troops and equip them with ideas and institutions that will allow us to live together as the global tribe we have become.[55]

Appiah cautions us about a twentieth century tendency. During the last century, it became common practice among liberal members of western cultures to distance and disdain their own religious or cultural tribe as a way to accommodate the difference of strangers. We might add that many women threw away being female due to the hindrances their gender identity suffered, something Bourdieu felt he had to do as well, in his context. In Appiah's view, this move is a mistake. Throwing away important aspects of personal and social identity in order to make other people appear comfortable (keep their power unhindered) is not something we should require of the *other* and therefore, not something we should demand of ourselves.

Perhaps the core issue when we face *otherness* has more to do with a kind of relaxed attentiveness—a humility that no longer worries about whether we're right or good—or seen by others as right or good. But *otherness* does pose a threat to our current way of being. Spiritual care rests on a willingness and ability to exercise relaxed attentiveness to others, what we call thick listening, while at the same time, listening compassionately to our own valued way of being ourselves.

Conclusion

Maybe we've heard someone say: "If you really knew me, you wouldn't like me." Maybe you've said that to others. The existential sense that our internal world is incongruent with our outward presentation is a spiritual issue. Even in groups that privilege individualism, being the same inside as outside, is a difficult, troubling and arduous task human beings take on, no matter their global pattern. But what we need to be aware of is that being the same inside as outside has a different complexity for white western women and strong group members, not to mention the African American woman Crenshaw describes using her term intersectionality. What if intersections of identity could be viewed as places of meeting and felt connection? What if they became places of thick listening at thin moments as well as I-Thou relating?

Throughout this chapter we've been looking at what it is that allows us to read and value the differences that *otherness* presents—whether those differences arise at home or at work. How do we manage tensions (emotional and cognitive) that arise as we encounter people who express different ways of being? Within strong groups and individualistic settings, affirmation follows a given script; subscribers receive social respect if they follow the script. Unpacking all three global patterns in concrete relational encounters is a significant aspect of spiritual care practice. If practitioners embrace the dichotomous tensions within someone's worldview dialectically, they can craft better spiritual assessments. In this regard, we've referenced theoretical and practical topics: the living human document, interpathy and dialogue, definitions and theories about empathy, an ethic of rights and an ethic of care, complexities of competing identities, social valuation, as well as intersectionality, liminality and cosmopolitanism. All of these concepts are well situated to help us rethink the worldviews we inherited when we were young.

The support some people get within a social system, that they come to believe is the way things are and should be, easily shows up as privilege and elitism to those who, systemically, don't get that support. Spiritual care professionals are trained in systems thinking and attuned to the implications of individualistic singularity and dyadic identities within personal narratives of those to whom they listen. Strong group members may seem weighed down when protocols privilege individualistic assumptions. Women may seem weighed down if they feel forcibly drawn in two compellingly strong directions that can't both be met adequately. As spiritual care practitioners sit with people who've maintained radical individualism as a way of life, they can begin to hear compassionately the relational losses that typify singularity, particularly at times of crisis.

Decoding what's going on in a global pattern is essential as we listen to someone's faith story. As spiritual care practitioners listen, they hear clues and use them to unlock the door into meaningful pathways to explore in the context of their professional relationships. We haven't presented these global patterns to privilege one against the other—but rather to point out the necessity of perceiving webs of meaning that have given them shape.

There's one strong belief we hold: given these different patterns, human beings can only afford to forget themselves and flourish if other people remember and offer them recognition. We need each other. If individualism tempts us to think otherwise, it's destructive. For all of us, challenges arise whenever we encounter *otherness* because there's emotional and conceptual tension inherent in our different ways of being human. The challenge may lead to competition, but the invitation is to be cosmopolitan.

Depending on personal and social awareness, we can navigate emotional and conceptual tensions while seeking to understand the other as *other*. In addition to tension, there's delay—there's a time lag between recognizing that someone is saying something we don't quite follow and the emergence of conceptual clarity that eventually comes as a result of thick listening. How we communicate with our bodies and words during these delays is significant. Using meaningful interpretive clues derived from research-based theories and insights, we shorten these delays, reduce the emotional tension, facilitate conceptual clarity and foster meaningful I-Thou relating.

Take Away Questions for Reflection

- What does Martin Buber's phrase "all real living is meeting" mean to you after reading this chapter?

- Have you had experiences in spiritual care where you distinguished sympathy, empathy and interpathy? What would it be like for you to write a verbatim, critical incident or case study featuring one or several of these qualities of relationship?

- How do you understand dialogue, dialectic and the relationship between them after reading this chapter? Based on your experience, what would a short verbatim of each type of discourse look like in your spiritual care practice?

- Which of the three global patterns discussed in this chapter resonates with your worldview? From within that perspective, how would you go about recognizing and meeting another as "other"? Is there a clinical vignette that comes to mind as you think about this?

- What sense did you make of Appiah's term "cosmopolitanism"? How might it factor into your spiritual assessment and interventions?

Chapter 6

The Role of Reason in Reconceiving a Worldview

Introduction

P erhaps it's because so many people live longer now that the opportunity to rethink our worldviews is more than an option, it's a requirement for living well in the twenty-first century.[1] With the influx of people from different cultures, with increasing diversity in our home cultures, the complexity we face calls for intentionality and reflection. Our expectations for intimate relationship depend on developing social and emotional skills that, perhaps, people in the past thought they could manage without. In addition, the social cost of refusing to rethink our concepts of peoples and groups that have been treated with disrespect, discrimination and systemic abuse is enormous. The attribution of blame on people of Asian descent during COVID-19 has been shocking. Indigenous peoples and cultures of African descent around the world refuse to live with the old status quo, and rightly so. Religious and sexual diversity are other examples of change that require us to reflect on habituated attitudes. Rethinking our sense of justice, inclusion and hospitality is urgently called for after the upheavals of 2020.

People of good will want to support the social need to find a way forward that genuinely counts everyone in. Rethinking ourselves is a personal, social and spiritual practice. In this chapter, our purpose is to focus on the aspect of being reasonable that's at the core of rethinking worldviews we acquired early in life. Being reasonable begins with, and is enhanced by, self-understanding, i.e., it's personal. Reason also plays a role in augmenting conceptual learning, a capacity every human brain offers its owner. This chapter focuses on healthy uses of reason in order to distinguish them from unhealthy uses and the twentieth century misdirection that reason took. We explore unhealthy reason in the form it takes in skepticism and the tyranny of negative thinking, as two examples. In addition, we examine healthy uses of reason by describing contemplative mindfulness, Socratic conversation and Aristotelian deliberation. At the end of the chapter, we connect patterns of healthy reason with spiritual care practice.

In chapter one, we outlined how worldviews form in the first place. The process of rethinking a worldview can be mapped on the progress of growth that begins with infancy. As the homunculus image reveals, the infant begins as a place where things happen and growth moves the infant to childhood and the child to adulthood. Growth implies that people move toward being intentional agents of their own thinking and acting. There's a social phenomenon that supports this growth—the rise of middle age. Brain research from the last few decades demonstrates the emergence of a period of time in which rethinking our worldviews is strongly supported by the maturing brain itself, during a period typically defined as the ages between 38 or 40 years to 65 or 70 years.[2] If people are made for relationship, as we argue in this book, they're also made for reframing worldviews they live by in order to integrate socio-cultural changes noted previously, but without thoughtlessly walking away from those early worldviews, although people may choose to walk away.

Twentieth century western cultures tended to follow Freud's advice, which was to abandon our inheritance. But he didn't follow his own advice, nor did his wife.[3] Right after his death, she returned to the Friday evening Shabbat rituals he had for years refused to let her celebrate. If we try to 'just forget' the past, it has a way of controlling the present. But we have opportunities to rethink our worldviews and make conscious, considered, wise decisions about the concepts by which we intend to live. Ideas assessment and sorting through the meaning we made early in our lives is spiritual work. Once again, this book takes stock of personal and social implications of rethinking ourselves. The goal is not to erase our way of being and replace it with an entirely new form, if that were even possible. But, since worldviews form in a particular social and family milieu, and since life experiences have a way of changing us over time, we may find the inherited content of our worldview no longer conveys the life we now live or the life we choose to live. There's a dance between past and present that calls for choreography comprised of clear thinking and a healthy use of reason. In what follows, we hope to offer several useful aspects of healthy reason that are capable of making the dance an artful presentation, the outcome of which is the cultivation of a beautiful soul.

Reconceiving Old Concepts

Recall from chapter one that worldviews form in a particular way that allows human beings to perceive more and more of what's going on in their environments. Conceptual learning allows them to strengthen and extend the meaning they organize and live by. Simply walking away from what's new and confusing isn't the best way to employ the brain's potential. Spiritual work is the ongoing task of grappling with meanings we've gathered about others, the world, the transcendent, nature and ourselves because the human brain is designed for ongoing conceptual learning. We get our worldviews initially not because they're true; we build them based on personal experience and family contexts.

Let's look at an example of conceptual learning. Suppose Nancy grew up with an absentee father. She learned from experience (e.g., her mother's behavior, her own disappointment) that he was away because he found other tasks, other people, and other places more interesting than spending time with family. Of course, everyone in her family may have misunderstood his motivation for being gone, and been unaware of the role played by his lack of the social and emotional skills needed to communicate his love convincingly. That being said, as a result of her early experience, Nancy built particular associations with and beliefs about the concepts for man, husband, father, in which she believed her dad didn't want to spend time with family because they weren't interesting to him. Then Nancy married Jim who, in his mid-thirties was required by his workplace to be away from home a lot of the time. As she pays attention to her spiritual needs and uses relational communication, Nancy comes to see that Jim is not her father. She is able to perceive his love for her and their children. By remaining open to what's going on, she revises her concepts for husband, father, man, in such a way that being absent is not the same as indifference. Jim is committed to family, prefers to be at home and is fully present when he's there.

The shift involved in Nancy's conceptual learning is enormous. Initially, the contradiction between her father-based husband concept (past) and her revised concept of Jim moves her thinking forward as she tries to understand herself. She begins to notice her relational environment and uses these perceptions to help her re-conceive her concepts. She takes in new information that allows her to reexamine the content of her old concepts, and to question her beliefs. She gets distance from her old concepts, and observes them change, based on her new experience. Most importantly, she trusts Jim enough to hear with fresh insight his reasons for why he's doing what he's doing. She releases her grip on old concepts and lets them be informed by her new reality.[4] By doing this work, Nancy is able to perceive Jim's humanity in a way she couldn't before.

She doesn't pretend she never had negative concepts, nor does she believe she can just walk away from them. Her emerging concepts interact with the old concepts and the old concepts influence the emerging ones; the old is part of the configuration of the new.[5] What she learns from being in relationship with Jim is new and challenges what she previously thought about all men. Up to now her old concepts controlled her assumptions. When she experiences a conceptual shift,[6] she can intentionally weigh and reflect on her concepts of man, father, husband, rather than being controlled by them. Through mental awareness, as an aspect of mindfulness, she's able to consider past and present at the same time. She practices trusting Jim. Trust is a choice, and sometimes a difficult one. Her conceptual tension is between old concepts and emerging ones. This is a struggle Nancy has to engage in herself. Jim can participate, but the conceptual learning is essentially hers.

This conceptual movement is seldom sudden and requires awareness of what's going on between past and present. The old concepts can still pop up, but less so as trust builds. When Nancy reflects on what she's thinking, her idea of Jim moves closer to his actual being. The outcome of rethinking her concepts is that Jim can show up as the person he is.[7] Up to now, he was hidden from view, covered by her patchwork cloak of old concepts. Rethinking one's worldview has other benefits as well. As her father ages, Nancy loves being in his presence and has released him from her youthful anger. In this chapter, we focus on how reason plays out in conceptual shifts like the one Nancy experienced. We also look at examples of people who refuse to let new experiences reshape old concepts.

On Being Reasonable

Being reasonable begins with, and is enhanced by, self-understanding, i.e., it's personal. How we think matters to spiritual health. In an earlier chapter, we focused on sociology and anthropology and used these discourses to unpack global patterns of human experience. In this chapter, we rely on philosophy and theology to underscore the role of reason in spiritual care. Our purpose is to offer approaches that help people understand the use of reason and imagination as they reflect on faith stories.

Philosophy has had significant impact on how we think about spiritual care. At the end of the 1700s, around the beginning of modernity, philosopher Immanuel Kant (1724-1804) proposed that people should use their own understanding as they make their way through life.[8] He thought this was the most courageous way to live, i.e., by finding one's own way, using one's own thinking as a guide—so long as thinking was shaped around reason as he understood it. He reflected on the beginnings of Enlightenment and proposed that people shouldn't thoughtlessly follow authority figures, be they religious or political.

Kant was clear that reason is more than personal, it's also social:[9] healthy reason allows us to make sense to other people, as well as to ourselves, as we tell our faith stories. During COVID it became clear that there were groups of people who were deeply divided over their interpretations of what was going on. Many of us asked how we could bridge those differences so that we could hold the personal and social together in a healthy tension.

While Kant believed people should have courage to use their own understanding, it may have been a reaction to the times he was living in, after European feudalism and in the wake of the French Revolution (1789). If we reflect on twentieth and twenty-first century insights conveyed in chapter one, we acknowledge that we're born into the influence of others. We might say Kant underestimated the influence of becoming human in the company of others and privileged the personal over the social. But there are issues around reason and imagination and limits on freedom that matter to spiritual care. How are these issues detected in the process of spiritual assessment? How are they engaged relationally? While he focused on personal freedom, Kant didn't believe reason was limitless or that imagination had no boundaries.[10]

Yet Kant's proposal to use our own understanding may influence people who feel uncomfortable with the idea of being companioned by others as they sort through their personal thoughts and feelings. What creates continuity between Kant and the approach of spiritual care is the importance of using healthy reason when reflecting on one's thought life.

Spiritual care practitioners help people hear how they currently use reason.

In addition, we look at the trajectory of reason over the centuries. We acknowledge that its movement is based on western understandings of how reason functions, as well as what it is. This analysis also relies on Christian traditions. That being said, we respect and seek to learn from thinkers and practitioners of different traditions who respond to our explanations from their own perspectives. The chapter presents readers with interpretive clues based on patterns of unhealthy and healthy reason. We don't intend to privilege a western notion, so much as to unpack how it works, in particular, to note its uses and misuses, as a way to help people rethink spiritual health.

In the chapter, we define reason as a peculiarly stubborn effort to get clear about something.[11] British writer and historian of ideas, Anthony Gottlieb defined reason this way in his book, *The Dream of Reason*. He relies on a western, secular (also atheistic) view and focuses on reason's role as an arbiter of thought. For Gottlieb, reason has less to do with the content of thought it produces, and more to do with showing people how to think about anything at all. Our intention in this chapter is to point out that the worldview we form from personal experience is shaped by particular uses of reason. That is to say, unhealthy reason may be deeply embedded in one's worldview and in the way people speak about themselves. Noticing, questioning and sometimes facilitating the elimination of unhealthy reason by listening thickly to the way people speak about themselves and other people is central to accompanying them during spiritual care.

Unhealthy Reason and Spiritual Care

As mentioned in the chapter on Human Development, Erik Erikson used an expression that's helpful when we talk about reason. His phrase *"a sense of"* explains what it's like to focus on our own thinking. He defined the phrase by identifying its three dimensions:

- Experiencing that's accessible to introspection (personal awareness)
- Behavior that's observable to others (social awareness)
- Emerging inner states that are determinable through testing and analysis.

As we focus on our own thinking and try to hear the reasons that drive our behavior, we have access to personal and social awareness at the same time. When people are in this state of awareness, spiritual care practitioners bring an ability to open up space, through thick listening, and foster the kind of stubborn effort that can allow people to find increased clarity.

Interpreting *a sense of* can include becoming self-aware of one's well-being, or its lack, by relying on the three dimensions listed above because they're available to testing and analysis. When conscious personal awareness is involved in *a sense of,* it can aptly be called 'a felt sense'.[12] As spiritual care practitioners listen to faith stories, they are cued through thick listening to hear the reasons people use to describe why they did (or do) one thing rather than another. A capacity to listen effectively is informed by a distinction we can make about reason itself.

First, let's look more carefully at 'a felt sense'.[13] This expression was discussed in the chapter on Exploring the Territory. It also undergirds the definition of spirituality we use in this book. In terms of its relevance to reason, we become aware of a felt sense in a friendly environment as someone listens to us compassionately: we expose a truth, without feeling a need to protect ourselves or wanting to cover it up. What we unearth is interesting to us and speaking about it relieves a burden we've been carrying because of its effects on us. We often come to see contradictions that present themselves as we become aware of our own thinking. Then, as we reflect on these contradictions, we become curious, not defensive. We refuse to use unhealthy reason because it can't free us from the trap we're caught in. Rather, our curiosity about what we've unearthed, including the contradictions, unlocks a desire for greater self-honesty.

As part of becoming aware of and assessing the ideas in a worldview, in the company of a spiritual care practitioner, we may come to identify ways of thinking that are unhealthy. Reason is unhealthy if we use the following ways of talking and thinking about what puzzles us. We're using unhealthy reason if we

- Belittle the problem
- Analyze it by grabbing at reasons that effectively dismiss it as a real problem
- Blame someone else or focus on someone else's part in the situation

- Suppress the problem by 'gritting our teeth and bearing it'
- Lecture ourselves about how stupid we are to take it seriously
- Drown in the feelings attached to the problem.[14]

Reason is misused if we try to pretend a potentially meaningful (thin moment) situation isn't serious, has a simple solution, or signifies that we're worthless, hopeless and alone. In addictions theory and twelve-step programs, this is frequently referred to as "stinking thinking" insofar as it describes the human tendency to pursue lines of unhealthy reasoning that don't serve us well.

It's important to notice patterns in the reasons people use to explain themselves. As spiritual care practitioners walk alongside those who tell their faith stories, they begin to work with aspects of reason so as to help people move away from unhealthy reasoning. In addition, recall what was said in the chapter on Otherness about the web of meaning that acts as a metaphor for someone's worldview. As we listen to reasons people give, and consider the health of those reasons, we ask ourselves about the web of meaning in which those reasons hold a place.

Another way to think about these worldview webs of meaning is to consider them as an idea system. In his book on learning organizations, American systems scientist Peter Senge identifies what he refers to as event explanations,[15] which is a way of describing a situation by paying attention to 'who did or didn't do what to whom'. To him, if people in organizations focus attention on event explanations, other people react to the explanation rather than paying full attention to what's really going on. He distinguishes event explanations from structural explanations in which people ask about and observe behavior that underlies the patterns of action they see occurring. A distinction between event and structural explanations also applies to spiritual care.

Suppose Steve comes for spiritual help. He grew up in a religious home and went to church with his family every week. He's in his early thirties. No one in his family attends church now. Steve writes code for computer games. When he was 15, he developed a successful game that got attention and provided him with a lot of spending money. At this point, he works for a company that invents games. He lives with his parents and spends a lot of time in the basement playing computer games when he's not working for the company.

You're a family friend. You were surprised when he called you because he knows you practice spiritual care professionally. He tells you he's tired of living in the basement. As you listen to him, you begin to notice a pattern of isolation that characterizes his current behavior. As you consider his faith story, and his spiritual needs, you hear him tell you about people who make it hard, if not impossible, for him to find meaningful human connections (event explanation). He gives you plenty of reasons why he can't find intimacy during social interaction.

Over time, you encourage him to look beneath the surface of what's going on until you both acknowledge that, in fact, he simply hasn't honed the social skills he needs to connect well with others. The structural explanation is that the more he isolates himself, the fewer opportunities he has to practice these skills. At present his pattern is snowballing, in the same way addiction behavior gathers momentum and covers over underlying sources of stress and discomfort. This insight about structural explanations is similar to Freud's substitution theory based on his repetition complex.[16] A structural explanation could come into focus if Steve sees connections between his action and his deeper needs, i.e., the way he stays isolated in contrast to his need to connect with others.

There's another dimension to the structural explanation. Steve has faith issues. He needs the spiritual resources of courage, hope and trust to persist in finding ways to connect. As you listen, you notice the underlying structure (web of meaning) that his reasons currently fit into and you invite Steve into a space for learning in which he begins to see the difference between unhealthy and healthy reason. Steve could also find spiritual resources by reconnecting with his faith tradition. Two important ideas from chapter one apply here. Robert Kegan points out that Steve's family religion isn't the same as Christianity itself. Further, as a Jewish woman, Lisa Miller makes it clear that a faith tradition must be taken on willingly and personally if it's to offer the benefits she identifies in her research. In Exploring the Territory, the section on forming a worldview offers the perspective that growing into maturity is an opportunity to reflect on inherited content in one's worldview and to come to terms with it in a way that's compellingly and personally attractive, and that provides people with the resources they need to go on living well. Steve has this option.

Belief, Disbelief and Unbelief

Let's say there are three possibilities for assessing the ideas that populate our worldviews: we may express belief, disbelief or unbelief. These are very different ways to think about the world and our place in it. Belief, as the affirmation of an idea or way of life, is straightforward. Unbelief is at the opposite end of a continuum and is something like indifference or lack of interest. Disbelief, on the other hand, is a mid-way point between belief and unbelief and has particular characteristics. These may include incredulity, doubt, mistrust and suspicion. Suppose people disbelieve their own value and refer to themselves as worthless. For them, disbelief is a form of skepticism that acts like a killing frost on their attempt to live a meaningful life. What may not at first be noticeable in their skepticism, however, is a paradox. In this case, disbelief in one's own value is also a strongly held belief. That is to say, in the nature of disbelief itself, belief plays a peculiar role that's not always recognized. Let's drill down a bit deeper into this line of thinking.

Skepticism (extreme disbelief) is an important pattern to consider because spiritual care tries to comprehend the roles of belief and disbelief if it's to be effective in its attempt to help people face life circumstances. But let's make a distinction. As mentioned, there are three possibilities for ideas assessment: belief, disbelief and unbelief. At this point, we're interested in the relationship between the first two. Unbelief[17] has a different nature. It's characterized by an absence of interest; belief and disbelief are often characterized by passion and strong interest, as well as by a desire to persuade others of the value and worth of the ideas or practices in question.

If the nature of skepticism begins with disbelief (rejection, mistrust) in an idea, person or event, thick listening in spiritual care can attend to the personal experience that initially moved an individual toward disbelief. Further, it may be appropriate for the spiritual care practitioner to introduce a challenge to the way the person is thinking; an invitation to reflect, to think about thinking. If skepticism is unchallenged by the personal experience of others, by empirical evidence or an education, there may be no end to its strength until one is locked inside its ethos—referred to earlier as a fortress of thought that's cut off from other peoples' understanding and isn't open to letting later life experience inform and heal the wounds of early life experience.

When applied to the self, skepticism can be self-sabotage. When someone is a relentless skeptic, there's little to offer as evidence that it's reasonable to believe in the idea, person or event in question. Yet skeptics often say they're just using reason. They fail to see that reason is personal, and not just personal, it's also social—if we're reasonable, we make sense to other reasonable people. Relentless disbelief is a lonely, dark place in which to take up residence. What's odd about disbelief is the way it deals with evidence and with other people's life experience.

Let's talk about Judy, a woman who says she doesn't believe the U.S. landed a spacecraft on the moon in 1969. She argues with people who say they did land on the moon, but she goes away without being persuaded by their arguments. Now landing on the moon is a claim that can be tested using empirical evidence. They did or didn't do so. There are no third options. The statement is true—they did land—or false—they didn't land someone on the moon. But what will Judy accept as evidence? That's the issue for her.

As discussed earlier, when it comes to disbelief, beliefs are also involved. These beliefs move disbelievers in a particular direction when arguing a topic. Judy believes she's right in her assessment that the moon landing didn't take place. What's interesting about skepticism, is that underlying beliefs—found in a person's worldview web of meaning—are more important to the skeptic's reasoning than the topic itself. If one thing is disbelieved, other observations or assessments are believed.

Teasing out these thoughts in terms of the moon landing, let's say Judy was 18 years old in 1969. As you listen to her, you realize she believes very strongly in two observations of the world in the 1960s. Her first observation is that the globe was divided between two world powers, the U.S. and Russia, and these two countries were in a Cold War over who was the strongest and most advanced scientifically, educationally and technologically. The first country to put a person on the moon would win the contest. Judy's observation is a reasonable account of that time in history.

It would be hard to convey the extent of the Cold War between the U.S. and Russia to people who were born in the first two decades of the twenty-first century, because nothing has happened between two countries on that scale since those times. Our skeptic points out that tension was tangible; it was breath stopping for those who knew of it. Given the degree of contestation between them, Judy came to believe that one of the countries would cheat in order to win. Social theorists have observed that injustices were happening in other parts of the world and went unnoticed because the two world powers were absorbed in this Cold War conflict, and little else mattered. The modern world of that period held its breath to see who would win. The contest was often described as a test between democracy and communism—the winner would impact the lives of people not only within these two countries, but also globally. Some people thought the conflict might result in World War III.

Judy's second observation, which led her to disbelieve the moon landing, had to do with the media event that occurred. How, she asks herself, was it possible to generate a visual account of the moon landing in 1969 that could be seen by millions of people around the world when they turned on their television sets? It wasn't simply that the U.S. got someone to the moon first; they did so in a way that demonstrated their victory to the whole world. Everyone could see it happen! Doesn't that prove it actually happened? But for Judy, it was *too much* to believe. Her conviction that one country would cheat supported her belief that the media blitz was just for show—it was a trick.

So with skepticism, it's not a question of simple disbelieving. It's a question of the competition between what's believed and what's not believed. If beliefs, such as the two pertaining to our moon-landing skeptic, are strong enough, no amount of empirical evidence outweighs that strength. The skeptic can appeal to the 'someone will cheat' belief and arrive at reasons why the media event was a charade.

One response to Judy, when she says she doesn't believe in the moon landing—especially if she hasn't given her underlying reasons—is to mock her disbelief, as might occur at a dinner party. This response may be common. The surface disbelief is so out of whack with what others think that they easily shift to mockery, perhaps in the hope she'll be embarrassed out of her disbelief. Mockery seldom works. If it's impactful at all, it's likely temporary. When Judy goes home she'll restore her disbelief.

How does this happen? Her reaction is based on mockery's misdirection. It focuses on a surface disbelief not on the underlying beliefs. The problem is similar to the difference between event explanations and structural explanations, mentioned earlier. An underlying structure of beliefs supports a surface disbelief. In addition, mockery is unkind. It may drive the skeptic deeper into a fortress of disbelief. The resulting isolation may form a higher wall around her thinking. These are the complexities to which thick listening in spiritual care attends. Peeling back the layers of disbelief and belief, while remaining respectful and kind, is integral to professional spiritual care practice. Within the context of a spiritual conversation, it's possible to get beneath Judy's surface disbelief and provide the safety needed for her to lay bare the underlying beliefs. If a skeptic is unable—due to a lack of safety, respect or kindness—to reveal these beliefs, the truth may not emerge. While not believing in the moon landing may seem trivial, spiritual care addresses beliefs and disbeliefs that have sharp edges within a tender soul. These can emerge in thin moment experiences. People are stories, not snapshots. If people get caught up in someone else's surface disbeliefs, they miss the story that lies behind what that person thinks, feels and does.

There's a helpful tool available to spiritual care practitioners who may be called upon to accompany someone questioning a belief.[18] Clark uses this tool with groups of students and as part of spiritual care conversations. The process begins with attentiveness to what someone believes. It then proceeds through questioning the belief. The practitioner remains open to the shifts and changes that arise as filters of disbelief, belief and unbelief are identified and paradigms and worldviews are revealed. Here are the questions used during the process:[19]

Name a belief:
The practitioner invites a client to name a belief or a disbelief. For example, I don't believe the moon landing actually happened in 1969. I believe that one of the countries would cheat in order to win.

Question the belief:
- How does your belief match how you understand what happened (fact-checking)?
- How does it feel to hold this belief?
- How does the belief limit me?
- How is this belief helpful to me?
- What do I get out of holding this belief?
- How would it feel to let go of this belief?
- How does this belief affect my overall sense of well-being?

Questioning a belief, while someone is taking great care to listen, may allow a skeptic to hear herself think about the moon landing and reflect on her belief and disbelief.

Yet, would a skeptic readily come for spiritual care? It's a fair question. In the growing isolation that accompanies skepticism, it's hard to reach out for help. Those who live or work with a skeptic may be more willing to ask for help. If they have to deal daily with relentless disbelieving, they may sense that their resources are so depleted they're open to spiritual care. If practitioners perceive a pattern of skepticism, they can effectively walk someone through relational issues that surround those who live in the isolation of skepticism or those who aren't skeptics themselves, but who live or work with people who powerfully disbelieve.

Healthy Reason

Healthy reason is essential to healthy reflection. It allows us to perceive what's in our own hearts and gives our perceptions and conceptions voice. It enables us to step back from our worldview webs of meaning in order to test and analyze our emerging inner states. If reason is a peculiarly stubborn effort to get clear about something, making the effort allows us to think about our thinking and to see how personal meaning shapes the way we live.

Healthy reason is also social. We want the way we think and speak to make sense to others so we can continue to be in meaningful relationship with them. For reason to be healthy, it must not become relentlessly skeptical. It's essential to healthy reason that we refuse to let unhealthy reason distract and confuse our thinking. This may sound easy, but it's not. It takes effort and deliberation. How tempting it can be to think the way everyone else does and passively comply with the multitude. How self-soothing it may seem to substitute the rigors of reason with the easy conclusions someone can reach by accepting social media trending or groupthink.

Refusing to let unhealthy reason distract and confuse our thinking requires a fundamental state of mental alertness that's determined to resist the belittling dismissal or suppression of real problems, and works tirelessly to question patterns of blame, intolerance, self-sabotage and abandonment when it comes to dealing with disturbing situations. Healthy reason is a fundamental state of mind that's unwavering in the face of unhealthy reason. It's the willingness and ability to counteract it if it shows up. Unhealthy reason prevents spiritual conversations from tapping into bedrock elements of one's faith story, worldview, and meaning making capacities where thick listening at thin moments can flourish. The exercise of healthy reason pursues ever deepening and expanding layers of personal and social meaning within one's idea system, or worldview. As people assess their ideas, using healthy reasoning, they experience a renewed sense of felt connection with their own thinking. In this light, healthy reason and spirituality are helpmates.

Twentieth Century Misdirection about Reason

In order to get clear about healthy reason, there's a twentieth century shift that's essential to understand. The shift emerged in response to philosophical investigations of reason that characterize Western thinking since the 1700s. Immanuel Kant is at the core of that shift but he didn't intend his view of reason to produce it. Many who followed Kant privileged ideas he specifically rejected. This section outlines a mistaken path reason took and describes its impact on a major misdirection in the last century—a mistake that specifically undermines and devalues faith-based belief and curtails what believers think is possible if they use reason to sort through ideas that populate their worldviews.

The shift in question has two strands that denigrated belief. With the first, spun through myths produced by Freud (as one example) God was to be rejected. That rejection was the primary evidence that a person was reasonable and had achieved maturity. As a consequence, people came to believe self-observation was nothing more than psychological self-preoccupation. God was dismissed as a source of insight. This strand could be used to weaken faith's reliance on the trustworthiness of transcendent experience. Further, it could discount the validity of spiritual experiences and spiritual practices that focus on, for example, forgiveness as genuinely felt, as linked to transcendent experience and as affirmed through community belonging. We fail to realize what's lost if psychology plays the sole role in self-observation. That is to say, self-preoccupation is not self-reflection; nor does it necessarily move us toward healthy reason. Revitalizing spiritual conversation requires getting past worrying whether spiritual work is psychology, and realizing that healthy spiritual self-observation renews unity between knowing, being and doing as people become mature and hold their beliefs with existential confidence and epistemological humility, a stance we probe further by describing Socratic conversation.

To pick out a second strand of twentieth century misdirection, we investigate what it means to know anything at all. The study of how we know what we know is epistemology and comes from two Greek words *episteme* (knowledge, understanding, acquaintance) and *logos* (word, argument, reason). The question of how we know what we know is as old as philosophy itself.[20] So let's explore some modern assumptions about the role of reality in learning. It's common to hear an assertion that reality is unknowable. Let's look at ordinary experience that disputes that skepticism.

To begin with, if we say reality is unknowable, how could it be available in cues we use to evaluate and alter our understanding of what's going on? If reality were unknowable, how could we learn anything? In addition, the claim is vague. Reality is multi-dimensional. For example, we can know *about* someone. We can also know someone personally. We can know what people who are no longer alive think on a topic by reading what they wrote or listening to those who knew them personally. We can know a country we've not visited by viewing films, taking virtual tours, talking with people who've emigrated from that country, and we can learn facts that those who live there may not know because we have access to global resources unavailable in local districts. At the same time, we know what it's like to live in our own country in a way outsiders don't know.

We know the taste and smell of coffee. We know what an expression on someone's face signifies so we can respond appropriately. We know what people are feeling by getting a sense of it while we're in their presence, or by reading a book about their experience. We know what a teddy bear feels like and can make sense of what it means to a young child to have one to hold. We know about atoms but can't see them. We may know God though we can't see God. We know some of these things because we experience their effects, just as we can't see the wind but we can see its effects on the tree branches in our own backyard.

To say reality is unknowable, without distinguishing different ways we know something, is misleading; it limits reality to its most complex, ineffable form. For example, Nancy came to know the real Jim when she paid attention to the way he described himself. While initially Nancy laid the concept of her father over Jim, eventually he showed up as a real object of Nancy's experience.

If we couldn't know real objects, and come to trust them, we couldn't make sense of the world and conceptual learning would be impossible.

The knowledge that infants acquire as they explore the world forms a basis for making the world meaningful so they can be sane. In terms of making the world meaningful, people continuously encounter objects, including people, and make sense of them. The terms objective and subjective have roots in this early experience. A subject, an infant, learns about objects by tasting, touching, smelling, hearing and seeing, as described in the section on worldview formation in chapter one. During infancy, the young also come to know that objects they can't sense directly, continue to exist outside the range of their sense perceptions.[21] In this way they come to trust that parents exist even though they're not in the room with them.

An element of experience that distances the subjective from the objective is the multi-dimensional nature of reality. Each object has more to it than a subject perceives. Some objects (atoms, God) can't be seen or assessed the way we experience teddy bears in a nursery. In addition, knowledge is partial. While we say we know what an expression on someone's face means, we acknowledge that the data are only a beginning point, a theory. We need to ask other people questions in order to check out the perception we're forming about them. When we believe we know something, it doesn't mean there's nothing more to know. The role of imagination allows us to fill in gaps between what we can and can't sense directly. Scientists also rely on imagination.[22] Healthy reason allows us to develop healthy imagination. We discuss imagination in the final section of the chapter.

The Trajectory of Reason

The pathway reason took in the last two centuries impacts what we think is reasonable to believe. To understand how reason functioned prior to a modern privilege given to human reason alone, we're well advised to consider the ancient world's nuanced ways of describing thought, for example in Greek culture. Our purpose in this section is to point out how historical ways of thinking about reason came back together, as one example, in Action Science.

In ancient times, there was a tendency to divide the power of thinking into two broad categories, reason and intuition, a division the ancient Greeks captured with two terms, *dianoia* or reason (διανοια)[23] and *nous* or intuition (νοῦσ).[24] *Dianoia* referred to cognitive understanding grounded on mathematics that offered explanations to guide knowledge that's pursued for its own sake, which is affirmed by the more recent use of the scientific method. *Dianoia* is built up by looking around at the world of objects and seeing them as measurable, which was a method typically used by Aristotle. However, *dianoia* has the potential to debase objects of thought that can't be perceived by the five senses, as happened after Kant.

Nous, on the other hand, was concerned with immediate apprehension or flashes of insight that came from outside the human mind. *Nous* is received thought, not dependent on human effort. In the past, Christians also used a Latin term *intellectus* to signify knowledge got directly from God. Even ancient Greeks had a sense that *nous* was knowledge received through a cosmic connection, an approach typical of Socrates' reliance on flashes of insight. During the Medieval European period, philosophically informed religious practice descending from *nous* was companion to attention paid to the motion of one's soul and the continual refinement of meaning derived through experience.[25] God was involved in self-reflection.

The use of these two ways of knowing was well understood among thinkers of the Italian Renaissance period. Italian artist Raphael (1483-1520) depicted *dianoia* and *nous*, and their association with Socrates and Aristotle in a fresco titled *The School of Athens*. In the fresco, the two ways of knowing are represented: Socrates exemplifies looking up as he points to the sky; Aristotle exemplifies looking around as he sweeps his hand toward the world that's right in front of him.

In Greek tradition, there was a relationship between *dianoia*, looking around at the world, and *nous*, looking up to receive flashes of insight that together help to understand human thought and the use we make of reason. Yet, for centuries, and perhaps up to Kant's era, *nous* was regarded as the superior means of knowing; knowledge received from God was more dependable than mere human thinking alone, primarily because sin was thought to distort human thought. For the most part, the Fall, recorded in Genesis, was considered as evidence that the human mind was less reliable than knowledge got from God, although some Christian scholars relied on both ways of knowing to understand the world in the fullest possible manner.

But unity between *dianoia* and *nous* lost its value during a philosophical period following Kant that focused admiration for (we might say worship of) what could be described as a belief in the limitless capacity of human thought to go wherever it wants, and the limitless potential of the scientific method to explain everything.[26] Human knowing and human knowledge (*dianoia*) took precedence over other ways of knowing. Yet preference given to *dianoia* over *nous* was based on a philosophical move made by Kant.

Early in the modern period, Kant developed two German terms, *Vernunft* (reason) and *Verstand* (intuition, intellection) that were linked to the Greek terms *dianoia* and *nous*. But he introduced new roles for the German terms. To put it briefly, he reversed the previous positions the Greek terms held, although he never excluded God from healthy reason.[27] Kant's move to explain the complexity of reason, as he introduced it, also rested on his suspicion of intuition when it became what he called Enthusiasm. He reacted against some of the cult-like excesses in his century. He saw examples of those who claimed to have insight from God but who appeared to be promoting the excesses of what was in their own minds only.[28] Kant observed that flashes of insight got from God could be little more than emotional excess, as happens with cult leaders. After Kant, his intellectual followers strengthened the role he gave to human reason in ways that shaped twentieth century approaches to faith and science. Ultimately, faith was reduced in value and was thought of as an absence of reason, but this move didn't have its origin in Kant's philosophy.

In an essay titled "What does it mean to orient oneself in thinking?" Kant analyzed reason while also looking around at the world in which he found himself. He proposed that reason must have an orienting starting point. He argued for freedom to think that was unconstrained by political or religious authorities, but didn't argue for unlimited freedom to think *per se*. To him, freedom to think had to be grounded on something. To Kant, the orienting point for reason was "a first *original being* as a supreme intelligence and at the same time as the highest good."[29] The existence of this original being allowed reason its freedom from external supervision, but not freedom to go wherever fancy took it. In his essay, Kant argues for the limits of healthy reason. Unmoored reason was nonsense to him, as was atheism.

Modern Reason's Impact on Belief

Much of the philosophical and scientific thought during the nineteenth and twentieth centuries created an inhospitable environment for faith in God. Discursive thinking (*dianoia*) thrives by looking around at the world of objects (including people) and sees them as measurable. *Dianoia* highlights the benefits of science and medicine and applauds comfort and plenty. Yet, focusing solely on what's measurable leaves out aspects of reality that aren't available through measurement and the scientific method. As a consequence of the privilege given to the five senses as primary means for knowing anything, the concept of divine revelation was reduced to non-relevance or non-existence. *Nous*, as received knowledge and immediate apprehension, was belittled.

But many people affirm a way of knowing that's conveyed and expressed in transcendent and spiritual experiences, as described in chapter one. Awareness associated with this way of knowing allows for the kind of knowing resonant with Buber's understanding of *a meeting* and with Stern's description of a present moment. It's an awareness that can't be measured; it isn't based on mathematical propositions. It's an activity of mind based not merely on looking around but also looking up and within, in order to gain knowledge of things beyond mere sight. Intuition, in this sense, implies a way of knowing born of connections to something larger than oneself, and links to our sense of knowing what other people might be going through.

There's a sense of Being implicit in *nous*—a sense of felt connection to the object of one's attention. In this view, people have potential to know things through flashes of insight. Yet, one must be purposeful about received knowledge and be attentive to distractions that can arise from a lack of self-awareness, self-understanding, unresolved internal conflicts, the refusal to participate in mutual regulation and the absence of self-regulation. Knowing isn't something we work out in isolation. The role of community was part of training apprentices in ancient Christian traditions and remains integral to the education of spiritual care practitioners. In CPE, for example, one's supervised peer group experiences afford learning that challenges isolated reasoning. The voices and experience of other people in community with us have a balancing influence on our tendency to run to excess. *Nous* was, and is, part of the process required in order to make meaning from experience; it's spiritual work. Thus, for spiritual care practitioners to use reason in healthy ways in the thick listening that undergirds their practice, it's essential to make connections between looking around (observing and quantifying through the five senses) and looking up (receiving knowledge as flashes of insight).

Healthy reason, as previously mentioned, is a way of thinking rather than the content it produces. The way we use reason has a character that remains consistent, a peculiarly stubborn effort and a sharply inquisitive cast of mind.[30] The combination of stubborn effort and this cast of mind moves someone to consider the vastness, variety, disagreement and dissonance among the intellectual products harvested from reasoning processes. Products of reason are variable and alterable, as evidenced by the philosophical tradition itself. The products of reason produce ideas that sharply disagree about the nature of thought, human experience, the world we can see and the world we can't see. Thus, we must maintain this emphasis on reason's character not on the content it produces alone. In this way, Gottlieb provides a basis for identifying the misdirection taken in the twentieth century, which forgot to remain true to the holistic character of reason.

During the time following Kant, people misled the West about reason, even though, as Freud would declare, reason was his god. The modern privilege given to *dianoia* and *Vernunft*, that constituted what we're calling the misdirection within reason's trajectory, *substituted the content of reason for the process of reasoning itself*. Freud's assertion that unbelief is the only trustworthy evidence of a reasonable person's maturity is one example. He mistook unbelief—a product of reason—for the process of reasoning itself. Rather than promoting a cast of mind and a stubborn effort, Freud held his position during a powerfully influential period in the West's history, in which the belief that there's no such thing as a human soul and that the human body is a machine, nothing more, held sway.[31] Freud gave credence to reason that's used when someone is looking around, and dismissed interest in looking up as a way to get clear about something.[32] Confidence in intuition (*nous*) got lost during modernity due to what we might call the idolatry of reason.[33]

This summary outlines a twentieth century misdirection in reason's trajectory that upended traditional understandings of *dianoia* and *nous*—two historic ways of knowing—in a manner that removed reason's self-transcending human capacities from the exercise of human thought. This error undermined and devalued faith-based reasoning and curtailed what people think is possible when they use reason to sort through thoughts that populate their faith stories. For spiritual care professionals, schooled to integrate psychological and spiritual/religious/cultural frameworks, there's great value in understanding not only the historical context of such misdirection but also to realize some of the correctives found in the scientific inquiry of human spirituality itself, as outlined in chapter one.

Healthy Reason and Spiritual Care

Healthy reason includes *dianoia* and *nous*. Reason's cast of mind is as appropriate in spiritual conversation as anywhere else because engagement that moves to dialogue unites intuition (looking up) and reason (looking around). Healthy reason is informed by looking around at the world as a way to hold intuition accountable and by looking upward to receive insights through transcendent experience. Yet healthy reason is humble and knows its appropriate place as a servant of truth and of truth telling.

As one example of unity between looking up and looking around, in *Learning While Leading*, Anita Farber-Robinson explains a relationship between *dianoia* and *nous* (without using the Greek terms) as they enhance human learning. Her book applies *Action Science* to theological reflection.[34] Her purpose is to improve the ability to look around at the world of objects, including oneself, as a way to become effective in reflecting on one's own thinking. Her book helps people improve their professional practice by inviting them to assess a central aspect of Action Science, i.e., directly observable data (looking around), and note their own responses to cues they get from the data they take in from the world of objects, at the same time as they engage in self-observation. According to her model, which we also discussed in an earlier chapter, connecting spiritual insight and self-knowledge while assessing reality is essential to personal learning that's also socially informed.

Healthy reason includes *dianoia* and *nous*, distinguishes subjective and objective elements, appreciates the connection between knowing something and making sense of something, and values reason's orienting starting point. It's noteworthy to mention that Kant's point about reason's need for orientation brings us back to something mentioned in the chapter on Faith. In the book *On Certainty*, Ludwig Wittgenstein noted that people can't think at all without holding some assumptions they no longer question, any more than they could go through a doorway, if the door had no hinges to allow it to swing open.

Contemplative Mindfulness

With the benefits of healthy reason, we want to pursue a mindful use of reason that's available as we reflect on our own faith stories, or listen to other people's stories. We use the term *contemplative mindfulness* to describe reflecting on faith stories, in ways that unite looking up (intuition) and looking around (reason). This approach to thinking isn't employed if people isolate themselves or become relentlessly skeptical. Contemplative mindfulness is characterized by two kinds of awareness—emotional and mental. Emotional awareness is an ability to identify feelings before, during and after an encounter. It's the skills, strategies and knowledge that allow people to recognize and account for emotions that arise within them and in other people.[35] These are some of the skills Steve needed to acquire to connect well with others. Mental awareness refers to what minds can do, their capabilities. Mental awareness includes a mind's capacity to focus attention so that learning occurs, to expend energy on paying attention, to see what's going on, to understand, reason, make decisions and put them into play, to make new decisions and to be conscious of past and present experience simultaneously.[36] This is what Nancy achieved through reconceiving her concepts.

If we stay with the trajectory of reason—pursuing ever deepening and expanding layers of personal and social meaning in one's idea system—we can consider its Latin tradition as well. In that tradition, reason has a division similar to the two Greek terms discussed earlier. Latin terms for the Greek notions of *dianoia* and *nous* are *scientia* and *sapientia*. The Latin term is like *nous,* but also has additional qualities: *sapientia* refers to engaged knowledge that connects the knower to the known. It's a form of knowing that comes to assume a need for trust in the object of its attention or awareness. It's interesting to note, in our examples given earlier in the chapter, that Nancy, Steve and Judy have difficulty with trust.[37] *Sapience* affects a knower positively and supports his or her well-being. American theologian Ellen Charry defines *sapientia* as having three characteristics: knowledge is assumed, reason is employed and trust is essential.[38] *Scientia*, like *dianoia*, is factual knowledge on which to make rational judgments, while *sapience* refers to discernment and thinking that leads to a felt sense of connection with self and others. To Augustine, *scientia* was preparation for *sapience;* the two ways of knowing worked together in making sound, meaningful judgments.

Sapientia is a deep, rich concept that indicates a capacity for healing those who practice it. As with *nous, sapientia* implies a connection to something larger than the person who seeks to be discerning, and comes "through insight, reflection, discernment, and inspiration as a result of thinking and guidance from a higher source."[39] It's fair to say that whenever we stand back and theorize, we engage with something larger than ourselves because wisdom is based on accumulated human experience condensed into transferable knowledge or insights.

From the perspective of contemplative mindfulness, people can be in the presence of another, can experience the transcendent, and have a heightened awareness of immediacy based on relational consciousness of the other.[40] *Sapience* has within it the power to renew relationship and to heal and refresh those who enter into contemplative mindfulness. Healing is experienced during time spent in transcendent experience and with other people who are genuinely listening to us. In this sense, contemplative mindfulness has affinity with thick listening and I-Thou relating. In summary, healthy reason contemplative mindfulness moves a person to look around and also upward, to look across in dialogue and to look within through self awareness.

The Tyranny of Negative Thinking

We describe a pattern of thought in this section that's far removed from healthy reason and soulful thinking.[41] Throughout the book, we've noted connections among the ways people think, feel and act. We've highlighted authors who say that how we think shapes how we feel and directs how we act.[42] In Appendix #2, we explore these connections more fully by providing an Awareness Wheel Exercise. As well, we discuss Action Science and the critical reflective thinking that Action Science promotes. In all of this, we assert that attending to reason is an element of thick listening. It's also a way to engage the wide-ranging faith stories offered to spiritual care practitioners as they walk alongside clients and patients. Thinking is powerful. Sometimes we have our thoughts; at other times our thoughts have us and hold us captive. They can oppress and bully us just as easily as they can inspire and motivate us. In this regard, Freud wrote about the tyranny of thinking.[43] If we take his point seriously, we could say that *we are what we think*. Those who practice spiritual care listen to the use being made of reason, as well as to the reasons themselves, as an essential part of their practical skill.

In the interest of teasing out a theme that cautions against depicting an exclusively positive perspective on spirituality, a standpoint that would miss the full range of experiences that accumulate within the human spirit, let's unpack some typical patterns of negative thinking. How can healthy reason assist someone who's entangled in unhealthy reasoning, encountering shadow aspects of human nature and wrestling with the underbelly of painful thoughts, emotions, situations and events? In general, we could say that all unhappiness has a substratum of loss at its foundation.

Due to unresolved loss, people slip into thought patterns that are self-defeating. In this section, we outline ways of thinking that spiritual care practitioners can attend to in order to discern the faith story hidden behind negative thoughts and unhealthy reasoning. The following examples identify specific trains of negative thought:

- I'm a failed project; I'm just a loser.
- This is what I'm missing. It's what I haven't done; it proves I'm not good enough.
- I feel disappointed with myself; I'm a disappointment to others; this is what I lack.
- Life is polarized and I feel split in myriad directions—my life is full of darkness, and there's no light at the end of the tunnel.
- I don't get things perfectly right and so I'm a complete failure—no excuses.
- There's no middle ground—there's no joy or hope at small successes.
- Once this happened (a negative event), it will always happen if I try again.

As we listen to someone's negative thinking, the following traits may show up:
- Mind-reading: a negative interpretation is offered and not checked out.
- Fortune-telling: a negative interpretation is anticipated and thought of as an already established fact.
- Magnifying: Negative experience is magnified; positive experience is minimized, or blown off.[44]

For those stuck in negative patterns, there's no option but to continue failing. All reality is dark. Positive experiences are rejected because they don't count. Reasons are found that dismiss anything positive or hopeful. A person focuses on negative events even if they can be contradicted by experience. A negative interpretation is offered and accepted even though there are no definite facts to convincingly support it. All activity and planning is moved by what dutifully must or should be done—nothing is capable of bringing joy or hope. Creativity isn't an option.

Frequently, people trapped in negative thinking will say they're just being 'realistic.' As British author and lay theologian, G.K. Chesterton pointed out, "Reason itself is a matter of faith. It is an act of faith to assert that our thoughts have any relation to reality at all."[45] Teasing out the associations that someone is making who is caught up in negative thinking involves giving one's attention to what the person describes as their reality; their snarl of losses, thoughts and feelings. It involves listening to a mix of beliefs/disbeliefs, grounding assumptions, orienting starting points, stubborn effort and its absence, which have brought this person to the current impasse—what Winnie the Pooh would call a 'stuck place.'

Notice the losses. Unresolved loss provides a platform for believing the world is fundamentally disappointing so that people put faith in the certainty that life won't measure up. At its core, negative thinking must come face-to-face with the way a person is dealing with faith and trust. Being present as someone sorts through threads of negative thinking, and grieving with them as they let go of what isn't helpful, is a profound privilege for someone offering spiritual care. At the heart of spiritual care is a particular attitude that allows for growth and healing that's possible for someone to gain through their investment in this practiced way of caring.

Socrates and Reason's Attitude

Personal authenticity is at the heart of healthy reason. One thing that's clear about the historic Socrates (470-399 B.C.E.) is that he was self-assured. In the speech he gave at his trial (the Apology), he's sure of his mission in life, sure of what he'd uncovered about Athenian society and its elite and powerful, and sure that, at the end of his life, he would remain true to his mission, regardless of the outcome of his trial. At his trial, he had the emotional integrity to affirm that, at the end of his life, his had been the one and only life he could have lived. Socrates was dis-content with simply following the crowd or remaining entrenched in his early ways of understanding the world. It remained a lifelong conviction that his fully examined life was well worth living.

Plato wrote the Apology (Socrates' defence of himself; it's not apolo-getic) soon after Socrates' death due to swallowing hemlock his accusers offered him as the option to exile. He lost his case at the trial. Since Plato was present at it, the speech is likely very accurate.[46] It's fair to claim, as Canadian philosopher Charles Taylor does, that Socrates is the model for personal authenticity that's so important in modern Western cultures.[47] For Socrates, reason is personal and is obeyed despite the mis-direc-tions that held hostage so many of the elite Athenians he conversed with during his lifetime, who were trapped conceptually by their own power and privilege. The word *obey* belongs to Socrates. He felt the sway of reason so powerfully he was compelled to challenge people on the street and implore them to consider the health of their own souls—the soul being the site for thinking and acting. Socrates was deeply spiritual. He followed reason at the expense of his own life.

What's equally true about Socrates is his humility. His friend travelled to the oracle at Delphi to ask who was the wisest person in the world. The answer was Socrates. But Socrates was puzzled at the oracle's answer. He didn't think himself wise. He finally came to describe his wisdom as a sense of knowing in which, as he put it, "I do not think I know what I do not know."[48] In conversation, he met many who thought themselves wise, yet talking together revealed that what they thought they knew con-tained contradictions and confusion. He upset a lot of people. But Socra-tes was a unique, rigorous combination of the existential confidence and epistemological humility we suggest is reason's appropriate attitude—an attitude that's also central to professional spiritual care practice.

Socratic conversation is an art of asking questions. He began by tak-ing seriously what someone else believed. He remained respectful. He inquired. He had an excellent memory of what the other said. As con-versations moved along, he listened so carefully to another's thinking that he was able to follow their thought until they arrived together at a point of truthfulness, if his interlocutor was willing. He was motivated by truth-telling. He listened and named the theory-in-use[49] that charac-terized the beliefs of his interlocutor (conversation partner). He followed out the implications of a theory-in-use by using clarification, analogies, restatement, by calling out 'straw-man' arguments[50] and by revealing circular arguments. In terms of circular argument, he showed that a theory-in-use ended up exactly the same point at the end of a conversation it was at the beginning. Nothing said supported the belief. A circular argument is one in which someone basically believes an idea because they believe it, but they have no support for it that would make it appealing to other people—it has no social value.

An example from Jesus of Nazareth points out how Socratic reason works. The example is brief, unlike most of Socrates' conversations. In the second part of the Christian scriptures (Matthew 12:24) some of the Pharisees make an accusation. They propose a theory as their theory-in-use: "It is only by Beelzebub, the prince of demons, that [Jesus] drives out demons." Jesus replies by using reason and offers an analogy to test their theory. He says, "Every kingdom divided against itself will be ruined, and every city or household divided against itself will not stand." His statement appeals to ordinary knowledge about the world and would be hard to dispute. Jesus supports his challenge by making three separate points that follow from it: "If Satan drives out Satan, he is divided against himself. How then can his kingdom stand?" His second point follows from a combination of the initial theory-in-use and his challenge to it: "If I drive out demons by Beelzebub, by whom do your [own] people drive them out?" His third response is another analogy that supports his challenge: "how can anyone enter a strong man's house and carry off his possessions without first tying up the strong man? Then his house can be plundered." Jesus invites these Pharisees to reconsider their theory about him. He invites them to reflect on their Messiah concept and offers an opportunity for them to challenge their initial theory-in-use. (Matthew 12:24-29 NIVUK)

In general, Socratic conversation aims to deconstruct commonly held beliefs or settled opinions. If we reflect on the section in chapter one of this book that describes how worldviews form, we might say Socrates and Jesus invite people to reflect on concepts from their inherited worldview content that were formed when they were young. Socrates wanted Greek citizens to reconsider concepts they'd held over time and to notice the implications of those concepts on their life and practice. He wanted people to think. He wanted people to unlearn some of their thinking so their concepts could receive the fresh accountability gained by assessing the world and using reason. He wanted them to see the world with new vision.[51]

If we consider for a moment how Socrates might interact with Judy, much would depend on what she felt safe to reveal. But what's clear is that the conversation would be respectful, Judy would be taken seriously, Socrates would be humble yet confident; and the aim of talking together would be an opportunity for Judy to reconsider her disbelief. Through attentive conversation and the thickness of Socratic listening, her concept of trust and her sense of how evidence about the moon-landing functions for her, might open up a fresh vision of 1969. If all goes well, Judy may gain self-understanding. She might open a door in her intellectual fortress. She may gain new ways to explain herself to others. She might change her view completely. Her imaginative response to her own scepticism may offer her new vitality and the social contexts she finds herself in might allow her to converse rather than argue her point.

We can also apply Socratic conversation to the negative thinking outlined in the previous section. Socratic conversation is not argument. It's dialogue that seeks understanding. The listener isn't trying to win or prove they're right. The listener is trying to converse in such a way that people who are telling their faith story can accurately hear themselves think. Socrates calls himself a midwife of thought. It's the birthing of ideas, truth and insight he aimed at conversationally. Socratic conversation is an invitation to allow questions and evidence (support of some kind) to direct our thinking. An image of being a midwife to thought applies to spiritual care practice as well. Spending time with people as they think about their thinking is motivated by a desire that they might live their lives to the full. In the next section, a second pattern for healthy reason, Aristotelian deliberation, also aims at helping people be wide-awake to living a spiritually satisfying, fully human life.

Healthy Reason and Aristotelian Deliberation

While Bellous was teaching at seminary, Peter, a former student and Prison Chaplain, came to her and related his story. Peter enjoyed a successful career in financial development and took early retirement to do something he'd always wanted to do—work with prisoners in jail. After completing his Master of Divinity degree and taking education courses from Bellous, he set up a learning event for ten prisoners he worked and worshipped with regularly. All of the men had told him stories about significant loss early in their lives. He began to think that most of the prisoners suffered from unresolved loss. He offered a ten-week small group experience to address the concept of loss. He wasn't at all sure what would happen, but he had come to trust Aristotelian Deliberation as a learning method.

The small group experience was powerful for all eleven men. During the sessions, eight of the prisoners told Peter they wanted to be Christian, even though he'd said nothing about salvation or becoming a person of faith. Two weeks after the sessions ended, the other two men came with the same request. Peter reflected on this shift. In his experience, the men lived in mental prisons as well as a physical one. The Deliberation method moved the men beyond the fortress of their habitual ways of thinking, to critically and imaginatively reflect on loss more broadly. Deliberation allowed them to step outside the prison of their past experiences into a new way of thinking and acting, just as Nancy did.

Aristotelian Deliberation[52] is a method for conceptual learning that focuses on the formation of character. In deliberating, we ask ourselves what sort of people we want to be. As we reflect on this question, we intentionally choose a path that's situated between two extremes and we walk toward that goal. Deliberating implies taking action. It isn't just

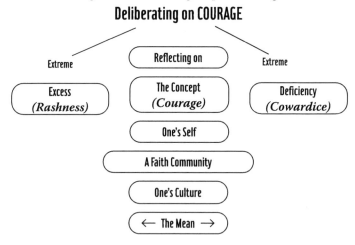

Figure 7 - Aristotelian Deliberation

thinking about what we want to do. As we deliberate, we think about what we have opportunities to become and take action based on that reflection. Taking action continues to inform our deliberations. We think and act; we act and think. Deliberation opens up people to other possibilities. Its creativity tends to open closed doors in a mental fortress. It has a tendency to loosen the places where people are stuck in their thinking.

Suppose a group of students sets out to deliberate on courage. As they consider what the word means and what it looks like in action, they establish a range of words to describe an excess of courage—they choose words such as rash, reckless, undisciplined, undependable, showy, self-promoting, risk-taking—to convey some of what too much courage looks like in action. Think of a game of hockey in which a rookie takes outrageous risks, grabs the puck whenever possible and refuses to pass it to other players, even though they're available and experienced. The rookie demonstrates an extreme of courage, too much of it, which now is no longer courage. It's best described by the words chosen by the group of students. After they identify an excess of courage, these students list words to describe its deficiency—i.e., too little courage. They choose words such as coward, intimidated, refusing to take risks, hiding, fearful, selfish, undisciplined and unconcerned with the team's success.

It's interesting to note that 'undisciplined' shows up in both lists. These students realize that the concept of courage has a lot to do with discipline. The concept carries the social value of remaining in place even when we're scared, and showing up for our team even if we feel threatened, anxious and unsure of ourselves. For Aristotle, courage had to do with a warrior who stood his ground, despite his fear, and acted bravely so he could be counted on by other warriors not to falter or act foolishly on the battlefield. In today's world, courage is a quality of character shared by men and women, often in the interests of peace and justice rather than war.

Aristotle also examines the concept of courage from a personal perspective. As part of deliberating, the group of students reflects on their own tendencies: they each ask themselves, Do I tend to act foolishly or do I tend to act in fear and let a situation overwhelm me? Everyone chooses a number to describe themselves from 1 to 10, with 1 representing cowardice and 10 representing rashness. The students discuss the range of numbers in the whole group and add insights from personal experience to help understand their current self-evaluations. The outcome of their discussion conveys more about what courage is and what it looks like in action, as far as these students can see at the present time.

As mentioned, the concept of courage has two extremes: an excess (rashness) and a deficiency (cowardice). For Aristotle, the mean holds a position between these extremes and is the most excellent way to think about courage and to act courageously. But the mean is conceptually nearer to one extreme than to the other. Courage it's more like rashness than it is like cowardice because it always relies on a degree of risk-taking. As these students deliberate, they move into self-awareness and social awareness as they invite each other to consider how the current social context expresses courage. Self-awareness is situated within social-awareness. For example, a game of hockey requires players to take risks. If hockey culture promotes fighting as a way to help one's team, it may overstep courage and become reckless; it may encourage players to take unnecessary, unwise risks, some of which could end someone's career. However, being willing to stand up for oneself is an essential attribute of an effective hockey player. Being effective as a hockey player requires each person to be deliberative rather than rash or cowardly when on the ice.

As we consider the insights gained through deliberation, self-reflection and social observation, and depending on whether a person tends to one extreme or the other, deliberation helps people understand what action to take to be closer to the mean. There are two reasons why the mean isn't in the middle; it's not 5 out of 10. One reason lies in the thing itself, courage is more like rashness than cowardice; the other lies in the people who are trying to be courageous, and the context in which courage is lived out. In general, people are pulled toward one extreme, not the other. If we tend toward cowardice, we learn to lean toward taking more risks as we engage in deliberation. If we tend toward rashness, we learn to lean away from recklessness so that others can count on us. Aristotle summarized deliberation by saying that to act virtuously is to act and feel towards the right person to the right extent at the right time for the right reason in the right way. He acknowledged that this isn't easy.[53] But once again, the complexity of twenty-first century social interaction makes Aristotelian Deliberation necessary.

Deliberation and Spiritual Care

The formation of character involves ongoing deliberation. This reasoning process tends to revolve around qualities of personal and social interaction that promote healthy and optimal functioning of organizations, countries, and systems of every kind. The concepts of courage, trust, honesty, kindness, generosity, integrity, loyalty, devotion, sincerity, self-control and gratitude are qualities that lend themselves to Aristotelian Deliberation. How many times have we heard someone say, "she's generous to a fault", or "even with all his good fortune, he's a penny-pincher"? These excesses and deficiencies are the kind of comment that can easily arise in conversations between spiritual care professionals and clients or patients. Noticing an extreme can alert a practitioner to issues of deliberation that may be going on within the person making such a comment. They may be searching for a mean, situated somewhere between the excess and deficiency. Listening to the reasoning in another person's thinking by drawing on principles of Aristotelian Deliberation can support clients as they consider opportunities to take action based on that reflection.

Ethical dilemmas can give rise to deliberation. Whether in a personal circumstance, a health-related situation, or some other realm, crises give rise to choice. Choice, in turn, manifests a person's character. Principled action is not always easy to tease out amidst the plethora of a client's personal and social options. For the spiritual care professional, hearing a person's character trait (e.g., grateful, honest, loyal) can assist in noticing where excesses or deficiencies may be in evidence. It's not uncommon for several character traits to be in conflict. For example, Mark is an excessively grateful parent and expresses his gratitude for the healthcare system that's supporting his daughter. However, when he's required to have his daughter fast before treatment, he's less than honest with staff about how difficult fasting is for his girl, especially when staff members keep delaying her treatment. Fasting is a burden for his daughter but his tendency to praise the healthcare system gets in the way of accurately conveying his daughter's difficulty. Sometimes a family member will benefit from spiritual care advocacy that arbitrates the need to say what's really going on. Leaning into honesty can also enable leaning away from the kind of gratitude for healthcare services many patients and family members express without realizing the excessive gratitude is actually tied to a sense of helplessness and powerlessness. If parents don't express their concerns, they remain in the trap of helplessness and powerlessness, and healthcare professionals aren't allowed into what's actually going on.

Taking action continues to inform our deliberations. We think and act; we act and think. Deliberation opens up people to other possibilities; the creativity implied has a tendency to unlock the places where people are stuck in their thinking. By having familiarity with using Aristotelian Deliberation, spiritual care practitioners can play an important role with thick listening at thin moments.

Reason and Imagination

Whether we consider the prisoners Peter guided, Judy, who couldn't believe in the U.S. moon landing, or Steve, who's locked in a pattern of isolation, the purpose of promoting healthy reason in spiritual care is to foster opportunities for people to gain access to what's going on, within them and in their environments. If someone has a sense of themselves, others and the broader scheme of things, they are more likely to imagine their release from a fortress of stuck thinking that has them locked inside. Using imagination in spiritual care can foster discourse between *dianoia/ scientia* and *nous/sapientia*. It can unlock conflicts of belief/disbelief and turn down the volume of tyrannical stinking thinking by allowing access to the pathway of contemplative mindfulness. Reason and imagination offer a bigger picture of the world and our place in it. It's the way out of a mental prison.

The relationship between imagination and spirituality isn't new. Sacred texts and objects in world religions and faith traditions depict imagery that fosters a full spectrum of creative thinking. For example, during his lifetime, St. Ignatius of Loyola (1491-1556) cultivated an approach to imaginative prayer that remains the backbone of Ignatian contemplation. Having referred to his 'application of senses' in the chapter on Faith, we now point to his use of imaginative prayer to foster spiritual exercises designed to bring reason and intuition together. Ignatius was convinced that God can speak to us as surely through our imagination as through our thoughts and memories.[54] People who self-describe as spiritual but not religious often turn imaginatively to nature, art, music or literature for a sense of felt connection to something greater and outside themselves. Healthy reason, in combination with healthy imagination, has a long history of inspiring philosophers and theologians, as well as authors and artists as they engage in reflection.

In summary, we highlight the importance of imagination in pursuing healthy reason. We also point to an affinity between imagination, Action Science and systems thinking. Thick listening at thin moments is not only a matter of asking someone "How do you feel?" It's also a matter of asking, "What do you think?" Thick listening takes into account the emotional vicissitudes of lived experience and tensions arising in the way people think about what's happening to, within and around them. This kind of listening frees people to reconsider the concepts that have, up to now, shaped their interpretations about what's going on. Deliberating on concepts such as courage, unpacking what we actually don't know about a situation but thought that we did, all contribute to using healthy reason to reconceive our worldviews. When we enhance our personal and social awareness we can live in greater harmony with the world as the way it really is.

Conclusion

This chapter focused on reconceiving personal worldviews by using healthy reason. Reason is more than personal; it's social. We need to be self-aware and make sense to other people. The complexity of the twenty-first century is an invitation to reconsider our inherited concepts and ask ourselves whether these concepts are the ones we want to continue using. As one example, Nancy's experience of reconceiving Jim as man, father, husband enriched her life in myriad ways. Likewise, with the help of a spiritual care practitioner's advocacy, Mark was able to be more honest about what he and his daughter were really going through.

The chapter has taken several deep dives into topics not usually taught in clinical forums where practical theology and lived spiritual care experiences meet. That being said, we offer these topics to the reader as pieces of a two-sided puzzle that depicts a human face on one side and the world on the other. Distinguishing unhealthy from healthy reasoning, appreciating the trajectory of reason and its misdirection spawned in the twentieth century, and observing skepticism and negative thinking patterns are all foundational to the activity of meeting people in Buber's I-Thou relating.

As well, seeing how belief, disbelief and unbelief factor into dynamic relational scenarios has implications for the diverse conversations in which spiritual care practitioners find themselves. Knowing how to attend to others in their soulful thinking, and remaining present to those stuck in stinking thinking, takes understanding and contemplative mindfulness. Acquiring tools, such as Socratic Conversation and Aristotelian Deliberation, can assist spiritual care professionals with knowing how to follow the thinking of another person to the point where that person says to a practitioner, "Yes, you understand me."

Take Away Questions for Reflection

- What did you think of Nancy's story? Are there any parallels in your experience? If so, describe your experience in writing or share it with someone else.

- What distinctions do you make between belief, disbelief and unbelief after reading this chapter? What complexities of reasoning do you notice in each?

- Try using the "questioning a belief" exercise with one of your own beliefs. After completing this, ask yourself: What did I learn in the process? What do I consider the pros and cons of using such a tool with a patient or client?

- Reflect on a time when you witnessed unhealthy reasoning in a patient or client. How did you engage with this person? What impact did the experience have on you?

- After reading about Socrates's and Aristotle's approaches to healthy reasoning and deliberation, how might you integrate these methods into your spiritual care practice?

- What would it be like for you to reconceive some element(s) of your worldview using one or other of the approaches to reasoning featured in this chapter? How does this work of reconceiving a worldview relate to Nancy's story?

Chapter 7

Competency and Competence in Spiritual Care Practice

Introduction

Throughout the book, we've focused attention on *thick listening at thin moments* as an interpretive lens for spiritual care practice. Each of the book's chapters has introduced theoretical content germane to what it means to engage another with the fullness of one's awareness and attention, i.e., by perceiving elements of worldviews, faith stories, developmental dynamics, I-Thou relating, and healthy reasoning in the midst of one's personal and professional functioning. We've looked at how essential it is to carry forward careful assessment that offers appropriate and helpful intervention. Likewise, we've highlighted the importance of intentional reflection as integral to the pre-briefing and post-briefing of spiritual care experiences.

In this chapter, our emphasis is *competency* and *competence*, and how these two distinguishable concepts are lived out in the practice of spiritual care as thick listening at thin moments. We point out that it's important to distinguish thick listening as one competency and the ability to recognize a thin moment as another. Further, it's important to observe that there are degrees of competence in the exercise of each competency. But viewing these competencies separately is not enough. They're intended to be integrated as the cohesive, seamlessly exercised complex competency of *thick listening at thin moments*. In combination, and when carried forward by neophyte as well as proficient spiritual care practitioners, this twofold competency comes alive in here-and-now social interactions that foster healing and wholeness within a felt sense of connection.

The integration of distinctive competencies into a single cohesive and seamlessly exercised complex competency mirrors work occurring in spiritual care associations around the globe. Over the past several decades, education programs and professional associations dedicated to the formation, certification and ongoing peer review of spiritual care practitioners have formulated competencies considered essential to effective professional practice in this field. Likewise, assessment tools and rubrics are now in use to assess a practitioner's movement along stages of knowledge, skill development and integrated competence. Our hope is that, by focusing attention on a single unified complex competency—thick listening at thin moments—and delving into theoretical groundwork for its use, broader understanding and appreciation of what it means to exercise complex competencies can result. While it's the educational centers, colleges and professional associations that differentiate and classify competencies, it's spiritual care practitioners who integrate, embody, and unify these competencies into their spiritual care practice, thereby expressing their competence.

The entry point to this chapter is a series of questions. While we won't thoroughly probe each one, we list them as the springboard from which we intend to proceed. In many ways, exploring this field of inquiry is like peeling an onion. Each question is intended to pull back a layer of a multidimensional topic that is ripe with insight and meaning for further investigation.

- What does hermeneutics have to do with competency and competence?
- What's important about considering hermeneutics as a reading strategy for thick listening at thin moments?
- What's a hermeneutic of social interaction?
- What are the types of literacy needed to practice a hermeneutic of social interaction as a reading strategy for thick listening at thin moments?
- What's involved in the construction of a competency?
- What's important about the safe and effective use of self in spiritual care practice?
- How is spiritual care competence assessed?

Peeling the Onion

Our investigation into competencies and competence begins with a discussion about hard sciences and soft sciences as forms of inquiry that contribute to the development of theoretical groundwork for spiritual care practice. On this foundation, we look at the topic of *hermeneutics*, including Hans-Georg Gadamer's (1900-2002) contribution. Of special note are his insights into (a) how "change" impacts what we come to know, (b) what a hermeneutic of social interaction looks like, and (c) how Gadamer's hermeneutical perspectives of horizon, circle and tact help navigate social interactions. Interpretive clues that surface during social interaction, detected in real time and drawn upon in assessment and intervention, foster attentiveness to the presence of thin moments. If spiritual care practitioners are grounded in interpretive frameworks that nurture thick listening and facilitate the recognition of a thin moment, they're well equipped to meet another as "other".

Once there's a theoretical rationale for the use of hermeneutics in spiritual care practice, we'll look at four types of literacy (cognitive, emotional, imaginative and social)—each with its interpretive functions—that inform practical aspects of spiritual care competence. These literacies are reading strategies. Spiritual care practitioners learn to read people, situations, and relationships through informed and skilled use of interpretive clues perceived in concrete clinical interactions. According to Bellous, "the acquisition of a literate stance with respect to cognition, emotion, imagination and social engagement is based on human capacities we all have as we acquire experience and make meaning about life, the world and our place in it."[1] Knowing how to maintain a hermeneutical stance that's informed by the four literacies when exercising thick listening at thin moments, can ground a spiritual care practitioner not only in practical, but also imaginative and optimal spiritual care interventions.

This hermeneutical approach to competency and competence development underscores a consistent theme in the book, the interconnectedness of personal and social underpinnings in all aspects of human experience. Behind the personal is the social, and within the social is the personal. No one is formed in isolation. Thick listening requires spiritual care practitioners to engage in contemplative mindfulness—a posture that understands and appreciates the deep interface between everyday experience and thin moments in which separation between worlds becomes increasingly thin and transparent. Working out an adult worldview that we intentionally choose to hold, by reflecting on the one we formed when we were young, is meaningful spiritual work—and integral to the process of competence development in spiritual care. Faith stories, spiritual experiences and spirituality come alive when both personal and social interactions are taken into account. The theme of taking the personal and social together to create an interpretive framework is informed by our analysis of reason, three global patterns (western individualism, strong group culture, and caught between-ness), an examination of otherness, and an overview of poverty among the working poor, to name some subjects that help build connections between the personal and the social.

When engaged with patients and clients, spiritual care practitioners enter a relational learning environment in which they draw on interpretive clues from their own worldview map and those communicated by the patient or client. It's an I-Thou model moment of "meeting" where entry onto the worldview map of the other can occur. In social interactions of this nature, relational learning can lean in the direction of both client and spiritual care provider. For example, in the chapter on Faith, Rose catches herself struggling when an unexplored aspect of her worldview map is triggered as she's invited onto the worldview map of the elderly man nearing death from lung cancer, who has asked her to assure him of God's forgiveness by offering a prayer.

This is a relational learning situation potentially skewed in Rose's direction. The interpretive clue from the man's worldview map is his reference to having acted sexually toward his daughters. The interpretive clues from Rose's worldview map are her flashbacks. To her credit, she stays present to the man even though both worldview maps are activated. Later, in a lengthy process of debriefing that includes CPE peers, therapeutic work, and shared reflection with her husband, Rose becomes better able to acknowledge the inherited quality of this aspect of her worldview map and take steps to re-conceive it in keeping with the spiritual care professional she seeks to become.

This is an important dimension of competence development in spiritual care and highlights why CPE's emphasis on self-knowledge and personal formation is considered not only foundational but also far-reaching. Without knowing ourselves, we can't truly know another as "other". It takes a unique combination of self-awareness, ethical integrity, theoretical knowledge, literacy skills, intentional reflection and emotional availability to demonstrate the safe and effective use of self—a marker of competent spiritual care.

Learning about competence is a process. It requires a myriad of threads of personal and professional integration, woven together over time and with intentional reflection to achieve mastery. In this regard, initial learning in CPE is followed by lifelong learning in one's professional practice. This is to be expected. Toward the end of the chapter, and more fully in the book's concluding chapter, we'll look at how spiritual care competence advances and is assessed over time, and what this can look like clinically.

The Importance of Differing Approaches to Scientific Inquiry

Practitioners in spiritual care are part of an established, long-standing ministry and a nascent allied health profession seeking to achieve respect and credibility among more established professional groups. In this context, it's important to ask: How do spiritual care professionals understand human experience? This question opens the topic of hard and soft sciences insofar as the field of healthcare brings together the expertise of practitioners who rely on both. Hard sciences include subject areas such as physics, mathematics, biology, and chemistry, while so-called soft sciences include areas of study such as psychology, sociology, philosophy, and theology.

The terms hard and soft refer to the way the scientific method—an approach to seeking knowledge systematically through observation, theorizing, testing and analysis—is used within each type of investigation. In our book, these two approaches have been in evidence throughout. The chapter on spirituality provided perspectives of British zoologist Alister Hardy's research while also highlighting contributions of American psychologist Lisa Miller. When delving into the topic of forming a worldview, we drew on the neurological research of British psychologist Josephine Klein. Later, we introduced Action Science, the brainchild of American business theorist Chris Argyris and philosopher David Schön, to focus attention on their hypothesis that behind every action is a theory-in-use or mental model. When looking at reason's role in reconceiving a worldview, we presented enduring insights of the classical philosophers Socrates/Plato and Aristotle to underscore use of the patterns of *dianoia* (looking around at the world) and *nous* (looking up to receive flashes of insight). Both approaches to inquiry are needed if spiritual care practitioners are to understand human experience.

The language of hard and soft sciences represents two windows into human experience. Spiritual care practitioners need to look through both windows. In this combined exploration, empirical methodologies and wisdom traditions can be studied, reflected on intentionally, and mined for meaning. In her book *Braiding Sweetgrass* (2013), Robin Wall Kimmerer is an excellent example of what can happen when differing worldviews are brought together with respect, sustained reflection, and depth of insight. Traversing the book's pages transports us into Kimmerer's worldview and engages us in a number of model moments in which she's brilliantly bilingual in speaking about her Indigenous Potawatomi roots and her scientific knowledge about the teachings of plants. Her work not only illustrates personal integration; it affirms the social behind the personal. For example, she describes Anishinaabe knowledge keepers as historians and scholars of the narrative of this culturally related group of indigenous peoples—a narrative that existed long before the arrival of offshore people (her word for European settlers) and includes what came after. She writes, "our histories are inevitably braided together with our futures."

Spiritual care practitioners often carry forward their activities in settings dominated by the hard sciences. When we speak about competencies that characterize spiritual care practice, however, we want to be clear that spiritual care relies on the human sciences to understand human experience. It's the soft sciences that open space for developing an emergent sense of expectancy, careful attention and quiet wonder as someone engages in thick listening at thin moments. This focus on human sciences resonates with words written by Killen and de Beer (1994) when they describe the human drive for meaning by saying "all of our lives are remembered and embodied, and so are available to be explored for their fuller meaning."[2] Interpreting human behavior and social interaction using methods that transcend what's immediate, observable, and quantifiable (as hard sciences do) has become the preference of spiritual care practitioners for nearly a century.[3] It's an emphasis that supports thick listening at thin moments as the centerpiece for coming to understand human experience.

So, what is our penchant for the soft sciences rather than hard sciences? As Claude Levi-Strauss (1908-2009), (a linguist who was the most prominent exponent of structuralism) put it, science has only two ways of proceeding as it tries to understand a text: reductionism and structuralism. Reductionism is an approach that takes complex phenomena and reduces them to more fundamental phenomena at a simpler level of analysis;[4] sometimes reductionism is the right thing to do. Reductionist approaches, to Levi-Strauss, can be applied to all complex phenomena we might try to understand; however, something may be lost or remain unexamined after a reductionist analysis is finished with a text. As one example, in Kimmerer's book, specifically in her chapter on Skywoman Falling, she departs from her indigenous creation narrative to compare Skywoman with Eve of the Christian Bible. This departure makes important points relevant to Kimmerer's story. At the same time, it reduces the Judeo-Christian creation narrative to the banishment of Eve from the garden and shows how easy it is to lose essential elements of a storyline through a reductionist analysis.

To Levi-Strauss, the second scientific approach is structuralism, which refers to keeping a text as a whole entity. When we approach complex phenomena that can't be reduced to a simpler explanation without losing something essential, we do so by seeing an interplay of relationships within it and by trying to understand it as a system. The idea that faith stories are belief/disbelief/unbelief systems was addressed in the discussion of scepticism in the chapter on Reason. When we try to comprehend complex phenomena (e.g., surface versus underlying beliefs) we're drawn to tools of appraisal and comparison for illumination.

In spiritual care learning, Anton Boisen, one of the founders of Clinical Pastoral Education (CPE), used a case study method[5] to look at the big picture of a patient's experience. He said, "I have sought to begin not with the ready-made formulations contained in books but with the living human documents, and with actual social conditions in all their complexity."[6] This approach includes details in patient/client appraisal, and moves away from reductionist assessments. We've all had conversations in which the few details we gave someone were reduced to such simplicity we felt unheard, misunderstood, and possibly angry. Being reduced to a simple solution is offensive at the deepest level. In this regard, it's significant to note that some spiritual care associations include the writing of a thoroughly documented case study as a requisite for certification.[7] Looking at living human documents and paying attention to actual social conditions contributes to competence in thick listening at thin moments.

In terms of how spiritual care professionals can broaden their approaches to scientific inquiry through the human sciences, we've seen that having an ability to listen (i.e., observe, theorize, test and analyze) and explore ways of interacting that incorporate insights from fields of study such as Action Science, worldview studies, common human themes, and global patterns hold great promise. These areas of learning need not replace traditional and existing resources for spiritual care education; rather, they expand on them. Rich nuances of theories-in-use and meaning-making can be uncovered by studying the Awareness Wheel and Ladder of Inference, traversing cycles of double loop learning and fostering fourth order thinking in the emergence of self/other understanding. In addition, the ability to listen is deepened by an approach to understanding taken by Gadamer, who was at pains to reveal a type of inquiry that suits the kind of empathetic consideration spiritual care practice relies on—a hermeneutic that applies to what spiritual care is best at uncovering. It's to Gadamer we now turn.

Use of Hermeneutics and Insights from Gadamer

The word "hermeneutic" has its origin in *hermeneuein*, a Greek term meaning to interpret or understand. How people perceive a situation or event, and the people in it, can have significant ramifications for the safe and effective use of self in spiritual care practice. In this respect, when spiritual care practitioners use the phrase "spiritual assessment", they're speaking about exercising an interpretative framework, a hermeneutic. Likewise, when they begin to learn about spiritual care, it's not uncommon for CPE students to use a spiritual screening tool—such as FICA or HOPE[8]—to frame their understanding. Such tools are a type of hermeneutic that provide new practitioners with a reading strategy for interpreting what patients or clients are communicating about their spiritual resources and needs. Gaining deeper insight into hermeneutics is important for the development of competence in thick listening at thin moments.

The following section looks at German philosopher Hans-Georg Gadamer's approach to hermeneutical theory in combination with insights from psychologist Daniel Stern, Persian poet Rumi (1207-1273) and theologian Edward Schillebeeckx (1914-2009). First, we look at Gadamer's thoughts about experiencing the world and how change impacts what we come to know. Next, we discuss what a hermeneutic of social interaction might look like for spiritual care practitioners. Lastly, we look at the importance of a hermeneutic perspective and the use of "tact" when navigating thin moment experiences. These theoretical inroads recognize that spiritual care practitioners learn to read people, situations, and relationships through informed and skilled use of interpretive clues perceived in concrete clinical interactions.

How Change Impacts What We Come to Know

Gadamer wrote at a time in history when the hard sciences stood as the only measure of truth and exactness. In comparing the human sciences as a form of inquiry, he didn't want to describe them as "inexact sciences."[9] Rather, he observed that how we experience our world, e.g., objectifying and attaining distance from it, versus opening and entering it, has an impact on our approach to observation, theorizing, testing and analysis in the systematic pursuit of knowledge. The hard sciences require a severing of one's bond with others and a distancing from one's own history for scientific knowledge to be gained. By contrast, inquiry into the world by way of human sciences doesn't require severing oneself from life. Accordingly, although many medical practitioners take distance from their patients as an essential feature of their professionalism, spiritual care practitioners see that distancing oneself risks I-It relating rather than I-Thou engagement. Empathetic sensitivity is required, and this means maintaining bonds of felt connection with patients and clients. In Gadamer's approach to inquiry, professional boundaries co-exist with entering the world of the client through genuinely listening to and understanding the other person's story.

Gadamer's quest was to find an approach to inquiry that would speak into the human sciences and their truth, so that truth could "come to speech."[10] He asserted that, like the hard sciences, human science is concerned with establishing similarities, consistencies, and patterns that make it possible to predict and interpret personal phenomena and processes. This happens if someone relies on personality theory, for example. In addition, Gadamer noted that with the human sciences, "we can't always achieve the goal of (the hard sciences) because it's not always possible to secure sufficient data to make our predictions reliable."[11] He makes the point that behind the observable, measurable aspects of experience (e.g., measuring what's possible between repeatable events), there exist the phenomena of social interaction. In the language of this book, among these phenomena are thin moments.

Gadamer made several observations about phenomenological experience. First, he noted that when our goal is to "make understanding the object of our reflection", "things that change force themselves on our attention far more than those that remain the same."[12] If you recall the swimmer's experience in an earlier chapter, spiritual care came into play when the swimmer sat on the edge of the pool, said she believed the water would hold her up, but refused to move into the water. Seeking to understand her drew a spiritual care practitioner into shared reflection, to explore what had changed for her.

Second, Gadamer believed that noting a change was a type of reflection that allowed for new critical consciousness to emerge. His fundamental hermeneutical question was: "what kind of knowledge is it that understands that something is so because it understands that it has come about so?"[13] Third, Gadamer reflected on this notion of coming about. As abstract as his question may sound at first reading, it's worth contemplating deliberately. Personal history and one's faith story come about; this coming about is relevant to the critical consciousness necessary for thick listening at thin moments. Unlike the hard sciences, spiritual care practitioners aim to see behind the self-presentation of a person; to observe, discern and interpret how something that's evident in a patient or client may have come about. This process of interpreting requires a practitioner to read a situation in a multidimensional way.

For Gadamer, a hermeneutic is a reading strategy that takes account of change, critical consciousness and coming about. It's a reading strategy that seeks to understand and interpret social interaction as a whole and in its parts. A hermeneutic always includes three elements: You, something you look through and something you look at. Throughout the book, we've emphasized the "you" that is the spiritual care practitioner. In terms of what spiritual care practitioners look through, their interpretive lenses, in addition to Gadamer's insights, they use and apply perspectives from spiritual, religious, cultural, and psychological frameworks. All these elements are brought to bear on personal and social aspects of the other person that a spiritual care practitioner observes.

When it comes to thick listening at thin moments, the ability to understand other people and oneself is foundational to all other competencies in spiritual care. As Gadamer points out, "understanding is a special case of applying something universal to a particular situation."[14] The kind of knowledge that understands that something is so because it understands that it has come about so also requires a spiritual care practitioner to look at complex phenomena within thin moments. All thin moments are phenomenological experiences that invite hermeneutical understanding.

A Hermeneutic of Social Interaction

Interpretive clues that surface through social interaction, detected in real time and drawn on in assessment and intervention, spark attentiveness to the presence of a thin moment. If spiritual care practitioners are grounded in interpretive frameworks that nurture thick listening and facilitate the recognition of a thin moment, they're well equipped to meet another as "other". Social interaction is the situation in which spiritual care practitioners become masterful at thick listening and recognizing thin moments, in themselves and in others.

A social interaction is any contact between two or more people. It can be verbal, non-verbal, brief, lengthy, unobtrusive, problematic, and so forth. In spiritual care practice, I-Thou relating most often occurs at a thin moment of social interaction where the "I" of the practitioner meets the "Thou" of the client at a time when the client's worldview map has been triggered by dissonance. Behind immediately observable elements of the interaction, a moment of meeting will register on worldview maps of all who are involved. Personal histories and faith stories not only of the client, but also family members, other involved professionals, and the spiritual care practitioner interact with one another.

How does Gadamer describe a hermeneutic of social interaction? For him, it's a reading strategy that allows us to understand and interpret a social interaction as a whole. His perspective is significant for spiritual care practitioners as they read living human documents. This reading occurs in what Daniel Stern calls "a present moment"[15] in which the quality of listening is so thick and focused that an intuitive reading of the other's thoughts goes hand in hand with a feeling—within the practitioner's body—of the other's feelings. This occurs not in any mystical way, but by carefully observing a client's facial expression and body posture, hearing their tone of voice, and noticing the immediate context for their behavior, even though this intuitive reading needs verifying and fine-tuning. Appreciating self and others through interpretive frames of reference, as suggested by Gadamer, broadens the scope of one's reading strategies when approaching a living human document in the sacred space of a thin moment. It's the social behind the personal and the personal within the social that one is reading during the complex competency of thick listening at thin moments.

For example, the pastor of a large urban church hears on the radio that a family in his congregation has suffered the loss of their home in a fire and that arson is suspected. In this situation, the initial social interaction is the pastor's hearing the news. He's motivated to contact the family and see if he can join them, to comfort them at this stressful time. When he calls the family, his call is answered by a first responder. The pastor is told the family is doing fine and doesn't need him to join them. The first responder will make sure the family knows he called. This telephone experience provides a second social interaction—one involving the worldview maps not only of the family and pastor but also of the first responder. While the pastor's worldview map includes the self-concept of a caring and compassionate helper, he's blocked from exercising his knowledge and skill by a restrictive intervention on the part of the first responder. He's frustrated and unconvinced that the family—whom he knows quite well—is doing fine. The confluence of these two social interactions triggers the pastor's worldview map, but rather than act impulsively, he takes time to think about what to do next.

Social interactions of this kind are complex and benefit from tools found in Action Science. What does the pastor understand initially? What further insight is needed? As he sits by the phone, he begins to deliberate. Gadamer summarized deliberation by saying that a particular person becomes what they are through what they do and how they behave—and they behave in a certain way because of what they have become. The purpose of their self-knowledge is to govern their action.[16] In this way, Gadamer's understanding links a hermeneutical stance to spiritual care practice and to Action Science and reveals a kind of knowledge and field of inquiry that helps people explore their own reasoning and attitudes, as they align what they say with what they do. This approach is helpful to the pastor as he reflects on his thoughts and feelings following the phone call. He realizes he's not only frustrated; he's angry. He feels dismissed as unimportant.

Using a hermeneutic of social interaction, the pastor looks at the complex dynamics involved. He reflects on his motivation to call the family. He ponders the first responder's involvement, especially insofar as it prevented him from communicating directly with the family, whom he's known for more than a decade. If he were to talk with any of them, he would be able to read their situation by hearing their tone of voice. This kind of inquiry into a social interaction reads the whole and its parts as a living human document, along with the benefits gained from reading oneself. The social and personal within the interaction come together in a field of inquiry that, to quote the poet Rumi, is "out beyond ideas of wrongdoing and rightdoing, where two worlds touch."[17] Self-knowledge, acquired by ongoing intentional reflection on one's worldview map, its model moments and one's theories-in-use, cultivates a spiritual care professional's capacity to engage another's worldview map at a thin moment.

The inquiry open to the pastor in his deliberation becomes a field of I-Thou meeting and relating. He becomes a place for understanding that something is so because it has come about so—for the family, the first responder and himself. This pastor focuses his attention on his own thin moment experience in which he felt rebuffed and ponders the personal and social dimensions of his current thinking, feeling and acting as well as what he might do next. He trusts that his careful assessment will lead him to optimal interventions.

It's reasonable to imagine that the pastor, benefitting from his hermeneutical deliberation, will act in beneficial ways not only toward his traumatized congregant family but also toward the first responder. He begins to wonder what has caused the first responder's refusal to connect him with the family. How did this behavior come about? Was it because he's a pastor? He considers the first responder's worldview map, wondering if spiritual and religious experiences have triggered the refusal. Was she being protective of the family? These are questions for which the pastor has no answers as yet, but they highlight the phenomena of social interaction operating behind what's observable. In summary, a hermeneutic of social interaction reads the social behind the personal and the personal within the social. The pastor's hermeneutical deliberation shifts his interpretation of the event. This is thick listening at thin moments as he reflects on the phone call. This pastor focuses his attention on his own thin moment experience in which he felt rebuffed and ponders the personal and social dimensions of his current thinking, feeling and acting as well as what he might do next.

The Hermeneutical Perspectives of Horizon, Circle and Tact

What we learn from Stern about "a present moment" includes the need to verify and fine-tune our interpretation of what's going on. Is our perspective on the situation accurate? Is our understanding superficial, comprehensive, or something else? The pastor will have to ask himself these questions when he meets the family and the first-responder. He'll need to carefully consider their facial expressions and body posture, hear their tone of voice, and notice the immediate context of their behavior. Are there questions arising from within the situation that will lead him into further inquiry? As he looks for answers, he discerns how his hermeneutical perspective helps him understand the situation more fully.

There are two metaphors related to a hermeneutical perspective in Gadamer's writings: the idea of a horizon and the image of a circle. Gadamer proposes that the concept of horizon suggests itself because it expresses the superior breadth of vision that a person who is trying to understand must have. People acquire a horizon by learning to look beyond what is close at hand—not in order to look away from it but in order to see it better.[18] Reading a living human document has parallels with reading a horizon and may have differences as well.

Reading a horizon includes seeing, imagining, knowing, discerning, and judging. Why is that? Some of what we're doing as we contemplate another person is sensing, e.g., we hear sounds and see movement occurring. We extrapolate from what we can see, taste, touch, smell, and hear to phenomena of social interaction that exist behind what's observable. Some of what we're doing as we look at the other is imagining. The same goes for knowing. We bring what we know from lived experience and theoretical resources to a client's experience of trauma or loss. Once we work with sensing, imagining, and knowing, we begin to discern aspects of the personal within the social and the social behind the personal. We make tentative assessments, such as "she's devastated," or "I need to call his children". Our reflections impact the way we see the other. However, judging, as it applies to reading a living human document, must remain open to inquiry and refuse to become judgmental.

Up to this point, we've explored the 'you' element of a hermeneutic of social interaction. What about the "something you look through" element? As we look at the other, we're using one or several interpretive lenses. Our perceptions are influenced by the particulars of our lens. The idea of reflectively looking at a living human document through an interpretive lens (e.g., eyeglasses) is that we can clean or repair our lenses, and sometimes get a new prescription. When we take our glasses off to have a look at them, to perceive first-hand how we see the world, we're engaging in a process of critical reflection, of coming to know how it is we see the world, rather than simply looking through lenses we've always been wearing. In addition to recognizing the lens we're using, for Gadamer, finding one's horizon involves discerning the significance of what's near, what's far off, what's great or small. It's a matter of finding perspective. This has parallels for spiritual care practitioners as they approach a living human document with thick listening at thin moments. They seek to see what's behind the observable; what's invisible to the eye.[19]

The third element of a hermeneutic is the "something you look at". Spiritual care practitioners prefer to say *someone* rather than *something*. But the who and the what both need to be seen. This means looking at the personal and the social with an inquiring mind. In the same way that people are stories, not snapshots, understanding requires a listener to get a sense of the whole story and its specific parts. It's a circular process: the whole narrative points to its parts and the parts point to the whole. Propelling this circular inquiry are questions that arise within spiritual care practice. The hermeneutical rule for Gadamer is that "we must understand the whole in terms of its detail and the detail in terms of the whole."[20] Theologian Edward Schillebeeckx links circular understanding and questioning when he writes:

> All understanding takes place in a circular movement—the answer is to some extent determined by the question, which is in turn confirmed, extended or corrected by the answer. A new question then grows out of this understanding, so that the hermeneutical circle continues to develop in a never-ending spiral... There is no definitive, timeless understanding which raises no more questions.[21]

In spiritual care practice, listening to the questions that arise within the exercise of thick listening at thin moments is integral to accurate assessment and intervention and keeps the practitioner from becoming judgmental. As noted earlier, Boisen described the living human document we meet as a whole person needing to be appreciated along "with actual social conditions in all their complexity."[22] Respect for the spiraling activity of circular inquiry contributes to the safe and effective use of self in spiritual care practice.

Delving deeper into circular inquiry, we turn again to Action Science insofar as it points out that all action is theory driven; listening, just like speaking, is action. Questioning is action. As we listen, we cannot not have theories about what someone is saying or will say next. We anticipate someone's meaning because that's how the brain works. A hermeneutical approach asks what to do with the theories and expectations that present themselves to us. Circular inquiry allows our listening to adjust expectations as we realize our theory-in-use doesn't fit the direction the other is taking. As we remain open and attentive to ourselves in the presence of the other, we learn to release our expectations and allow the other person's story to provide us with a different theory to explore. That is, movement of understanding is constantly from the whole to the part and back to the whole, because "a text must be understood in its own terms."[23] Gadamer summarizes his description of understanding by saying that "the harmony of all the details with the whole is the criterion of correct understanding."[24] Finding hermeneutical perspective by drawing on Gadamer's metaphors of horizon and circle, helps spiritual care practitioners hold the tension of perception, standpoint and questioning as they listen thickly at thin moments.

A final concept provided by Gadamer is that of tact. He uses this term to refer to "a particular sensitivity and sensitiveness to situations and how to behave in them, for which we cannot find any knowledge from general principles."[25] This understanding has resonance in Boisen's words, "I have sought to begin not with the ready-made formulations contained in books but with the living human documents"[26] It's tact that allows us to read interpretive clues that are available, starting with what's in front of us while also realizing we may miss essential elements of a story we're seeking to hear. As we genuinely listen to another's experience and insight, and draw on a peculiarly stubborn effort to get clear about it, we discover some validity in it, something about it that wouldn't have shown itself if we looked through our own lens only. In that sense, two participants in a conversation belong to each other; they belong to the subject matter being discussed and participate mutually in the process that brings out the nature of that subject.[27] In making his point about hermeneutical listening, and the role of tact in this interpretive approach, Gadamer uses Socratic conversation—discussed in the chapter on Reason—as his best example.

In its etymological roots, tact comes from the Latin "tangere", which means to touch. For Gadamer, tact is a way of getting in touch with the phenomena of social interaction that exist behind what is observable. He came to see that the human sciences needed a different way to investigate situations to which we can't apply the scientific method. Tact offers an investigative method that does not require distance from the other.

For him, tact has a great deal to do with asking the questions: What am I hearing? What's the relationship between what I'm hearing and this person's life?

To Gadamer, tact is not only a special sensitivity and sensitiveness to complex phenomena and situations, it's also the knowledge of how to behave in them. It includes sensual perception, awareness, mindfulness, and a quality of reasoning that arrives at results that may come as flashes of insight (the concept of *nous* previously discussed). Gadamer cautions that tact can't be put into a simple formula, for "an essential part of tact is that it is tacit and unformulable".[28] Once again there is resonance with Boisen's spurning ready-made formulations. To be tactful in one's hermeneutical listening, a spiritual care practitioner is comprehensively aware of the other. In that awareness, practitioners come to understand what to say and what to leave unsaid. When something is unsaid, it's not ignored. Practitioners realize that tact requires a passing over of the observation, if or until it's timely to address it in the conversation.

The exercise of tact creates a safe space, without becoming distant. It avoids an offensive, intrusive violation of the intimate sphere of the other, while at the same time conveying one's willingness to bring the fullness of one's awareness and attention to the conversation at hand. Tact is a viewpoint that's open to the viewpoint of others. It's a sense, like the other five senses, that can be cultivated as competent awareness increases. In the language of Rumi's poem, tact operates "where two worlds touch", as demonstrated by the pastor referred to earlier.

Types of Literacy Required to Develop Competence in Spiritual Care

In distinguishing superior from average performance in the complex competency of thick listening at thin moments, spiritual care practitioners need to draw on more than one way of knowing. The human brain is capable of multiple intelligences,[29] and these factor into the work of competency integration. We stated earlier that an I-Thou model moment of "meeting" opens a relational learning environment between the practitioner and client. Navigating this environment involves practitioners in the exercise of cognitive, emotional, social, and imaginative literacy. These types of literacy are required in a hermeneutic approach to social interaction. They are reading strategies that contribute to thick listening at thin moments. What do we mean by this point of view?

For many in the field of spiritual care, hermeneutical analysis began with the study of Jewish and Christian scriptures and includes the valid reading of a text along with its exegesis, and on interpretive contributions based on other forms of knowledge that are brought to the text.[30] In keeping with Boisen's insights, spiritual care reads a living human document and this living human document is an embodied sacred text layered with social conditions in all their complexity. This exegesis requires a valid reading not only of the person but also the locus of meeting (social interaction) and the worldview maps and models that are activated. The next section of the chapter looks at how emotional, social, cognitive and imaginative types of literacy contribute to the exegetical work of reading a living human document competently.

Emotional Literacy and Social Literacy as Developing Competencies

In a workbook used by the Korn Ferry Hay Group (2009),[31] to assess emotional and social intelligence, the core terms describe competent adults in the following way:

> Emotional and social intelligence is the capacity for recognizing our own feelings and those of others, for motivating ourselves, and for managing emotions effectively in ourselves and in others. It describes behaviors that sustain people in challenging roles, or as their careers become more demanding, and captures the qualities that help people deal effectively with change.[32]

This view of emotional and social intelligence is built on American psychologist and science journalist Dan Goleman's two books, *Emotional Intelligence* (1995) and *Social Intelligence* (2006). Together with American psychologist Richard E. Boyatzis, an expert on emotional intelligence, Goleman and Hay Group personnel developed an assessment known as the *Emotional and Social Competency Inventory* (ESCI). The ESCI assessment highlights four areas of ability:

- Self-Awareness: recognizing and understanding our own emotions
- Social-Awareness: recognizing and understanding the emotions of others
- Self-regulation (self-management): effectively managing our own emotions
- Relationship-Management: applying emotional understanding to

social interaction

Emotional literacy, as a reading strategy, develops on the strength of emotional intelligence, which is a capacity human beings have from birth. Recall that infants engage with parents in affect attunement due to emotional intelligence that deepens over time. While emotional intelligence is primarily about self-awareness and self-regulation, social intelligence realizes that every interaction produces change. We influence others; they influence us. From the perspective of emotional and social literacy, we engage in an intimate brain-to-brain connection whenever we're with other people. Again, research on affect attunement supports this brain-to-brain interaction during infancy, as children collect percepts and organize concepts about the world. Chapter one includes essential aspects of learning that are active in the brain: perceptual learning (sensations linked to the external world and to the body) and conceptual learning (stimuli that activate internally linked neurons to organize meaning). Conceptual learning works with perceptual experience, which is the centerpoint of Action Science. These capacities have implications for navigating a relational learning environment between practitioners and clients.

During social interaction, the more strongly connected we are, the greater the mutual effect our interactions have on all involved. During an interaction, our brains engage in a dance of feelings. Feelings are contagious: they ripple through our bodies and send out a cascade of hormones that regulate biological systems among our organs and immune system. Every interaction has emotional subtexts, so that relationships we find nourishing have beneficial impacts on health; toxic relationships can act like a slow poison in our bodies.

As a science journalist, Goleman summarized extensive research on human interaction to say that social intelligence is an ordinary capacity people have that allows us to be in relationship with one another. To him, it rests on caring about other people's needs in addition to our own, as one of its core values. Goleman is clear: social intelligence always includes concern for others. Without concern for others' well-being, social intelligence could incline toward manipulation and bullying. Human beings are designed to connect. Children learn from their environment what to expect through those connections, as the little girl on the slide and the little boy on the step demonstrated in the chapter on Faith. People use those connections to steer their behavior in a particular direction, whether it's a healthy choice and direction, or not.

Along with emotional intelligence, social intelligence is a range of capacities from instantaneously sensing another's inner state, to understanding someone else's feelings and thoughts. It's an ability to comprehend complex social situations and act appropriately while they're taking place. Socially literate people think on their feet. Being literate implies that the ability to read ourselves and others during an interaction is seamless. Literate people use social intelligence ground rules in a skilled manner. Using social intelligence as a reading strategy allows a socially literate person to negotiate interactions, repair mis-directions as they arise, and remain engaged with others. Ground rules for social literacy include the following achievements: having the ability to

- Attend to another person
- Pace an interaction
- Engage in conversation
- Tune in to another's feelings
- Manage one's own feelings during the encounter

In spiritual care contexts, emotional and social reading strategies act together to achieve meaningful social engagement. The outcome of their union is an artful ability to be true to oneself—to be authentic—while in the presence of people who matter to us, but who may differ from us. Emotional and social types of literacy form two ways of knowing needed by practitioners as they engage diversity that characterizes human encounters. The developed capacity of embodied social and emotional literacy is integral to thick listening at thin moments.

Cognitive Literacy and Imaginative Literacy as Developing Competencies

In addition to social and emotional literacy, the use of reason and imagination foster types of literacy that help spiritual care practitioners navigate relational learning environments. As already mentioned, human beings have the capacity to be active agents in the process of making meaning. Spiritual care is about helping people (including the practitioner) to be intentionally reflective, mindfully active agents of their own thinking by being self-aware of what's currently in their thoughts, as Rose and Nancy demonstrate in the chapters on Faith and Reason. Cognitive and imaginative types of literacy form, reform, and transform the meaning people make. The human capacity for using reason and imagination is grounded on brain activity.

The first chapter included an analysis of the brain's role in forming a worldview. To recap, and to apply these insights to spiritual care, some of our neurons link the body to objects in the world, so that percepts form through experiencing people and things. Percepts produce representations in the mind that appear as impressions, thoughts, memories, ideas, images. These mental representations resemble material objects (and events) in the world so that a distinction is made between actual material objects and their representation in the mind.[33] In the process of perceiving, each percept involves an association, "to perceive is to associate,"[34] so that, if a child experiences mother/father as warm and loving, the child will associate mother/father with love, comfort, and safety.

As mentioned in chapter one, another set of neurons are connected internally to each other. Through their communicative interaction concepts form in the mind, e.g., the concept of a triangle. What's central for spiritual care practice is to hear the percepts, associations and concepts that populate the narrative which shapes how people see the world and informs the meaning they've been making over time. Thick listening at thin moments seeks to detect percepts, associations, thoughts, images, memories, and ideas as they are spoken or embodied by a client or patient and use them as interpretive clues as they listen thickly. As spiritual care practitioners listen, they notice clues from their own worldview map of percepts, associations, concepts, memories, thoughts, and images. In spiritual care practice that's informed by a hermeneutical persective, it's the interplay of both worldview maps to which practitioners listen. As they are guided in the conversation by patient/client narratives, they notice and release interpretations that come from their own worldview maps if they don't fit the map of the other person. Growth in understanding for client and practitioner comes about as concepts currently in use shift and change with the entry of new insight, perspective and information that's introduced into the encounter.

As part of the hermeneutic skill of being with someone as they tell their faith story, practitioners pay attention to what's in someone's thinking and are aware that conceptual learning and perceptual experience work together. Conceptual learning remains open to perceptual experience so that people can acquire new thoughts and alter those that were previously held by gaining insight into the concepts they currently use (theories-in-use) and by asking themselves whether these are the concepts they want to continue relying on, as Rose and Nancy exemplify. Both women learn to trust, cope with trauma, or tell a faith story by using reason and imagination as organizing principles for gathering meaning into new patterns that provide them with greater life satisfaction, and they do so by remaining open to new understanding, largely gained from other people.

All learning moves through change—loss and recovery—and has implications for reconceiving one's worldview. As examples, a child leaves a teddy bear on the shelf, which up to that point signified comfort as well as companionship, and runs outside to play with other children, who now constitute friendship, at least potentially. A father leaves his macho image behind, which up to that point signified self-protection and garnered respect from others. He allows his tears to fall freely as he stands beside his wife, as he feels secure and valued in their companionship, while they attend the funeral of their youngest son who was killed in a motor vehicle accident. Change occurs as new data enter a worldview map; change requires people to pay attention to what they currently think, feel, and do. Paying attention—an identifier of thick listening—is a central organizer of human meaning.[35]

Reason and imagination help to shape the meaning that people are making. While they work together, imagining refers to forming a mental concept or image of what is not actually present to the senses but that produces ideas and images. Imagining always has the quality of something that's not in evidence. Imagining and outcomes of imagination are usually linked to creativity. Imagination plays with pictures, thoughts, opinions, objects in the world and objects not available to the senses and invents something new. There's a sense with imagination that one is going beyond the ordinary to form new or composite ideas, worlds, opinions, or practices that aren't known with certainty. In existential contexts (as opposed to neurotic, psychotic) people know when they are imagining, just as they can distinguish dreaming from being awake.

Reason also helps organize meaning, and generally produces statements and facts, either in written or spoken form. German social theorist Hannah Arendt[36] proposed that thinking is always about the past; reason uses what's already available through percepts and concepts and works with that mental material, while imagination moves us into the future. Reason typically relies on patterns or approaches that can be learned, such as asking prior questions or recognizing a circular argument.

Reason has to do with using selected ideas that ground or lead to a conclusion. The result may be an idea or an action. Reason relies on evidence, whether it's empirical (e.g., the accuracy of counting chairs in a room), conventional (e.g., definitions that rely on the way we tend to understand a word) or theoretical (e.g., arguments that are cogent because they match the way the world is, or are internally consistent—i.e., the ideas hang together). As we use reason, we may argue or discuss, but if what we write or say is reasonable, it comes across in a connected, sensible manner so that conclusions follow from points we make along the way to support those conclusions. As a result, other reasonable people can follow us to those conclusions, whether they agree with them or not. Socratic conversation and Aristotelian deliberation are patterns that structure well-reasoned positions and points of view. If the point of imagination is creativity, the point of reason is clarity and making sound judgments.

Given the earlier discussion of brain activity, it's compelling to consider how Immanuel Kant (1724-1784) conceived of imagination. In his view, without benefit of brain research, he positioned imagination at the mid-point between the activity of receiving percepts and forming concepts, so that imagination works with percepts and concepts. Aristotle also distinguishes imagination from perceiving and conceptualizing by saying that, imagination is "different from either perceiving (*aesthesis*) or discursive thinking (*noesis*) though it is not found without sensation, nor is judgement found without it."[37] For these philosophers, imagination functions with perceiving and conceptualizing (though differs from both) and plays out in making judgments as well. Based on this view of imagination, we recall that, even in dire circumstances, there's a spiritual need to look forward to and imagine a hopeful future and find one's place in it.

The following clinical vignette captures the four types of literacy as they are lived out between and among a military couple, spiritual care practitioner/chaplain, a neonatologist, and other hospital staff members during a unique and meaningful birth event. As previously stated, a holistic, embodied, and unified use of the four reading strategies distinguishes superior from average performance in spiritual care practitioners when exercising the complex competency of thick listening at thin moments.

The incident occurred in the Neonatal Intensive Care Unit (NICU) wing of a large, urban hospital. A young military couple, deployed from England to western Canada, pregnant and struggling with the complexities of a developing fetus, were in a thin moment experience. As they approached the delivery time, they could foresee that the baby's viability would be slim, and they wanted to have their newborn baptized.

The spiritual care practitioner carried the on-call pager, signaling her availability to be called anywhere in the hospital over a 24-hour period. She received a referral to meet the military couple, and thus had an initial opportunity to talk with them prior to their going to the delivery area of the NICU. Their faith was strong, but so was their heartache. Together with the chaplain, the couple spoke about this being their first pregnancy and how devastating it had been to cope with the baby's abnormalities. It was their desire to have the baby baptized following birth. The chaplain asked if they had a name in mind. They didn't. They said they'd think about a name for their baby.

The call came to the chaplain at about 11:00 p.m. and she made her way to the NICU. Once there, she prepared for the baptism. A small bottle of sterilized water was provided by a nurse. Following the birth, a neonatologist gathered the quite disfigured female baby in his arms and carried her to where she was placed in an isolette for critical care. The chaplain made her way to the baby's isolette. There she was greeted by the neonatologist who said, "Her name is Hope. They have decided to call her Hope." At this exact moment, nurses from the birthing room wheeled the baby's mom into the NICU, accompanied by the baby's dad, so they could take part in the baptism. Several staff members gathered around to provide a community of faith for baby and parents. The chaplain poured water, spoke the words, and baptized "Hope". This infant lived only several hours. Her brief existence remains a testimony to her parents' deep faith at a touch point that took place between their suffering and their imaginative response.

Emotional, social, cognitive and imaginative reading strategies are at play in this scenario as the spiritual care practitioner enters into a series of social interactions with a military couple, a neonatologist, NICU staff members and baby Hope. The entry point into the parents' worldview map was *tradition*, in particular their faith tradition. Reasoning brought them to a decision to have their baby baptized. Imagination provided them with her name "Hope". The chaplain, grounded in procedural details related to the baptism (water, words, action), engaged compassion and reason when inquiring about a name for the baby during her pre-meeting with the parents. Imaginative literacy was triggered when she heard the neonatologist's pronouncement, witnessed the forming of a community of faith around the newborn in her isolette, and had the experience of "baptizing Hope". It was a complex and multifaceted social interaction, but the scenario unified the four types of literacy—each one playing a part in the relational learning environment. Brain-to-brain neural resonance joined together with a heart-to-heart felt sense of connection. A spiritual care practitioner perceived a need to draw on and use differing ways of knowing as she sought not only to be ritually accurate but also emotionally and imaginatively aligned with the parents as they navigated this profound and meaningfully thin moment.

Following such an impactful experience, and after allowing sufficient time for the chaplain to absorb what's occurred, it's beneficial—not only for the practitioner but also for others on his or her spiritual care team or professional peer group—to spend time collegially debriefing the critical incident. This is an opportunity to explore specific aspects of the relational learning environment involved in this clinical vignette. What took place in this limited space and time conveys a wide range of implications about what it means to listen thickly, read a living human document as sacred text, and recognize a thin moment as it emerges and plays out meaningfully.

Noticing where this chaplain's professional competencies surfaced during the incident sheds light on her stage of competence, i.e., how integrated, unified, and holistic it has become. On a broader plain, many spiritual care associations are identifying and assessing competencies in professional practice, and benefit from the use of rubrics that distinguish superior from average performance.[38] These rubrics are referenced in the endnotes for anyone who wishes to know more about them. In this chapter, we now move to the following topics: (a) constructing a competency and the development of competence in spiritual care practice and (b) assessing competence in thick listening at thin moments. Once again, we express our hope that, by focusing attention on a unified complex competency—thick listening at thin moments—and looking at how it plays out in practice from entry level to seasoned expertise, there will also be a broader application of other theories and principles explored in this book.

Constructing a Competency and Developing Competence in Spiritual Care

Our understanding of how a competency is constructed and how competencies operate in spiritual care practice grows out of two assertions made by Richard Boyatzis:[39] (i) a theory of performance is the basis for the concept of competency, and (ii) maximum performance is believed to occur when a person's capability or talent is consistent with the needs of a particular job. Competency-based learning—as distinct from content, context, or course-based learning—has fast become a focus of attention in spiritual care education. But what does this mean in practical terms?

The words "competency" and "competence" derive from the same Latin source as *compete*—to seek together—from com (together) + petere (to aim at, seek). Its Latin source involves seeking, striving, and pursuing a common objective. If competing has implications for winning/losing, besting and defeating one's opponent, competence has a step-by-step, self-improvement focus. For our purposes, interest in competency development and competence assessment is directed by two questions:

- What do these notions have to do with thick listening at thin moments?

- How can understanding the development of competence in spiritual care practice contribute to a practitioner's approach to and use of competencies listed by their education programs and professional associations in such a way that distinct competencies become seamlessly integrated and unified in a complex competency?

What follows is an effort to spell out what competency is and how it comes to be, and to point spiritual care practitioners to a hermeneutical reading of underlying clues and behaviors embedded in their educational/professional lists of competencies.[40]

To begin with, a competency is an ability that relies on basic attributes of a person's character. In the process of learning, these attributes or characteristics are either already present in an adult or are learned through practice, until they become durable and enduring. As a result, people can be counted on to demonstrate them as they carry out tasks that are part of their work. To say a competency is a set of underlying characteristics that are recognizable within a given work setting, implies that they express specific values for that occupation and convey how to do the job correctly and well. This view of a competency means that these characteristics include more than the requisite knowledge and skills to do a job. There are attitudes and behaviors associated with a competency. Taken together, all dimensions of a competency, listed below, create the possibility of successful achievement. All of them matter in the successful carrying out of a role or function because they are interdependent and interwoven within a given competency.

Aspects of a competency are visible in action and can be observed by others. When assessed, competencies predict who will perform well and who will perform poorly.[41] Again, the words competency and competence are related in that the first term describes the underlying characteristics and the second term, competence, refers to a person's degree of accomplishment as compared with an ideal performance of these characteristics. As we consider competencies associated with spiritual care practice, in particular the complex competency of thick listening at thin moments, we understand every competency to be an interwoven ability that includes six dimensions:

- Motives: what a person constantly thinks about that causes action
- Traits: physical characteristics and consistent responses
- Self-concept (1): the picture one has of oneself and the value one places on that picture
- Self-concept (2): the difference between the map and the model (see Forming a Worldview in chapter one.)
- Knowledge: the information/data one has accrued about mental, emotional, physical and spiritual tasks
- Skill: the ability to perform physical, mental, emotional, imaginative and spiritual tasks.[42]

To represent the inter-relatedness of the dimensions noted above, Spencer and Spencer introduced the image of an iceberg.[43] While a competency is always demonstrable and observable, there are visible and hidden features to it. For the most part, an iceberg model of competence represents skills and knowledge above the water line; motives, traits, and self-concepts lie below the water line. It's important to approach this iceberg image with thoughtfulness, however, insofar as competence is embodied and not dissected into parts. The exercise of any competency is holistic, authentic, and unified.

Toward a goal of seamless and integrated competence, when using the iceberg model, spiritual care practitioners learn to look inward and scan their thoughts and feelings while they're listening to someone. As they listen, they may ask themselves: What moves me? What comes or doesn't come naturally to me? What ideas do I have about myself and about the patient/client? What's me and what's not me? How do I see myself in this social interaction? What's important and not important? Such questions accompany an assessment of what a practitioner knows and doesn't know, as well as an understanding of what they can or can't do. This kind of reflective questioning underscores the importance of self-knowledge and self-awareness throughout the process of gaining mastery in spiritual care practice. Rose's story, as mentioned earlier, demonstrates that practitioners can't ignore themselves as they listen to others.

There's a second feature of the iceberg image to consider. While the iceberg is helpful, what fits above or below the water line is not rigid in human experience. Spiritual care practitioners realize that something coming from below the client's water line can express itself bodily and provide interpretive clues. For example, degrees of emotion are embodied and can appear gradually. In seeking to recognize a thin moment, recall that emotion is embodied, as was presented in the chapter on Made for Relationship. Practitioners attend carefully to embodied clues and remain open to what the other might be conveying that they can explore together. What's depicted as hidden in the iceberg diagram conveys itself to a perceptive spiritual care reader. That is, a thin moment is both visible and hidden. Reading what's visible and interpreting what's hidden is central to thick listening. Competence increases as spiritual care practitioners discern signs of a thin moment by recognizing their own embodied thoughts and those of their clients or patients.

Taking a Closer Look at Six Dimensions of a Competency

Looking at each of the six dimensions of a competency in greater depth, we start with *motives*. Motives cause, initiate or drive action. A motive is an assumption, thought, insight, reason, or impression that prompts, induces, causes, or moves a person to take a particular course of action. Motives are largely hidden whereas action taken based on those motives is observable. Further, motives may be evident to the person taking the action but could be somewhat hidden from the agent of the action. Becoming consciously aware of one's motives, and learning to be transparent about them, is part of developing mastery in the competencies associated with thick listening at thin moments.

The second dimension is *traits*. These are consistent and enduringly dependable qualities of a person's character or way of being. The word trait has its origin in art and refers to a line or stroke made by pen or pencil, or the feature of a line in someone's face. In the military, it referred to a shot, missile or arrow that followed a particular trajectory as it moved through space. A trait has a trajectory; it follows a path, so that if someone becomes competent in a complex ability, other people can generally predict where their behavior is leading. Trait also refers to a particular feature of mind or character, i.e., a distinguishing quality of someone's dependable or habitual way of being or acting. While depicted below the water line in the competency iceberg image, traits are observable. As they get to know someone, others come to count on traits that characterize that person. For example, if someone is late to a meeting, those present might say, "Oh, he's always late. He'll probably show up in 20 minutes." Or they might say, "She's never late. I wonder if she's alright?"

The third and fourth dimensions, self-concepts, are both hidden and evident. A healthy self-concept may show up as self-confidence. The way a confident person walks, talks and interacts with others reflects genuineness, poise, and grounded-ness. In many ways, the definition of *self-concept* is straightforward. It's the image or picture we have of ourselves along with the value we place on that picture. In other ways, the term self-concept is complex. For example, according to Michael Argyle,[44] American psychologist Carl Rogers differentiated three parts to a self-concept: the person you want to be (ideal self), the person you present (self-image), and how much you like and value yourself (self-esteem). Often it's tension between the ideal and the presented self that's a source of internal conflict. Thus, it's important to notice that we may see ourselves quite differently than others do. Likewise, we may see ourselves the way we want to look, rather than the way we do look. In this regard, there can be blind spots to our self-concept. Furthermore, we may present to others a masked image, a presentation of self that Swiss psychiatrist Carl Jung referred to as a "persona".[45] This is a public face that puts to the side what's true and real. While not the ideal, at times this is what's called for when a spiritual care practitioner is required to show up in their professional role, while coping with personal grief, trauma, fatigue, or other stressors. Developing healthy self-concepts is important work for those who seek to be competent in thick listening at thin moments.

Based on Josephine Klein's work, a second dimension of a self-concept involves different aspects of learning. Klein uses a worldview map and a model moment to depict meaning systems that contain three elements: a sense of self, a sense of other people and things, and a sense of what goes on between them.[46] We've added this dimension to Spencer's and Spencer's analysis because of it's relevance to thick listening at thin moments.

The worldview map and model each contain a self-concept. A person shows up both as the sense they have of themselves that has accumulated over time and the here-and-now person involved in an event. In the encounter, under favorable conditions, the map agrees with the model. For example, you're studying about spiritual care at a theological college and meet a new course instructor for the first time. This person recognizes your role at the college and has a sense of accomplishments you've accrued in your degree work thus far. When there's congruence between map and model, we hardly notice. It's just the way things are supposed to be. But suppose you're called to the bedside of a dying patient and the person dies shortly after you arrive. The patient's family is there and looks to you for emotional support. It's the first time you've seen a dead body. You're thrown off balance. Map and model are incongruent.

Of course, you have options. But the model moment is out of whack with your existing experience and sense of self; you need to adjust to this new situation. Adjustment requires you to be attentive to potential conflicts between your ideal self and the self you present. Learning competencies associated with thick listening at thin moments calls for assessing worldview map and model incongruence. This assessment focuses outwardly to involve the use of tact while engaging with the bereaved family. It also focuses inwardly and invites reflective reassessment of self-concepts awakened and/or challenged during the model moment. The work of attending to this second sense of self-concept involves the use of contemplative mindfulness and healthy reasoning as practitioners take steps to re-conceive their view of themselves and of what's going on, while with the deceased person's family.

Lastly, we turn to dimensions five and six. If some dimensions of a competency are somewhat hidden, knowledge and skills are evident and lie above the water line of a person's practice. *Knowledge* refers to the accrued information, academic degree work, supervised practice, insights, spiritual practices, and related experiential learning that a person has acquired. Its use can be easily witnessed by others, as can the *skills* that the spiritual care profession relies upon. The development of knowledge and skill is a distinguishing feature of those who are competent, i.e., who do a job effectively. But not all competencies necessary for a job will differentiate good performance from performance that needs to improve.

Distinguishing Between Threshold and Differentiating Competencies

According to Richard Boyatzis,[47] competencies are divided into threshold and differentiating groups. Of note in this regard, when referring to

, we're distinguishing competencies that exist *within* the profession of spiritual care. By contrast, it's not uncommon for spiritual care practitioners to be asked to describe what they do that's different from what other professionals who have similar skill sets might do. They're often asked what makes them unique. But that's not the kind of differentiation we refer to here.[48] Our focus is two groups of competencies that cluster into threshold and differentiating groups, as identified by Boyatzis, which we will apply to spiritual care practice.

Threshold competencies are foundational to the practice of spiritual care. Examples include communication skills (verbal/written), interpersonal skills, organizational skills, decision-making and problem-solving skills. These competencies highlight *what a person does*. They can be found in most job descriptions for spiritual care practitioners and are often a component of the screening process for Clinical Pastoral Education (CPE) applicants. A beginning spiritual care practitioner needs to be able to initiate a conversation, ask appropriate questions, provide suitable reflective responses, and document an interaction for referral and/or learning purposes. Insofar as threshold competencies are foundational to and required for most spiritual care interventions, their presence is incorporated into the language and tools used for Basic/Level I learning in the context of North American CPE programs.

For the purposes of this chapter, threshold competencies for thick listening at thin moments can be clustered as follows:

- Listening competencies—such as expertise with multi-dimensional, in-depth listening; assessing social interactions when meeting another as "other"; noticing elements of the life narrative and faith story of the other; and integrating spiritual, religious, and cultural traditions alongside psychological theories and frameworks.

- Integrative competencies—such as experience with drawing on knowledge gained through academic as well as supervised clinical learning; bringing both book knowledge and a felt sense of connection to engaging another in shared reflection on the other's immediate concerns about faith, spirituality and/or life in general; and facilitating meaning-making with the other by using spiritual reflection and/or theological reflection.

- Relational competencies—such as an aptitude for providing a safe interpersonal space; using cognitive skills to pay close attention to a social interaction that is unfolding; noticing verbal and nonverbal interpretive clues; and being attentive to not only heart but also head by using healthy reasoning while communicating empathetically.

Differentiating competencies distinguish superior from average performance in spiritual care practice. Examples include communicating empathetically while observing another's distress, documenting efficiently and effectively when writing a chart note, assessing the ethical implications of delaying a critical procedure while discerning whether or not patient advocacy is called for, and knowing when one's scope of practice is at its limits, as one tries to solve a complex problem. These aspects of a competency indicate *how well a person does what they do* when they communicate, relate with others, make decisions, and solve problems. Differentiating competencies are incorporated into the language and tools used for Advanced/Level II, Certification and Peer Review assessment in North American spiritual care associations.

For the purposes of this chapter, differentiating competencies for thick listening at thin moments can be clustered as follows:

- Systems competencies—such as the ability to recognize a thin moment, notice relational patterns, see connections between a whole and its parts (within a faith story or a healthcare concern) and to think systemically; to attend to the dynamics of one's own social location, beliefs, power, vulnerability and boundaries as these impact relationships with individuals and groups.

- Contemplative mindfulness competencies—such as an aptitude for self-awareness and other-awareness as these coexist within reflective and contemplative practice; discerning thin moments within a social interaction; opening space for the emergence of expectancy, careful attention and quiet wonder when engaged in thick listening at thin moments; simultaneously accessing one's own worldview map while also reading the relational clues communicated by a client that indicate a point of entry onto the worldview map of that other person; appreciating layered aspects of humility (i.e. intellectual, epistemological, hermeneutical, cultural, racial, gendered); and being able to stand alone as well as in solidarity with others.

- Social interaction competencies—such as the safe and effective use of self in the practice of thick listening at thin moments; engaging compassionately and with awareness of socio-political dynamics, and knowing how to navigate these complexities with tact, clarity, skill and empathy; demonstrating awareness of and sensitivity to trauma's intergenerational impacts on the body, mind, and spirit as these manifest in thin moments; and exercising leadership while also functioning collaboratively both within and beyond one's spiritual care profession.

To summarize, the construction of a competency and the development of competence in spiritual care practice involves acquiring a set of specific competencies, usually provided by one's theological college or professional association. These concrete abilities bring together basic attributes of a person's character (motives, traits, self-concept), knowledge (theological/spiritual/religious, psychological, cultural), and the exercise of skills (listening, relational engagement, ethical discernment, for the work of spiritual care). Among more advanced spiritual care practitioners, there are threshold behavioral habits that integrate with differentiating relational abilities to unify competencies into what homeopathic practitioner Will Taylor calls *reflective competence* and Hubert Dreyfus calls *practical wisdom*.[49] As stated previously, it's the educational centers, colleges and professional associations that articulate and classify competencies, but it's the spiritual care practitioner who integrates and unifies these competencies into competent spiritual care practice.

Assessing Competence in Thick Listening at Thin Moments

The task of assessing competence in spiritual care practice usually takes place in two ways: supervisors assess students and colleagues assess peers. For CPE students, assessment involves students and supervisors in writing evaluations and summary assessments. These parallel documents, crafted with reference to lists of competencies, are used to measure a student's progress from Basic/Level I to Advanced/Level II learning.

For those who have completed CPE, certification and peer review are processes wherein ongoing assessment and professional accountability occur. To begin with, a designated number of practice hours are required after completing CPE and before applying for professional certification. During this interim, practitioners self-scrutinize what they've learned, seek to align their actions with evidence-based criteria inherent in the competencies listed by their professional associations, and allow themselves to be informally apprenticed by colleagues within their spiritual care work settings.

Practitioners apply for certification through their professional associations. While each association has its own requirements, materials gathered for application tend to fall into two categories: (1) formal documents (evidence of association membership, academic qualifications, copies of CPE unit assessments, faith group endorsement, professional ethics course completion, and letters of reference) and (2) reflective documents (an autobiographical statement, an essay or narrative statement demonstrating personal/professional integration of theory and practice, and one or several examples of the provision of spiritual care, e.g. verbatim or thoroughly documented case study, as this practice applies to listed competencies. In the application and review process, certification candidates engage with already certified colleagues who deliberate about the candidate's becoming a peer. The function of certification review is more about collegial reflection and peer affirmation than giving approval or granting permission. Based on their assessment of a candidate's application materials, reviewers consider whether the person is ready to be welcomed as a Certified Spiritual Care Practitioner or Board Certified Chaplain. Is there evidence of an ability to exercise complex competencies with personal and professional as well as theoretical and practical integration? Does the candidate demonstrate competence at an expert stage?

Once certified, spiritual care practitioners continue their ongoing assessment and professional accountability by means of peer review. In most cases, every three to five years they meet again with selected peers to discuss their professional functioning. Here the questions have to do with demonstrating mastery. Are there strengths or limitations in evidence related to a practitioner's safe and effective use of self? Are there ways the practitioner is advancing personally, and are there ways they are advancing the profession of spiritual care as a whole?

So, what does this mean for assessing competence in thick listening at thin moments? As previously noted, while thick listening and the ability to recognize a thin moment are two distinct competencies, they're integrated as the cohesive, seamlessly exercised complex competency of *thick listening at thin moments*. The exercise of a complex competency occurs during social interactions that take place in relational learning environments, as already mentioned. Each social interaction is comprised of three parts: a *before*, a *during*, and an *after*. If participants in a social interaction 'meet', there's an intersection of personal and social diversity. Everyone present brings who they are to the encounter; pasts come in to the present and possibilities flow out to the future. Thus, every I-Thou meeting calls for thoughtful attentiveness. This attentiveness, or contemplative mindfulness, welcomes thick listening on the holy ground of worldview maps that are meeting in a model, and often thin, moment.

During patient/client interaction, thin moments are detected through interpretive clues carefully read by the spiritual care practitioner. Emotional, social, cognitive and imaginative reading strategies interpret the situation and discern specifics of the thin moment. If, for example, a chaplain has been called to be with a family in the Emergency Department of a hospital, it's reasonable to assume there's a crisis thin moment unfolding. By contrast, if a congregational pastor is invited to dinner at the home of an aging couple, it may not be clear what to expect. In the hospital emergency room, while all four reading strategies are embodied holistically, practitioners draw more intentionally on emotional and cognitive literacies for that specific situation. In the second situation, social and imaginative literacies may foster a safer environment for social discourse, and readiness on the part of the pastor to engage whatever questions or disclosures the couple may bring forth. Using one's knowledge and skill for thick listening at thin moments—as a chaplain or pastor—involves conscious deliberation and spontaneous intuition. Within thick listening, there's ongoing discernment about thin moments.

Spiritual care practitioners are adult learners. While spiritual care may be a new field of study for someone, after an initial orientation, adult learners tend to be less instructor-dependent and more self-directed. This dynamic is built into CPE program design insofar as the focus is on experience and less on content. An assumption made in the CPE learning model is that learners will take responsibility to inform themselves and/or pursue a knowledge gap by selecting related topics for theory seminars. Thus, in CPE, it's clinical events and their reflective debriefing that have greatest weight in program time allocation. Accordingly, both patient/client social interactions and supervisor/peer social interactions comprise the relational learning environments where spiritual care expertise develops.

To summarize, learning how to practice thick listening at thin moments is a complex and multifaceted proficiency that coheres around someone's preparedness and ability to effectively read situations, people, stories and patterns. It draws on threshold and differentiating competencies in spiritual care practice, as summarized previously. For a spiritual care practitioner, thick listening at thin moments begins with anticipatory vigilance as a particular social interaction starts to unfold. This vigilance recognizes there is a *before* to the encounter and is alert to ways one's own worldview map may be intersecting with—and, perhaps, triggered by—other people in the encounter. *During* the event a spiritual care professional may discern it to be a thin moment, in which there's dissonance occurring for patient, client, practitioner and/or both. Listening to this dissonance, this thin moment, raises Gadamer's fundamental hermeneutical question, *"what kind of knowledge is it that understands that something is so because it understands that it has come about so?"*[50] and is the essence of thick listening at thin moments. As spiritual care practitioners learn to listen thickly, their expertise can be measured by how well they draw on more than one way of knowing and how effectively they discern both what is so and what has come about so. When expert interventions occur during a spiritual care encounter, they have ramifications for what happens *after* the social interaction. Thus, a traumatic death or conflicted family situation will be remembered by the patient or client, and this memory will include the actions of the spiritual care practitioner.

Assessing progress in the exercise of thick listening at thin moments requires a lifetime commitment to reflective practice and peer accountability. Learning doesn't end with completion of the twelve-to-sixteen hundred hours of CPE. From formal academic studies to the use of competency lists, and to the integration of competencies into expert competence, spiritual care practitioners are always engaged in experiential learning. Thus, there is merit to forming post-CPE peer groups for shared debriefing of significant clinical experiences—as did the chaplain who baptized Hope—where ongoing learning about thick listening at thin moments can occur. This is an important resource not only prior to but following professional certification. Ideally, spiritual care practitioners who choose to foster mutual relationships with colleagues, and share the journey of growth in self-knowledge and skills development, will become masterful practitioners. Developing mastery in thick listening at thin moments follows a pattern that's outlined in the final chapter of the book. By following this pattern for acquiring mastery, nuances of learning coalesce throughout a lifetime of personal and professional reflection as complex spiritual care competencies are integrated and unified into seamless, confident, embodied competence.

Conclusion

This chapter contains a number of topics relevant to competencies for and competence in spiritual care practice. These topics include a perspective on inquiry and hermeneutical interpretation as they apply to social interaction. We've outlined the construction of a competency, and distinguished its threshold from differentiating aspects. Throughout this chapter, by drawing on insights from previous chapters of the book, we've given special attention to learning the complex competency of thick listening at thin moments. In the next chapter, we'll examine the approach to skills acquisition developed by American philosopher and educator Hubert Dreyfus (1929-2017), applying his insights to spiritual care competence development. Our focus is on lifelong learning that coalesces around personal and professional reflection and growth, as distinctive spiritual care competencies are integrated and unified into seamless, confident, embodied complex competence.

Take Away Questions for Reflection

- In which of the so-called soft sciences, i.e., human sciences, do you feel best grounded? How do these approaches to inquiry inform your spiritual care practice?

- What do you make of the sentence, "For Gadamer, a hermeneutic is a reading strategy that takes account of change, critical consciousness, and coming about"? Are you aware of the reading strategies you use in your spiritual care assessments and interventions?

- How do you understand the idea of a relational learning environment? Are there elements in your understanding that are present or missing in your current context? What do you see yourself contributing to your relational learning environment?

- Can you recall a time when you experienced engaging a patient/client with emotional and social literacy and/or cognitive and imaginative literacy? If so, write down your experience and highlight how these literacies impacted your perspectives on the spiritual care encounter.

- What's the difference between "competency" and "competence"? What did you learn about a competency when reading about the six dimensions of a competency, and differences between threshold and differentiating competencies?

- From what you've read about a "complex competency", where in your spiritual care practice do you see this complexity in action?

- Can you develop a case study based on your enactment of complex competencies derived from your spiritual care association's list of competencies?

Chapter 8

Skills Acquisition in the Assessment of Spiritual Care Practice

Introduction

This chapter flows out of the previous chapter and sharpens the theoretical ideas found there by concentrating on two questions: (1) What does competent spiritual care practice look like clinically? and (2) What's involved in mastering the complex competency of thick listening at thin moments? In taking up these questions, there are two theoretical and educational constructs that frame the chapter. First, we sketch the importance of *case study* usage, research and publication as ways to make spiritual care practice visible and assessable. Second, we look in depth at the work of American philosopher and educator Hubert Dreyfus (1929-2017), and his approach to skills acquisition, which covers stages of competence development from novice to practical wisdom. Incorporated into the section on Dreyfus, are clinical vignettes depicting what spiritual care practice as thick listening at thin moments looks like as one progresses toward mastery of spiritual care competence.

What does Competent Spiritual Care Practice Look Like Clinically?

The origins of Clinical Pastoral Education (CPE) in the mid-1920s saw the use of case studies as integral to the work of Anton Boisen.[1] At a website of the Universidad Interamericana de Puerto Rico one can find a collection of Boisen's documents, donated by Chicago Theological Seminary, that includes a file of thirty-five downloadable case studies.[2] There's also a "Case Analysis (Blank Form)" provided by Boisen as a didactic tool by which to approach living human documents "with actual social conditions in all their complexity."[3] While these archived resources are outmoded and no longer used in CPE programs, their existence is testimony to the longstanding use of case studies in spiritual care education. Today most CPE programs, and their partners within theological colleges and seminary field education programs, see the use of case study reports as a mainstay for personal and collective reflection. Likewise, and noted in previous chapters, a thoroughly documented case study is required by some spiritual care associations as part of the professional certification process. Case studies are a respected means by which to visualize and assess spiritual care practice.

This book includes several case studies and clinical vignettes. Of special note are Mary's story and Rose's intentional reflection during her CPE learning. Vignettes and case studies matter. They tell stories, paint pictures and put flesh on the bones of theoretical constructs. Case studies, alongside verbatim and critical incident reporting tools, make spiritual care visible. They are reflective instruments. Students and practitioners use them to incorporate principles of Action Science, foster contemplative mindfulness, integrate theological and spiritual reflection, explore empathy and interpathy, facilitate deliberation and spark imagination. In addition, case studies offer the opportunity to practice the four reading strategies discussed in the previous chapter, and to focus awareness on interpretive lenses being used by spiritual care practitioners as they reflect on clinical experiences. Case studies are based on real life events with patients and clients—who tell their stories of faith, grief, trauma, discovery, celebration and more. Spiritual care students and practitioners, as they listen to these thin moments, become increasingly aware of strengths and limitations in their own developing competence.

Previously noted in the chapter on Faith, when teaching CPE, Clark makes a distinction among verbatim, critical incident and case study tools in terms of what each is looking at. The verbatim tool studies a single conversation by capturing initial impressions about the context, person or people involved, and the reason for choosing that particular experience. Developing the verbatim includes writing out a spiritual care conversation in detail, examining the conversation from theological, spiritual, psychological, cultural and sociological points of view, and then reflecting on one's spiritual care functioning through self-critique and learning aptitudes.

A critical incident is an experience of significance to the report writer—something that has triggered dissonance and/or raised questions—perhaps questions about the spiritual care practitioner's beliefs, values, attitudes and behaviors. Here again, resources from theology, spirituality and the human sciences are used to carry forward the reflection. Lastly, case studies are used to view more long-term, multidimensional and nuanced spiritual care experiences. They usually encompass more than one contact with a patient or client, focus attention on patterns of social interaction, and spell out details relevant to spiritual assessment and interventions. Two excellent resources for seeing what a good case study looks like are George Fitchett's article titled "Making our Case(s)"[4] and the chapter on Certification in the Policy and Procedure Manual of the Canadian Association for Spiritual Care/Association canadienne de soins spirituels (CASC/ACSS).[5] Features of this latter resource are spelled out in the chapter on Faith. Each tool is a means by which self-disclosure, shared reflection and growth in awareness can occur. Each tool makes visible what spiritual care practice looks like clinically.

In addition to using case studies for spiritual care educational purposes, the advancement of case study research in spiritual care is noteworthy, particularly during the past decade. Case study research advancement has gone hand in hand with the publication of articles and books that provide case studies relevant to a variety of spiritual care contexts. References to a selection of these articles and books are found in Appendix #3.

Given that case studies tell stories, paint pictures and put flesh on the bones of theoretical constructs, the authors wonder what a collection of case studies based on this book's theoretical groundwork might look like. Wouldn't it be exciting to see spiritual care students and seasoned practitioners give their accounts of engaging with patients and clients through thick listening at thin moments? What might a hermeneutic of social interaction look like in case study form? How would a practitioner describe their experiences of I-Thou relating with another who is "other" than they are? What about the spiritual care practitioner who accompanies a patient or client struggling with unhealthy reasoning or with reconceiving their worldview? Such possibilities are proposed for further research. Who knows what the outcome of such reflection might be!

Introducing the Dreyfus Approach to Skills Acquisition

Twenty-first century spiritual care educators and practitioners are giving increased attention to competency-based spiritual care education and evidence-based spiritual care practice.[6] These approaches focus on treatment planning, outcomes and efficiencies. As described in a recent article, the shift is from "pastoral care and counselling to multi-faith, evidence-based spiritual care and psycho-spiritual therapy".[7] So, what does this look like clinically and how is it assessed?

The previous chapter provided information about rubrics for assessing CPE student learning and the writing of professional papers for spiritual care certification. Whenever assessment is involved, elements of subjectivity and objectivity come into play. How well a student or practitioner feels or believes they're doing exists alongside how well that person appears to others to be doing. In a rating scale, a learner's self-assessment may be higher or lower than the assessment given by others. This discrepancy may be due to a variety of subjective factors, including personal beliefs, attitudes, values, self-image and self-esteem. Likewise, those who observe might not be objective in their assessments. All parties look through particular interpretive lenses. The observed and observer lenses may not be compatible. In order to address these discrepancies, we need a theoretical framework that describes what spiritual care competence can look like at various stages.

The following pages address this need by offering a framework that considers the second question noted at the beginning of the chapter: What's involved in mastering the complex competency of thick listening at thin moments? Our purpose is to look at the skills acquisition framework developed by Hubert Dreyfus using a spiritual care practitioner lens. Based on his framework, which covers seven stages of competence development, we believe it's possible to design a rubric or rating scale to assess the complex competencies that comprise spiritual care practice.

Our approach is rooted in the belief that it's complex competencies—rather than single competencies—we need to assess. This belief is reinforced by reading two broadly referenced lists of competencies used by spiritual care associations in North America. From the authors' perspective, each single ability listed is part of a group of abilities that belong to a more comprehensively identified ability. For example:

- The Competencies of CASC/ACSS Certified Professionals[8] document lists the competency "Embodies a holistic and spiritually-oriented approach to care and therapy" as one of six single competencies that comprise the category of "Professional Identity." This comprehensive category is spelled out as "A Certified Member is rooted in one's spiritual/religious/cultural tradition that connects with self, other and the sacred for a holistic and spiritually-oriented approach to care and therapy. From this foundation, a CASC/ACSS Certified Professional reflectively integrates the wisdom of spiritual/religious/cultural traditions with psychotherapeutic modalities as a way of being with and for others during times of crisis, challenge and change." This comprehensive category constitutes a complex competency that can be observed and assessed using Dreyfus' seven stages of skills acquisition, but that work hasn't been done yet.

- The Board of Chaplaincy Certification Inc.'s document, Common Qualifications and Competencies for Professional Chaplains,[9] lists as a single competency the following: "Provide spiritual care that respects diversity and differences including, but not limited to culture, gender, sexual orientation and spiritual/religious practices." This competency is grouped as one of eleven single competencies that comprise the category of "Professional Practice Skills Competencies". As authors we wonder how these single competencies might be unpacked in terms of the abilities implicit in each one. As well, how might the cluster of eleven be described as a comprehensive unified whole? This unified whole could then be observed and assessed, using Dreyfus' seven stages, within the category of professional spiritual care practice.

Viewing distinct competencies separately isn't enough. They're intended to be in relationship with one another in such a way they can be observed as integrated, cohesive, seamlessly exercised complex competencies. As has been the case throughout this book, we hope that by focusing on the complex competency of thick listening at thin moments, and delving into its theoretical groundwork, a broader understanding of and appreciation for what it means to exercise complex competencies can result. Toward this end, we turn to Dreyfus.

Hubert Dreyfus identified seven stages of learning that culminate in mastering complex skills. He believed that later stages depend on and grow out of earlier ones. According to him, moving from novice to master involves a learner in instruction, practice and apprenticeship. His contributions to skills acquisition began in the 1980s in collaboration with his brother Stuart.[10] At that point, they developed a five-stage model that's widely used in professional literature.[11] They became concerned with whether learning to be masterful could be achieved via computer-mediated communication. Hubert came to believe it couldn't. Integrated competence is achieved bodily in face-to-face encounters. For him, to omit the body from learning environments leads to a multitude of losses, e.g., the capacity for recognizing relevance, skills acquisition, a sense of the reality of people and things, and ultimately of meaning.[12] Thick listening at thin moments in spiritual care practice couldn't function in the presence of these losses.

As an embodied approach to spiritual care competence, the use of Dreyfus' skills acquisition stage theory is well-suited to the observation of competence development in thick listening at thin moments. His theory could also be used by spiritual care associations seeking to further the benefits of competency-based spiritual care education and evidence-based spiritual care practice, all of which depend on face-to-face embodied interaction.

Applying Dreyfus to Thick Listening at Thin Moments

What follows is a summary of Dreyfus's seven stages as they apply to the complex competency of thick listening at thin moments. His staged approach effectively shapes the practice of *embodied*[13] spiritual care activities. It goes beyond the five stages mentioned earlier to include stages six and seven. Six and seven focus on developing personal authenticity and cultural astuteness. Descriptions of his ideas and principles for each stage are viewed through a spiritual care lens. Rather than following the professional life of a single spiritual care practitioner, we've chosen to feature several practitioners and carry the thread of learning from stage to stage by means of patient and client focused examples.

Competence advancement is discussed at each stage. As previously noted, for Dreyfus, progress is step-by-step: first steps are necessary before you can take the next steps. For spiritual care practitioners, growth in competence moves along a path situated in relational learning environments that are encountered and navigated. The outcome is cumulative and holistic. It's by picturing this movement from step to step that one gains an appreciation of what spiritual care competence can look like at each stage on a rubric or rating scale.

In our use of clinical vignettes for each of Dreyfus' stages, we acknowledge that we emphasize healthcare settings. This is due to Clark's healthcare background. We can only write authentically out of who we are. We recognize the limitations of this focus and invite readers to continue authoring articles and books with case studies that highlight spiritual care practice in its broadest scope, its multiple contexts and cultural diversity.

Stage #1 Novice

When they commence their education, inexperienced spiritual care learners are given *features and rules*. CPE Supervisors begin by decomposing the task to be learned into its context-free features that beginners can recognize from everyday life, e.g., how to listen. This involves using threshold spiritual care competencies, as referred to in the previous chapter. For example, when learning to initiate a spiritual care conversation, students recognize domain-independent features such as basic listening skills and pre-briefing (tuning into self and tuning into the patient/client).

Listening begins to become *thick* listening as students also receive a list of features to demonstrate stages of entering and then leaving a patient's/client's room, home, or workspace. These features may include the following:

- Introducing oneself and providing a brief explanation of what spiritual care is (say why you're there),
- Establishing rapport (ask the patient's/client's permission to engage in conversation),
- Using reflective listening techniques (pay attention to what's said, and navigate issues of importance to the patient/client, while picking up on the patient's/client's spiritual needs and resources),
- Knowing when to leave (end appropriately, while assessing follow-up, referral) and
- Taking time for initial debriefing after leaving (tune into self, tune into patient, follow-up planning).

For CPE students, all early spiritual care experiences are documented (e.g., recording the number of contacts and time spent with each one, writing reflective reports, presenting verbatim or critical incident reports). These documents are shared with students' supervisors as required assignments. Other documents may be shared with both the supervisor and a clinical preceptor,[14] (e.g., clinical activity report) and/or one's peer group (in clinical seminars). In these ways, students receive feedback from different sources (supervisor's comments and verbal feedback, preceptor's modeling and observation, peer group responses). This process, and these tools, encourage inexperienced learners to recognize in their practice what Will Taylor[15] calls the "unconscious incompetence" of a naïve mind. This expression refers to realizing *when we don't know what we don't know*. The novice stage allows a learner to correct their practice by paying attention to features and rules as a way to become more aware of what they don't yet know. At this stage a novice experiences the scope of thick listening through observation and the rigor of regular (daily, weekly) practice. A series of steps are followed in the learner's mind, and each new patient or client is approached in such a way that the student tries to build on previous successes as well as mistakes, until there's a felt sense of basic competence that's also affirmed by external observers.

When Howard Meets Mrs. Corazón

Howard is in his first Basic/Level I CPE program in a community hospital. His clinical placement is two medicine units. Over the past week he's been involved in an intensive orientation process to both CPE learning and his clinical location. After spending time with his preceptor, watching her spiritual care engagement with several medicine patients, Howard is now being observed by his preceptor. Although he's nervous about being watched, he's eager to apply the method for initial visits he's been taught.

The following is an excerpt from Howard's first verbatim document. As he was encouraged to do, the document is organized in such a way that his conversation with Mrs. Corazón identifies her as "P" (patient) and himself as "C" (chaplain), with indications of his interior thoughts written parenthetically.

C1 Mrs. Corazón, my name is Howard Alma. I'm from spiritual care and a student member of the healthcare team on this medicine unit. Spiritual care seeks to provide spiritual and emotional support to patients and their loved ones. I'd like to spend some time with you if that's okay.

P1   Sure, Howard. I'd be happy to have you visit me.

C2   I notice you have some beautiful flowers on your bedside table. (Inner thoughts: I've been told to notice what's in the patient's immediate space, such as cards, flowers, etc.)

P2   Yes, my husband brought them when he visited me last night.

C3   Does your husband come to visit you every evening? (Oh, oh, I asked a closed ended question. But I'm curious about her family.)

P3   No. He can only come to see me a couple times a week due to his work schedule. And I'm afraid I'm going to be in here for another week.

C4   Oh? How does that feel? (Hope I didn't jump to the feelings too quickly.)

P4   I'm okay with it. We've been through this a number of times now.

C5   What brought you to the hospital? (That's better; an open-ended question. I wonder if she'll tell me what's wrong with her.)

P5   I have a chronic condition that requires periodic adjustments to my medicines. The only way they can achieve an accurate modification is by admitting me to hospital for several weeks. It's been like that for a number of years now.

The spiritual care encounter continues for another ten to fifteen minutes. When it's time to bring the visit to a close, Howard draws on the outline for initial visits he was given and is careful to end his conversation with Mrs. Corazón appropriately, saying he'll try to come see her again later in the week.

Debriefing (applying rules/guidelines as a Stage #1 Novice learner): Howard uses what he's been given during the CPE orientation process in terms of rule and features. His inner thoughts reveal some of the lessons learned, e.g., noticing the flowers, detecting his closed versus open ended questions, and paying attention to what's said. As novices, CPE students tend to be focused on "doing things right." There's a meticulous quality of interacting with patients and clients that fits with paying attention to the features and rules being learned.

Stage #2 Advanced Beginner

Learners now have some experience and are given *maxims*. A maxim is a principle of action that learners take on and try out. For example, with reflective listening techniques, a maxim might be: *Say what you see and reveal what you feel.* Unlike rules, a maxim requires that learners already have some understanding of the domain (e.g., healthcare, prison, school, faith community, etc.) to which it applies. *How* one says what they see and reveals what they feel will look different in different situations. Learners must become discerning in using maxims by trying things out in new situations and learning from lived experience.

An advanced beginning spiritual care practitioner uses situational aspects such as patient/client location (surgery, medicine, long-term care, community agency) as well as non-situational features such as urgency (on-call, staff referral, client request, self-selected) to decide when to initiate contact and how to focus a spiritual assessment. As an example, for some spiritual care students taking CPE in an acute care hospital, in addition to features and rules acquired as novices, students might learn the maxim: *If at all possible, respond to an on-call page within five minutes, follow up on staff referrals or client requests the same day, and use information provided in patient/client lists to prioritize self-initiated contacts.* Location and urgency aren't always immediately evident. Students can no longer simply follow rules. With maxims, advanced beginners use personal choice while learning through their mistakes. At this stage, CPE students might be intentional and focused in their use of spiritual assessment tools provided by their supervisor or preceptor, e.g., FICA or HOPE.[16] They might also experiment with more complex assessment tools available to them in spiritual care literature.[17]

Once again, the value of supervision, preceptorship, and peer sharing emerges as integral to acquiring skill. Where the novice gains from instruction and application, the advanced beginner benefits from a coaching stance. Growth in a student's approach to patients/clients may sometimes come to light by a supervisor or preceptor who asks "What led you to go in that particular direction in the conversation?" Or, "Did you notice what she said about her sense of foreboding?" Maxims take spiritual care beginners from novice to competent as learning occurs not only within the clinical sphere but also within one's educational community. This is where Will Taylor's term "conscious incompetence" can unsettle the beginner mind, but in beneficial ways. *It's when we know that we don't know.*

In CPE, this stage is a time for exercising independent functioning while also making intentional use of one's supervisor, preceptor, and peers for modeling and feedback. Thick listening is taking shape in the spiritual care practitioner as he or she discerns variations in relational learning environments, such as urgency, confusion, conflict, or subtlety. Evidence-based competence is emerging. This is where a purposeful use of learning tools (critical incident, case study, verbatim reports) can integrate with self-awareness, theoretical knowledge, and skills development, and when thin moments start to be noticed and considered by the learner.

Providing Spiritual Care Following a Death

Barbara is in her second Basic/Level I CPE program. She's the assigned student on-call chaplain. In the early evening, she's paged to be with the wife and children of a man who just died as the result of a heart attack that was being treated over several days. Barbara responds to the page within five minutes (in keeping with the maxim she's learned). She checks in at the nursing station and then proceeds to the patient's room. She introduces herself and brings a sense of caring presence as she meets the deceased man's family, listening attentively while each person speaks. They ask her to say a prayer and, because she's listened to them so carefully, she's able to incorporate, in the words of her prayer, the maxim to say what she sees and reveal what she feels. She's noticed the family talks about feelings comfortably, so she feels free to use feeling words in her prayer. This makes her prayer quite personal to the unique circumstances of the grieving family. They express their appreciation in words and hugs.

Following the prayer, attendants from the hospital's morgue arrive. Barbara steps out of the room with the family while nursing staff and the attendants prepare the deceased man's body for transport to the morgue. Once this is completed, Barbara walks with the family as they follow their deceased loved one's gurney to the elevator. There the family says goodbye and their husband/dad is taken to the morgue. Barbara remains with the family and walks with them to the exit location of the hospital nearest to where their car is parked. In bidding the family farewell, she again says what she sees and reveals her caring in an appropriate way. After the family is gone, Barbara returns to the patient care unit where the man died and checks in again with staff to see how they are.

Debriefing (using maxims alongside learned protocols as a Stage #2 Advanced Beginner learner): Barbara has accrued some experience during her CPE learning and knows what to do when called to a patient's death. She knows how to attend to the details of checking in with unit staff, providing a religious intervention when asked, and accompanying family members from the unit to the hospital exit. She's also integrating maxims into her learning, such as the timing applied to an urgent call, using assessment to guide interventions, and uses her ability to say what she sees and reveal what she feels in ways that are appropriate and helpful to the grieving family. She's aware that another family may have been less comfortable with the free use of feelings in her prayer. She is less dependent on rules and more focused on discerning helpful spiritual care, based on her careful attention to body language and to what the family is comfortable saying and doing.

Stage #3 Competent Learner

Competent spiritual care learners have accumulated diverse situational experiences and can identify a variety of interventions in keeping with patient/client focused goals. They continue to be more cognitive in their analysis and in monitoring their intervention options. At times, this sense of having a plethora of options can feel overwhelming, nerve-racking and exhausting insofar as a sense of what's important in a particular situation is often missing. Learners wonder how anyone ever gains know-how or masters the skill of thick listening at thin moments in spiritual care practice. To cope with overload and achieve competence, student practitioners learn, through instruction and modelling, to devise a plan, and choose a perspective that determines which of the aspects of the situation must be treated as important, and which can be put to the side. This is a time when inner resources are getting tapped in new ways and when motives, traits and self-concepts come into play. Learners may ask themselves: Who am I in this situation? How do I need to conduct myself? As they learn to restrict themselves to a few of the many possible relevant features and aspects of a situation, their understanding and decision-making become more paced and measured; they can self-monitor their interventions. Thick listening concentrates not only on external circumstances but also on internal reasoning and deliberation of the practitioner. Learners need to recognize the approaches to inquiry they use to help them understand and engage with complex spiritual care experiences.

The sequencing of skills acquisition that's now occurring moves from relying on features and rules (application), to maxims (testing options), to planning (grasping the big picture and weighing priorities in becoming the spiritual care practitioner one wants to become). For the competent learner in spiritual care, assessment is now more complex and becomes a locus for thick listening. While paying attention to patient/client sharing of what they're dealing with—including a faith story and immediate concerns—the competent spiritual care learner also assesses the following:

- Elements of social location: Gender, race, social class, age, ability, religion, sexual orientation, geographical variables, understanding of the language being used.

- Aspects of systems issues: Power advantage/disadvantage, use of scarce resources, high risk/low risk concerns, whether patient/client advocacy is called for, or not.

It's this complex quality of thick listening that enables practitioners to formulate spiritual care plans and execute spiritual care interventions that are based on their comprehension of social location and systems issues.

A Story of Intersecting Narratives

Leon is an Advanced/Level II CPE student chaplain on-call. He's paged to the Pediatric Intensive Care Unit (PICU) of a large acute care hospital. After he arrives, scrubs in, and checks with unit staff, he's directed to an isolation room where a child, 4 years of age, is being treated for terminal cancer. The boy's parents are from two different Christian denominations—mom is Lutheran, dad is Roman Catholic. Following their lengthy and painful discussions over a few weeks time, the parents decided to have their child baptized by a Roman Catholic priest. This information is communicated to Leon by the boy's maternal grandmother, who is Lutheran and is with the boy's parents in the hospital room. Once he receives the request for a Roman Catholic priest, Leon leaves the room for a few minutes to telephone the priest on-call. He returns to be with the parents and grandmother, knowing it will take about thirty minutes for the priest to arrive.

During the interlude, Leon observes how stressed and exhausted the parents look. He learns more about their decision related to baptism. Both are devout in their faith, but also committed to their distinct denominations. It has been impossible for them to choose between having their child baptized by a Lutheran pastor or Roman Catholic priest. In the end, their compromise was to flip a coin—heads Lutheran and tails Catholic—and live with the outcome. The coin turned up tails. Thus, the request for a priest.

While he continues waiting, Leon also speaks quietly with the boy. He notices several very disfiguring tumors on the child's chin and neck. These growths seriously affect the boy's appearance, to a point of grotesqueness. There's a quality of self-consciousness in the child's mannerisms, which are awkward and uncertain. He's also in pain and seems to move in and out of consciousness. Leon feels a great deal of compassion for the boy, his parents, and his grandmother. He also knows that his role will be as a liaison between the priest and family.

Before long the priest enters the unit, talks with staff at the front desk, and makes his way to the boy's isolation room. Upon entering the room, the priest greets Leon, the parents and grandmother. He's kind and engaging in his mannerisms, and spends some time quietly listening to the mom, dad and grandmother. Then he turns to talk with the boy. All of a sudden, his demeanor changes. He stops moving and is speechless. The boy's disfigurement is so striking, the priest can't continue. He remains frozen in place for several minutes. Parents and grandmother are alarmed and appear annoyed. It's at this point that Leon intervenes, facilitating communication between the priest and the boy, and lets the priest know of the boy's rare and terminal diagnosis. With this liaising, the priest regains his composure and carries on with the baptism. All ends well.

The next day, while in the hospital's chaplaincy office, Leon finds out that the priest is new to the city, having arrived at his assigned parish only hours before receiving the call to the hospital for the baptism. Everything the priest did while in the PICU was for the first time. Even though he was able to communicate warmth and compassion, the priest was feeling tentative, disoriented, and unsure about exact procedures. Leon's intermediating role was critical to the priest's feeling welcome, meeting the parents and grandmother, and being able to find equilibrium after seeing the disfigured boy.

Debriefing (exercising complex spiritual care assessment and intervention, as a Stage #3 Competent Learner): As he reflects on this experience, Leon realizes there were two intersecting narratives in the dying boy's isolation room: that of the conflicted and grieving family and that of the relocated and disoriented priest. In the meeting of these two narratives, Leon's role as liaison served to stabilize things. He had already established rapport with the parents and grandmother and could welcome the priest into this rapport. Leon perceived a wordless thin moment in the priest's initial response to the sick child. While assessing the situation in the room, and observing the family's annoyance, Leon was aware that his ability to recognize a thin moment prevented him from getting caught up in the parents' negative reaction to the priest's initial moment with the boy. In this awareness, he could see how important it is to remain open to everyone involved in a spiritual care encounter and be non-judgmental in his assessment. Leon engaged the priest with respect and compassion, calling him out of his silence to the immediacy of the baptism. He realizes in hindsight that his interventions were integral to the positive outcome of the critical care incident. He also realizes how beneficial using the Awareness Wheel Exercise in clinical seminars has been to increase his competence in recognizing thin moments. [See Appendix 2]

At this stage there's new rigor for the spiritual care practitioner in terms of self-assessment and how one feels about one's role, comportment, and comfort in the midst of all the complexity at hand. CPE students must decide for themselves in each new situation what perspective to adopt, without being sure it will turn out to be correct or helpful. Given this uncertainty, becoming competent can be frightening and exhausting. Prior to this stage, spiritual care students can rationalize they were not given adequate rules for doing what they needed to do. When there's someone else to blame, a person can feel no remorse for their errors. But, at this point, results depend on learners themselves. They feel responsible for their choices and the sense of success or failure that results. In the clinical vignette that follows, the spiritual care learner goes through a series of feelings: frightened, embarrassed, culturally humbled, disappointed with self, and discouragement with the result of choices made. In chapter one, referring to the work of Evelyn Whitehead, we discussed how difficult emotions often come bearing gifts. Such is the case here.

An Unintended Boundary Breach

Marta is part way through a year-long CPE Residency Program at a tertiary care hospital in a large city. She's concluded two Basic/Level I courses and is soon to be assessed for Advanced/Level II standing. In the months of her clinical placement within a surgery and trauma unit, she's become well known and trusted. She regularly attends inter-professional rounds, follows up on referrals, and takes the initiative to see as many patients as possible during her time allotment each week. Her spiritual care chart notes are viewed by others on the team as exemplary, adding to the high standard of collaborative care being pursued.

Today Marta is spending time with patients in a curtained off area of the unit where people are post-op. They're sitting in recliner chairs and readying for discharge. She's decided to visit all ten patients, starting at one end of the curtained area, and working her way to the other. It's here that she meets an Indigenous woman in her fifties, dressed in a hospital gown, and sleepily leaning back in her recliner. She's partially covered with a thin blanket, but it had slipped off her lap so the woman was somewhat exposed.

Looking directly into the woman's eyes, Marta introduces herself. She also spontaneously reaches to adjust the blanket in order to cover up what is exposed. The woman is startled from her semi-sleep and starts to cry out in distress at Marta's actions. Even though Marta speaks in calm and apologetic words, the woman settles only after Marta moves away. By this time, Marta feels embarrassed by the patient's distress. A nurse comes over to assist and the patient relaxes.

Debriefing, Part I (feeling responsible for her choices and the sense of failure that resulted, as a Stage #3 Competent Learner): Marta feels awful. She decides to leave the unit for awhile to reflect on what just happened. At first, she goes outside for a walk, ruminating over her inept and somewhat impulsive need to adjust the blanket. She's disappointed with herself and discouraged by her very public error in offering care.

Debriefing, Part II (demonstrating emotional investment in herself and the patient, and using consultation to learn and grow, as a Stage #3 Competent Learner): After calming down, Marta's attention shifts away from herself and toward the patient. What was the experience like for this recently post-op Indigenous woman? Marta makes the decision to learn from her mistakes. She goes to the hospital's chaplaincy office. There she looks for her trusted Indigenous colleague who is part of Spiritual Care Services, who also serves Indigenous patients as a cultural liaison. Marta gets some tobacco from where it's stored in the office and gives it to her colleague. He receives the tobacco, and she shares what occurred on the surgical unit. He points out that using direct eye contact with Indigenous people is considered rude and can be experienced as aggression. A better way to engage the woman would have been to look down and off to the side when making the introduction, and to follow this with respectful silence. Likewise, entering the woman's personal space by trying to adjust her blanket could easily be perceived as further aggression. Marta didn't have the woman's permission. Her action alarmed and frightened the patient. Naturally, the woman cried out for help.

As they debriefed together, Marta's colleague was kind, respectful and encouraging in his comments. She found herself at a thin moment, aware that her self-image as a spiritual care practitioner didn't include being viewed as aggressive. At the same time, and as the result of her consultation, she was aware of significant cultural ignorance about Indigenous people. She knew she needed to reconceive her worldview, correct her cultural ignorance, and use this experience of embarrassment and discouragement as an opportunity to grow. She felt true gratitude for her Indigenous colleague's counsel.

It's at the stage of competent learner that the function of emotional literacy takes on significant value. As spiritual care students become more and more emotionally involved in their complex task of thick listening at thin moments, it's increasingly difficult to draw back and adopt a maxim-following stance, as advanced beginners can do. The strangeness of this phase is felt deeply: learners believe they're getting better but feel worse about what they're doing. Emotional involvement is disconcerting. One response to this distress may be to pull back and play it safe. But this is the wrong move. Unless spiritual care learners stay emotionally involved and accept the joy of a job well done, as well as remorse for mistakes, they'll not develop further in mastery. They burn out trying to keep track of all the features, aspects, rules, and maxims that a domain requires. In general, resistance to emotional involvement and risk-taking leads to stagnation, and even to wanting to quit altogether. Staying connected—remaining in the room like Rose did when she was thrown off balance or like Marta did when she consulted her Indigenous colleague—means committing to and demonstrating emotional investment in oneself and others. This is key to advancement.

The goal for a competent learner in spiritual care by this point is to have spent enough time on self-reflection to have (a) sorted out personal and professional strengths and limitations, (b) gained a sense of "what's me and what's not me", and (c) seriously engaged not only with book knowledge (spiritual/religious/cultural/psychological) but also with relational health resources (therapy, spiritual direction, topic-specific consultation) to promote professional growth. This is the work of taking seriously implications for the safe and effective use of self while being with and for others during times of crisis, challenge, and change. In the practice of thick listening at thin moments, this is a time for surveying the terrain of one's own worldview map in light of its historical thin model moments. What relational patterns have been learned? Are they still useful and helpful, or do they need to be reconceived? How have the four points of entry discussed in the chapter on Faith served as inroads to one's worldview map exploration?

At stage #3 competent learning, supervisors and preceptors matter a great deal. They influence whether students will withdraw into dis-embodied minds or become emotionally involved in learning. A supervisor's or preceptor's manner and embodied perspective provides a model for learners: educators and employed practitioners may be involved or detached; either way, learners pick up their approach, responses, hope or despair. If supervisors and preceptors are open and involved, if they take risks and continue to learn from their own failures and successes, their courage is transmitted to learners. Courage constitutes the best possible embodied perspective for CPE learners to experience as they grow in autonomous functioning while initiating more complex interventions. Continuing with language from Will Taylor, competent learners exercise what he calls a learning mind, and they act with "conscious competence": *they know they know something.* Thus, confidence builds, and mastery evolves.

Stage #4 Proficient Learner

Proficient learners are characterized by their involvement in the positive as well as negative experiences that drive the acquisition of *embodied* competence. Holding on to the detached, information-consuming stance of novices and advanced beginners is no longer helpful. Rather, it's the positive and negative emotional experiences themselves that strengthen successful responses and inhibit unsuccessful ones. In proficient learning, thick listening at a thin moment can take on the appearance of the following scenario.

Proficient Compassionate Engagement

Ruth is in her second unit of Advanced/Level II CPE. During an on-call rotation, she engages compassionately with an out-of-country tourist who is weeping loudly in the face of his wife's sudden and unexpected death. It's late at night in the hospital emergency room. The man is shocked to the core, incredulous, and utterly bereft. He doesn't know what to say or do. Ruth offers comfort while also inquiring about whether the man knows anyone locally or not. She asks where he's staying, and who he might need to contact in his home country. She learns that he and his wife are tourists. They don't know anyone in the city. They hadn't made a final decision about accommodations for their first night in town. Ruth tells the man there's a hotel across the street from the hospital where he can stay. He can also return to the hospital the next day to consult with the physician who was present with his wife at the time of her death. She says he can complete any pending paperwork the next day. Eventually the man is ready to leave the hospital.

While it's not unusual for spiritual care practitioners to accompany bereaved family members from the location of their loved one's death to a hospital exit, Ruth decides to walk the bereaved widower to the hotel across the street. She stays with him while he checks in. As she does so, she observes the disoriented man pull a large wad of mixed currency bills out of his pocket in full view of all who are in the hotel lobby. When she accompanies him to the elevator and says goodbye, she can imagine him being robbed for the cash in his pocket. She cautions him to be watchful as he copes with his shock and disorientation, and entreats him to be vigilant about his safety at such a vulnerable time. She's aware of and emotionally connected with the man's thin moment experience of acute grief. Her embodied responses to him guide her spiritual care.

Debriefing (embodied engagement and drawing on multiple intelligences as a Stage #4 Proficient Learner): While walking back to the hospital, Ruth reflects on her experience. She takes a second look at how she's stepped outside her usual practice in this incident. She decides to write up the event and bring it to her CPE peer group for feedback. Her initial thoughts take her to the four literacies she's learned about as a theoretical resource in spiritual care practice. Clearly, her emotional and social literacies were in evidence as she engaged and related with the man. She was both self-aware and socially aware. She self-regulated while observing the relationship in ways that communicated her empathy by accompanying this newly bereaved tourist through what he'll probably always remember as the worst day of his life. For the first time,

273

Ruth felt she understood what Daniel Stern meant when he described a "present moment." The quality of her listening to the man was so thick and focused that her intuitive reading of his thoughts went hand in hand with a feeling—within her body—of his feelings.

What she wasn't so sure about was how well she'd used cognitive and imaginative literacies. Did she do the right thing when she walked the man to the hotel? What impact did her imaginings about him being robbed have on her assessment and decision to caution him at the elevator? These were the questions she brought to her CPE group. They, like Ruth, looked at the action of accompanying the man beyond the hospital exit as unusual, as it was technically outside her professional scope as a spiritual care practitioner. At the same time, it was only at the hotel registration desk that she became aware of the man's wad of money and could assess his vulnerability, which was not only emotional but also physical. One of her peers asked, "While you were focused on the man's trauma and grief, what prevented you from paying attention to the fuller picture of resources that might be available to him at the time of leaving the hospital?" In the face of this question, Ruth thought about possible alternatives to the actions she took. She could have talked to the security guards at the Emergency Department exit and asked one of them to accompany the man. She could have noticed the taxis parked outside the exit and discussed this mode of transportation with the man, due to his disoriented condition. She could have asked him if he had enough money for the hotel—at which point she might have become aware of his wad of money. In essence, and in keeping with learning gained from Action Science theory, there was directly observable data present for her to draw on that she could have incorporated into her thinking, imagining and action. Yet, after probing the incident with the CPE group, Ruth still felt she'd done the right thing in this case.

Ruth concluded her reflections by affirming the proficiency with which she met and engaged the newly widowed man. Her response was embodied and a-theoretical. The actions she took were natural and uncalculated. It was a situation where she took a risk and, reflecting on that risk, she felt true to herself. In a different situation she may have simply walked the patient's family to the exit. The process of thinking through these aspects of the encounter with her peer group, and considering ways she could have acted differently at the time the man was leaving the hospital, strengthened her self-confidence as a spiritual care professional.

Proficiency develops if, and only if, experience is assimilated in an embodied, a-theoretical way. Only then are intuitive reactions unified with reasoned responses. This shift gives concrete meaning to the insights of Socrates/Plato and Aristotle, where *dianoia* (looking around at the world) and *nous* (looking up to receive flashes of insight) work together effectively. Both *dianoia* and *nous* are needed to understand and engage in thick listening at thin moments during complex spiritual care experiences.

In proficient spiritual care learning, action becomes less stressful and more natural as practitioners simply see and do what needs to be done, rather than calculating among several possible alternatives. Thus, interventions are less cognitive and more spontaneous. There is less doubt about what action to take, even when taking some calculated risks. In this sense, spiritual care practitioners don't focus exclusively on deliberation; they begin to trust some flashes of insight when choosing an intervention. In the scenario, Ruth knew the bereft widower needed a place to stay that night. Her intuitive choice was to walk with the man and accompany him due to his acute grief, emotional vulnerability, and because he was a tourist who knew no one in the city. Staying connected and emotionally available to him resulted in her witnessing his disorientation with the wad of currency and cautioning him to be self-protective. That said, even as she was walking back to the hospital after leaving the man, reasoned responses were kicking in and questions were surfacing about the appropriateness of her action. To her credit, these reasoned responses lead her to bring this experience to her supervisor and peers for shared reflection. In that context, additional learning occurred.

Proficient learners have a balanced grasp on rules, features, maxims and embodied engagement. Decisions are made that flow with organic integrity. According to Will Taylor, this is where a practitioner is moving from "conscious competence" to "unconscious competence." The learner mind is active, involved and gains an ability to be self-supervising. One not only knows *they know something, but also that they don't know it all.* They have resources available for further learning, such as integrating emotional and social with cognitive and imaginative literacies.

Stage # 5 Expert

By the time a spiritual care practitioner has progressed to the stage of expert, they're more than likely post-CPE and, hopefully, recognized as

Certified Spiritual Care Practitioners or Board-Certified Chaplains. An expert spiritual care practitioner sees what needs to be done, establishes spiritually integrated therapeutic relationships of trust and can carry forward spiritual assessments and interventions with advanced integration of the safe and effective use of self, theoretical knowledge, systems awareness, and collaborative functioning. He or she regularly gives evidence of balancing initiative and adaptability, maturity, autonomy, collaboration, confidence, and naturalness. This constancy of refined as well as subtle discernment in one's spiritual care practice is what separates an expert from a proficient learner.

As experience accrues in a variety of situations—all seen through the perspective of spiritual care professional practice but requiring different tactical decisions—the flow of experiential learning re-emerges for the practitioner and can be embraced at new levels. For example, some spiritual care practitioners gain expertise in palliative care, while others become knowledgeable in care for those living with dementia, or care for the homeless or incarcerated. Each area of expertise within the profession of spiritual care can be viewed as a subclass of spiritual care practice. Applying Dreyfus to spiritual care, the brain of the expert gradually decomposes a class of perspectives (spiritual care practice) into subclasses that are specially developed areas of spiritual care expertise— each of which requires a specific response—but all of which require thick listening at thin moments. Thus, the embodied presence of a spiritual care practitioner unifies the dimensions of a complex competency no matter where he or she may be. This embodiment of practice opens space for immediate intuitive situational responses that are characteristic of an expert. Accordingly, someone in spiritual care who is at this stage, while having accrued expertise in a specific subclass, can also demonstrate thick listening expertise when meeting a homeless man or woman at a street corner while waiting for a traffic light to change. Discerning the emergence of a thin moment in that encounter occurs insofar as expert competence is embodied and available as needed. At the expert stage, spiritual care has become an attitude toward the world—a way of being oneself— as discussed in the chapter on Made for Relationship.

It's hoped that Spiritual Care Practitioners and CPE Supervisors are counted among those who are expert when they work with CPE students. If they are, students will be able to observe their authentic, holistic practice. In supervisor-student and preceptor-student relationships, observation and imitation of experts replaces the random search for better ways to act.

CPE students benefit when they learn with more than one CPE supervisor, are placed in more than one clinical location and work with more than one preceptor. Experiencing the holistic practice of different experts assists students in their personal and professional identity formation. The point, for a learner, isn't to copy any one spiritual care practitioner. Rather it's to observe how several expert professionals implement spiritual care competencies and demonstrate competence. Each experienced practitioner serves as a model alongside whom learners make choices in establishing a unique and embodied personal style that's authentically their own. Observing, imitating and differentiating self from others is a way of being in relationship with CPE supervisors and clinical practitioners that's existed for nearly a century of CPE history. It mirrors what Dreyfus calls apprenticeship.

For Dreyfus, learning competence progresses from instruction, to practice, and then to apprenticeship. When CPE students emulate expert clinical practitioners or supervisors, they're learning abilities for which there are no rules. In both clinical and educational settings, they learn through brain-to-brain neural resonance that merges with a heart-to-heart felt sense of connection. Mannerisms and turns of phrase, or a sense of when to continue in a conversation or when to bring it to a close, are picked up and used as one's own. According to Dreyfus, in apprenticeship relationships, it's the expert's style more than anything else that a learner picks up and imitates. He gives the example of Ludwig Wittgenstein—referred to previously in this book—as an inspiring teacher "who left several succeeding generations of students not only imitating his style of questioning but even his gestures of puzzlement and desperation."[18]

By observing experts in the field of spiritual care, learners—particularly those who see themselves as life-long learners—are continually growing in their professional expertise. This occurs with what Will Taylor calls self-study and peer review, as "unconscious competence" grows into "reflective competence." Interestingly, in Taylor's Conscious Competence Diagram, it's the circle for reflective competence that is largest and overlaps with all other circles. Thus, we can distinguish the circular and ongoing nature of competence development. The beneficial use of a peer group, something that constitutes an essential element of CPE programs, need not cease with completion of these programs. Rather, bringing clinical scenarios—like that involving the baptism of Hope—to collegial settings for debriefing, peer discussion and shared reflection can lead to improving the profession of spiritual care as a whole. Expertise grows as spiritual care practitioners become more and more themselves in their spiritual care professional practice.

Returning to Rose's Intentional Reflection in Clinical Pastoral Education

In the chapter on Faith, we met Rose, a middle-aged woman in a life transition that led her to CPE learning. Throughout her CPE experience, Rose used intentional spiritual and theological reflection to navigate four points of entry to self, others, tradition, and culture. She found that, by attending to thin moments at each point of entry, she was able to learn a great deal about professional spiritual care in a multi-dimensional and multi-layered way. This involved her plunging deeply into several psychological theories, Erik Erikson's stages of psychosocial development, and specific therapeutic modalities for spiritual care practice. She worked with theological, spiritual, religious, and cultural understandings in ways that integrated what she knew conceptually with how she related to others so that she could incarnate her beliefs and values relationally. From within the rigor of CPE, Rose grew to better appreciate the map of her life narrative and faith story as she reflected on it deeply and in the company of supervisors, peers, and her husband. In this work, Rose recognized thin moments in her lived experience, and wrestled with the bedrock as well as shifting sands of reconceiving her worldview. She grappled perceptually and conceptually, but gradually came to a sense of self that she believed was tested, trusted and open to further growth. After completing her Master's degree, Rose proceeded to become a professionally certified Spiritual Care Practitioner.

By the time she reached Dreyfus's Stage #5 Expert, Rose had gained expertise in palliative care chaplaincy to a degree that she was invited to be part of a research project on validating competencies for spiritual care practitioners in palliative and bereavement care in Canada.[19] She went on to complete the Sacred Art of Preceptorship Course (referred to in the chapter on Competencies for Spiritual Care Practice) and worked with several CPE students placed with her at the community palliative home care agency where she was employed. Over time, her professional transition story came full circle, from novice learner to expert practitioner.

Expert spiritual care practitioners demonstrate thick listening at thin moments as second nature. It has become a seamlessly practiced complex competency that authentically and holistically integrates what a person knows with what the person does. Expert spiritual care competence is practiced primarily as the embodiment of differentiating competencies. To be an expert, however, is not to arrive at a plateau of satisfaction and contentment. Further development will occur as the complex competence of thick listening at thin moments remains a motivation for ongoing learning.

Stage # 6 Being Masterful: Personal Style

According to Dreyfus, the role of a master is to pass on to an apprentice the ability to apply context appropriate theory to real life situations. For acquiring personal style, Dreyfus believed that apprenticeship is the only method available. Master and apprentice must be immersed in a common context. As it applies to spiritual care practice, in transmitting an informed understanding of their spiritual care domain, master practitioners can't help demonstrating their perspective on the way they do things. Thus, less experienced spiritual care practitioners observe a diversity of embodied, personalized styles and—based on their observations—sort out elements of "what's me and what's not me". Over time, maturing practitioners adopt a personal style of their own. As a result, during stage six, expert practitioners become more and more themselves as they practice spiritual care.

When CPE learners complete their formal programs and move toward professional certification, apprenticeship transfers from supervisors and preceptors to peers and colleagues. It's now apprenticeship among equals, some of whom are more experienced than others. Dreyfus points out that working with different master practitioners becomes a way of finding one's own style. One master has a whole style; another master has a different whole style. When apprenticing with more than one master, less experienced spiritual care practitioners are destabilized and puzzled. They can't copy any one master so they must develop their own style. This is the process of mastery acquisition. It goes well beyond formal learning and is essential to reaching one's full capacity in the exercise of thick listening at thin moments in spiritual care practice. While becoming personal begins in earlier stages, as noted with the risk Ruth took, at this stage that process needs to be fully realized. At stage six, a practitioner confidently and consistently demonstrates their true personal style.

In the profession of spiritual care, one of the ways people grow from expert to master is through a change of perspective and/or context. CPE learning usually occurs in a specific setting, e.g., hospital, prison, social agency, faith community and so forth. Further, within a particular setting, spiritual care learning and expertise may develop as part of a subclass of spiritual care practice, e.g., in an urban or rural faith community, with deployed, garrisoned or reserved military companies or squadrons, or on a forensic, surgical, ICU or long-term care unit within diverse healthcare facilities. Completing one's formal CPE program usually results in a person having expertise that's context specific. Thus, a person can be an expert acute care hospital spiritual care practitioner but know little about military or prison chaplaincy.

While thick listening at thin moments in spiritual care practice is a complex competency that applies to all contexts, in different settings this complex competency will take specific features and rules into account. These features and rules are informed by distinguishable systems, theoretical approaches, and operational protocols that are unique to each setting. As one example, there are features and rules in a prison setting that must be taken into account. These are different than features and rules in a military setting, faith community or a hospital setting. If a practitioner moves from faith community-based spiritual care to a hospital-based setting, or an institution to a community-based agency, new learning for the new context is necessary to gain perspective and proficiency. Given these necessary shifts, an expert spiritual care practitioner may experience regression in their growth toward mastery. Personal style needs to be resituated. This, too, is a process of embodied proficiency attainment. It takes confidence in one's existing expertise, coupled with motivation to broaden one's knowledge and skill, for the expert to become a master.

Charlie and Jack

Charlie is a priest who has served rural parishes in the western US for many years. Jack is a Presbyterian minister who has worked at small rural hospitals in the same geographical location as Charlie. The two men are long-time friends. They've known each other since taking some of the same theology courses at a biblical institute affiliated with their different seminaries.

Soon after ordination, Charlie was assigned to be the priest chaplain at a large urban hospital in the same city as his seminary. He had taken a unit of CPE as part of his internship year while completing his Master of Divinity degree, and was observed as being quite skilled. His religious authorities were willing to fund him while he completed more CPE through a year-long chaplain residency program. In this experience, Charlie grew in character, attitudes, knowledge, and skill. He went on to work as a professional spiritual care practitioner, employed at several large as well as smaller health facilities, for a period of ten years. It was then that Charlie grew restless and discussed a possible change with his bishop. He was assigned to a rural parish in eastern Montana. There he came alive in new ways, while also bringing his rich learning through chaplaincy with him into the new setting. By the time he'd completed several more years of spiritual care practice as a parish pastor, he knew his heart was in parish-based ministry. Throughout his time as a hospital chaplain and parish pastor, Charlie stayed in contact with Jack.

Unlike Charlie, Jack began his years of service in a mid-sized congregation in the southern US, developing quite a reputation as a good administrator and personable pastor. He, like Charlie, had taken a unit of CPE during his internship year in seminary. It was a parish-based CPE program rather than hospital-based. He loved meeting people, visiting their homes, organizing bible studies, running fund-raising campaigns for various social justice causes, visiting parishioners at the local hospital and preaching a message of God's love during weekly worship services. After several very happy years, Jack's happiness grew when he met Gloria. They shared a plane ride as Jack was traveling to his denomination's conference in Louisville, Kentucky. Gloria, a registered nurse, was on her way home to Billings, Montana, after being the keynote speaker for a Parish Nursing conference in St. Louis, Missouri. Over the next several years, Jack's and Gloria's relationship grew and deepened, and they decided to marry and settle in Billings. Gloria was well established in her combined hospital and parish nursing career, and Jack believed he could find a congregation that would call him to serve as pastor. As things turned out, there were no congregational openings and Jack approached the chaplain at a local hospital to see what might be available there. To his surprise and delight, CPE[20] was offered at the hospital. Jack was accepted to the program, which he saw as a temporary learning opportunity until he could apply to be called by a congregation. Before long, he was fully engaged in his hospital spiritual care experiences and loving it. He moved from Level I/Basic to Level II/Advanced CPE and, from there, applied to become a Board-Certified Chaplain. Just as he had loved the mix of experiences he found in congregational ministry, he also loved the mix of experiences in hospital ministry. It was in Billings that Charlie and Jack reconnected after not seeing one another for five years.

Before long, Jack and Charlie were meeting twice monthly over coffee at a local bakery-and-beverage shop. It was during these times that their conversations turned to shared reflection on their experiences of spiritual care. Both men were familiar with the work of Hubert Dreyfus but had never thought about it in terms of their own lives. As they looked back over the years, they could point to some of the junctures in their stages of learning.

The irony of Charlie's beginning in hospital and going on to thrive in parishes, while Jack began in congregations and was now thriving in a hospital, was not lost on them. Both developed expertise in two distinct subclasses of spiritual care practice. Both loved both, but each man said I can "really be myself" in the setting where he now served. When Charlie visited his parishioners at the local hospital, he knew how to check in with unit staff, notice posted signs related to gowning and masking, and implement appropriate confidentiality and documentation protocols. At the same time, he was always "Charlie" in the ways he related to his congregational members. They didn't experience him differently than when he was leading worship or facilitating a parish council meeting. He had a personal style that was recognizable, embodied, and natural.

Jack, who was sometimes asked to preach on weekends, or officiate at weddings and funerals, likewise found he felt at home in a congregational setting even though it was in hospital spiritual care where he wanted to focus his passion and expertise. When preaching or officiating, he was always "Jack", and brought his wit and insight to whatever he did. But his real love was hospital chaplaincy. There he could thrive in the fullness of his personal style as he related to patients, their loved ones, and the hospital's staff.

In their coffee conversations, Charlie and Jack deepened in appreciation of their ministry stories. They reflected on some of the things they'd learned in seminary that stayed with them through their ministry years. For example, Erik Erikson's eight developmental ages were meaningful to Charlie in his parish work. He often noticed youth struggling with identity vs. role confusion, and his aging congregation struggling with generativity vs. stagnation. Jack, too, found Erikson helpful as he observed patients go through times of trust v. mistrust while dealing with stressful diagnoses. He also detected struggles with autonomy vs. shame and doubt as patients and their families tried to decide on treatment options, or the cessation of treatment all together.

While both men could see parallels in their congregational and hospital spiritual care, they also saw differences with regard to the ways they listened thickly to thin moments. Charlie, for example, was a regular presence at youth group gatherings in his parish. He felt comfortable being direct with red-faced youth by asking them "How's your love life with Jesus?" Alongside his directness, and based on what Charlie learned about Lisa Miller's spirituality research, he shared how important it is to have a relationship with God that's real, personal and accessible through the ups and downs of being a teen and becoming a grown up. For his part, Jack sought to embody trustworthiness in such a way that patients and their loved ones could turn to him with whatever they were going through. He laughed with them and wept with them, being his witty as well as compassionate self in a variety of circumstances.

When they talked about Dreyfus' stage of mastery, both men remembered people who served as masterfully skilled pastors and chaplains. They shared stories about the men and women who modelled for them what compassionate care, common sense, and prayerful lives that were coupled with humor and humility can look like. It was through their apprenticing with these masterful colleagues that Charlie and Jack learned how to be fully themselves—each exercising thick listening at thin moments through a different personal style.

Before leaving the discussion of Stage #6 Being Masterful: Personal Style, we turn our attention to three subclasses of spiritual care practice that are worth noting: spiritual care education, management and research. In addition to those who are expert and masterful in a broad spectrum of frontline spiritual care proficiencies, there are those who are expert and masterful in CPE supervision, department and/or regional spiritual care management, and the carrying forward of research in spiritual care. Thick listening at thin moments is no less needed in these areas than it is in frontline clinical areas. The personal styles and modelling of these spiritual care practitioners is important to highlight insofar as—

like their clinical colleagues—they are contributing to the profession of spiritual care as a whole.

Credible and competent frontline spiritual care clinicians model the importance of this profession's unique skill set through excellence in thick listening at thin moments with patients, clients, families, staff, and colleagues. In a similar manner, credible and competent spiritual care managers, supervisor-educators and researchers model the importance of bringing theoretical and practical knowledge about thick listening at thin moments to research projects, articles, CPE curriculum design, and program evaluation initiatives. Management, research and supervisory education are distinctive, and also extremely valuable, subclasses of spiritual care expertise.

Using the insights of Dreyfus, we propose that people who are drawn to spiritual care education, management and research can learn through apprenticeship opportunities to emulate master practitioners, acquiring abilities that are fostered through brain-to-brain neural resonance and merged with a heart-to-heart felt sense of connection. Inexperienced CPE supervisors apprentice with seasoned supervisors as provisional supervisor-educators (used in CASC/ACSS) or certified educator candidates (used in ACPE). Inexperienced spiritual care managers apprentice with knowledgeable managers by serving as "acting" managers and during overlap periods when an outgoing manager and incoming manager work together to transition knowledge and expertise. And novice researchers apprentice with accomplished and published researchers through participation in team research projects and/or by becoming a principal investigator as competence with research design and implementation grows.

As with the development of clinical competence, learning to be a spiritual care educator, manager or researcher is embodied, personal and social. Similar to their clinically-based masterful colleagues, spiritual care practitioners who seek to excel in research, management and clinical/supervisory education do so within specialized relational learning environments where neural resonance and a felt sense of connection thrive in collegial apprenticeship. Thick listening at thin moments, as it's exercised in research, management and supervisor-educator relational learning environments, holds—in creative tension—the dynamics of *dianoia* (looking around) and *nous* (looking upward) as these practitioners interact with topical questions, accumulated data, and the work of building a body of knowledge related to evidence-based practice within the profession of spiritual care.[21]

Stage #7 Acquiring Practical Wisdom: Cultural Style

To arrive at Dreyfus' seventh stage in developing the complex competency of thick listening at thin moments, a spiritual care practitioner has grown in competence by means of the previous six stages. To briefly summarize what we've written to this point:

- Novice: Applying rules and features that are relevant to basic spiritual care practice (listening skills; initial spiritual care relating; reflective pre-briefing and debriefing);

- Advanced Beginner: Using maxims and testing options as inexperience translates into limited experience (discerning variations in relational learning environments; purposeful use of reflective learning tools);

- Competent Learner: Accumulating experience within contexts where there are multiple perspectives and intervention options (listening to one's own internal reasoning and deliberation processes; making informed decisions; beginning to grasp the big picture and weigh priorities in becoming the spiritual care practitioner one wants to become);

- Proficient Learner: Embodying one's listening capacity through awareness of and attentiveness to global patterns and personal uniqueness within "otherness" (listening to emotional clues in oneself and others; assessing systems; remaining present while experiencing the emotional highs and lows involved in one's spiritual care interventions);

- Expert: Integrating, embodying and holding as one's own what one has learned through imitation, reflective practice, the observation of expert modelling and engaging supervisory/peer feedback (personalizing one's approach to thick listening at thin moments in such a way that it's available in a variety of spiritual care contexts); and

- Master: Embodying and broadening one's personal style as a spiritual care practitioner (discerning "what's me" and "what's not me"; accruing ongoing apprenticeship experiences within collegial/peer relational learning environments; being fully who one is when exercising thick listening at thin moments in one's spiritual care practice).

For Dreyfus, *practical wisdom* is "the general ability to do the appropriate thing, at the appropriate time, in the appropriate way."[22] This understanding derives from Aristotle's concept of *phronesis*, a type of wisdom or intelligence that's relevant to practical action. For the spiritual care practitioner, practical wisdom is viewed as the personal and social embodiment of one's accrued competence. In our analysis of the Dreyfus model as it applies to the complex competency of thick listening at thin moments, stage six looks at personal aspects of its embodiment and stage seven looks at cultural aspects.[23]

Just as mastery involves personal style, practical wisdom involves cultural style. But what do we mean by cultural style at stage seven? To begin with, the learning of culture goes hand in hand with acquiring a worldview. All human beings are apprenticed to their family of origin's culture. Dreyfus observes that our cultural style is so embodied and pervasive that it's generally invisible to us. Thus, we come to perceive our cultural style only when we encounter people from other cultures. For example, how to cook food, nurture infants, organize labor, worship, and bury the dead are all embodied differently within diverse cultures. This observation returns our attention to the chapter on Meeting Another as "Other". The issue here is to understand how meaning is constructed differently in another culture and to *read the meaning* rather than being distracted by the practices we're observing that are so different from our own. At this stage, a cultural style that's reflective and discerning allows people to remain authentic but also to adapt to the meaning of another cultural practice, as that meaning is conveyed through an *outwardly* different way of doing things. For example, when she encountered the practices of people from other cultures and faith backgrounds, Rose was beginning to explore this kind of cultural discernment and flexibility.

Stage seven broadens the sorting process described earlier when a practitioner reflects on "what's me" and "what's not me", and extends that inquiry to "what's us" and "what's not us". The practitioner moves from the personal to the cultural. Spiritual care experts who listen thickly to their own cultural style, and simultaneously to the cultural clues of others, revisit Gadamer's fundamental hermeneutical question and understand *that something is so because they understand that it has come about so.* They're able to appreciate cultural style and its nuanced complexity.

To demonstrate thick listening at thin moments at the stage of practical wisdom, a spiritual care practitioner has an embodied cultural awareness and can recognize when intersectionality is triggering dissonance based on gender, race, faith tradition, social class, and the like. Listening at thin moments has become a way of being in the world. Looking inward while also looking outward to discern the activation of one's own and/or another's worldview map is a trait of contemplative mindfulness and intentional reflection. In this realm of skills acquisition, it's noteworthy that a number of resources on cultural diversity can be found by searching the websites of spiritual care associations in North America and the *Journal of Pastoral Care & Counseling*. Information about cultural variances and their complexity—about one's own culture and that of others—needs to be part of one's spiritual care interpretive lenses and reading strategies.

Finally, on the topic of cultural diversity and style, we believe it's important to ask a systems question. That is, how does practical wisdom apply to the history of CPE as an educational method? Originating in New England, in the United States during the mid-1920s,[24] CPE migrated throughout the US and internationally as CPE supervisors moved within the US and relocated to countries around the world. International students also traveled to CPE centers in North America. Although an analysis of the cultural style of CPE learning is not within the purview of this chapter, it would be interesting to investigate how a global pattern of western individualism—discussed in the chapter on Meeting Another as "Other"—has influenced CPE learning processes not only in the US but also globally.

For example, the use of personalized student learning covenants (or contracts), the dedication of supervisory time to reading student reports and scheduling individual supervision, and the writing of student-specific evaluation/assessment documents at the end of each CPE course provide indicators of a focus on individualism that's integral to the cultural context for CPE in North America. When CPE is offered in countries where strong group dyadic membership is more valued than individualism, what adaptations need to occur? How do CPE programs in diverse cultures resemble and/or differ from those in North America? As authors, seeking to align this inquiry into CPE's history with Dreyfus' acquisition of practical wisdom, a core question for us is: which CPE learning elements are considered essential across cultures, and which are culturally flexible? One example of struggling with this question is found in the following story about two CPE supervisors, one North American and one East Asian.

If You Like, We Can See Each Other as a Walkway Between Our Cultures

Pre-briefing (background to the scenario): Anita first encountered In-Su by chance. He dropped by the Spiritual Care Services office of the large acute care hospital in Canada where she worked as CPE Supervisor. In-Su was inquiring about CPE. Anita just happened to be there. She spoke with him briefly and gave him a CPE information packet. Several weeks later he sent her an email saying he had read over everything and would like to schedule an appointment. It was during their appointment that Anita felt she really "met" In-Su. Gaining a window into his background and CPE hopes, she was impressed. Reading his theory paper and doctoral dissertation, she was captivated and curious. After several further meetings, they could both see some possibilities taking shape.

Unknown to In-Su was Anita's long history of seeking supervisory colleagueship within the site. Due to budget restrictions, additional CPE Supervisors could not be hired. There was, however, interest on the part of several spiritual care practitioners to pursue supervisory certification. For Anita, this felt a long way off.

In-Su seemed like a gift from God, dropped into the hospital setting out of the blue. He was from South Korea, an experienced congregational minister who also served in the Philippines for several years. It was in the Philippines that In-Su became involved with CPE, and achieved Associate Supervisor certification in the Asian Clinical Pastoral Education Association (ACPEA). He was in Canada to serve as interim senior pastor for a local congregation. In their initial meetings, In-Su expressed interest in volunteering at the hospital in order to gain familiarity with Canadian CPE standards and procedures. Within a short period of time the wheels were set in motion to include In-Su in some limited ways as part of the site's CPE and supervisory learning processes.

As things turned out, Anita and In-Su ended up collaborating over a period of four years. It was a time of mutual learning. The following event captures a moment, early in their relationship, when it became clear to them that a core question for their shared consideration needed to be: Which CPE learning elements are considered essential across cultures, and which are culturally flexible?

Significant scenario: In-Su arrived at Anita's office for a scheduled meeting. As they commenced their time, he told the story of walking to her location from the spiritual care office in the main hospital building. He used a pedway to get to the building where her office was located. He went on to say that people in east Asia and the Philippines like to talk about important topics by telling a story. They like to circle a topic before landing on it. That way there's a sense of meaning that forms in the relationship, so it's the relationship that supports the insight they reach. In-Su then went back to talk about the pedway. He pointed out that it was a bridge between two buildings. Sometimes, in order for them to meet, he walked in her direction and sometimes she walked in his direction. This movement between buildings, he said, can be compared to the movement between cultures. Sometimes he brings cultural wisdom to her and sometimes she brings cultural wisdom to him. Then he spoke the words that stuck in her mind and heart: "If you like, we can see each other as a walkway between our cultures."

Debriefing I (exploring the question about CPE's essential learning elements while honoring cultural adaptability): During the years he was in Canada, In-Su encountered a number of barriers related to transferring his certification credentials from the Philippines to Canada. That said, while he experienced obstacles and setbacks, In-Su accomplished a great deal—going through two regional and one national certification reviews to become recognized as a clinical Specialist (now called Certified Spiritual Care Practitioner) and Provisional Teaching Supervisor (now called Provisional Supervisor-Educator). Since returning to his home country, In-Su has exercised leadership and creativity in furthering the development of CPE where he works. As he joins with others to celebrate over twenty years of CPE in South Korea, In-Su continues to explore cultural knowledge and wisdom. One way this has occurred is through his communications with Anita. Together they've been pondering the question about which CPE learning elements are considered essential across cultures and which are culturally flexible. The following points have surfaced.

First, an important reality to name whenever cultures meet is the impact *language* has on what's communicated and understood. When In-Su arrived in Canada, he had a mother tongue that was rich with nuance, meaning, and imagination. But it was a language he could not speak to Anita insofar as English was the primary language of the CPE center and programs within which he participated. In order to communicate on the topics of spiritual care and CPE, In-Su studied English. This was no small feat, and had an impact on his self-image as a competent practitioner and supervisor. In terms of the global patterns discussed in the chapter on Otherness, In-Su experienced *caught betweenness*. That is to say, when he tried to express the true depth of his knowledge and understanding, he was repeatedly hampered by a limited English vocabulary. This was a thin moment place for him insofar as he recognized language as a barrier to bringing his personal, professional and cultural resources into relationship with Anita. She was attentive to this and communicated her respect to him in such a way that, together, they were able to persevere in collegial supervisory collaboration. Both In-Su and Anita grew in an awareness of cultural style through this appreciation of problematics related to language.

Second, In-Su and Anita talked on a number of occasions about differences between formal and informal structures for CPE programs. North American spiritual care associations are known for their highly developed Standards pertaining to education and practice. In-Su found this emphasis both attractive and disconcerting. On the one hand, he appreciated the strong system of support for CPE found in Canada. On the other, these Standards closed doors to him being recognized within the Canadian association. While there is reciprocity between spiritual care associations in Canada and the United States that allows practitioners to be recognized in both countries, there was no formal agreement of reciprocity between Canada and the Asian Clinical Pastoral Education Association (ACPEA) in the Philippines. In order for In Su to gain recognition in Canada, he and Anita looked for some open space (a walkway) in the Standards. They found what In-Su called a "guest house" in an Appendix used for certification applicants who came from alternative educational backgrounds. In-Su used this Appendix to prepare for his certification reviews in Canada, and was successful in gaining recognition. While he didn't return to the Philippines when he left Canada, In Su brought his Canadian learning and recognition to his home country of South Korea where he currently lives.[25]

Beyond his own experience with differences between formal and informal structures, In-Su could see that individually focused practices in the Canadian Standards would not be a good fit for his Korean context. However, he and Anita agreed that the personal style of every spiritual care practitioner is an essential aspect of learning mastery. So they puzzled over what the personal looks like in a North American CPE context and in his Korean setting. The chapter on Otherness explores some of these differences.

For both Anita and In Su the role of an effective CPE supervisor is to call forth the "real person" of each student while also maintaining a sense of group solidarity. For In Su, group solidarity has a different meaning than it has in North America. In his experience, the role of a CPE supervisor is not to stand out but rather to translate standards into practice by way of embodied modelling and by fostering group solidarity based on his knowledge of dyadic membership. In-Su and Anita spoke about the value of a CPE supervisor spending personal time with each student (referred to as Individual Supervision, or IS, in CPE practice) as a locus for bridging student competence with shared group learning and feedback. While arriving at this conclusion from different cultural perspectives, Anita and In Su agreed that personalized supervision (IS) is an essential element of CPE.

Third, on the matter of CPE program design and development, In-Su spoke about how much he valued taking the adult education course (required of CPE supervisors) while he was in Canada. From that course, he was able to bridge insights gained in writing his theoretical paper for Provisional Supervisor consultation with experiences of the CPE students he supervised.[26] In their ongoing dialogue about CPE's essential learning elements, he and Anita explored several diagrams in which In-Su depicted self-directed, egalitarian and experiential/somatic learning. They spoke of *learning to know* as having a good fit with theoretical/didactic seminars and *learning to do* fitting well with clinical seminars. When it came to Interpersonal Relationship Group (IPR) and Individual Supervision, Anita and In-Su used different phrases. For In-Su, it was a matter of "learning to live together" (again, the value of a strong group). For Anita, it was a matter of "learning appropriate self-disclosure and peer feedback" (valuing individualism). Lastly, they spoke about *learning to be* as having to do with personal and professional identity formation.

Finally, when it came to how a supervisor can best accompany and apprentice a spiritual care learner through various CPE stages, i.e., Basic/Level I to Advanced/Level II, In-Su shared what he considers to be four phases of the supervisor-student relationship. Anita added insights from Dreyfus.

- Dependent learners need expert authority supervisors (Anita noted similarities in Dreyfus' novice and advanced beginner stages)
- Interested learners need motivator supervisors (Anita noted the role of motivation provided by skilled practitioners in the advanced begin-

ner and competent learner stages)

- Involved learners need facilitator supervisors (Anita noted the role of involvement and emotion arising during competent and proficient learner stages), and

- Self-directed learners need delegator/collaborator supervisors (Anita noted the role of reflective questions and risk-taking in the proficient learner and expert stages).

In their continuing discussions, In-Su and Anita found common ground as they envisioned CPE through different cultural lenses. In-Su shared a diagram he developed to show what he considers are essential CPE learning elements across cultures (see Figure 8).[27] Anita found this diagram confirmed her own thinking. They agreed that it's the lived experience of providing spiritual care, coupled with theoretical input, IPR and clinical elements of this educational method that are essential to CPE learning in all cultures. The role of a CPE supervisor—especially through Individual Supervision—is central to cultivating personal and professional integration among students. Other elements of CPE, such as curriculum design and clinical placement locations, can vary and need to be culturally flexible.

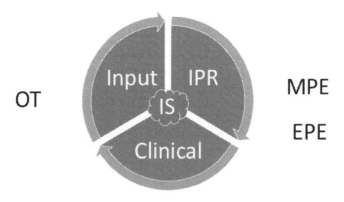

Figure 8: Essential CPE Learning Elements Across Cultures

In Figure 8, there's a circle with letters outside and words inside. Letters outside the circle describe the linear movement of a CPE program, from entry to midway to exit. Letters and words inside the circle depict the circular movement of CPE learning processes. These two types of movement are further described under the following headings:

Linear movement from entry to exit:

OT   Orientation to a CPE program; mapping and information

MPE   Midpoint evaluation; draft of personal and professional integration halfway through a CPE program

EPE   Endpoint evaluation; summary of personal and professional integration, and completion of collective learning processes, at the end of a CPE program

Circular movement of core learning processes:

Input   Theoretical and Practical information needed by CPE learners; this can differ according to context and culture, and be learned through independent study and/or group seminars

IPR   Interpersonal Relationship Group Seminars; peer group sessions where personal and professional issues, and group culture are explored

Clinical   The Seminars where case study, critical incident and/or verbatim documents are reflectively reviewed with peers and supervisor.

IS   Individual Supervision is pictured as the hub around which theoretical input, IPR and clinical learning experiences circle.

Debriefing II (exploring the question about how practical wisdom applies to the history of CPE as an educational method): In reflecting on In-Su's cultural approach to CPE, as distinct from her own, Anita had a thin moment experience with implications for international CPE learning. She listened to the ways In-Su talked about authority, i.e. embedded in and explained by strong group cultural theory. As she thought about his approach to authority, she saw in a new light her embedded western individualism, and how her understanding of authority was colored by an emphasis on singularity. Without the benefit of their dialogue about essential CPE learning elements across cultures, this awareness about how authority is viewed through different cultural lenses would not have occurred to Anita. In a flash of insight, she realized that when CPE expands beyond its North American roots, cultural walkways like the one discovered by In-Su and Anita are essential for strong group cultures and western individualism cultures to "meet". But what does this mean?

In order for Dreyfus' insights into practical wisdom and cultural style to flourish in CPE programs for the twenty-first century, some of the relational tools discussed in the chapter on Otherness need to be studied, integrated and embodied. Specifically, the tool of dialectical communication offers the potential for two points of view (or two worldviews) to interact and form a third view.[28] Yes the "meeting" of cultures may involve learning through "caught betweenness"—as was the case when In-Su's credentials were not recognized in Canada. But "meeting" may also involve establishing liminal learning environments within CPE programs where dialectical discussion and reasoning are encouraged. The dialectical works at points of liminality. It invites communication among the global patterns of western individualism, strong group culture and caught betweenness. It requires CPE learning processes that seek to understand how meaning is constructed differently in another culture and to *read the meaning* rather than being distracted by practices that are different from one's own.

Using systems thinking, what walkways are needed for North American CPE programs to welcome and benefit from the cultural wisdom found in strong group cultures like In-Su's? Similarly, what walkways are needed for CPE programs located in strong group cultures to welcome and benefit from western individualism's cultural wisdom like Anita's? And, what walkways are needed for those who find themselves in places of *caught betweenness*? In their dialogue, Anita and In-Su came up with the following possibilities, for others to consider and broaden:

First, having parallel experiences can bring us closer: Just as In-Su travelled to Canada to learn about how CPE is offered there, what if Anita were to travel to Korea to learn about how CPE is offered there? According to In-Su, his experience with language barriers and different procedures and practices, evoked his imagination and deepened his emotional understanding. In this book, imaginative and emotional intelligence are two of the four literacies discussed in the chapter on Spiritual Care Competencies. In another vein, parallel experiences open space for "empathy," as understood by Edith Stein and discussed in the chapter on Otherness, to come alive in concrete relationships. According to Stein, the primary notion in empathy is a realization that the object of our contemplation is "foreign" to us in the sense that a particular event is not happening to us in this way at that time. For her, empathy refers to acts in which we grasp foreign experience by sensing not only what's presented by another person, but also what's *behind* that self-presentation, i.e., a narrative that brought someone to this point by way of experiences about which the one empathizing doesn't know.

Second, hosting certified CPE supervisors who are bilingual and from different cultural contexts can open space for dialectical communication: Imagine (with the benefits of videoconferencing technology like Zoom) CPE programs where bilingual CPE supervisors—from cultural contexts in Australia, Cameroon, Kenya, South Korea, North America, or the Philippines as examples—are guests of CPE programs in other cultures than their own. Student participants in the CPE programs hosting these guest CPE supervisors would learn about cultural style by talking with each other, using the benefits of translation. They'd grapple with and better understand differences among the global cultural patterns of western individualism, strong group dyadic membership and "caught betweenness" discussed in the chapter on Otherness. Making space for CPE participants to interact and better know each other across cultural differences can lead to what Brian Hall wrote about, which he called "forming a third" point of view.

Third, incorporating translation services for CPE programs with students from several countries and cultures: As In-Su and Anita learned, an important reality to name whenever cultures meet is the impact *language* has on what's communicated and understood. What if a Korean translator, bound by a confidentiality agreement, had been hired for the CPE programs In-Su supervised while he was in Canada? Or what might happen if a translator were part of a CPE program comprised of students from Cameroon and Kenya, or Korea and the Philippines? It's a complicated idea, but something worth considering.

What Anita and In-Su discovered through their relationship and dialogue is that cultural apprenticeship—like all apprenticeship discussed by Dreyfus—occurs as embodied learning through brain-to-brain neural resonance that merges with a heart-to-heart felt sense of connection. Wherever CPE programs imagine, cultivate and structure possibilities for students to participate in cultural apprenticeship, new walkways will become visible across which cultural wisdom can be carried and meaningfully shared. These walkways may contribute to the flourishing of CPE— in acquiring practical wisdom and cultural style—as it moves out of the twentieth century and more fully into the twenty-first century.

To summarize this section, according to Dreyfus, learning practical wisdom is so embodied that it can't be captured in a theory. It's passed from body to body. Yet he notes that cultural style is what makes us human and provides the background for all our learning. The practical wisdom of cultural style is learned relationally. In terms of the language of our book, practical wisdom aligns with contemplative mindfulness as a quality of thick listening that can turn inward as self-observation and outward as perceptive accompaniment of others. Contemplative mindfulness is about embodied thick listening at thin moments. It transcends reflective practice and participates in what Drake and Miller have called contemplative practice—a quality of being that's experienced as unmediated awareness characterized by openness, a sense of relatedness, and by the awe and wonder involved in practical wisdom.[29]

Conclusion

This chapter has looked in depth at two questions. First, what does competent spiritual care practice look like clinically? Second, what's involved in mastering the complex competency of thick listening at thin moments? The chapter outlines the importance of vignette and case study usage in research and publications as ways to make spiritual care practice visible and assessable.

We've also taken a detailed look at the work of Hubert Dreyfus and his seven stages of skills acquisition. Incorporated into this section, we've provided clinical vignettes to depict what spiritual care practice as thick listening at thin moments looks like as one moves toward mastery in spiritual care competence.

The complexity and embodied expertise found in spiritual care practice needs to be better understood, recognized and respected. It's our hope that a collection of case studies based on theoretical constructs developed from the book's chapters might evolve. Such a collection would need to highlight spiritual care practice in its broadest scope, multiple contexts and cultural diversities. With greater visibility, together with the theoretical framework provided by Dreyfus, spiritual care associations are better positioned to assess students and professionally certified practitioners by using scales and rubrics developed on the strength of the framework for spiritual care mastery described in this chapter.

Take Away Questions for Reflection

- How have you learned about what spiritual care looks like by writing verbatim, critical incident and case study reports? What additional understanding have you gained by reading articles and books that feature spiritual care case studies?

- What do you make of Dreyfus's emphasis on step-by-step competence development through seven stages? How do you see instruction, practice and apprenticeship fitting with your experiences of spiritual care learning? Does the idea of moving from novice to master make sense for you? Does it appeal to you? If so, why? If not, why not?

- What does Dreyfus's emphasize on in-person learning and embodiment say to you about competency development? How does CPE foster this learning? How do theological colleges, seminaries and other educational centers foster this learning?

- At which of Hubert Dreyfus's seven stages of skills acquisition do you find yourself? What are your reasons for choosing this stage? Have those who are supervising and/or observing your spiritual care practice affirmed your choice? Why? Why not?

- How might Dreyfus's theoretical framework inform the development of rubrics and scales for assessing professional spiritual care practice in your professional association?

- Having learned a great deal about "thick listening at thin moments" by reading this book, in what ways do you see this complex competency operative in your spiritual care practice?

Appendix 1

References to Definitions of Spirituality

Initial Overview:
- When exploring the literature for definitions of 'spirituality', there is a lot of discussion on differences between use of spirituality clinically vis-à-vis in research (Reinert & Koenig).
- Differentiation had to do with certain *beliefs* being characteristic of spirituality, but noting problems with using *beliefs* as indicators of spirituality in research surveys.
- Spirituality as 'self-defined' and/or subjectively defined.
- Process of arriving at consensus definition of spirituality (Puchalski).
- Spirituality and religion situated within culture in DSM-5 (Ellor).

Definitions
1. Brown, Brene (2010). *The Gifts of Imperfection*. Center City, MN: Hazelden Publishing. "Defining Spirituality," March 27, 2018 https://brenebrown.com/articles/2018/03/27/defining-spirituality/.

    Spirituality is recognizing and celebrating that we are all inextricably connected to each other by a power greater than all of us, and that our connection to the power and to one another is grounded in love and compassion; practicing spirituality brings a sense of perspective, meaning, and purpose to our lives.

2. Buck, H. (2006). "Spirituality: Concept analysis and model development". *Holistic Nursing Practice*, November/December, 288-292.

A definition of spirituality is presented, and a model constructed from a review of the literature and reflection. Spirituality is
defined as: that most human of experiences that seeks to transcend self and find meaning and purpose through connection
with others, nature, and/or a Supreme Being, which may or may
not involve religious structures or traditions.

3.   Chiu, L., Emblen, J., Van Hofwegen, L., Sawatzky, R., Meyerhoff,
      H. (2004). "An integrative review of the concept of spirituality in
      the health sciences". *Western Journal of Nursing Research*, 26 (4),
      405-428.

      Spirituality has been described in a multiplicity of ways. A
      thematic analysis of current definitions was done to reveal the
      following themes: existential reality, transcendence, connected-
      ness, and power/force/energy. (409).

4.   Cohen, M., Holley, L., Wengel, S., & Katzman, M. (2013). "A
      platform for nursing research on spirituality and religiosity:
      Definitions and measure". *Western Journal of Nursing Research*,
      34 (6), 795-817.

      Spirituality may be defined as an individual's sense of peace,
      purpose, and connection to others, and beliefs about the mean-
      ing of life. Spirituality may be found and expressed through
      an organized religion or in other ways. Patients may think of
      themselves as spiritual or religious or both. (http:www.cancer.
      gov/cancertopics/pdq/supportivecare/spirituality/Patient).

5.   Ellor., J. (2013). "Religion and spirituality among older adults in
      light of DSM-5". *Social Work & Christianity*, 40, 4, 372-383.

      Koenig, McCullough and Larson (2001) offer the following
      definition, "Spirituality is the personal quest for understanding
      answers to ultimate questions about life, about meaning, and
      about relationship to the sacred or transcendent, which may
      (or may not) lead to or arise from the development of religious
      rituals and the formation of community" (18).

6. Hodge, D., & Holtrop, C. (2012). "Spiritual assessment: A review of complementary assessment models". In T.L. Scales & M.S. Kelly (Eds.), *Christianity and Social Work* (pp. 255-281). Botsford, CT: North American Association of Christian Social Workers.

Spirituality is defined as an existential relationship with God (or perceived transcendence) (Hodge, 2001a). Religion flows from spirituality, expressing the spiritual relationship in particular beliefs, forms, practices that have been developed in community with other individuals who share similar spiritual experiences (Hodge, 2000). Accordingly, spirituality and religion are overlapping but distinct constructs (Canda, 1997; Carroll, 1997).

7. Lasair, Simon, "What's the Point of Spiritual Care? A narrative response," *Journal of Pastoral Care and Counseling*, 73(2) (2019): 115-116.

Spirituality has typically been defined as an individual's beliefs and practices relating to ultimate meaning, including an individual's capacity to make meaning of their life and situation (Lasair, 2018a, forthcoming; Lasair & Sinclair, 2018; McBrien, 2006; Sinclair and Chochinov, 2012, Swinton, 2012). Religion includes this, but also formulates understandings of ultimate meaning in terms stemming from the teachings, rituals, practices, and institutions of established faith traditions (Sinclair & Chochinov, 2012; McBrien, 2006; Swinton, 2012; Lasair, forthcoming; Lasair & Sinclair, 2018). A person may express their spirituality within the context of religion. However, there are aspects of a person's spirituality that can never be encompassed by their religion, such as the main driving forces in their life—their loves, their hobbies, their relationships, their life goals—all of which are important aspects of a person's spirituality, but which may or may not be given specific religious meanings (Lasair, 2018a, 2018b). The challenge is thus to define and understand spirituality in such a way that it can be meaningfully engaged and treated with readily identifiable outcomes (Handzo et al., 2014; Snowden & Telfer, 2017; Steinhauser et al., 2017). Currently, many discussions of spirituality, particularly in heathcare, fall short of meeting this goal, remaining instead with the basic notion that a person's spirituality ought to be included in their overall treatment plan, but not moving much beyond this (cf. e.g., Balboni et al., 2017; Puchalski et al., 2009; Puchalski, Vitillo, Hull, & Reller, 2014; Steinhauser et al., 2017).

8. Pesut, B. (2010). "Ontologies of nursing in an age of spiritual pluralism: Closed or open worldview?" *Nursing Philosophy*, 11(1), 15-23.

   Although spirituality has many definitions in the nursing liter-ature, in this paper spirituality means the following: The accep-tance of a level of reality beyond the observable world known to science, to which are ascribed meanings and purposes complet-ing and transcending those of the purely human realm (Martin, 1978, p. 12). Spirituality includes, but is not limited to, religion and assumes a supernatural reality that has implications for human health and flourishing. Therefore, the terms spirituality and religion will be used interchangeably depending upon the common usage within the body of knowledge upon which I am drawing (e.g. sociology and philosophy of religion vs. nursing spirituality).

9. Puchalski, C., Ferrell, B., Virani, R., R., Otis-Green, S., Baird, P., Bull, J., Chochinov, H., Handzo, G., Nelson-Becker, H., Prince-Paul, M., Pugliese, K., & Sumany, D. (2009). "Improving the qua-lity of spiritual care as a dimension of palliative care: The report of the consensus conference". *Journal of Palliative Medicine*, 12(10), 885-904.

   Spirituality is the aspect of humanity that refers to the way individuals seek and express meaning and purpose and the way they experience their connectedness to the moment, to self, to others, to nature, and to the significant or sacred. (p. 887).

10. Reinert, K.G. & Koenig, H.G. (2013) "Re-examining definitions of spirituality in nursing research". *Journal of Advanced Nursing* 69(12), 2622-2634. doi: 10.1111/jan.12152

   As such, we submit that an appropriate definition of spirituality in nursing research is: Spirituality is distinguished from other things—humanism, values, morals and mental health—by its connection to the transcendent. The transcendent is that which is outside of the self, and yet also within the self—and in Western traditions is called God, Allah, HaShem, or a Higher Power and in Eastern traditions is called Ultimate Truth or Reality, Vishnu, Krishna, or Buddha. Spirituality is intimately connected to the supernatural and religion, although also extends beyond religion (and begins before it). Spirituality includes a search for the transcendent and so involves travelling along the path that leads from non-consideration to a decision not to believe, to questioning belief to devotion to surrender (Koenig et al. 2012, p. 46). The above definition for spirituality allows researchers to adequately measure spirituality in the context of religious involvement with more consistency in research, while using constructs that are in nature distinct from mental health. Implications for practice and/or policy:

- The definitions of spirituality in research aimed at evaluating mental health outcomes should be distinct from definitions used in the clinical setting for purposes of providing spiritual care.

- Spiritual care or spiritual assessment in the clinical setting should be inclusive and open to cultural and individually appropriate definitions and conceptualizations.

- Appropriate definitions of spirituality can transform nursing research aimed at determining the relationship between spirituality and mental health, while facilitating the identification of protective factors and resilience mechanisms.

11. Zinnbauer, B., Pargament, K., Cole, B., Rye, M., Butter, E., Belavich, T., Hipp, K., Scott, A., Kadar, J. (1997). "Religion and Spirituality: Unfuzzying the Fuzzy", *Journal for the Scientific Study of Religion*, Vol. 36, No. 4, pp. 549-564.

Current definitions of spirituality are...diverse. Spirituality has been variously defined by theorists as 'the human response to God's gracious call to relationship with himself' (Benner 1989: 20), "a subjective experience of the sacred' (Vaughan 1991: 105), and 'that vast realm of human potential dealing with ultimate purposes, with higher entities, with God, with love, with compassion, with purpose' (Tart 1983:4). Furthermore, the terms spirituality and religiousness have been used interchangeably and inconsistently by some authors. For example, Miller and Martin (1988:14) frequently interchange the terms even after they explicitly state that spirituality 'may or may not include involvement in organized religion'.

12.   The formulation of psyche—in which the human mind is part and parcel of living spiritual reality—expands psychology.... [and] demands that we move beyond the exclusive mechanistic and materialist view of the human mind....[a human mind which is 'postmaterial' (p. 611) and] which is in dialog with a conscious and sacred world and emanates from the same source as the world around us. Lisa Miller, (Ed.) *The Oxford Handbook of Psychology and Spirituality*, Oxford: Oxford University Press, 2012.

13.   In comparison to the view of spirituality presented so far, from a nursing perspective, spirituality may be defined as "whatever or whoever gives ultimate meaning and purpose in one's life, [and] that invites particular ways of being in the world in relation to others, oneself and the universe." Nursing themes associated with the concept of spirituality include meaning, purpose, hope, faith, existentialism, transcendence, a sense of peace and connectedness among others. This definition and its expansion describe content and ways of life implicit in spirituality. The nursing point of view addresses *the what* of spirituality; spiritual care also addresses *the how* of and rests on assumptions about *the why* of spiritual care. Wright, 2005 in *Canadian Nurses Association*; World Health Organization, 2005 in *Canadian Nurses Association.*

14.   Defines spirituality as 'relational consciousness' in which children express an unusual level of consciousness or perceptiveness...regarding how they related to things, other people, to themselves, and God. It's a distinctive quality of mental activity, profound and intricate enough to be termed consciousness and refers to something more than being alert and mentally attentive and is more than awareness, it's a distinctly reflective consciousness and in the research was often apparent as objective insight into a child's subjective response that fostered a new dimension of understanding. Rebecca Nye, "Identifying the

Core of Children's Spirituality", in David Hay and Rebecca Nye, *The Spirit of the Child*, London: Fount, 1998, 113-114.

15. Spirituality is an inner sense of relationship to a higher power that is loving and guiding. The word we give to this higher power might be God, nature, spirit, the universe, the creator, or other words that represent a divine presence. But the important point is that spirituality encompasses our relationship and dialogue with this higher power. Lisa Miller, *The Spiritual Child: The new science on Parenting for health and lifelong thriving.* New York: St Martin's Press, 2015, 25.

16. Murgia, C., Notarnicola, I., Rocco, G., and Stierano, A. (2020). "Spirituality in nursing: A concept analysis". *Nursing Ethics*, 20(10), 1-17. doi: 10.1177/0969733020909534.

Appendix 2

The Awareness Wheel Exercise and Intentional Reflection

We recommend this tool as a complement to other learning instruments used by Clinical Pastoral Education (CPE) programs and practical theology courses fostering self-awareness in spiritual care learners. It brings together writing and reflection steps for using the Awareness Wheel Exercise. Readers are invited to write, investigate theoretical groundwork, reflect on and personalize what's learned. In this way, it's hoped they will discover how Action Science's assumption that every action is theory driven is applicable to the practice of thick listening at thin moments in spiritual care practice.

Preparatory Step

Provide an account of approximately 300 words to depict a "helping incident" in which you were the person who provided the help. Choose an incident you still have questions about, and about which you still feel unsettled. Describe the incident as fully as you can, including the location, circumstances and individuals or groups involved. Provide a detailed description of your role in the experience, including aspects of the incident you're unsure about. Discuss the spiritual care interventions you selected and what the outcome of your helping incident looked like. Ensure that you protect confidentiality by using initials for participants in the incident.

Write this account before you move on to the rest of the Appendix.

Introduction to the Awareness Wheel Exercise

When considering the complex competency of thick listening at thin moments, the central skill required is self-awareness that extends to an awareness of what might be going on in other people. The Awareness Wheel Exercise is at the heart of learning that skill. In this Appendix, we go over theories that elaborate elements of self-awareness and an awareness of others so that spiritual care can offer human understanding to all those involved. First, we look at relevant theory contained in several of this book's chapters. Second, we spell out the skills involved in understanding self and others by exploring five aspects of awareness that are explained by the Awareness Wheel and support the practice of Action Science.

The third part of the Appendix invites readers to reflect on the Preparatory Step, which they've already written, and develop it by using steps of the Awareness Wheel for gaining insight into self and others. It's hoped the theory, five aspects of awareness and reflection on one's helping incident—when taken together—will provide a framework for increasing mastery in the acquisition of thick listening at thin moments as a complex competency that involves an in-depth awareness of self and others in spiritual care practice.

Relevant Theories

Recall that the complex competency of thick listening at thin moments requires a person to learn and practice thick listening and to practice recognizing thin moments. Acquiring this complex competency calls for a type of thinking and intentional reflection that's supported by theories contained in a number of this book's chapters.

In chapter one, we outline the formation of a worldview and point to brain research that describes how people think—a process that includes perceptual and conceptual learning. In perceptual learning, from infancy onward, certain neurons in the brain are linked to the outside world via the body's organs, e.g., eyes see shapes and ears hear sounds. An infant can recognize its mother's face and its father's voice. In the chapter on Competencies for Spiritual Care Practice, we reference Freud's theory that every percept has an association attached to it. An infant's recognition of its mother's face and father's voice links to a set of associations about mother and father that are eventually included in the concepts of mother and father for this infant.

Initially, infants are a stream of percepts (sense perceptions). It takes time and a great deal of experience before concepts form based on experience. Conceptual learning relies on a second set of neurons that aren't linked to the outside world, as is the first set, but to each other to form an internal communication system. As mentioned in the chapter on Competencies for Spiritual Care Practice, imagination also plays a role in conceptual learning. Theories in preceding chapters about thinking, perceiving, and conceiving help to understand how we become more fully aware of what's going on, within ourselves and in other people.

Action Science plays a central role in the practice of becoming aware of self and others because its practice depends on the capacity neurons have for perceptual and conceptual learning. Using the Awareness Wheel Exercise, we become more intentionally attentive to what we're sensing: hearing, seeing, touching, tasting, smelling by focusing on Directly Observable Data (D.O.D) as outlined in Action Science. Through being intentional about perceptual awareness, we become more fully aware of what we sense is going on in a situation or event. As we focus on what we're sensing, we take in more of what there is to see, hear, touch, taste and smell. In addition, as we practice intentional perceptual awareness (sensing more of what there is to perceive) we learn to distinguish what we sense from what we think and from feelings that immediately arise due to interpretations we make about what's going on (a feature of mindfulness from the chapter on Made for Relationship).

A capacity to be self-aware, and aware of others, is an ordinary ability all people have access to if they give attention to it. In Made for Relationship, we propose that spiritual care could become an attitude toward the world everyone shares in and benefits from. We ask readers to consider what would happen if everyone saw homes, friends, communities, and workplaces as opportunities to seed, cultivate and nourish the human spirit. To explore these capacities for self-awareness and awareness of others, the list below contains ideas from various chapters of the book that support spiritual care based on ordinary human attributes. Awareness includes noticing and reflecting on telltale signs of embodied communication that show up as interpretive clues as we listen to another person:

- There are patterned, embodied ways human beings express themselves and we can learn to read, interpret, and understand these patterns.

- People can engage in Daniel Stern's present moment in which they give their full attention to another person or group of people, and show interest in them.
- As we show interest in another person, we become aware of slight or significant changes in their embodied communication, and interpret potential meanings of that communication, while remembering that interpretations must be affirmed by the other person as accurately expressing their thoughts and feelings, or of not doing so.
- We may show interest in ourselves and discern our own thoughts and feelings.
- Embodied communication may include leaning forward to show interest, widening the eyes, tilting the head, nodding, brighter facial coloring, or conversely, gripping a pen, tightening hands into fists, turning away, sitting back, a sharper tone of voice, changing the subject, as examples of changes in embodied communication.
- In the chapter on Competencies for Spiritual Care Practice, a hermeneutical stance takes note of changes such as these and realizes they're opportunities for follow-up inquiry.
- The possibility for creating these telltale signs relies on content explained in the chapter Made for Relationship that includes:

  ◊ Charles Darwin's observations about the relationship between facial muscles and the expression of feeling
  ◊ Paul Ekmann's website that teaches people to recognize feelings in others and in themselves (https://www.paulekman. com)
  ◊ The Vagus Nerve Complex (the body's internal social engagement system)
  ◊ The practice of mindfulness and various skills associated with offering our full attention in a present moment experience
  ◊ Intentional reflection based on attending to another as a conveyer of information and as an embodied living human document.

The Awareness Wheel: Sensing, Thinking, Feeling, Wanting, Doing

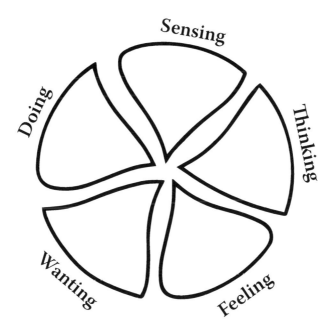

Look at the Awareness Wheel Diagram and note that sensing, thinking, feeling, wanting, and doing are five aspects on the spokes of the Wheel. It's important to realize that awareness may begin along any of these spokes. People may sense they feel angry by noting a change within their own body, such as one of the telltale signs noted above. Self-awareness may be the first step. However, awareness may also be directed toward something that's changed in an other person—an embodied shift that signals a change—e.g., the swimmer in the chapter on Faith who sits on the pool edge and refuses to dive into the water. For spiritual care practitioners, intentionally reflecting on the safe and effective use of self requires one to interpret the embodied communication of self and other through reading the body's telltale signs. This move is necessary for practitioners to create environments of safety for others, so the human spirit is free to flourish. The safe and effective use of self begins with a well-rounded awareness of what may be going on based on sensing, thinking, feeling wanting and doing.

As an essential part of this reflection, perspectives from other chapters come to our aid:

- Asking how change influences how we come to know what's going on
- Understanding that something is so because it has come about so
- Recognizing and resisting unhealthy reason as we interpret an event
- Reviewing relevant beliefs, disbeliefs and unbelief as they impact interpretation
- Reflecting on the expression of empathy toward oneself and the other(s)
- Considering what hospitality looks like in this situation
- Asking ourselves what we want in this situation
- Considering possible actions and their impacts on ourselves and others

As we consider all of these dimensions of awareness, we increase our confidence about taking ourselves and other people more fully into account.

At the center of spiritual care as thick listening at thin moments, there's a pattern for Awareness that has five aspects: sensing, thinking, feeling, wanting, and doing. The Awareness Wheel Exercise allows someone to give attention to these five activities, identify relationships among them, and develop masterful, complex skills by practicing in-depth awareness of self and other.

Sensing (Sense data or Percepts)

Sensing relies on the ability to perceive and be conscious of the properties of something. Infants have a capacity to acquire percepts through brain/body interactions outlined in chapter one. Sensory data or percepts are based on seeing, hearing, tasting, touching, and smelling. In addition, in the chapter on Competencies for Spiritual Care Practice, we noted Freud's research observation that every percept is accompanied by associations once infants have accumulated enough experience. So, for example, an infant may learn to associate mother (object) with smile. Percepts and their associations are the outcome of experiencing people, things and nature and noticing or observing these objects, e.g., faces and body movements, postures, or tone of voice. Sensing and associating produce descriptions, visualizations, stories, facts, recollections, fantasies, and intuitions. Sensory data may be verbal or non-verbal (body language: e.g., gestures, facial movements) or both simultaneously. Sensing and associating move forward in a developing, accumulating awareness so that someone may perceive something vaguely, then realize something about it more clearly, and then detect its characteristics or qualities precisely.

- Suppose Fred enters a room and sees Jerry sitting in a chair drinking coffee. Fred focuses on Jerry's facial expression. As he stops in the doorway, Fred becomes aware that he's made his hands into fists and he's sure his face is red. He pauses for a moment. He looks more carefully at Jerry, who is looking directly at him. The muscles in Jerry's face have shifted the corners of his mouth so that they turn upward. Fred pauses to wonder what's going on within himself and in Jerry.

Thinking and Imagining (Interpreting)

Thinking produces the meaning we attach to what we sense. As mentioned elsewhere in the book, thinking is about the past and relies on numerous factors, e.g., associations, thoughts, beliefs, interpretations, expectations, impressions, ideas, opinions, assumptions, theories, evaluations, judgments, conclusions, reasons, possibilities, objections, predictions, explanations, benefits, and principles. For many people, thinking also involves the making of risk or odds assessments, e.g., by asking about the probability or likelihood that one is right about what's going on in a particular situation. While thinking works with past experiences, imagining is also involved in interpreting a situation but goes beyond the present to include elements that aren't observable. If we recall mindfulness as presented by Wilder Penfield, it has a capacity for attending to past and present at the same time; imagining invites us into the future.

- As Fred focuses on Jerry's expression, he may interpret Jerry's mouth as a smile, or he may interpret Jerry's mouth as a sneer. These are very different interpretations of what's going on and what Jerry's mouth is conveying. Fred shifts his attention to his own thoughts. He asks himself what he imagines Jerry thinks of him. He realizes he doesn't know. and his hands relax.

Feeling, Emotions and Mood

Feeling refers to a general sensibility in the body. Feeling is a physical sensation or perception in which people are emotionally affected by something. Feeling can be a sensation of pleasure or pain. It may refer to the general tone of something that leaves an impression on someone, e.g., a piece of art that has 'the right feel to it' or a room where people are meeting that has 'an uncomfortable feel to it'. Feeling also refers to 'feeling out', seeking out something or probing for a sense of it to ascertain or discover its features.

Emotions are based on responses to something or someone. The word emotion conveys a sense of motion. Its original meaning has to do with moving, as in the expression 'this moves me'. It may refer to a disturbance of mind, a warm or cold affective response in contrast to a cognitive (thought-based) response to something. Emotions include feeling proud, frustrated, confident, trustful, excited, hesitant, cautious, angry, comfortable, uneasy, fascinated, agitated, disappointed, eager, disinterested, irritated or bored, as some examples.

- Suppose Fred is feeling sad and is in a gloomy mood as he enters the room where Jerry is sitting. The interpretation he makes of Jerry's facial expression is likely to be influenced by his mood and his feelings.

In addition to feelings and emotions, a mood is an affective state. Its purpose is to inform a person of their general state of being and their needs. The effects of mood are general and pervasive, whereas emotions are relatively specific. A mood may be a lingering, pervasive, in-the-background quality that can influence a broad array of potential responses, many of which may be quite unrelated to a mood-precipitating event. Weariness, irritability, restlessness and distraction, to name some examples, may describe a particular mood. Becoming aware of a mood—such as Fred's gloomy mood—is an opportunity to shift one's focus, pause, and care for self and others as one adjusts to the situation at hand.

One way to distinguish mood and emotion is to think of a painting in which emotion is in the foreground, like a solitary figure, and mood is the background. The solitary figure in the foreground of Edvard Munch's *The Scream* (1893) is a very different scenario than the solitary figure in Vincent van Gogh's *The Sower* (1888), or figures in the Mieklejohn's graphic *The Village Toy Shop* (2017). If we want to know what the emotion in the figures signify, we look at the hands, face, shoulders, as some examples, to see what they convey about their emotions. (Please note that in this book, we don't focus on mood disorders, but on existential attributes of mood that influence how people address daily life and relationships.)

- As Fred considers his interpretation of Jerry's mouth, whether a smile or a sneer, his feelings will be directed by the interpretation he pays the most attention to as he looks at Jerry.

Wanting (Intentions)

Our wants are intentions or desires that reflect our goals, objectives, motives, hopes, drives, aspirations, interests, values, desires, our wishes, and our needs. We may have wants that pertain to ourselves, to another person or to a group of people. Our wants may not be evident to others, or even to ourselves. In terms of intentional reflection, it's essential for Fred to pause at this point to consider what he wants, and to become aware that he may have multiple wants, or even competing or conflicting wants. Sorting through our wants is an aspect of awareness that people may under-analyze. Worldview concepts, expectations and self-images are elements that inform what people have come to believe they can legitimately want from a situation or a relationship.

- What Fred wants, as he enters the room, will have to do with his relationship with Jerry and his past experiences of him and of people like Jerry. Wanting directs him toward the future, as does imagining, so Fred's intentions will be influenced by what he wants from the relationship as an outcome of how he interacts with Jerry in this present moment. Recall that mindfulness allws someone to be simultaneously aware of past and present experiences.

Doing (Actions)

Doing refers to action, to carrying out a deed, initiating, performing, executing, accomplishing, completing, or ending an action. Doing is about someone's conduct, such as carrying out activities, action plans, suggestions or solutions. Action has to do with patterns of observable behavior made visible through our responses, promises, gestures, or words.

What we do may be about the past, the present or the future. Actions are evident to other people, although what we want, think, feel and imagine may remain hidden.

- As Fred walks across the room to where Jerry is sitting, he interprets Jerry's expression as a sneer, and he laughs out loud. Fred and Jerry have been playing chess every afternoon since Fred moved into the extended care home. He moved in after his wife of 62 years died of cancer. Fred usually wins at chess. Jerry is letting him know that it might not be so easy to win today. Fred welcomes the challenge.

Pausing to Reflect: Attending to Awareness through Intentional Reflection

The five parts of the Awareness Wheel work together during daily experience, whether a person is attending to them or not. At a point of intentional reflection, people come to discern what's going on during awareness and gain agency over how they think, feel, and act, so they can steer their behavior in the direction they want it to go. While the five aspects of awareness may typically move in one direction: from sensing to thinking to feeling to wanting to doing, they may also go in the reverse direction. We can begin to intentionally reflect at any point on the Awareness Wheel.

When Fred notices he's made his hands into fists and feels his face turning red, he asks himself what he's assuming about the situation. If he pauses in the space between sensing and thinking (interpreting), he knows he needs to ask himself about what's going on. In that pause, he realizes he doesn't know what Jerry wants to convey. If he changes his interpretation during this pause, and wonders about what's really going on, his feelings will respond to that shift in his thinking.

The richest opportunity for intentional reflection opens in the space between sensing (the stimulus) and thinking (the interpretation of the stimulus). As American psychologist Rollo May observed, "Human freedom involves our capacity to pause between the stimulus and response and, in that pause, to choose the one response toward which we wish to throw our weight,"[1] and by doing so, we steer our behavior in a desired direction. The action of pausing and reflecting supports the practice of Action Science. As Fred pauses to become more aware of his feelings (tight fists), his mood (gloomy), and of his thinking, desires and needs, he's able to relax and consider what's going on and how he wants to respond so that he can be consistent with the kind of person he wants to be.

The chance for changing how one feels and interprets a situation generally requires a person to reflect on information taken in through the senses that they relied on for their feelings and thoughts in the first place. The following Diagram shows how pausing between sensing and thinking is the best opportunity to reframe our interpretations and therefore to entertain different feelings, desires, and actions.

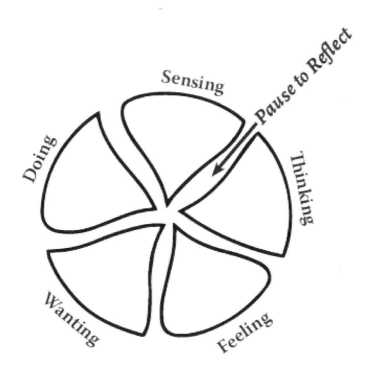

Return To Your "Helping Incident" and Use the Awareness Wheel

The following reflective exercise is intended to support Action Science by using the Awareness Wheel Exercise to explore the helping incident you've already written as a Preparatory Step. We invite you to participate in all parts of the exercise as it rolls out from step to step. Write down your observations and insights as you go through the exercise. This approach provides readers with an additional option for intentional reflection to the traditional practices of verbatim, critical incident and case study report writing.

STEP ONE

Read over your account of the helping incident you selected.

STEP TWO

Look at the two images of the Awareness Wheel. We've described it as a wheel with spokes, but it also looks like the blossom of a flower with five petals. Each petal represents an aspect of awareness: sensing, thinking, feeling, wanting and doing. Before moving to step three, spend a few minutes reflecting on insights gained from the theoretical pages you've just read. Imagine this theory as it relates to your helping incident.

STEP THREE

Using the helping incident account as your point of reference, start with the SENSING petal and work your way around the Awareness Wheel from sensing to thinking to feeling to wanting, and to doing. Use the following questions to guide your movement around the Wheel and write under each section the points of awareness and discovery that emerge for you.

SENSING: What sensory data is in evidence: through the lens of being the helping person in the incident, what can you see, hear, touch, taste and/or smell? What's the directly observable data? What's provided verbally, non-verbally? Who are the key players in the scenario? What is their body language, e.g., their posture, gestures, facial movement and any other changes in their bodily communication? What, if any, spontaneous associations arise for you out of your sensory perceptions—i.e., visualizations, stories, descriptions, recollections, fantasies, and/or intuitions?

THINKING: What meaning do you find yourself making based on your perceptions? What thoughts are going through your mind? Toward whom or what are you directing these thoughts (can be more than one person or thing)? What qualities do these thoughts have—e.g., beliefs, interpretations, expectations, impressions, ideas, opinions, assumptions, theories, judgments, reasons, possibilities, explanations or principles and the like? Do you find yourself making any risk assessments, e.g., considering the benefits and risks of what you're perceiving? Do you find yourself imagining what might occur in the immediate or long-range future?

FEELING: What are your emotional responses to what you are experiencing: e.g., glad, fearful/cautious, frustrated/angry, agitated/concerned, sad, serene/anxious? What's your "feel" about the situation? E.g., Is it safe/unsafe, comfortable/uncomfortable, problematic/relaxed? What aspects of the incident suggest the presence of a mood? If you were to make a painting of the incident, what figures would be in the foreground and what would the background look like? What do the hands, face, shoulders, etc., of figures in your scenario convey about their emotions?

WANTING: What do you desire from the situation? What are your hopes, aspirations, interests, goals, objectives, motives, drives, wishes, intentions or needs? Which of these desires are directed toward the person(s) you are seeking to help, and which are directed toward yourself?

DOING: What actions are present in the scenario? Who does what, and to whom? Are actions in the form of gestures, movement toward or away from, speaking, listening? Are there elements of doing that are pro-active, re-active? Is there evidence of action planning, problem solving, promise making and the like? Do you notice any patterns in the activity? Which actions appear to come from the past, emanate from the present, and/or move toward the future?

STEP FOUR

Review what you've written. What do you notice? What's new? What connections are you making? What didn't occur to you before? How has your awareness shifted?

STEP FIVE

Now, go back to the awareness aspects of sensing and thinking, and consider inserting a "pause" between these two petals, as depicted in the second Awareness Wheel image. How would such a pause apply to your helping incident? Reread what you've written in the sensing section of

Step Three, and follow this by reading again what you've written in the thinking section. Then drawing on Rollo May's words cited previously, ask yourself: What alternative choices and responses come to your awareness? How would a different choice or response from the one you made have an impact on your feeling, wanting, and doing? Are there thoughts, feelings, objectives, actions etc., in evidence that indicate you may have missed directly observable data available through your senses? If you were able to have a "do over" of the incident, what would you change? What would you keep the same? What value does sensory data have in developing awareness?

In summary, the very nature of this book, *Thick Listening at Thin Moments: Theoretical Groundwork in Spiritual Care Practice*, aims at empowering readers to become more aware of theories that drive their action and reaction. As people grow in self and other awareness, they're better able to perceive their theories-in-use and assess the match between theory and what's going on in a particular situation. In that assessment, spiritual care practitioners establish whether previous theories-in-use should continue to be applied or whether a new theory needs to be taken on and integrated because it fits better with the circumstances and people involved in the experience. Theoretical touchpoints for, and the practical application of, using the Awareness Wheel that are found in this Appendix, offer a framework for putting flesh on the bones of spiritual care practitioners' experiences as they proceed with mastering the complex competency of thick listening at thin moments.

Appendix Three

A Selection of Case Study References

In the chapter on Skills Acquisition in the Assessment of Spiritual Care Practice, we address the question: What does competent spiritual care look like clinically. A conclusion we reach is that *case studies* make spiritual care practice visible for shared reflection and learning. What follows is a selection of case study references. They've been organized in order to look first at foundational information, followed by several published articles where a case study is the main focus of attention. Then reference is made to two further cases studies where, in addition to the case study articles, reader responses have been published. In the first case study, responses are of a theoretical and educational nature. In the second, the responses are inter-professional. This approach highlights the value of inviting and receiving feedback as part of learning competence in spiritual care practice.

Following cases studies published as articles, there's a list of books that feature spiritual care case studies. These have been collected and published between the years 2006 and 2020. Each book features settings and themes that arise in spiritual care practice. Each makes competence and learning in spiritual care practice visible.

Lastly, there is reference to two excellent online resources for information about spiritual care/chaplaincy and case studies. The first, Chaplaincy Innovation Lab, includes four case studies that a person can work through in a self-paced way. They offer learning not only about the topic/title of each study but also about a variety of educational approaches to case study learning in spiritual care practice. The second online resource, Transforming Chaplaincy, operates in collaboration with the Joint Research Council to promote evidence-based spiritual care and integrate research into professional spiritual care practice and education. Its goal is to fostering a culture of inquiry. A search at the website homepage, using the term "case study", yields an abundance of information about case study research and resources.

Foundational Information

G.H. Asquith, "The case study method of Anton T. Boisen," *Journal of Pastoral Care*, 34 (2), 1980, 84 – 94.

Brown, L. (2010). Making the case for case study research. *Chaplaincy Today, 26*(2), 2-15.

Fitchett, G. (2011). Making Our Case(s). *Journal of Health Care Chaplaincy*, 17, 3-18.

McCurdy, D., & Fitchett, G. (2011). Ethical issues in case study publication: "Making our Case(s)" ethically. Journal of Health Care Chaplaincy, 17, 55-74.

Nolan, S. (2021). Lifting the lid on chaplaincy: A first look at findings from chaplains' case study research. *Journal of Health Care Chaplaincy, 27*(1), 1-23.

Universidad Interamericana de Puerto Rico. (n.d.) *Colección Especial / Special Collection: Anton Boisen*. Retrieved January 21, 2022, from http://web.metro.inter.edu/facultad/esthumanisticos/anton_boisen. asp.

Articles with Cases Studies Featured

Almog, R., Shafrir, O., Shavit, R., & Ulitzur, N. . (2021). Three Short Case Studies of Non-Religious Spiritual Care: Connecting with Nature, Gentle Touch, and Non-Theistic Personal Prayer. *Health and Social Care Chaplaincy, 9*(1), 113–124.

Blakley, T. (2007). Murder and faith: A reflected case study of pastoral interventions in traumatic grief. *Journal of Pastoral Care and Counseling, 61*(1-2), 59-69.

Cousineau, A., Chow, M., & Brezden, P. (2003). "Worlds apart": Truth telling in the case of Mrs. VV. *Journal of Pastoral Care and Counseling, 57*(4), 415-426.

King, S. (2012). Facing fears and counting blessings: A case study of a chaplain's faithful companioning a cancer patient. *Journal of Helath Care Chaplaincy, 18*, 3-22.

Risk, J. (2013). Building a new life: A chaplain's theory based case study of chronic illness. *Journal of Health Care Chaplaincy, 19*, 81-98.

Rodriguez, J. (1999). Chaplains' communications with Latino patients: Case studies in non-verbal communication. *Journal of Pastoral Care, 53*(3), 309-317.

Timbers, V., & Childers, M. (2021). A case study in group spiritual care for residents of a post-acute care facility. *Journal of Religion, Spirituality & Aging*, 33 (1), 86-96.

Van Loenen, G., Körver, J., Walton, M., De Vries, R. (2017) Case study of "moral injury": Format Dutch case studies project. *Health and Social Care Chaplaincy* 5(2), 281-296.

Case Study with Theoretical Feedback

Cooper, R. (2011). Case Study of a Chaplain's Spiritual Care for a Patient with Advanced Metastatic Breast Cancer. *Journal of Health Care Chaplaincy*, 17(1/2), 19-37.

Canada, A. (2011). A psychologist's response to the case study: Application of theory and measurement. *Journal of Health Care Chaplaincy*, 17(1/2), 45-54.

King, S. (2011). Touched by an angel: A chaplain's response to the case study's key interventions, styles, and themes/outcomes. *Journal of Health Care Chaplaincy, 17*(1/2), 38-45.

Case Study with Inter-Professional Reflection

Nolan, S. (2016). "He needs to talk!": A chaplain's case study of nonreligious spiritual care. *Journal of Health Care Chaplaincy, 22*, 1-16.

Hess, D. (2016). Myths and systems: A response to "He needs to talk!": A chaplain's case study of nonreligious spiritual care. *Journal of Health Care Chaplaincy, 22*, 17-27.

Pesut, B. (2016). Recovering religious voice and imagination: A response to Nolan's case study "He needs to talk!" *Journal of Health Care Chaplaincy, 22*, 28-39.

Books

Adams, C. (2006). *Pastoral Care for Domestic Violence: Case Studies for Clergy.* Seattle, WA: Faith Trust Institute.

Fitchett, G. & Nolan, S. (Eds.) (2015). *Spiritual Care in Practice: Case Studies in Healthcare Chaplaincy.* London, UK: Jessica Kingsley Publishers.

Fletcher, J. (Ed.) (2019). *Chaplaincy and Spiritual Care in Mental Health Settings.* [Part 3: Case Studies.] London, UK: Jessica Kingsley Publishers.

Nolan, S., & Fitchett, G. (Eds.) (2018). *Case Studies in Spiritual Care.* London, UK: Jessica Kingsley Publishers.

Wirpsa, M.J. & Pugliese, K. (Eds.) (2020). *Chaplains as Partners in Medical Decision-Making: Case Studies in Healthcare Chaplaincy.* London, UK: Jessica Kingsley Publishers.

Swift, C., Cobb, M., & Todd, A. (Eds.). (2015). A Handbook of Chaplaincy Studies: Understanding Spiritual Care in Public Places. [Case studies included at the end of Parts III, IV, V & VI.] Burlington, VT: Ashgate Publishing Co.

Online Learning Resources

Chaplaincy Innovation Lab. (n.d.) *Case Studies in Effective Chaplaincy*. Retrieved January 31, 2022, from https://chaplaincyinnovation.org/training-credentials/case-studies

Transforming Chaplaincy. (n.d.) Homepage includes access to educational, research, and evidence-based resources under a number of headings at the top of the page. Retrieved February 1, 2022, from https://www.transformchaplaincy.org

End Notes

Front Matter

1   M. Clark & J. Olson, *Nursing Within a Faith Community: Promoting health in times of transition* (Thousand Oaks, CA: Sage, 2000).

2   D. Pranke, and M. Clark, "Out of the ashes: The Alberta Consortium for Supervised Pastoral Education Program," *Journal of Pastoral Care and Counseling*, 74(4) (2020): 241-249.

3   Calzone, K., Jenkins, J., Culp, S., Caskey, S. & Badzek, L. "Introducing a new competency into nursing practice," *Journal of Nursing Regulation*, 5(1) (2014): 40-47.

Fehér, P., Aknai, D. & Czékmán, B. "Complex competency development with augmented reality supported digital storytelling," *Hungarian Educational Research Journal*, 1 (2018): 93-96.

Nikitina, G. A. "Complex competency-based model of the intending foreign language teacher," *Perspectives of Science and Education*, 53 (5) (2021): 223-237.

Wiemeyer, L.; Zeaiter, S. "Social media in EFL teaching: Promoting (oral) communication skills in complex competency tasks," *Dutch Journal of Applied Linguistics*, 4(2) (2015):193-211.

4   In this book, attention is given to differing certification titles use by spiritual care associations in North America to describe those who practice spiritual care professionally, i.e., Certified Spiritual Care Practitioner and Board Certified Chaplain. As such, the terms chaplain and spiritual care practitioner are used interchangeably throughout the book. Each concept has its unique meaning, scope of practice, and pros as well as cons with regard to how it's perceived. That said, both spiritual care practitioners and chaplains can apply the theoretical groundwork found in the book to their professional practice.

5   C. Dickens, and H. Dunn, A *Tale of Two Cities* (New York, Cosmopolitan Book Corporation, 1921).

Chapter 1 - Exploring the Territory

1   Peter Senge, *The Fifth Discipline* (New York: Penguin Random House, 2006).

2   Tom Gerken. "Coronavirus: Kind Canadians start 'caremongering' trend." *BBC News*, 2020.

3   A. Kipp and R. Hawkins, R. *CareMongering in Canada: How does a community care?* (Guelph, ON: University of Guelph, Department of Geography, Environment and Geomatics, 2020). [https://www.amykipp.com/research].

H. Seow, K. McMillan, M. Civak, D. Bainbridge, A. van der Wal, C. Haanstra et al., "Caremongering: A community-led social movement to address health and social needs during COVID-19," *PLoS ONE* 16(1): e0245483 (2021). https://doi.org/10.1371/journal.pone.0245483

D. Vervaecke and B. Meisner, "Caremongering and assumptions of need: The spread of compassionate ageism during COVID-19," *The Gerontologist*, Vol. 61, No. 2 (2021): 159-165.

4   In a treatise on loneliness and love, Belgian philosopher Libert Vander Kerken (1910-1998) wrote that "man alone" is an ontological contradiction, hence unthinkable and impossible. At the same time, he pointed out that this fundamental human bond does not endanger personal subjectivity. L. Vander Kerken, *Loneliness and Love* (New York, NY: Sheed & Ward, 1967), 17-18.

5   Throughout this book the terms "faith story" and "faith stories" are used to describe those aspects of a person's narrative that emerge with worldview development, evolve at intersections of lived experience as well as social connection, and have to do with beliefs and practices related to being in relationship, as developed in the chapter on Faith. Spiritual care involves listening to someone put their faith story into words (both verbal and non-verbal).

6   David Hay, *Something There: The biology of the human spirit* (Philadelphia: Templeton Foundation Press, 2007), 34.

7   Joyce E. Bellous, *Educating Faith: An approach to Christian formation* (Toronto: Clements, 2006; 3rd printing Tall Pine Press, 2015), 219-225.

8   *Something There*, 37.

9   *Something There*, 39.

10   Lisa Miller, *The Spiritual Child: The new science on parenting for health and lifelong thriving* (New York: St. Martin's Press, 2015), 7.

11   *Spiritual Child*, 7-8.

12   *Spiritual Child*, 6.

13   *Spiritual Child*, 7.

14   *Spiritual Child*, 8.

15   *Something There*, 9.

16   *Something There*, 11.

17   Evelyn E. Whitehead and J.D. Whitehead. *Shadows of the Heart: The spirituality of painful emotions* (Lincoln NE: iUniverse, 2003), 5.

18   *Shadows of the Heart*, 8.

19   *Shadows of the Heart*, 10.

20   *Shadows of the Heart*, 7.

21   David Hay and Rebecca Nye, *The Spiritual Child* (London: Fount, 1998).

22   *Educating Faith*, 9-20.

23   Spirituality is a mid-point reality between subjective and objective realities; e.g., what Martin Buber calls a relation that he thought of as a spiritual connection. As he put it, "In the beginning is the relation—as a category of being, as readiness, as a form that reaches out to be filled...." He identified a spiritual link between self and object by using childhood as an actual and metaphorical ground for describing subject/object relations, i.e., for his own theory of object relating, although he didn't use that term. *Educating Faith*, 26.

24   Some would use the word religion here but we think we need a broader expression so chose way of life.

25   Joyce E. Bellous, adapted from *Educating Faith: An approach to Christian formation* (2006, 2012).

26   See *The Spiritual Child*.

27   Josephine Klein, *Our Need for Others and its Roots in Infancy* (London: Tavistock, 1987).

28   *Our Need for Others*, 76.

29   Unless otherwise noted, the analysis of concept formation and intentional behaviour is a summary of Klein research on the capacity to make meaning that creates a mental system that forms a worldview, pp. xv-71.

30   *Our Need for Others*, 77.

31   *Our Need for Others*, 86.

32   *Our Need for Others*, 87.

33   Daniel Stern, *The Interpersonal World of the Infant: A view from psychoanalysis & developmental psychology* (Basic Books, 1985 & 2000).

34   *Interpersonal world*.

35   *Our Need for Others*, 12.

36   Canadian psychologist Donald O. Hebb identified the process of

thinking and its connection to neurons in a book he wrote, *Organization of Behaviour* in 1949. He posited that the process of thinking depends on neuron cell-assemblies. He wrote *Essay on Mind* in 1980 to further his investigation of human thought and its reliance on the brain.

37   *Our Need for Others*, 26.

38   Essay on Mind, 148.

39   Ana-Maria Rizzuto, *The Birth of the Living God: A psychoanalytic study* (London: The University of Chicago Press, 1979).

40   *Essay on Mind*, 12.

41   *Essay on Mind*, 162.

42   *Essay on Mind*, 134.

43   *Essay on Mind*, 174.

44   F.A. Hayek, *The Sensory Order: An inquiry into the foundations of theoretical psychology*. The book was first published in 1952 and the paperback in 1976. Kindle version 8.1. Hayek wrote the book by using section numbers in each chapter. 8.1 refers to chapter 8, section 1. We've maintained his numbering system.

45   *Our Need for Others*, 36.

46   *Our Need for Others*, 26-48.

47   *Our Need for Others*, 27.

48   *Our Need for Others*, xv.

49   *Our Need for Others*, 41

50   *Our Need for Others*, 42

51   Wilder Penfield and Edwin Boldrey, "Somatic motor and sensory representation in the cerebral cortex of man as studied by electrical stimulation," *Brain* 60 (1937): 389–440.)

52   Wilder Penfield, *The Mystery of the Mind: A critical study of consciousness and the human brain* (Princeton: Princeton University Press, 1975). Penfield and Hebb both worked at McGill University. Penfield expanded brain surgery's methods and techniques, including mapping the functions of various regions of the brain such as the cortical homunculus.

53   Joyce E. Bellous, *Conversations That Change Us: Learning the arts of theological reflection, Second Edition* (Edmonton: Tall Pine Press, 2017), 31-42.

54   Eugene T. Gendlin, *Focusing* (New York: Bantam Books, 1981); and *Experiencing and the Creation of Meaning* (New York: The Free Press of Glencoe, 1962).

55   *The Sensory Order*, 5.33ff.

56   *Our Need for Others*, 130

57   *Our Need for Others*, 131.

58   *Our Need for Others*, 65

59   *Our Need for Others*, 42-43.

60   *Our Need for Others*, 34.

61   *Our Need for Others*, 42.

62   *Our Need for Others*, 50.

63   Clinical Pastoral Education (CPE) is an experience-based approach to learning practical skills and competencies in the profession of Spiritual Care. Programs of CPE are overseen by professionally certified Supervisor-Educators. A typical CPE learning experience includes classroom instruction, peer group feedback, intrapersonal reflection and guided clinical placements in healthcare facilities, congregations, prisons, military settings, and/or community-based agencies. CPE aims to assist learners in achieving their full personal, vocational and professional potential. This form of experiential education has parallels in Field Education Programs offered through Theological Colleges and Seminaries. The main focus is twofold: personal formation (self-awareness, reflective practice, safe and effective use of self) and competency development (growth in Spiritual Care abilities that rely on basic attributes of a person's character and are exercised with knowledge and skill).

64   *Our Need for Others*, 53-57.

65   G.A Miller, E. Galanter, E., and K.A. Pribram, *Plans and the Structure of Behavior* (New York: Holt, Rhinehart, & Winston, 1960).

66   *Our Need for Others*, 55-57.

67   *Our Need for Others*, 62.

68   *Our Need for Others*, 68.

69   Harold Bloom, *Shakespeare: The Invention of the Human* (New York: Riverhead Books, 1998), xvii.

70   *Our Need for Others*, xv.

71   Peter Berger and Thomas Luckman, *The Social Construction of Reality* (Vintage Books, 1966).

72   Examples of the work of Pierre Bourdieu include *The Logic of Practice, Rules of Art, Acts of Resistance*. Pierre Bourdieu (1930-2002) was the first sociologist to take prominent intellectual leadership in France following in the footsteps of Jean Paul Sartre (1905-1980) and Michel Foucault (1926-1984). Also see F.A. Hayek's section 6: The order of sensory qualities not confined to conscious experience, in *The Sensory Order* (Chicago: University of Chicago Press, Kindle version), 1.68-1.74. Originally published, 1952. As one example, a worldview is based on a mental system that "is shaped by the

conditions prevailing in the environment in which we live, and it represents a kind of generic reproduction of the relations between the elements of this environment which we have experienced in the past; and we interpret any new event in the environment in light of that experience." *Sensory Order*, 8.1.

73   Robert Kegan, *The Evolving Self: Problem and process in human development* (Cambridge, Massachusetts: Harvard University Press, 1982); *In Over Our Heads: The mental demands of modern life* (Cambridge, Massachusetts: Harvard University Press, 1994).

74   *The Evolving Self*, viii.

75   *The Evolving Self*, 1.

76   James B. Pratt, *The Religious Consciousness: A psychological study* (New York: MacMillan Company, 1956).

77   *In Over Our Heads*, 267.

78   See *The Birth of the Living God*.

79   R. Kinast, *Making faith sense: Theological reflection in everyday life* (Collegeville, MN: Liturgical Press, 1999).

80   An extremely useful approach to Action Science is found in the Alban Institute book by Anita Farber Robinson, *Learning While Leading* (Alban Institute).

81   *In Over Our Heads*, 134.

82   *Learning While Leading*, 82.

83   R. Sinclair, "Identity lost and found: Lessons from the sixties scoop," *First Peoples Child & Family Review*, 3(1) (2007):, 65–82.

         A. Stevenson, *Intimate integration: A history of the sixties scoop and the colonization of indigenous kinship.* (Toronto, ON: University of Toronto Press, 2020).

84   Barbara Ehrenreich, *Nickel and Dimed* (New York: Henry Holt and Company, 2001).

85   Jane Jacobs, *Cities and the Wealth of Nations: Principles of economic life* (New York: Vintage Books, 1984). Martha Nussbaum, *Sex and Social Justice* (Oxford: Oxford University Press, 1999), 39-42.

Chapter 2 - Faith, Thick Listening and Intentional Reflection

1   Margaret Clark, "Characteristics of faith communities", M. Clark and J. Olson, *Nursing Within a Faith Community: Promoting health in times of transition* (Thousand Oaks, CA: Sage, 2000), 17-29.

2   L. Vander Kerken, *Loneliness and Love* (New York, NY: Sheed & Ward, 1967), 17-18).

3   R. Panikkar, "Faith: A constitutive human dimension", *India International Centre Quarterly*, 26/27 (1999): 34-47.

4   M. Clark, "Day 1: Contextualizing theological reflection: Overview of core concepts," Retrieved from St. Stephen's College, Edmonton, AB: SSC589/789 *Theological Reflection in Professional Practice*, (2000/2016).

5   M. Harris, *Proclaim Jubilee! A spirituality for the twenty-first century* (Louisville, KY: Westminster John Knox Press, 1996).

6   Proclaim Jubilee, ix.

7   T. Groome, *Sharing faith: A comprehensive approach to religious education and pastoral ministry, the way of shared praxis* (New York, NY: HarperCollins, 1991).

8   Robert Kinast, *Making Faith-Sense* (Collegeville, MN: The Liturgical Press, 1999)

9   A. M. Rizzuto, *The Birth of the Living God: A psychoanalytic study* (Chicago, IL: University of Chicago Press, 1979).

10   John Polkinghorne, *The God of Hope and the End of the World* (New Haven and London: Yale University Press, 2002), xxii.

11   *The God of Hope*, xxii.

12   James B. Pratt, *The Religious Consciousness: A psychological study* (New York: MacMillan Company, 1956), 2.

13   Pratt used this definition and others to describe religion itself. His perspective is particularly instructive when applied to faith, which to us is the more appropriate term for the psychological aspect of religion that he wished to explain. See *Religious Consciousness*, 2-3.

14   *Religious Consciousness*, 1-44.

15   Immanuel Kant, "What does it mean to orient oneself in thinking?" *Religion Within the Boundaries of Mere Reason* (Cambridge: Cambridge University Press, 1998), 1-14.

16   A. Saint-Exupery, *The Little Prince* (Boston, MA: Mariner Books, 1943/2000).

17   M. Heidegger, *Poetry, Language, Thought* (New York, NY: HarperCollins, 1971).

18   *The God of Hope*, 31.

19   Hebrews 11:1, paraphrased.

20   *The God of Hope*, 49.

21   G.H. Asquith, "The case study method of Anton T. Boisen," *Journal of*

Pastoral Care, 34 (2) (1980): 84 - 94. G. Fitchett, "Making Our Case(s)," *Journal of Health Care Chaplaincy* 17 (2011):1-18.

22   Canadian Association for Spiritual Care/Association canadienne de soins spirituels (CASC/ACSS), *Policy and Procedure Manual*, Chapter 4: Certification (3.2.1). (Newmarket, ON, 2020).

23   D.A. Schön, *The Reflective Practitioner: How professionals think in action* (New York: Basic Books, 1983).

24   S.M. Drake and J.P. Miller, "Beyond reflection to being: The contemplative practitioner," *Phenomenology + Pedagogy* 9 (1991): 319-334. In addition to this article, J. P. Miller has written a book that articulates in greater depth the conceptualization of contemplative practitioner. J.P. Miller, *The Contemplative Practitioner: Meditation in Education and Workplace* (Toronto, ON: University of Toronto Press, 2014).

25   M. Buber, *I and Thou* (New York, NY: Scribner, 1958).

26   M. Buchman, "The careful vision: How practical is contemplation in teaching?" *American Journal of Education* 98(1) (1989): 35-61, 39).

27   P.O. Killen and J. de Beer, *The Art of Theological Reflection* (New York, NY: Crossword1994/2002).

28   Ludwig Wittgenstein, *On Certainty* (Oxford, England: Basil Blackwell, 1979), 96.

29   *On Certainty*, 141.

30   *On Certainty*, 94.

31   *On Certainty*, 336.

32   *On Certainty*, 357.

33   *On Certainty*, 358.

34   George A. Buttrick, ed., *The Interpreter's Dictionary of the Bible* (New York: Abingdon Press, 1962), 222.

35   *Interpreter's Dictionary*, 228.

36   G. Ganss, *The Spiritual Exercises of St. Ignatius – St. Ignatius of Loyola* (author), George Ganss (translator), (Chicago, IL: Loyola Press, 1992).

37   F.A. Hayek, *The Sensory Order: An inquiry into the foundations of theoretical psychology.* The book was first published in 1952 and the paperback in 1976. Kindle version 8.1. Hayek wrote the book by using sections numbers in each chapter. 8.1 refers to chapter 8, section 1. We've maintained his numbering system.

38   T. O'Connor and E. Meakes, *Spiritual and Theological Reflection: A Canadian qualitative study on spiritual care and psychotherapy* (Waterloo, ON: Waterloo Lutheran Seminary, 2013), 3.

39   On this matter, we draw attention to two well crafted chapters in

O'Connor's and Meakes' book that summarize models of theological reflection as well as models of spiritual reflection. Their chapters draw attention to the fact that much has been written about theological reflection, especially in the final decades of the twentieth century, including three summaries that describe various models and styles of theological reflection. S. Bevans, *Models of Contextual Theology* (New York, NY: Orbis, 2001). E. Graham, H. Walton and F. Ward, *Theological Reflection: Methods* (London, UK: SCM Press, 2005). E. Graham, H. Walton and F. Ward, *Theological Reflection: Sources* (London, UK: SCM Press, 2007). R. Kinast, *What Are They Saying About Theological Reflection?* (Mahwah, NJ: Paulist Press, 2000).

40   *The Sensory Order*, 5.33ff.

41   Josephine Klein, *Our Need for Others and its Roots in Infancy* (London: Tavistock, 1987).

42   J. Whitehead and E. Whitehead, (1995). *Method In Ministry: Theological reflection and Christian ministry* (New York, NY: Sheed & Ward, 1995). P.O. Killen and J. de Beer, (1994/2002). *The Art of Theological Reflection* (New York, NY: Crossword, 1994/2002). R. Kinast, *Let Ministry Teach: A guide to theological reflection* (Collegeville, MN: Liturgical Press, 1996). R. Kinast, *Making Faith-sense: Theological reflection in everyday life* (Collegeville, MN: Liturgical Press, 1999). R. Kinast, *What Are They Saying About Theological Reflection?* (Mahwah, NJ: Paulist Press, 2000). J. Stone and J. Duke, *How to Think Theologically* (Minneapolis, MN: Fortress Press, 1996).

43   Thin model moments of social interaction open points of entry to the landscape of one's worldview map. Thick listening at a point of entry brings one to the terrain that needs to be explored. Once on the ground, so to speak, there are tools and exercises offered by a number of authors cited in O'Connor and Meakes that can facilitate environmental scans and topographical studies of one's life map and faith story. In this regard, we recommend: (1) the exercises in Chapter 4, "Personal Theological Reflection", of P.O. Killen and J. de Beer, (1994/2002). *The Art of Theological Reflection* (New York, NY: Crossword, 1994/2002), (2) Chapter Two, "How to Make Faith Sense: Getting Started", in R. Kinast, *Making Faith-sense: Theological reflection in everyday life* (Collegeville, MN: Liturgical Press, 1999), and (3) Part IV, "Theological Reflection at Work", in J. Whitehead and E. Whitehead, (1995). *Method In Ministry: Theological reflection and Christian ministry* (New York, NY: Sheed & Ward, 1995). Other helpful resources include: (1) G. Fitchett (1993, 2003), *Assessing Spiritual Needs: A Guide for Caregivers* (Minneapolis, MN: Augsburg), (2) J. Holland and P. Henriot (1986, 2000). *Social Analysis: Linking Faith and Justice* (Maryknoll, NY: Orbis Books), and(3) W. P. Jones, *Theological Worlds: Understanding the Alternative Rhythms of Christian Belief* (Nashville, TN: Abingdon Press, 1989). In addition to these theological tools and exercises, there are many helpful psychological, sociological and cultural tools for exploration.

44   In the context of this chapter, the term tradition is mostly used to refer

to one's faith tradition. That said, tradition is a concept that has broader meaning. It speaks to inherited customs, values, beliefs and practices passed on from generation to generation. In this sense, tradition is a significant contributor to worldview development.

45   A previous understanding of points of entry in theological reflection is found in M.B. Clark, "The nurse and theological reflection", M. B. Clark and J. K. Olson, *Nursing Within a Faith Community: Promoting health in times of transition* (Thousand Oaks, CA: Sage, 2000), 91-110. In addition to this published reference, we acknowledge the benefit of collaborative visioning and conceptualization shared with Dr. Zinia Pritchard, Instructor for St. Stephen's College, Edmonton, AB: SSC589/789 Theological Reflection in Professional Practice.

46   In many healthcare settings, a spiritual care practitioner is expected to carry an on-call pager—signaling availability to be called anywhere in the hospital or long-term care facility over a 12, 24 or 48 hour period.

47   R. Steinhoff-Smith, "The tragedy of clinical pastoral education," *Pastoral Psychology* 41(1) (1992): 45-54.

48   C. Puchalski, B. Lunsford, M. Harris and T. Miller, "Interdisciplinary spiritual care for seriously ill and dying patients: A collaborative model," *The Cancer Journal* 12 (5) (2006): 398-416.

49   P. Hall, L. Weaver, F. Fothergill-Bourbonnais, S. Amos, N. Whiting, P. Barnes and F. Legault, "Interprofessional education in palliative care: A pilot project using popular literature," *Journal of Interprofessional Care* 20:1 (2006): 51-59.

50   Zinia Pritchard, *The Dark Night of the Soul: A sacred anatomy of dying* (Doctoral dissertation, St. Stephen's College, 2014), Education and Research Archive, University of Alberta.

51   J. Swinton, "Attributes of spirituality", *Spirituality and mental health care: Rediscovering a 'forgotten' dimension* (London: Jessica Kingsley Publishers, 2001).

52   *The Art of Theological Reflection.*

53   *Fiddler on the Roof.* A movie directed and produced by Norman Jewison, 1971.

54   University of Victoria, *Cultural Safety Module 2: Peoples Experiences of Oppression* (2021 March 15). Social location is defined as follows: The groups people belong to because of their place or position in history and society. All people have a social location that is defined by their gender, race, social class, age, ability, religion, sexual orientation, and geographic location. Each group membership confers a certain set of social roles and rules, power, and privilege (or lack of), which heavily influence our identity and how we see the world.

55   Canadian Association for Spiritual Care/Association canadienne de soins spirituels, *Competencies of CASC/ACSS Certified Professional* (Newmarket, ON, 2019).

56   *The Final Report of the Truth and Reconciliation Commission of Canada. Volumes 1-6* Truth and Reconciliation Commission of Canada (Montreal and Kingston: Truth and Reconciliation Commission and McGill-Queen's University 2015).

57   Robin DiAngelo, *White Fragility: Why it's so hard for white people to talk about racism* (Boston, MA: Beacon Press, 2018).

58   Donella Meadows, *Thinking in Systems: A primer* (White River Junction, VT: Chelsea Green Publishing, Inc., 2008). Peter Senge, *The Fifth Discipline: The art and practice of the learning organization* (New York, NY: Random House, 1990, 2006).

59   John Barry, *The Great Influenza: The story of the deadliest pandemic in history* (New York, NY: Penguin Random House, 2004).

Chapter 3 - Spiritual Care and Human Development

1   E.E. Thornton, *Professional Education for Ministry: A History of Clinical Pastoral Education* (Nashville, TN: Abingdon Press, 1970); C.E. Hall, Head and Heart: The Story of the Clinical Pastoral Education Movement (Decatur, GA: Journal of Pastoral Care Publications, 1992).

2   A.F. Tartaglia, "Reflections on the development and future of chaplaincy education," *Reflective Practice: Formation and Supervision in Ministry* 35,((2015): 116-133; S. Lasair, "What's the point of clinical pastoral education and pastoral counselling education? Political, developmental, and professional considerations," *Journal of Pastoral Care & Counseling* 74(1) (2020): 22–32.

3   Erik Erikson, *"The Eight Ages of Man," Childhood and Society* (New York: W.W. Norton & Company Inc., 1963), First published in 1950, 247-274.

4   NHSScotland, "Spiritual care matters: Introductory resources for all NHSScotland Staff", (2009), https://www.nes.scot.nhs.uk/media/3723/spiritualcaremattersfinal. pdf.

5   Hadrian Lankiewicz, *Languaging Experiences: Learning and Teaching Revisited* (Newcastle Upon Tyne: Cambridge Scholars Publishing, 2014).

6   Notably, in his essay, Erikson specifically mentions girls only once.

7   M. Syed and J. Fish, "Revisiting Erik Erikson's legacy on culture, race, and ethnicity," *Identity: An International Journal of Theory and Research* 18(4) (2018): 274–283. https://doi.org/10.1080/15283488.2018.1523729.

8   Stephen B. Graves & Elizabeth Larkin, "Lessons from Erikson," *Journal of Intergenerational Relationships* 4:2, 61-71, DOI: 10.1300/ (2006).

J194v04n02_05.

9   Eight Ages, 37.

10   Eight Ages, 247.

11   Eight Ages, 247.

12   Eight Ages, 249.

13   Key questions included in the text are taken from the "Erikson's Psychosocial Stages Summary Chart" found at the Office of Children and Families in the Courts website, http://www.ocfcpacourts.us.

14   Eight Ages, 253.

15   Eight Ages, 253.

16   Eight Ages, 254.

17   Eight Ages, 256.

18   Eight Ages, 258.

19   Eight Ages, 264.

20   Eight Ages, 265.

21   Eight Ages, 268.

22   M. Oliver, "The summer day," *New and Selected Poems* (Boston, MA: Beacon Press, 1992).

23   NHSScotland, 2009.

24   Martin Buber, *I and Thou* (2nd rev. ed.; R. G. Smith, Trans.), (New York: Scribner, 1958), 11.

25   T.S. Eliot, "East Coker", *The Four Quartets* (New York: Harcourt, Brace, Jovanovich, 1976). (Original work published in 1943).

Chapter 4 - Made for Relationship

1   Joyce E. Bellous with Jean Clinton, *Learning Social Literacy* (Edmonton: Tall Pine Press, 2016).

2   Charles Darwin, *The Expression of Emotion in Man and Animals* (Oxford: Oxford University Press, 2009), First published in Great Britain in 1872.

3   It's interesting that Genesis puts animal and human creation together on the 6th 'day' of creation.

4   Matt Ridley, *Genome* (New York: Perennial, 1999), 6. It's almost overwhelming to realize, even to a small degree, how our knowledge of the human body has exploded in the last two decades. As Ridley points out, on "June 26, 2000, scientists announced that they had completed a rough draft of the

complete human genome,", The human genome is the recipe for how to make a human body. It's the complexity that's so astonishing.

5   It's easy to search on-line to discover DNA comparisons between human beings and specific animals.

6   The site that helps people learn to recognize facial expressions to accompany emotions is found through www.paulekman.com.

7   Azarian, 2020.

8   Sigmund Freud, *An Outline of Psychoanalysis* (New York: W.W. Norton, 1949).

9   Daniel N. Stern, *The Interpersonal world of the Infant: A view from psychoanalysis and developmental psychology* (New York: Basic Books, 1985).

10   Daniel N. Stern, *The Present Moment in Psychopathology and Everyday Life* (New York: W.W. Norton & Company, 2004), 75-76.

11   Bessel van der Van der Kolk, *The Body Keeps the Score: Brain, mind and body in the healing of trauma* (New York: Penguin Books, 2015).

12   *The Body Keeps*, 81.

13   *The Body Keeps*, 83.

14   Polyvagal theory is a collection of evolutionary, neuroscientific and psychological claims pertaining to the role of the vagus nerve in emotion regulation, social connection and fear response. Psychological practices based on the polyvagal theory and related concepts are currently carried out by Stephan Porges, Mary Muller and Peter Levine, as some examples. These psychological approaches depend for their efficacy on the Vagus Nerve as a communication system that has so recently been developed into viable approaches to emotional healing. The shift in thinking these approaches introduce is to see a person as able to make changes if they can, rather that if they want to improve their situation. This approach shifts attention away from the exercise of the will, as it has been understood historically in moral action. The implication is to focus less on a person's will in the process of healing and to focus more on supporting what they can accomplish when people receive the well informed affirmation for the way we've all been created to connect with others.

15   R. Menakem, *My grandmother's hands: Raciaized trauma and the pathway to mending our hearts and bodies.* (Central Recovery Press, Las Vegas, NV, 2017).

16   Kipling D. Williams, et al, Eds. *The Social Outcast* (New York: Psychology Press, 2005), 5.

17   Peter Senge, *The Fifth Discipline: The Art and Practice of the Learning Organization* (New York: Doubleday, 1990, 2006).

18   Margaret Guenther, *Holy Listening: The Art of Spiritual Direction* (Lanham, Maryland: Rowman & Littlefield Publishers, 1992), 10.

19   Henri J.M. Nouwen, *Reaching Out: The three movements of the spiritual life* (New York: Doubleday, 1975), 50.

20   *Reaching Out*, 47.

21   *Reaching Out*, 69.

22   Edith Stein, *On The Problem of Empathy*, tr. Waltraut Stein (The Hague: Martinus Nijhoff, 1964).

23   Charles Derber, *The Pursuit of Attention: Power and Ego in Everyday Life* (Oxford: Oxford University Press, 1979).

24   Joyce E. Bellous, *For Crying Out Loud: Forty meditations on loss and recovery* (Edmonton: Tall Pine Press, 2008), 27-29.

25   Robert Kegan, *The Evolving Self: Problem and process in human development* (Cambridge, Massachusetts: Harvard University Press, 1982), 211.

26   R.F. Baumeister, *Escaping the self* (New York: Basic Books, 1991), 10.

27   *Evolving Self*, 17.

28   *Evolving Self*, 17-18.

29   *The Pursuit of Attention*, xxiv.

30   Josephine Klein, *Our Need for Others and its Roots in Infancy* (New York: Routledge, 2005), First published 1987 by Tavistock Publications.

31   Lisa Miller, *The Spiritual Child: The New Science on Parenting for Health and Lifelong Thriving* (New York: Picador, 2015).

32   For an understanding of Miller's concept of the nod, see *The Spiritual Child*, 79-101.

33   *The Spiritual Child*, 86.

34   *The Body Keeps*, 81.

35   *The Body Keeps*, 81.

36   *The Body Keeps*, 38.

37   *The Body Keeps*, 82.

38   *The Body Keeps*, 82.

39   *The Body Keeps*, 59.

40   Jean Clinton, *Love Builds Brains* (Edmonton: Tall Pine Press, 2020).

41   *The Body Keeps*, 26-27.

42   *The Body Keeps*, 81.

43   S. Broidy, *A Case for Kindness: A new look at the teaching ethic* (Gorham, ME: Myers Education Press, 2019); G. Pohaota, "Kindness - The teleological creed of human condition", *Cogito* VII(2),(2015): 18-33; S. Clegg and S. Rowland, "Kindness in pedagogical practice and academic life", *British Journal*

of Sociology of Education 31(6), (2010): 719-735.

44   Jerome Kagan, *Galen's Prophecy: Temperament in human nature* (New York: Basic Books, 1998).

45   *The Body Keeps*, 81.

46   https://www.cftre.com

47   *The Body Keeps*, 62; Wilder Penfield, *The Mystery of the Mind: A critical study of consciousness and the human brain* (Princeton: Princeton University Press, 1975).

48   Charles Derber, *Pursuit of Attention* (Oxford: Oxford University Press, 2000), xxiv.

49   Joyce E. Bellous, "Learning the Art of Self-Regard," *Journal of Christian Education*, edited by Allan Harkness Australian Christian Forum on Education Vol. 46., No.1, (May, 2003): 7-19.

50   Eugene Gendlin, *Experiencing and the Creation of Meaning* (New York: The Free Press of Glencoe, 1962), 3.

51   *Evolving Self*, 142.

52   *Evolving Self*, 126.

53   *Evolving Self*, 126.

54   *Evolving Self*, 162.

55   *Evolving Self*, 126.

56   Robert Kegan, *In Over Our Heads: The mental demands of modern life* (Cambridge, Massachusetts: Harvard University Press, 1994), 221-222.

Chapter 5 - Meeting Another as "Other"

1   Martin Buber, *I and Thou* (Edinburgh: T & T Clark, 1958).

2   The "living human document" metaphor was introduced by Boisen and Dykstra in 1930. For further detail see, B.J. Miller-McLemore, "The Living Human Web: A Twenty-five Year Retrospective". *Pastoral Psychol* 67 (2018): 305–321. https://doi.org/10.1007/s11089-018-0811-7.

3   Canadian Association for Spiritual Care/Association canadienne de soins spirituels (2019). *Competencies of CASC/ACSS Certified Professionals* (Competency 1.4 and 4.1.1). Newmarket, ON: Author.

4   Social Location: "The groups people belong to because of their place or position in history and society. All people have a social location that is defined by their gender, race, social class, age, ability, religion, sexual orientation, and geographic location. Each group membership confers a certain set of social roles and rules, power, and privilege (or lack of), which heavily influence our

identity and how we see the world." https://web2.uvcs.uvic.ca/courses/csafety/mod2/glossary.htm

5   David W. Augsburger, *Pastoral Counseling Across Cultures* (Westminster John Knox Press, 1986).

6   R. Karaban, "The sharing of cultural variation", *The Journal of Pastoral Care* XLV, 1 (1991): 25-34.

7   William Isaacs, Dialogue: *The Art of Thinking Together* (New York: Doubleday, 1999).

8   Pope Paul VI, *Ecclesiam Suam*, 1964.

9   N. Morton, *The Journey is Home* (Boston, MA: Beacon Press, 1985), 90-91.

10   Paulo Freire, *Pedagogy of the Oppressed*. (New York: Herder and Herder, 1972).

11   Brene Brown on *Empathy*, https://www.youtube.com/watch?v=1Evwgu369Jw.

12   Edith Stein, *On The Problem of Empathy*, tr. Waltraut Stein (The Hague: Martinus Nijhoff, 1964). Edith Stein (1891–1942) was a realist phenomenologist associated with the Göttingen school and later a Christian metaphysician. She was a Jew who converted to Catholicism in 1922 and became a Carmelite nun in 1933. She died in Auschwitz in 1942. She was subsequently declared a Catholic martyr and saint.

13   Joyce E. Bellous with Jean Clinton, *Learning Social Literacy* (Edmonton: Tall Pine Press, 2016), 271-306.

14   We acknowledge that many people are quite capable of thinking about their social context, as philosophers in particular are able to do. We refer to the many people who tend not to reflect on the truthfulness of the worldview they got when they were young. In the past, this would refer to most people.

15   Clifford Geertz, *The Interpretation of Cultures* (New York: Basic Books, 1973), 5.

16   In her book, *Cat's Eye*, (1988) Margaret Atwood describes aptly a process of bullying that's described by these three stages: the bully is significant to the bullied person, is capable of surveillance and the bullied person internalizes the harm and expresses the harm in self-sabbotage, self-harm and sometimes, suicide.

17   F. Chasma and G. Cousin, "Eco-brushing", *Br Dent J* 229 (2020): 399–400 (2020). https://doi.org/10.1038/s41415-020-2243-x.

18   Donald Schön, *The Reflective Practitioner: How professionals think in action* (New York: Basic Books, 1983).

19   Barbara Ehrenreich, *Nickel and Dimed: On (not) getting by in Ameri-*

ca (New York: Holt Paperbacks, 2001).

20   As an example, see the phrase 'a hermeneutics of disappointment in the article by Joyce E. Bellous, "Analyzing Atheism," in *Canadian Evangelical Review*, edited by Keith Bodner, Nos. 30-31 (Fall 2005 and Spring 2006): 61-77.

21   Rainer Maria Rilke, 1875-1926, *Letters to a Young Poet* (San Rafael, CA: New World Library, 1992), Letter 4.

22   As an example of women's embodied knowledge, see Mary Field, et al., *Women's Ways of Knowing: The development of self, voice and mind* (New York: Basic Books, 1986).

23   Geoff Dench, *Minorities in the Open Society: Prisoners of Ambivalence* (London: Routledge and Kegan Paul, 1986).

24   Mary Douglas, *Natural Symbols: Explorations in Cosmology* (New York: Pantheon Books, 1982).

25   We distinguish existential from spiritual issues by noting that spiritual concerns overlap existential ones but include aspects of the transcendent, an experience that is scientifically verifiable as a capacity to communicate with the Unseen. See for example, *The Spiritual Child*.

26   There were earlier forms of feminism, particularly in the move to get women the vote. In Canada, the Famous Five, all of whom lived in Edmonton Alberta during their adult lives, petitioned the Privy Council of the British government in 1927. In 1929, they secured for women the right to be called 'persons' under the law. The outcome of their success was the election of the first woman, Cairine Wilson, to Canada's Senate. During the mid-twentieth century, the focus for feminism shifted, particularly as many more women were allowed to attend university during the 1960s in order secure a post secondary degree in their chosen field. Also see Anabel Robinson, *Jane Ellen Harrison* (Oxford: Oxford University Press, 2002), in which she points out that English women were allowed to attend Cambridge and Oxford during the final two decades of the 19th century, but neither university would grant the degrees to women that they had paid for and earned until the middle of the twentieth century, at Oxford in 1948.

27   Carol Gilligan was Kohlberg's student. Lawrence Kohlberg studied the lives of 84 boys over a period of 20 years. As his student, her research pointed to different patterns emerging among the girls she studied. She recorded these differences in her book, *In A Different Voice* (Harvard University Press, 1982).

28   *Different Voice*, 18.

29   *Different Voice*, 2.

30   Pierre Bourdieu, "The Forms of Capital," in John G. Richardson, ed., *Handbook of Theory and Research for the Sociology of Education*, Ed. JG. Richardson (New York: Green, 1983). Pierre Bourdieu, *Acts of Resistance: Against the tyranny of the Market* (New York: The New Press, 1998).

31   In France, people value intellectuals the way North Americans value movie stars and musicians.

32   Martha C. Nussbaum, *Women and Human Development* (Cambridge: Cambridge University Press, 2000); Martha C. Nussbaum, *Sex and Social Justice* (Oxford: Oxford University Press, 1999).

33   Colin Morris, *The Discovery of the Individual 1050-1200* (London, Toronto: University of Toronto Press, 1972).

34   Harold Bloom, *Shakespeare: The invention of the human* (New York: Riverhead Books, 1998).

35   It's evident in the ancient literature about some strong groups, e.g., Greek myths, that there's no evidence of mind-body dualism and little evidence of critical distance or critical reflection on events. Perhaps, there's no distinction between fantasy and reality, although this is a theory applied to the text and the texts that move from the human world to the world of the gods without any adjustment may have other explanations.

36   As is evident in Homer's *Iliad* and *The Odyssey*.

37   Bellous worked with a Korean student at the Masters level who moved on to do a PhD at the University of Toronto. There were no other strong group students in her class at U of T. In one class she was asked to write about herself in a stream of consciousness style. She contacted Bellous to say she simply couldn't do the assignment. When she handed it in, her professor would hand it back and say it wasn't right. Bellous suggested that she write "I" every time she wanted to write 'We' or 'Korean' in the assignment. The student reflected back on her memories of childhood in which her elementary school classes was told over and over again to say We. She exchanged the word I for every We in her assignment, handed it in and got a good grade.

38   Guatemalan *Rigoberta Menchú* Tum is a K'iche' Indigenous feminist and human rights activist from Guatemala. She wrote of her experiences in the book, *I Rigoberta Menchu: An Indian woman in Guatemala* (New York: Verso, 1984).

39   In both global patterns (individual and strong group) maleness is developed, understood and expressed in terms of being "not like" femaleness. In both patterns, don't run, walk, or throw a ball 'like a girl' are stringent messages sent to adolescent boys. Women inhabit a typically domestic world. As a result, women can be uneasy in public spaces unless they become 'like men'.

40   Kimberle Crenshaw, "Demarginalizing the Intersection of Race and Sex: A Black Feminist Critique of Antidiscrimination Doctrine, Feminist Theory and Antiracist Politics", *University of Chicago Legal Forum*, Volume 1989, Issue 1, Article 8.

41   *Minorities in the Open Society.*

42   *Minorities in the Open Society.*

43   Franz Fanon, the philosopher and social activist from Martinique was one of the first to name racism's tendency to divide identities and subtract one from the other so that a person was left empty of identity. As one of the first theorists to initiate the Black Revolution in the mid-twentieth century, his books disrupted the status quo across the globe. See Frantz Fanon, *Black Skin, White Masks* (London: Pluto Press, 1952); *The Wretched of the Earth: The handbook for the black revolution that is changing the shape of the world* (New York: Grove Press, Inc., 1968); and a commentary on his life by Emmanuel Hanson, *Frantz Fanon: social and political thought* (Ohio, Mass.: Ohio State University Press, 1977).

44   This comment is by Courtney Wilson, written in a paper for Christian Ministry (CM1EO3) on April, 2003 at McMaster Divinity College, Hamilton Ontario. Used with written permission.

45   Robert Kegan, *In Over Our Heads: The mental demands of modern life* (Cambridge, Massachusetts: Harvard University Press, 1994).

46   As one example of the pressure households face as they try to raise families, work and find love satisfying showed up during 2020. Olivia Bowden, Global News, reported that "divorces have increased during the pandemic and lawyers are expecting more to follow." Posted July 19, 2020.

47   Rebecca Solnit, *Recollections of My Nonexistence: A Memoir* (New York: Penguin Books, 2020)

48   Khaled Hosseini, *A Thousand Splendid Suns* (Toronto: Viking Canada, 2008)

49   An additional question hovers around the corners of this discussion: how does Erikson's framework fit people who aren't in households the way he describes them or who have no wish to live within a heterosexual, monogamous one? This question is outside the scope of our book, but it must be raised, given our current circumstances in this century.

50   Brian P. Hall, *The Genesis Effect: Personal and Organizational Transformations* (Eugene, Oregon: Resource Publications, 1986).

51   Peter D. Kramer, *Against Depression* (New York: Penguin Books, 2005).

52   *The Genesis Effect.*

53   Charles Taylor, *The Ethics of Authenticity* (Cambridge, Massachusetts: Harvard University Press, 2002). Canadian philosopher Charles Taylor, makes the point that "the spiritual is most clearly seen when we consider the modern hubris of refusing limits to human nature." See the discussion on pages 33ff.

54   Kwame Anthony Appiah, *Cosmopolitanism: Ethics in a world of strangers* (New York: W.W. Norton & Company, 2006), xv.

55   *Cosmopolitanism,* xiii.

Chapter 6 - The Role of Reason in Reconceiving a Worldview

1   Barbara Strauch, *The Secret Life of the Grown-up Brain: The Surprising Talents of the Middle-Aged Mind* (New York: Viking, 2010); Norman Doidge, *The Brain that Changes Itself* (New York: Viking, 2007); Barbara Arrowsmith-Young, *The Woman who Changed her Brain* (New York: Free Press, 2012).

2   *The Secret Life.*

3   Ana-Maria Rizzuto, *Why Did Freud Reject God?* (Chelsea, Michigan: Book Crafters, Inc., 1998).

4   The process Nancy goes through in conceptual learning is mapped out by Hegel who introduced the notion of self-consciousness of self-conscious experiencing. See Martin Heidegger, *Hegel's concept of Experience* (New York: Harper & Row, Publishers, 1989). Also see Joyce E. Bellous, *Educating Faith, 3rd Edition* (Edmonton, Alberta: Tall Pine Press, 2015), 267-267.

5   *Hegel's Concept of Experience*, 23.

6   G.W.F. Hegel refers to the shift as sublation. See Hegel, *Phenomenology of Spirit*, trans. A.V. Miller (Oxford: Oxford University Press, 1977). For an explanation of sublation, see Michael Inwood, *A Hegel Dictionary* (Oxford: Blackwell Publications, 1992), 283-285.

7   *Educating Faith*, 260.

8   Immanuel Kant, "An answer to the question: What is Enlightenment" in *Kant: Political Writings*, edited by Hans Reiss and H.B, Nisbet (Cambridge, UK: Cambridge University Press, 1970), 54-60.

9   Immanuel Kant, "What does it mean to orient oneself in thinking," *Religion Within the Boundaries of Mere Reason*, edited by Allen Wood et al. (Cambridge, UK: Cambridge University Press, 1998), 3-14; in particular see p. 12.

10   See for example, Caygill's analysis of Enthusiasm, which was particularly offensive to Kant in *A Kant Dictionary* (London: Blackwell, 1995), 175. If a reader is interested further in the issue Kant foresaw in the analysis of reason, see also Caygill's analysis of the extremes that some of Kant's followers took to describe reason and freedom as having no limits whatsoever. Kant is clear that reason has limits.

11   Antony Gottlieb, *The Dream of Reason* (New York: W.W. Norton & Company, 2016), x-xi. Gottlieb is applying William James's definition of philosophy as "a peculiarly stubborn effort to think clearly."

12   A felt sense is described in two of his books: Eugene T. Gendlin, *Fo-*

cusing (New York: Bantam Books, 1981) and Eugene T. Gendlin, *Experiencing and the Creation of Meaning* (New York: The Free Press of Glencoe, 1962). To Gendlin, "there's a relationship between felt experiencing and thought itself. Thought, as we actually have it, always requires experiencing. Human thought is really a functioning relationship between mental symbols (words, images) and experiencing, *The Creation of Meaning*, 11.

13   *Focusing; Experiencing and the Creation of Meaning.*

14   Joyce E Bellous, *Conversations that Change Us: Learning the Arts if Theological Reflection* (Edmonton: Tall Pine Press, 2017), 37.

15   Peter Senge, *The Fifth Discipline: The art and practice of the learning organization* (New York: Doubleday, 1990), 52-54.

16   When one of Freud's daughters died, he was sitting in the living room watching his grandson. The boy ran his toy car along the floor and then immediately looked up at the kitchen door. He remained looking in that direction for a few moments. Then he ran his toy car across the floor again and immediately looked up at the kitchen doorway. The boy repeated the exact behavior over and over again. Freud surmised that he had seen his mother come into the doorway in the past, when he was running his car along the floor. As he played with his car, his mother had appeared in the doorway. The boy's behavior, to Freud, was an attempt to bring his mother back. He named the pattern the repetition compulsion. In terms of his substitution theory, Freud theorized, based on his observations, that when a patient experienced loss as an internal emptiness, he or she would choose a substitute as a way to fill the emptiness left by the loss. Since the substitute substance (as one example) wasn't capable of resolving the loss, the patient repeatedly relied on the substance without any resolution, a pattern he called substitution theory. Forms of addiction fit this pattern he identified.

17   In this chapter, the word "unbelief" has two different but related meanings. Here, unbelief is described as indifference, or an absence of interest. Later, when discussing Freud's role in mistaking reason's content for its process, unbelief has a slightly different meaning, i.e. for Freud, unbelief is viewed as the only trustworthy evidence of reason.

18   M. Clark, "Living in a time of transition", in M. B. Clark and J. K. Olson, *Nursing within a faith community: Promoting health in times of transition* (Thousand Oaks, CA: Sage, 2000), 182.

19   Recognition is given to Presbyterian minister Dr. Frank W. Kimper (1917-2009), who shared these questions during a workshop in 1979 at Angela Center in Santa Rosa, California.

20   J. Woleński, "The History of Epistemology", in: I. Niiniluoto, M. Sintonen, J. Woleński (eds) *Handbook of Epistemology* (Springer, Dordrecht, 2004). https://doi.org/10.1007/978-1-4020-1986-9_1.

21   *Educating Faith*, 84.

22   Donald O. Hebb, *Essays on Mind*, (Kindle Version, 2014), 212.

23   F.E. Peters, *Greek Philosophical Terms: An historical lexicon* (New York: New York University Press, 1967), 37.

24   *Greek Philosophical Terms*, 132-139.

25   *Conversations That Change Us*, 42-52.

26   See for example, the objections raised by John Polkinghorne and Canadian psychologist Donald O. Hebb, in *Essays on Mind*, e.g., p. 212. based on (the sometimes ignored) limitations of scientific inquiry.

27   Emmanuel Kant, "What does it mean to orient oneself in thinking" in *Religion Within the Boundaries of Mere Reason*, Allen Wood and George di Giovanni, Eds. (Cambridge: Cambridge University Press, 1998)

28   *Religion within the Boundaries of Mere Reason*, 13. It's interesting to consider some of the cults that came to America from Germany in the 1700s. One example is a community called, The Ephrata Cloister in Philadelphia. Bellous visited that community's historic site just outside of Philadelphia. It's leader, Johannes Kelpius was a German Pietist, mystic, musician, and writer, interested in the occult, botany, and astronomy, who came to believe with his followers in the "Society of the Woman in the Wilderness", a reference to the book of Revelation. They also believed that the world would end in 1694. This cult was established during Kant's lifetime. Kelpius motivated a group of people to leave their homeland and travel to America, a difficult voyage, to say the least.

29   *Religion within the Boundaries of Mere Reason*, 7.

30   *The Dream of Reason*, x.

31   *Educating Faith*, 191 -230.

32   *Why did Freud Reject God?*

33   Freud's perspectives on the world contain more myths than science. Many of his later works were based on fanciful thinking rather than on science. He was an influential twentieth century mythmaker. Apparently, the evening before he sent the Moses and Monotheism manuscript out for publishing, his Jewish friends begged him not to publish it. The book is the most outrageous, fanciful, flight of fancy. It has no basis in reason, science, historicity, although he claimed that reason was his god. He published the book, despite the protest.

34   Action Science is the product of thought by two people, Donald Schon and Chris Argyris.

35   Daniel Goleman, *Emotional Intelligence* (New York: Random House, 1995).

36   Wilder Penfield, *The Mystery of the Mind* (Princeton, New Jersey: Princeton University Press, 1975).

37   French sociologist, Pierre Bourdieu, was the first to define the term social capital in his essay "Forms of Capital" in which he noted that, "modern female labor, i.e., the vast work of reproduction, constitutes an "economy of practices" that sustains and supports other forms of capital accumulation. PierreBourdieu, "The forms of capital" in J. Richardson (Ed.) *Handbook of Theory and Research for the Sociology of Education* (New York, Greenwood), 242. Also see Robert Putnam, *Bowling Alone* (New York: Simon & Schuster, 2000).

38   Ellen T. Charry, *By the Renewing of your Minds* (Oxford: Oxford University Press, 1997), 4-8.

39   *By the Renewing Your Minds*, 133.

40   David Hay and Rebecca Nye, *The Spirit of the Child* (London: Fount, 1998), 53.

41   C. Robert Cloninger, *Feeling Good: The science of well being* (Oxford, Oxford University Press, 2004).

42   Jean Clinton, *Love Builds Brains* (Edmonton: Tall Pine Press, 2020).

43   Sigmund Freud, *Totem and Taboo* (New York: Vintage Books, 1918), 98-129.

44   Joyce E. Bellous, *Learning Social Literacy* (Edmonton, AB: Tall Pine Press, 2016), 142-144.

45   G.K. Chesterton, *Orthodoxy* (Mineola, New York: Dover Publications, 2004), 29.

46   Plato, *Five Dialogues*, translated by G. M. A. Grube (Cambridge, Mass: Hackett Publishing Company, 1981), 23. Socrates didn't write down any of his conversations. It was Plato, his most famous student that recorded the conversations Socrates had with other Athenians. It's not easy to distinguish the work of the two philosophers, which we signify by using the expression Socrates/Plato. Both Socrates and Plato are depicted in The School of Athens, as well as Aristotle and many other thinkers that the Renaissance held in high esteem

47   Charles Taylor, *The Ethics of Authenticity* (Cambridge, Mass: Harvard University Press, 1991).

48   *Five Dialogues*, 27.

49   We're applying an Action Science expression to his conversation, but he didn't use that expression himself.

50   A straw man argument is one that invents an extreme example of a particular way of thinking or being, and uses that example to support a point. However, the phrase straw man signifies that no reasonable person goes to the extreme that's described. Such a person doesn't exist. Therefore, a straw man (a scare crow in a field of corn) can't be used to support the point in question. It has no validity.

51   In Plato's *Republic*, there's the analogy of the cave that depicts how Plato, following Socrates, thought about the conventional world and the ordinary person's inability to really see what's going on in it.

52   Aristotle, *Nicomachean Ethics* (Oxford: Oxford University Press, 1980), 63-67.

53   *Nicomachean Ethics*, 80.

54   K. O'Brien, *The Ignatian adventure: Experiencing the Spiritual Exercises of Saint Ignatius in daily life* (Chicago, IL: Loyola Press, 2011).

Chapter 7 - Competency and Competence in Spiritual Practice

1   Joyce E. Bellous, "Spiritual care as the foundation for a child's religious education", *Religions* 12, 954 (2006): 12.

2   P.O. Killen and J. de Beer, *The Art of Theological Reflection* (New York, NY: Crossword, 1994/2002), x.

3   This statement is based on the emergence of Clinical Pastoral Education (CPE) in the early 1920s. It's understood that the history of spiritual and pastoral care is far longer than a century, rooted in the study of theology and philosophy, and usually taught in theological colleges and seminaries. In the early 1920s, however, with emergence of CPE as a learning model, psychology and sociology were added to theology and philosophy as theoretical mainstays. E. Brooks Holifield, *A History of Pastoral Care in America: From Salvation to Self-Realization* (Eugene, OR: Wipf and Stock Publishers, 1983); Stephen D. W. King, *Trust the Process: A History of Clinical Pastoral Education as Theological Education* (Lanham, MD: University Press of America, 2007).

4   Claude Levi-Strauss, *Myth and Meaning* (London: Routledge, 2003), 7.

5   G. Asquith, "The case study method of Anton Boisen", *Journal of Pastoral Care* 34(2) (1980): 84-94.

6   Anton T. Boisen, *The Exploration of the Inner World* (Philadelphia, PA: University of Pennsylvania Press, 1971), 185.

7   Canadian Association for Spiritual Care/Association canadienne de soins spirituels, *CASC/ACSS Policy and Procedure Manual* (Newmarket, ON: Author, 2020). Ch. 4, B, 3.2.1

8   T. Borneman, B. Ferrell and C. Puchalski, "Evaluation of the FICA Tool for Spiritual Assessment", *Journal of Pain and Symptom Management* 40(2) (2010): 163-173.

...and...

G. Anandarajah and E. Hight, "Spirituality and medical practice: Using the HOPE questions as a practical tool for spiritual assessment", *American Family*

Physician 63(1) (2001): 81-88.

9   Levi-Strauss, *Myth and Meaning*, 5.

10   Levi-Strauss , *Myth and Meaning*, xxiii.

11   Levi-Strauss , *Myth and Meaning*, 4.

12   Levi-Strauss , *Myth and Meaning*, vi, xxiv.

13   Han Georg Gadamer, *Truth and Method* 2nd Revised Ed, J Weinsheimer and D. G. Marshall (trans.) (New York: Crossroad, 1989), 5.

14   Gadamer, *Truth and Method*, 312.

15   Daniel N. Stern, *The Present Moment in Psychopathology and Everyday Life* (New York: W.W. Norton & Company, 2004), 75-76.

16   Gadamer, *Truth and Method*, 312-314.

17   J. Rumi, "The great wagon", Coleman Barks (trans), *The Essential Rumi* (New York, NY: HarperCollins, 1995), 35.

18   Gadamer, *Truth and Method, 2nd revised ed* (London: Continuum International Publishing Group, 2004).

19   In spiritual care practice, it's important to be self-aware about both one's interpretive lens and the standpoint one is taking when relating with others. In this regard, we refer to Antoine de Saint-Exupery's *The Little Prince*: "it is only with the heart that one can see rightly; what is essential is invisible to the eye". A. Saint-Exupery, *The Little Prince* (Boston, MA: Mariner Books, 1943/2000)]

...and...

We also point to the work of Patricia Killen and John de Beer, insofar as we tend to assume different standpoints in our use of an interpretive lens. Killen and de Beer describe three standpoints: certitude, self-assurance, and exploration (p. 1-19). Each standpoint is depicted in light of the critical reflection that brings life experiences into conversation with the wisdom of one's worldview and heritage. P.O. Killen & J. de Beer, *The Art of Theological Reflection* (New York, NY: Crossword, 1994/2002), 1-19.]

20   Gadamer, *Truth and Method*, 291.

21   R. Schreite (Ed.), *The Schillebeeckx Reader* (New York, NY: Crossroad Publishing, 1984), 104.

22   Boisen, *The Exploration of the Inner World*, 185

23   Gadamer, *Truth and Method*, 291.

24   Gadamer, *Truth and Method*, 291.

25   Gadamer, *Truth and Method*, 16.

26   G. Asquith, "The case study method of Anton Boisen", 84-94.

27   Gadamer, *Truth and Method*, xvi.

28   Gadamer, *Truth and Method*, 14.

29   Howard Gardner, *Frames of Mind: The theory of multiple intelligences* (New York: Basic Books, 1983).

30   M.H. Abrams and Geoffrey Galt Harpham, *A Glossary of Literary Terms* 11th Edition (Toronto: Cengage Learning, 2015), 178-186.

31   The Hay Group Emotional and Social Competency Inventory (ESCI) is now called Korn Ferry Hay Group Inventory. Korn Ferry is a management consulting firm headquartered in Los Angeles, California.

32   "Emotional and Social Competency Inventory, Feedback Report," Hay Group, 02/27/10, 1.

33   Ana-Maria Rizzuto, *Freud and the Spoken Word: Speech as a key to the unconscious* (London: Routledge, 2015), 28.

This mental representation is a human construction made out of sensations originating in the existing thing (object) in factual reality—it's a psychic representation that resembles a 'thing' that there is in the world. *Freud and the Spoken Word*, 28

34   Rizzuto, *Freud and the Spoken Word*, 67.

35   Robert Kegan, *The Evolving Self: Problem and process in human development* (Cambridge, Mass: Harvard University Press, 1982).

36   Hannah Arendt, *The Life of the Mind* (New York: Harcourt Brace Jovanovich, Publishers, 1978).

37   Howard Caygill, *A Kant Dictionary* (London: Blackwell, 1995) 246.

38   Rubrics for assessing CPE student learning and the writing of professional papers for spiritual care certification have existed in the education Standards of spiritual care associations for over two decades. Language used in these rubrics has tended to focus on the supervisors'/reviewers' subjective assessment. It's this subjectivity that raises concerns for three reasons. First, assessor subjectivity may interfere with a student's/colleague's developing authenticity in that the rubric situates *power over* the student or colleague in the person of the assessor. Second, while rubrics offer clarity about what competence development looks like, aspects of that development need to be situated in a theoretical framework that moves learners toward complex competency development and integration. Third, education generally is shifting toward student-centered learning. Outcomes of a well structured, theoretically sound rubric for assessing spiritual care competence provides the best learning environment for adults.

Several more recently developed rubrics include the following examples. These indicate a movement in the direction of a more comprehensive and less subjective approach.

In Canada, the Canadian Association for Spiritual Care (CASC/ACSS) distinguishes Basic, Advanced and Provisional Supervisor-Educator learning levels. Using member access to the CASC/ACSS Policy and Procedure Manual, one finds a "Scoring Rating—Alberta (AHS, AC-SPE) Competency Assessment Scale" (adapted from Dreyfus) used at all student learning levels and in the assessment of professional papers for practitioner Certification.

In the United States, there are several professional associations dedicated to the education and assessment of spiritual care practitioners. These include the Association for Clinical Pastoral Education (ACPE), Association of Professional Chaplains (APC), National Association of Catholic Chaplains (NACC) and Neshama: Association of Jewish Chaplains (NAJC). While each association has its unique learning and competency emphases, all North American associations also share a collaboratively developed "Common Qualifications and Competencies for Professional Chaplains" document. The stages of learning in the USA are Level I, Level II and Educator CPE. If one downloads publicly available resources from the ACPE website, one finds there are "End of Phase I" and "End of Phase II" assessment forms, and there's a "Theory Integration Presentation Rubric". Emphasis is on evidence-based assessment at emerging and competent levels.

39   R. Boyatzis, *The competent manager: A model for effective performance* (New York, NY: John Wiley & Sons, 1982).

...and...

R. Boyatzis, "Competencies in the 21ˢᵗ century", *Journal of Management Development* 27(1) (2008): 5-12.

40   The following lists of competencies among spiritual care associations in North America are noteworthy:

(1) CASC/ACSS (2019). Competencies for CASC/ACSS certified professionals. Oakville, ON: Author.

(2) Manitoba Spiritual Health Care Partners (2017). Core competencies for spiritual health care practitioners. Winnipeg, MB: Author.

(3) Board of Chaplaincy Certification, Inc. (2017). Common qualifications and competencies for professional chaplains. Hoffman Estates, IL: Author. This document was first drafted in 2004 as part of the Council on Collaboration (2003-2006) and Spiritual Care Collaborative (2007-2012). It was endorsed by the follow entities in the United States and Canada: Association of Professional Chaplains (APC), Association for Clinical Pastoral Education (ACPE), National Association of Catholic Chaplains (NACC), Neshama Association of Jewish Chaplains (NAJC), and the Canadian Association for Spiritual Care (CASC/ACSS). It was updated in 2017, and is affiliated with the Association of Professional Chaplains.

41   Lyle M. Spencer and Signe M. Spencer, *Competence at Work: Models for superior performance* (New York: John Wiley & Sons, 1993), 9-15.

42   Spencer and Spencer, *Competence at Work*, 9-15.

43   Spencer and Spencer, *Competence at Work*, 11. The Iceberg Model of Competence defined by Spencer and Spencer.

44   M. Argyle, *Social encounters: Contributions to social interaction* (Oxfordshire, England, UK: Routledge, 2008).

45   C.G. Jung, "Definitions", *Psychological Types*. (Princeton, NJ: Princeton University Press, 1921/1971), 408.

46   Josephine Klein, *Our Need for Others and its Roots in Infancy* (London: Tavistock Publications, 1987), 131.

47   Boyatzis, "Competencies in the 21st Century", 5-12.

48   A good source of information relative to this topic of interprofessional competencies is the following:

Canadian Interprofessional Health Collaborative (2010). A National Interprofessional Competency Framework. Vancouver, BC: author.

49   Will Taylor, "Conscious Competence Diagram", (Department of Homeopathic Medicine, National College of Natural Medicine, Portland, Oregon, USA., 2007)

...and...

Hubert L. Dreyfus, *On the internet*. (London, UK: Routledge, 2001).

50   Gadamer, *Truth and Method*, 314.

Chapter 8 - Skills Acquisition in the Assessment of Spiritual Care Practice

1   G.H. Asquith, "The case study method of Anton T. Boisen," *Journal of Pastoral Care* 34 (2) (1980): 84 - 94.

2   Universidad Interamericana de Puerto Rico. (n.d.) Colección Especial / Special Collection: Anton Boisen. Retrieved January 21, 2022, from http://web.metro.inter.edu/facultad/esthumanisticos/anton_boisen.asp.

3   Anton T. Boisen, *The Exploration of the Inner World* (Philadelphia, PA: University of Pennsylvania Press, 1971), 185.

4   G. Fitchett, "Making Our Case(s)," *Journal of Health Care Chaplaincy* 17 (2011):1-18.

5   Canadian Association for Spiritual Care/Association canadienne de soins spirituels (CASC/ACSS), *Policy and Procedure Manual*, Chapter 4: Certification (3.2.1). (Newmarket, ON, 2020).

6   Literature on the topics of competency-based spiritual care education and evidence-based spiritual care practice is increasing all the time, and can be found by researching easily accessible data bases. References here have been selected to highlight early and more recent publications.

Competency-Based Spiritual Care Education (in the order of the year of publication)

G. Hilsman, "Grafting clinical pastoral education: Teaching competencies for the new spiritual care work," *Journal of Pastoral Care* 51(1) (1997): 3-12.

R. Anderson and M. Fukuyama (Eds.), *Ministry in the spiritual and cultural diversity of health care: Increasing the competency of chaplains* (New York, NY: Haworth Pastoral Press, 2004).

G. Fitchett, A. Tartaglia, K. Massey, B. Jackson-Jordan, and P. Derrickson, "Education for professional chaplains: Should certification competencies shape curriculum?" *Journal of Health Care Chaplaincy* 21, (2015): 151-164.

Evidence-Based Spiritual Care Practice (in the order of the year of publication)

T. O'Connor, and E. Meakes, "Hope in the midst of challenge: Evidence-based pastoral care," *Journal of Pastoral Care* 52(4)(1998): 359-367.

T. O'Connor, "Is evidence-based spiritual care an oxymoron?" *Journal of Religion and Health* 41(3) (2002): 253-262.

G. Fitchett, K. White, and K. Lyndes (Eds.) *Evidence-Based Healthcare Chaplaincy: A Research Reader.* (London, UK: Jessica Kingsley Publishers, 2018).

E. Snider, A. Erenay, T. O'Connor, C. Dotzert, S. Hong, R. Smith, L. Dolson, and M. Foulger, "Evidence-based spiritual care practice in the Canadian context: Twenty years later," *Journal of Pastoral Care and Counseling* 73(2) (2019): 88-95.

7   T. O'Connor, and E. Meakes, "Three emerging spiritual practices in the Canadian Association for Spiritual Care (CASC): From pastoral care and counselling to multi-faith, evidence-based spiritual care and psycho-spiritual therapy," *Journal of Pastoral Care and Counseling* 75(4) (2021): 278-283.

8   Canadian Association for Spiritual Care/Association canadienne de soins spirituels, 2019. Competencies of CASC/ACSS Certified Professionals (Competency 1.4 and 4.1.1). Newmarket, ON: Author.

9   Board of Chaplaincy Certification, Inc., 2017. "Common qualifications and competencies for professional chaplains." Hoffman Estates, IL: Author.

10   S. Dreyfus and H. Dreyfus, *A five-stage model of the mental activities involved in directed skills acquisition* (Washington, DC: Storming Media, 1980).

11   P. Benner, "Using the Dreyfus Model of Skill Acquisition to describe and interpret skill acquisition and clinical judgment in nursing practice and education," *The Bulletin of Science, Technology and Society Special Issue: Human Expertise in the Age of the Computer* Vol. 24 (3) (2005): 188-199.

...and...

P. Gonon, K. Kraus, J. Oelkers, and S. Stolz, (Eds.), *Work, Education and Employability* (Bern, Switzerland: Peter Lang AG, International Academic Publishers, 2008).

...and...

Ian McPherson, "Reflexive learning: Stages toward wisdom with Dreyfus," *Educational Philosophy and Theory* 37(5), (2005): 705-718.

12   Dreyfus, *On the Internet*, especially 32-49.

13   Embodied learning and embodied spiritual care practice are important themes throughout the book. Significant attention has been given to the role of brain research in worldview formation and re-conception, relational development, perceptual and conceptual learning, entering into "present moment" experiences with others, and acquiring the types of literacy required to develop competence in spiritual care practice. Listening thickly to oneself and others, and recognizing thin moment experiences in self and others are embodied activities.

When considering Dreyfus' approach to skills acquisition—with his strong emphasis on the embodied nature of this acquisition—it's important to ask: How do we learn to listen to our bodies? How does one go about integrating embodied learning when there's embodied trauma? How is embodied learning tied to race, gender, intersectionality, social location, etc.? How does self-regulation theory contribute to embodied learning? While these questions are beyond the scope of this book, we raise them here for further contemplation and speculation.

14   D. Pranke, and M. Clark, "Out of the ashes: The Alberta Consortium for Supervised Pastoral Education Program," *Journal of Pastoral Care and Counseling*, 74(4) (2020): 243.

In Alberta, Canada, preceptors are specially prepared spiritual care professionals who are clinically based in health facilities and/or community agencies. They prepare for their role by means of the Sacred Art of Preceptorship course offered through St. Stephen's College in Edmonton. In many other locations across North America and beyond, where clinically located spiritual care practitioners support the learning of CPE students, the terms "mentor" and "clinical liaison" are sometimes used.

15   Will Taylor, "Conscious Competence Diagram", (Department of Homeopathic Medicine, National College of Natural Medicine, Portland, Oregon, USA., 2007)

Diagram retrieved from

https://www.businessballs.com/self-awareness/conscious-competence-learning-model/#conscious-competence-theory-origins on February 18, 2022.

16   T. Borneman, B. Ferrell, and C. Puchalski, "Evaluation of the FICA Tool for Spiritual Assessment," *Journal of Pain and Symptom Management* 40(2) (2010): 163-173.

…and…

G. Anandarajah, and E. Hight, "Spirituality and medical practice: Using the HOPE questions as a practical tool for spiritual assessment," *American Family Physician* 63(1) (2001): 81-88.

17   Examples include the following:

G. Fitchett, *Assessing Spiritual Needs* (Minneapolis, MN: Augsburg, 1993).

T. O'Connor, E. Meakes, K. O'Neill, C. Penner, G. Van Staalduinen and K. Davis, "Not well known, used little and needed: Canadian chaplains' experiences of published spiritual assessment tools." *Journal of Pastoral Care and Counseling* 59(1-2) (2005): 97-107.

18   Dreyfus, *On the Internet*, 39.

19   While Rose's story is imagined, there is evidence of this study in the monograph: V. Stang, H. Koots, P. Barnes, and C. Enfield, "Final report: Validating competencies for spiritual care professionals specializing in palliative and bereavement care in Canada." Ottawa, ON: Authors, 2021.

20   Jack's story is imagined, but the story of CPE in Billings, Montana is worth reading. R. Becker, and A. Embry, "The Northern Rockies Clinical Pastoral Education Center, Inc., Billings, Montana," *Journal of Healthcare Chaplaincy* 9(1-2), (1999):73-79.

21   There are several people in North America that stand out as leaders in highlighting the importance of evidence-based spiritual care practice and integrated research literacy. In Canada, Thomas St. James O'Connor and Elizabeth Meakes are noteworthy. For several decades, they've dedicated themselves to conducting research, apprenticing Supervised Pastoral Education students and spiritual care/psycho-spiritual therapy colleagues in research literacy, and publishing articles and books relevant to evidence-based practice. There are a number of references to their work in several chapters of our book. In the United States, George Fitchett and Larry VandeCreek stand out as pioneers in spiritual care research, educating for research literacy, and providing apprenticeship for new researchers through their books, articles, and—more recently—Fitchett's founding of Transforming Chaplaincy to "promote evi-

dence-based spiritual care and integrate research into professional practice and education by fostering a culture of inquiry".

While naming names risks slighting other significant contributors to this subclass of spiritual care expertise, the following references speak to the accomplishments of many practitioners and scholars who make research and evidence-based practice visible.

G. Fitchett, K. White, and K. Lyndes (Eds.), *Evidence-Based Healthcare Chaplaincy: A Research Reader* (London, UK: Jessica Kingsley Publishers, 2018).

Journal of Pastoral Care and Counseling (2018). Research in pastoral care and counseling: A rich feast of articles published in the Journal of Pastoral Care and Counselling (1999 - 2017). Thousand Oaks, CA: Author.

P. McCarroll, "Taking inventory and moving forward: A review of the research literature and assessment of qualitative research in JPCC, 2010-2014." *Journal of Pastoral Care and Counseling* 69(4), (2015): 222-231.

L. VandeCreek, H. Bender, and M. Jordan, *Research in Pastoral Care and Counseling: Quantitative and Qualitative Approaches* (Eugene, OR: Wipf and Stock Publishers, 2008).

22   Dreyfus, *On the Internet*, 46.

23   Cultural Intelligence, cultural quotient or CQ, is a term used in business, education, government and academic research. Cultural intelligence can be understood as the capability to relate and work effectively across cultures. Originally, the term cultural intelligence and the abbreviation "CQ" was developed by the research done by Soon Ang and Linn Van Dyne as a researched-based way of measuring and predicting intercultural performance. The term is relatively recent: early definitions and studies of the concepts were given by P. Christopher Earley and Soon Ang in the book *Cultural Intelligence: Individual Interactions Across Cultures* (2003) and more fully developed later by David Livermore in the book, Leading with Cultural Intelligence. The concept is related to that of Cross-cultural competence but goes beyond that to actually look at intercultural capabilities as a form of intelligence that can be measured and developed. According to Earley, Ang, and Van Dyne, cultural intelligence can be defined as "a person's capability to adapt as s/he interacts with others from different cultural regions", and has behavioral, motivational, and metacognitive aspects. Without cultural intelligence, both business and military actors seeking to engage foreigners are susceptible to mirror imaging.

24   On the ACPE website one can download "ACPE Brief History" as a PDF file: https://acpe.edu/docs/default-source/acpe-history/acpe-brief-history.pdf. Other resources on the history of CPE can be found in the Journal of Pastoral Care & Counseling and the Journal of Reflective Practice: Formation and Supervision in Ministry, to name a few.

25   For several years, including those during which In Su applied for recognition in what is now the Canadian Association for Spiritual Care (CASC/

ACSS), there was a document in the Standards referred to as "Appendix V". This Appendix provided "Guidelines" for entry into or placement in the Association's "clinical educational process from an alternate or irregular clinical educational background." It's an Appendix that no longer exists. "Equivalency" is the current term used for exploring recognition by CASC/ACSS of a person's previous CPE learning and/or certification.

26   Of particular value to In-Su was the following article:

Gerald Grow, "Teaching Learners to be Self-Directed," *Adult Education Quarterly*, 41 (Spring 1991): 125–149.

27   Kim, Do Bong, "Essential CPE learning elements across cultures [Photograph]." Personal correspondence, 2022.

In addition to providing his diagram, Rev. Dr. Do Bong Kim contributed extensively to formulating the content of this Stage #7 Acquiring Practical Wisdom: Cultural Style vignette. It is collaboratively authored.

28   Brian P. Hall, *The Genesis Effect: Personal and Organizational Transformations* (Eugene, Oregon: Resource Publications, 1986).

29   S.M. Drake and J.P. Miller, "Beyond reflection to being: The contemplative practitioner", *Phenomenology + Pedagogy*, 9, (1991), 319-334. In addition to this article, J. P. Miller has written a book that articulates in greater depth the conceptualization of contemplative practitioner. J.P. Miller, *The Contemplative Practitioner: Meditation in Education and Workplace* (Toronto, ON: University of Toronto Press, 2014).

Appendix 2

1   Rollo May, *The Courage to Create*, (New York: W.W. Norton & Company, 1975), 100.

Index

B

C

G

H

L

M

S

T

U

Manufactured by Amazon.ca
Bolton, ON

31521001R00221